Messages

Building Interpersonal Communication Skills

Sixth Edition

Messages
Building Interpersonal Communication Skills

Joseph A. DeVito

*Hunter College of the
City University of New York*

PEARSON

Boston   New York   San Francisco
Mexico City   Montreal   Toronto   London   Madrid   Munich   Paris
Hong Kong   Singapore   Tokyo   Cape Town   Sydney

Executive Editor: Karon Bowers
Series Editor: Brian Wheel
Development Editor: Ellen Darion
Editorial Assistant: Jennifer Trebby
Marketing Manager: Mandee Eckersley
Associate Editor: Andrea Christie
Senior Production Editor: Annette Pagliaro
Editorial Production Service: Nesbitt Graphics, Inc.
Photo Researcher: Laurie Frankenthaler
Composition Buyer: Linda Cox
Manufacturing Buyer: Megan Cochran
Cover Administrator: Linda Knowles
Electronic Composition: Nesbitt Graphics, Inc.

For related titles and support material visit our online catalog at www.ablongman.com.

Between the time Website information is gathered and then published, some sites may have closed. Also, the transcription of URLs can result in typographical errors. The publisher would appreciate notification where these occur so that they may be corrected in subsequent editions. Thank you.

Many of the designations used by manufacturers and sellers to distinguish their products are claimed as trademarks. Where those designations appear in this book and Allyn & Bacon was aware of a trademark claim, the designations have been printed in caps or initial caps.

Library of Congress Cataloging-in-Publication Data

DeVito, Joseph A.
    Messages : building interpersonal communication skills / Joseph A.
DeVito.—6th ed.
        p. cm.
    Includes bibliographical references and index.
    ISBN 0-205-41489-3 (pbk.)
  1. Interpersonal communication—Textbooks. I. Title.

    BF637.C45D5 2004
    158.2—dc22

                                        2003063787

Printed in the United States of America

10 9 8 7 6 5 4 3   VHP 07 06

Brief Contents

Specialized Contents

Self-Tests

Skills Toolbox

Listen to This

Ethical Messages

Skill Building Exercises

Welcome to Messages

It's a great pleasure to present this thoroughly revised and updated sixth edition of *Messages: Building Interpersonal Communication Skills*. The book continues to have two interrelated purposes: (1) to present you with an overview of interpersonal communication—what it is and what we know about it—and (2) to improve your interpersonal communication skills. These two purposes influence everything included in the text—the topics discussed, the way each topic is presented, the specific skills highlighted, and the pedagogy incorporated.

Major Themes

Several themes highlight the skills of interpersonal communication and—taken together—define the uniqueness of this text:

- an emphasis on **skill building** with guidelines and experiences to help you master the crucial skills of interpersonal communication and relationships
- an integration of **listening** skills throughout the topics of interpersonal communication
- an integration of **critical thinking** principles and techniques to help you think more logically about interpersonal communication (or about anything else)
- an emphasis on **culture** and cultural sensitivity as it influences all forms of interpersonal and intercultural interactions
- a focus on **ethical issues** as they relate to a wide variety of interpersonal communication situations
- **power and empowerment** skills for increasing interpersonal effectiveness
- an **interactive presentation** to make learning about interpersonal communication more exciting and more personalized

Skill Building

With a more focused approach than in previous editions, this edition emphasizes the development of **interpersonal communication skills** such as increasing accuracy in interpersonal perception, using active listening skills more effectively, and dealing constructively with interpersonal conflict. These skills are integral to the text discussions and appear in all chapters. But several features further highlight these skills and will facilitate your mastery of them.

First, and new to this edition, is a set of 124 **Message Skills** that are highlighted in marginal notes throughout the text. These message skills are summaries of the most important interpersonal communication skills.

Noise

Noise is anything that interferes with your receiving a message someone is sending or with their receiving your message. Noise may be physical (loud talking, honking cars, illegible handwriting, "garbage" on your computer screen), physiological (hearing or visual impairment, articulation disorders), psychological (preconceived ideas, wandering thoughts), or semantic (misunderstood meanings). Technically, noise is anything that distorts or gets in the way of the message.

A useful concept in understanding noise and its importance in communication is **signal-to-noise ratio**. In this phrase the term *signal* refers to information that you'd find useful; *noise* refers to information that is useless (to you). So, for example, mailing lists or newsgroups that contained lots of useful information would be high on signal and low on noise; those that contained lots of useless information would be high on noise and low on signal.

Because messages may be visual as well as spoken, noise too may be visual. Thus, sunglasses that prevent someone from seeing the nonverbal messages from your eyes would be considered noise, as would blurred type on a printed page. Table 1.2 on page 13 identifies the four major types of noise in more detail.

All communications contain noise. Noise cannot be totally eliminated, but its effects can be reduced. Making your language more precise, sharpening your skills for sending and receiving nonverbal messages, and improving your listening and feedback skills are some ways to combat the influence of noise.

Message Skills

Noise Management: Reduce physical, physiological, psychological, and semantic noise as best you can; use repetition and restatement and, when in doubt, ask if you're clear.

Context

Communication always takes place within a context: an environment that influences the form and the content of communication. At times this context is so natural that you ignore it, like street noise. At other times the context stands out, and the ways in which

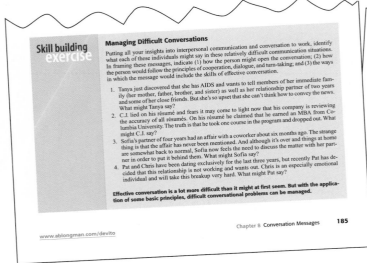

Skill building exercise

Managing Difficult Conversations

Putting all your insights into interpersonal communication and conversation to work, identify what each of these individuals might say in these relatively difficult communication situations. In framing these messages, indicate (1) how the person might open the conversation; (2) how the person would follow the principles of cooperation, dialogue, and turn-taking; and (3) the ways in which the message would include the skills of effective conversation.

1. Tanya just discovered that she has AIDS and wants to tell members of her immediate family (her mother, father, brother, and sister) as well as her relationship partner of two years and some of her close friends. But she's so upset that she can't think how to convey the news. What might Tanya say?

2. C.J. lied on his résumé and fears it may come to light now that his company is reviewing the accuracy of all résumés. On his résumé he claimed that he earned an MBA from Columbia University. The truth is that he took one course in the program and dropped out. What might C.J. say?

3. Sofia's partner of four years had an affair with a coworker about six months ago. The strange thing is that the affair has never been mentioned. And although it's over and things at home are somewhat back to normal, Sofia now feels the need to discuss the matter with her partner in order to put it behind them. What might Sofia say?

4. Pat and Chris have been dating exclusively for the last three years, but recently Pat has decided that this relationship is not working and wants out. Chris is an especially emotional individual and will take this breakup very hard. What might Pat say?

Effective conversation is a lot more difficult than it might at first seem. But with the application of some basic principles, difficult conversational problems can be managed.

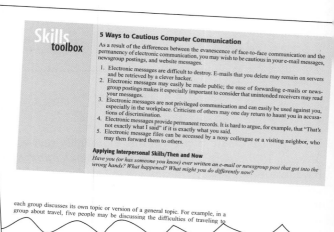

Skills toolbox

5 Ways to Cautious Computer Communication

As a result of the differences between the evanescence of face-to-face communication and the permanency of electronic communication, you may wish to be cautious in your e-mail messages, newsgroup postings, and website messages.

1. Electronic messages are difficult to destroy. E-mails that you delete may remain on servers and be retrieved by a clever hacker.

2. Electronic messages may easily be made public; the ease of forwarding e-mails or newsgroup postings makes it especially important to consider that unintended receivers may read your messages.

3. Electronic messages are not privileged communication and can easily be used against you, especially in the workplace. Criticism of others may one day return to haunt you in accusations of discrimination.

4. Electronic messages provide permanent records. It is hard to argue, for example, that "That's not exactly what I said" if it is exactly what you said.

5. Electronic message files can be accessed by a nosy colleague or a visiting neighbor, who may then forward them to others.

Applying Interpersonal Skills/Then and Now

Have you (or has someone you know) ever written an e-mail or newsgroup post that got into the wrong hands? What happened? What might you do differently now?

each group discusses its own topic or version of a general topic. For example, in a group about travel, five people may be discussing the difficulties of traveling to

Second, 35 **Skill Building Exercises** will enable you to apply the material in the chapter to specific situations and thereby to increase and perfect your own interpersonal skills. Positioned throughout the text, these exercises are practice experiences aimed at increasing your ability to formulate more effective messages. All exercises, in fact, ask you to construct specific types of messages to demonstrate your mastery of skills. Examples include exercises focusing on reducing apprehension, formulating excuses, managing difficult conversations, and confronting intercultural difficulties.

Third, a series of **Skills Toolboxes** (one per chapter) appear throughout the text. Each of these boxes identifies a cluster of related skills relevant to the chapter; for example, "5 Ways to Cautious Computer Communication," "3 Ways to Resist Pressure to Self-Disclose," "8 Ways to Create Sticky Relationships," and "6 Ways to Exert Power." Each Toolbox ends with a section called "Applying Interpersonal Skills/Then and Now" that asks you to recall a previous situation and the way you communicated in it—and to consider how you would communicate in that same situation now, ideally on the basis of insights from the chapter and the Skills Toolbox. A complete list of these Skills Toolboxes appears in the Specialized Contents on page xiii.

Fourth, each of the interior photos has a **Skills ViewPoint** caption that asks you to discuss the skills related to the case presented.

Apprehensive Behaviors

We can also look at apprehension in more behavioral terms (Richmond & McCroskey, 1996). Generally, apprehension causes a decrease in the frequency, strength, and likelihood of engaging in communication transactions. High apprehensives avoid communication situations; when forced to participate, they do so as little as possible. This reluctance to communicate shows itself in a variety of forms. For example, in small group situations, apprehensives not only will talk less but also will avoid the "seats of influence" in the group leader's direct line of sight. Even in classrooms high-apprehension individuals avoid seats where they can easily be called on, and they maintain little direct eye contact with the instructor, especially when a question is likely to be asked. Closely related to this behavior is the finding that apprehensives have more negative attitudes toward school, earn poorer grades, and are more likely to drop out of college (McCroskey, Booth-Butterfield, & Payne, 1989).

Apprehensives disclose little and avoid occupations with heavy communication demands (for example, teaching or public relations). Within their occupations, they're less desirous of advancement than others, largely because with advancement comes an increase in the need to communicate. High apprehensives are even less likely to get job interviews.

Apprehensives also engage more in steady dating, a finding that is not unexpected. One of the most difficult communication situations is asking for a date—especially a first date—and developing a new relationship. Consequently, once a dating relationship

? SKILLS VIEWPOINT

Research finds that in the classroom, increased instructor clarity and immediacy (language that creates a connection between sender and receiver) helps to reduce *receiver apprehension*—people's fear that they won't be able to understand the message to which they're listening (Chesebro & McCroskey, 1998). Assuming that these findings would also apply to the health care context, what specifically might health care professionals do to help reduce apprehension among patients?

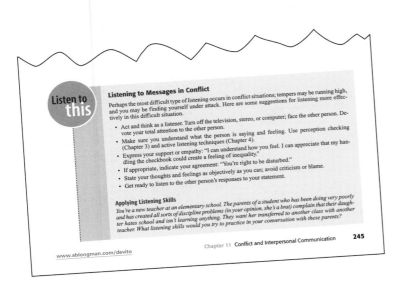

Listening

Messages covers listening in two ways. First, Chapter 4 focuses exclusively on listening. It covers the listening process from receiving to responding, provides guidelines for increasing listening effectiveness, and clarifies the role of culture and gender in listening.

In addition, to emphasize that listening is a part of all types of interpersonal communication, each chapter contains a **Listen to This** box. These boxes discuss listening skills as they relate to the chapter content; for example, skills such as listening to gender differences, listening to the emotions of others, and listening without bias. At the end of each box is a case for analysis that asks you to apply the relevant listening skills. A complete list of these boxes is given in the Specialized Contents on pages xiii–xiv.

Critical Thinking

On first glance, it might appear that the critical thinking material from the previous edition is absent here. But it isn't. To help streamline the presentation and to better integrate critical thinking concepts, the text now incorporates the best from the fifth edition's critical thinking boxes.

A separate booklet, *Brainstorms: How to Think More Creatively about Communication or about Anything Else,* which contains a variety of creative (and in many ways critical) thinking tools, is available.

Culture and Intercultural Communication

The text presents interpersonal communication as taking place in a context that is becoming increasingly intercultural. Chapter 9, "Interpersonal Communication and Culture," covers intercultural communication in depth, focusing on the nature of culture and of intercultural communication, the ways in which cultures differ (for example, in individualism and collectivism, high and low context, and masculinity and femininity), and the ways to improve intercultural communication.

In addition, **integrated discussions of culture** appear throughout the text. Some of the more important of these discussions include:

- culture and human communication, including cultural awareness, communication among blind and sighted, the relevance of culture, and the aim of a cultural perspective (Chapter 1)

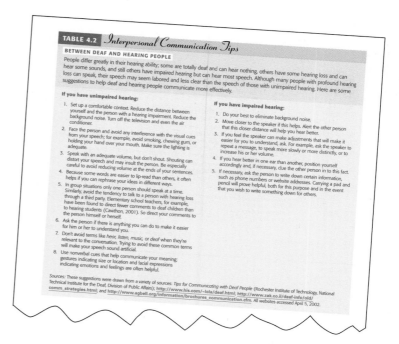

TABLE 4.2 *Interpersonal Communication Tips*

BETWEEN DEAF AND HEARING PEOPLE

People differ greatly in their hearing ability; some are totally deaf and can hear nothing, others have some hearing loss and can hear some sounds, and still others have impaired hearing but can hear most speech. Although many people with profound hearing loss can speak, their speech may seem labored and less clear than the speech of those with unimpaired hearing. Here are some suggestions to help deaf and hearing people communicate more effectively.

If you have unimpaired hearing:

1. Set up a comfortable context. Reduce the distance between yourself and the person with a hearing impairment. Reduce the background noise. Turn off the television and even the air conditioner.
2. Face the person and avoid any interference with the visual cues from your speech; for example, avoid smoking, chewing gum, or holding your hand over your mouth. Make sure the lighting is adequate.
3. Speak with an adequate volume, but don't shout. Shouting can distort your speech and may insult the person. Be especially careful to avoid reducing volume at the ends of your sentences.
4. Because some words are easier to lip-read than others, it often helps if you can rephrase your ideas in different ways.
5. In group situations only one person should speak at a time. Similarly, avoid the tendency to talk to a person with hearing loss through a third party. Elementary school teachers, for example, have been found to direct fewer comments to deaf children than to hearing students (Cawthon, 2001). So direct your comments to the person himself or herself.
6. Ask the person if there is anything you can do to make it easier for him or her to understand you.
7. Don't avoid terms like *hear, listen, music,* or *deaf* when they're relevant to the conversation. Trying to avoid these common terms will make your speech sound artificial.
8. Use nonverbal cues that help communicate your meaning; gestures indicating size or location and facial expressions indicating emotions and feelings are often helpful.

If you have impaired hearing:

1. Do your best to eliminate background noise.
2. Move closer to the speaker if this helps. Alert the other person that this closer distance will help you hear better.
3. If you feel the speaker can make adjustments that will make it easier for you to understand, ask. For example, ask the speaker to repeat a message, to speak more slowly or more distinctly, or to increase his or her volume.
4. If you hear better in one ear than another, position yourself accordingly and, if necessary, clue the other person in to this fact.
5. If necessary, ask the person to write down certain information, such as phone numbers or website addresses. Carrying a pad and pencil will prove helpful, both for this purpose and in the event that you wish to write something down for others.

Sources: These suggestions were drawn from a variety of sources: *Tips for Communicating with Deaf People* (Rochester Institute of Technology, National Technical Institute for the Deaf, Division of Public Affairs); http://www.his.com/~lola/deaf.html; http://www.zak.co.il/deaf-info/old/comm_strategies.html; and http://www.agbell.org/information/brochures_communication.cfm. All websites accessed April 5, 2002.

- culture's influence on self-concept, self-disclosure, and apprehension (Chapter 2)
- stereotypes and cultural sensitivity in perceptual accuracy (Chapter 3)
- listening, culture, and gender; communication between deaf and hearing people (Chapter 4)
- gender and cultural differences in directness; language as a cultural institution and cultural maxims; sexism, heterosexism, racism, and ageism in language; and cultural identifiers (Chapter 5)
- culture and nonverbal communication; for example, in touching, time, and color perception (Chapter 6)
- the role of culture and gender in emotions and emotional expression; societal rules and customs (Chapter 7)
- ethnocentrism, conversational taboos, cultural sensitivity, and cultural and gender differences in conversation; communication between people with and without speech and language difficulties (Chapter 8)
- interpersonal communication and culture: culture and intercultural communication, how cultures differ, and ways to improve intercultural communication; communication between those with and those without physical disabilities (Chapter 9)
- culture and gender differences in relationships (Chapter 10)
- conflict and the ways it is influenced by culture and gender (Chapter 11)
- the cultural dimension of power; culture and power distances (Chapter 12)

Ethics

A series of **Ethical Messages** boxes (one per chapter) highlight a variety of ethical issues in interpersonal communication; for example, the legitimacy of censoring messages and interpersonal interactions, outing, ethical fighting, culture and ethics, emotional appeals, lying, gossiping, and silence. These boxes will serve as frequent reminders that ethical considerations are an integral part of all interpersonal communication decisions you make. At the end of each box, you're given a specific real-life situation and asked, "What Would You Do?"

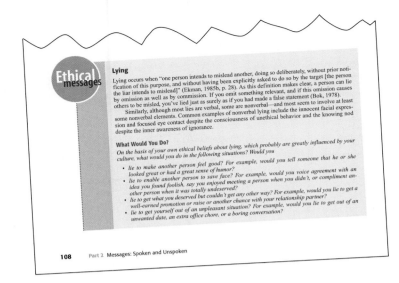

Power and Empowerment

Because power permeates all forms of interpersonal communication, **personal empowerment** and **empowering others** are integral parts of this text. *Messages* aims to give you the skills and experiences to become a more effective, more empowered, and more empowering individual. This orientation underlies the book's emphasis on building skills useful in a variety of contexts, and it comes into sharp focus in the final chapter. Chapter 12, "Interpersonal Communication and Power," examines the principles of power and discusses ways to increase self-esteem and assertiveness.

Interactive Pedagogy

Of course, a printed text cannot literally be interactive. But, given the limitations of print, the format of *Messages* is as interactive as possible, asking you to respond and get personally involved with the material. In addition to the text proper, which invites interaction at numerous points, the book also contains a variety of features to win your involvement:

- **Self-Tests** encourage you to assess yourself on a variety of interpersonal issues.

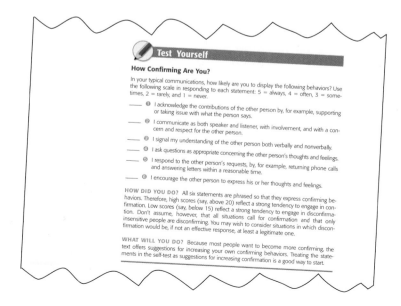

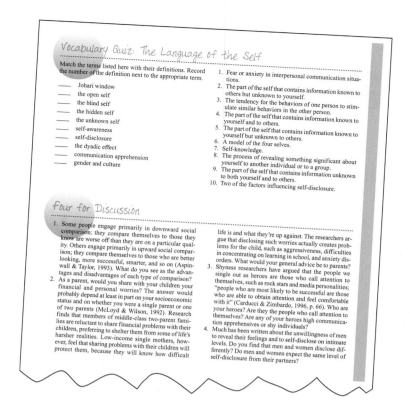

Vocabulary Quiz: The Language of the Self

Match the terms listed here with their definitions. Record the number of the definition next to the appropriate term.

—— Johari window
—— the open self
—— the blind self
—— the hidden self
—— the unknown self
—— self-awareness
—— self-disclosure
—— the dyadic effect
—— communication apprehension
—— gender and culture

1. Fear or anxiety in interpersonal communication situations.
2. The part of the self that contains information known to others but unknown to yourself.
3. The tendency for the behaviors of one person to stimulate similar behaviors in the other person.
4. The part of the self that contains information known to yourself and to others.
5. The part of the self that contains information known to yourself but unknown to others.
6. A model of the four selves.
7. Self-knowledge.
8. The process of revealing something significant about yourself to another individual or to a group.
9. The part of the self that contains information unknown to both yourself and to others.
10. Two of the factors influencing self-disclosure.

Four for Discussion

1. Some people engage primarily in downward social comparison; they compare themselves to those they know are worse off than they are on a particular quality. Others engage primarily in upward social comparison; they compare themselves to those who are better looking, more successful, smarter, and so on (Aspinwall & Taylor, 1993). What do you see as the advantages and disadvantages of each type of comparison?
2. As a parent, would you share with your children your financial and personal worries? The answer would probably depend at least in part on your socioeconomic status and on whether you were a single parent or one of two parents (McLoyd & Wilson, 1992). Research finds that members of middle-class two-parent families are reluctant to share financial problems with their children, preferring to shelter them from some of life's harsher realities. Low-income single mothers, however, feel that sharing problems with their children will protect them, because they will know how difficult life is and what they're up against. The researchers argue that disclosing such worries actually creates problems for the child, such as aggressiveness, difficulties in concentrating on learning in school, and anxiety disorders. What would your general advice be to parents?
3. Shyness researchers have argued that the people we single out as heroes are those who call attention to themselves, such as rock stars and media personalities; "people who are most likely to be successful are those who are able to obtain attention and feel comfortable with it" (Carducci & Zimbardo, 1996, p. 66). Who are your heroes? Are they the people who call attention to themselves? Are any of your heroes high communication apprehensives or shy individuals?
4. Much has been written about the unwillingness of men to reveal their feelings and to self-disclose on intimate levels. Do you find that men and women disclose differently? Do men and women expect the same level of self-disclosure from their partners?

- **Skill Building Exercises** encourage you to interact with and personalize the concepts discussed in the text.
- **Vocabulary Quizzes** highlight key terms and make learning new terms easier and more enjoyable.
- **Application exercises** (in the ethics, toolbox, and listen boxes) and **photo captions ("Skills ViewPoints")** invite your active participation in the analysis and management of interpersonal situations.
- **Discussion questions** appear at the end of each chapter, inviting debate and challenge.
- **Integrated discussions** throughout the text encourage personalization of the material; all of these discussions are denoted by a bulleted list on a blue background.

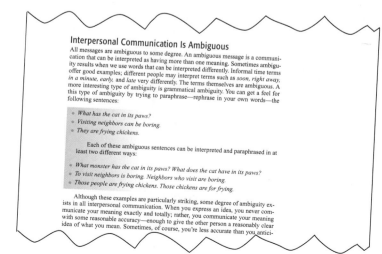

Interpersonal Communication Is Ambiguous

All messages are ambiguous to some degree. An ambiguous message is a communication that can be interpreted as having more than one meaning. Sometimes ambiguity results when we use words that can be interpreted differently. Informal time terms offer good examples; different people may interpret terms such as *soon, right away, in a minute, early,* and *late* very differently. The terms themselves are ambiguous. A more interesting type of ambiguity is grammatical ambiguity. You can get a feel for this type of ambiguity by trying to paraphrase—rephrase in your own words—the following sentences:

- *What has the cat in its paws?*
- *Visiting neighbors can be boring.*
- *They are frying chickens.*

Each of these ambiguous sentences can be interpreted and paraphrased in at least two different ways:

- *What monster has the cat in its paws? What does the cat have in its paws?*
- *To visit neighbors is boring. Neighbors who visit are boring.*
- *Those people are frying chickens. Those chickens are for frying.*

Although these examples are particularly striking, some degree of ambiguity exists in all interpersonal communication. When you express an idea, you never communicate your meaning exactly and totally; rather, you communicate your meaning with some reasonable accuracy—enough to give the other person a reasonably clear idea of what you mean. Sometimes, of course, you're less accurate than you antici-

Major Changes in This Edition

For those who used the previous edition, let me identify some of the major changes in each chapter (in addition to those mentioned already and in addition to updated research findings throughout):

Chapter 1. New elements are a discussion of "Message Overload," a topic especially relevant to beginning college students; an extended table on communication between blind and sighted people; and a discussion of the ambiguity of interpersonal communication.

Chapter 2. Ways to resist the pressure to self-disclose, apprehension and its influence on dating, and ways to empower apprehensive individuals have been added.

Chapter 3. The section on increasing accuracy in interpersonal perception has been totally revised, and there is a new exercise on checking perceptions.

Chapter 4. A new chapter opener, a revised table on the purposes and payoffs of effective listening, an extended table on communication between deaf and hearing people, and a section on "Reflections on the Model of Listening" have been added. The section on "Increasing Listening Effectiveness" (now called "Styles of Listening Effectively") has been totally revised to give more specific recommendations for increasing listening effectiveness.

Chapter 5. The discussion of politeness has been revised and integrated into the discussion of conversation (Chapter 8). The principle that "Messages Vary in Inclusion" has been added, as has a new section on ageism.

Chapter 6. New are a section on the functions of nonverbal communication and a clarified definition of nonverbal communication; the section on space and territoriality has been totally revised.

Chapter 7. The introductory material is now organized around six principles of emotions. New discussions cover the influential nature of emotions, "The Case of Anger," and how anger may be managed.

Chapter 8. The chapter has a new opening vignette and discussions of communication between people with and without speech and language disorders, the quantity maxim as it applies to e-mail, the principle of dialogue, the types of excuses and how they are used in romantic and workplace relationships, and closing a conversation in e-mail. In addition, the entire section on qualities of effective conversation has been rewritten to include more specific suggestions.

Chapter 9. New discussions address ethnic identity and communication between people with and without disabilities. In addition, there is a new self-test and an expanded explanation of ethnocentrism. The section on improving intercultural communication has been thoroughly revised and abbreviated to reduce overlap with the discussion in Chapter 8.

Chapter 10. This chapter has been restructured. The discussion of the advantages and disadvantages of relationships now takes the form of a self-test. There is new material on the characteristics of interpersonal relationships and on intimacy and risk as well as new statistics on the family. To avoid overlap with Chapter 8's presentation of the qualities of effectiveness, the section on improving relationship communication has been recast as a Skills Toolbox on "sticky" relationships.

Chapter 11. The chapter now opens with a section on "Principles of Interpersonal Conflict"; material on cultural norms about conflict and a new section, "Conflict Styles Have Consequences," have been added.

Chapter 12. This chapter has been restructured; it now presents the principles of power first, then explores improving self-power (through enhanced self-esteem) and interpersonal power (through assertiveness). The section on sexual harassment has been rewritten and updated, as has the section on affirmation.

Articles. The reprinted articles that appeared in the previous edition have been removed, with the best of the material integrated into the text proper.

Glossary of Interpersonal Skills. A new glossary devoted to interpersonal skills has been added. This glossary is an alphabetized presentation of the Message Skills that appear throughout the text in marginal notes.

In addition, all of the boxed features have been completely rewritten for greater clarity and a more focused presentation of skills. Among the new items:

Self-Tests: New tests address ethnocentricity and the advantages and disadvantages of relationships.

Skills Toolbox boxes: Cautious computer communication, resisting the pressure to self-disclose, talking on the phone, and creating sticky relationships are new topics.

Listen to This boxes: A new box focuses on listening to new ideas.

Ethical Messages boxes: New features cover communicating in cyberspace and ethical fighting.

Skill Building Exercises: Exercises now include giving effective feedforward, thinking in e-prime, managing difficult conversations, confronting intercultural difficulties, talking cherishing, responding to complaints, and rewriting unrealistic beliefs.

The Internet

This edition of *Messages* provides both text and Internet resources for improving your interpersonal communication skills.

- **Integration:** The text offers a variety of discussion topics, tips, and strategies to help you master important email and Internet communication skills for both personal and workplace use.

- **Web Exploration:** The accompanying text website provides a wide variety of resources including exercises and self-tests related to each chapter's concepts and skills. Writing resources and assignments are also available for your use. Each chapter ends with an overview of those resources that can be found at **www.ablongman.com/devito**.

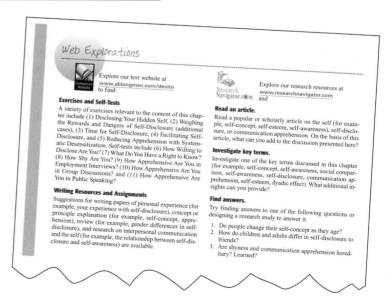

- **Allyn & Bacon's Research Navigator website** is a powerful and extensive on-line database of popular and academic articles in communication and other related areas of interest. Providing credible and reliable source material from, among others, the EBSCO Academic Journal and Abstract Database, *New York Times* Search by Subject Archive, "Best of the Web" Link Library, and *Financial Times* Article Archive and Company Financials, Research Navigator helps students quickly and efficiently make the most of their research time. At the end of each chapter you will be prompted to go to www.researchnavigator.com to read an article, investigate key terms, and find answers related to topics, terms, and questions based on the chapter content.

Supplements

Student Resources
Print Supplements

Study Guide/Activity Manual, by Sue Selk, El Paso Community College. The study guide contains learning objectives, chapter summary grids, study methods, chapter outlines, vocabulary review, sample tests, suggested readings and tips for learning. It also includes activities for reinforcing learning and demonstrating skills.

Research Navigator Guide for Speech Communication, by Terrence Doyle, Northern Virginia Community College. This resource guide is designed to teach students how to conduct high-quality online research and to document it properly. The guide provides access to Research Navigator (www.researchnavigator.com), which contains exclusive databases of credible and reliable source material, including EBSCO's ContentSelect Academic Journal Database and the *New York Times* Search by Subject Archive.

Brainstorms, by Joseph A. DeVito. A guide to thinking more creatively about communication, or anything else; a perfect complement to the text's unique emphasis on critical thinking. Students find 19 practical, easy-to-use creative thinking techniques along with insights into the creative thinking process.

Electronic Supplements

Companion Website with Online Practice Tests, by Joseph A. DeVito and Diana Murphy. Accessed at www.ablongman.com/devito, this site provides web links and Internet activities to enrich the course. The site also contains self-tests and skill development exercises designed exclusively for the Web.

VideoWorkshop for Interpersonal Communication Student Learning Guide, by Lynn Disbrow, Sinclair Community College. VideoWorkshop for Interpersonal Communication is a new way to bring video into your course for maximized learning! This total teaching and learning system includes quality video footage on an easy-to-use CD-ROM plus a *Student Learning Guide* and an *Instructor's Teaching Guide*—both with textbook-specific correlation grids. The result? A program that brings textbook concepts to life with ease and helps your students understand, analyze, and apply the objectives of the course. VideoWorkshop is available for your students as a value-pack option with this textbook.

Allyn & Bacon Communication Studies Website, by Terrence Doyle, Northern Virginia Community College, and Tim Borchers, Minnesota State University at Moorhead. This site includes modules on interpersonal, small group communication, and public speaking and includes web links, enrichment materials, and interactive activities to enhance students' understanding of key concepts. Access this site at www.ablongman.com/commstudies.

Tutor Center (access code required), www.aw.com/tutorcenter. Our Tutor Center provides free, one-on-one tutoring for students who purchase a new copy of participating Allyn & Bacon textbooks. Qualified instructors tutor students on all material covered in the texts. The approach is highly interactive, providing both knowledge of the academic discipline and methods for study of that discipline. Tutoring assistance is offered by phone, fax, Internet, and email during Tutor Center hours. For more details and ordering information, please contact your Allyn & Bacon publisher's representative.

Instructor's Resources
Print Supplements

Instructor's Manual and Test Bank with Transparency Masters, by Harriet Briscoe Harral. The Instructor's Manual provides chapter overviews, chapter outlines, skill objectives, and classroom strategies for each chapter. The manual provides ideas to activate class discussions and contains exercises to illustrate the concepts, principles, and skills of interpersonal communication. In addition, the Test Bank portion of the manual contains numerous multiple-choice, true/false, fill-in-the-blank, and essay test questions. The manual also includes more than 100 transparency masters that frame key concepts and skills.

The Blockbuster Approach: A Guide to Teaching Interpersonal Communication with Video, Third Edition, by Thomas E. Jewell, Bergen Community College. The guide provides lists and descriptions of commercial videos that can be used in the classroom to illustrate interpersonal concepts and complex interpersonal relationships. Sample activities are available.

Electronic Supplements

TestGen EQ: Computerized Test Bank   The user-friendly interface enables instructors to view, edit, and add questions, transfer questions to tests, and print tests in a variety of fonts. Search and sort features allow instructors to locate questions quickly and arrange them in preferred order.

PowerPoint Presentation Package, by Harriet Briscoe Harral. This text-specific package consists of a collection of lecture outlines and graphic images keyed to every chapter in the text. Available at http://suppscentral.ablongman.com.

Allyn & Bacon Digital Media Archive CD-ROM for Communication, Version 2.0   This CD-ROM contains electronic images of charts, graphs, maps, tables, and figures, along with media elements such as video, audio clips, and related web links. These media assets are fully customizable to use with our preformatted PowerPoint outlines or to import into your own lectures. (Windows and Mac)

VideoWorkshop for Interpersonal Communication Instructor's Teaching Guide, by Lynn Disbrow, Sinclair Community College. This guide provides teaching suggestions, quiz questions and answers, and discussion starters that will help you use the Video Workshop for Interpersonal Communication CD-ROM in class. A correlation guide helps you relate the materials to your text. The complete CD-ROM and Student Learning Guide are included in this guide. Go to http://www.ablongman.com/html/videoworkshop for more details.

Allyn & Bacon Interpersonal Communication Videos   Allyn & Bacon offers three Interpersonal Videos, ranging from 30 to 50 minutes, that contain scenarios illustrating key concepts in interpersonal communication. Accompanying user guides feature transcripts, teaching activities, and class discussion questions for each episode. Contact your Allyn & Bacon representative for ordering information. Some restrictions apply.

The Allyn & Bacon Communication Video Library   A collection of communication videos produced by Film for the Humanities and Sciences. Topics include, but are not limited to: *Business Presentations, Great American Speeches,* and *Conflict Resolution.* Contact your local Allyn & Bacon sales representative for ordering information. Some restrictions apply.

Interpersonal Movie Library   This collection is available to adopters and contains popular feature films dealing with a range of interpersonal topics. Contact your Allyn & Bacon representative for ordering information. Some restrictions apply.

Acknowledgments

I want to express my thanks to all those who reviewed the text at the various stages of revision; they gave generously of their time and expertise and I am in their debt. Thank you to Victoria Clements, College of Southern Maryland; Gretchen Harries, Austin Community College; Victoria Howitt, Grossmont College; Martin McDermott, Brookdale College; Patricia Minton, Hibbing Community College; and Julie Simanski, Des Moines Area Community College.

I also want to thank the many people who worked on the book, turning the manuscript into this great-looking text. Thank you to editors Karon Bowers and Brian Wheel for taking such good care of the book and for putting together a great supplements package; Ellen Darion and Sharon Geary, developmental editors, for contributing greatly throughout the entire revision process; Susan McIntyre, project manager at Nesbitt Graphics, for coordinating everything with great competence; Jay Howland, copy editor, for polishing this manuscript so expertly; and Laurie Frankenthaler, photo researcher, for finding such relevant and appropriate photos.

Joseph A. DeVito

Interpersonal Communication

1

▶ **Pat and Chris have been dating for the last three years and plan to move in together and enter into a permanent relationship. But one issue is creating serious conflict and has given Chris serious pause as to whether they should even continue this relationship: Pat is addicted to chat groups, often spending four or five hours a day chatting. Pat refuses to allow Chris to see any messages or to participate in the chat groups. This is private. Chris feels left out and wonders if Pat is really committed to the traditional relationship they originally envisioned. Pat minimizes this "problem" and says that love conquers all; once they commit themselves fully, chat-room communication will lessen.**

▶ **Reno has five children and works as a superintendent in a large condo complex in Boston. Although he's deeply interested in the lives of his wife and children, he feels ignored. His children rarely confide in him; whenever there's important news they go to their mother. Reno feels his only function is to earn money, and he has seriously considered leaving his family and starting another life in another city.**

▶ **For the last 14 years, Karla has worked in a toy factory in Michigan that was recently purchased by a Japanese investment firm. The production department, which Karla had headed for the last four years, has been reorganized and is now run by three people—two Japanese businessmen and Karla. Although production is up, morale is down. Karla used to handle most problems informally by talking with the crew over lunch or at company parties. Now, however, the managers handle all problems at formal business meetings. Karla feels that the new owners have virtually eliminated her job and that she is being kept on only because the union contract protects her. She's thinking of asking for a transfer or seeking a position with another company.**

These situations all revolve around problems in interpersonal communication. All of these people would profit from learning the principles and skills of interpersonal communication. Whether in a romantic or friendship relationship, a long-established family, or a work environment, the principles of interpersonal communication are powerful tools for dealing with problems such as these. Chris and Pat, for example, don't seem to know how to communicate with each other and derive the benefits that Pat is obviously receiving from chat communication. The belief that love will conquer all prevents Pat from seeing the difficulties this obsession with the Internet is causing Chris and the relationship. Pat seems unrealistic both about the power of love and about how deep-seated attachment to chat rooms is going to change so easily. Instead of dealing with the problem, Pat wants to ignore it as if it will go away once the couple exchanges vows. Pat needs to learn to see the situation from Chris's perspective, and Chris needs to see it from Pat's perspective (issues discussed in Chapter 3). Both need to confront and deal effectively with the differences that now only cause conflict (a topic covered in depth in Chapter 11).

Reno feels left out and doesn't know how to facilitate self-disclosures on the part of his children or his wife. Nor does he know how to communicate his own feelings. So it's not surprising that his children have learned that he's not the parent to go to with feelings. Reno wants involvement, but he doesn't know how to get it. The suggestions for facilitating self-disclosure and for communicating empathy and support discussed in Chapters 2 and 8 would prove helpful to Reno.

Karla is having trouble communicating in this new intercultural setting. Although morale is down throughout the plant, the new owners are unaware of it, largely because no one has voiced concern. Karla's self-esteem has been damaged; she feels she's lost her importance and doesn't know how to deal with the situation. Karla would profit from the discussion of self-esteem in Chapter 12 as well as from the discussions of culture throughout this text, especially Chapter 9's suggestions for improving intercultural communication.

As you'll see throughout this text, interpersonal communication is an extremely practical art. Your effectiveness as a friend, relationship partner, coworker, or manager will depend largely on your interpersonal skills. For example, in a survey of 1,001 people over 18 years of age, 53 percent felt that a lack of effective communication was the major cause of marriage failure—a factor significantly greater than money (38 percent) or in-law interference (14 percent) (http://www.natcom.org/research/ Roper/how_Americans_communicate.htm, accessed April 8, 2003). The relevance of interpersonal communication skills to relationships is a major theme of this text, and we will return to it repeatedly.

In a similar way, interpersonal skills are crucial to professional success, as has been widely documented (Morreale, Osborn, & Pearson, 2000). So important have interpersonal skills become that the U.S. Department of Labor, in its report, "What Work Requires of Schools"—a report based on interviews with managers, employers, and workers who described the skills they needed to function effectively at their jobs—identified interpersonal skills as one of five skills essential for a nation and an individual to be economically competitive in the world marketplace (*New York Times,* July 3, 1991, p. A17). In a study of more than 500 employers conducted by the Collegiate Employment Research Institute of Michigan State University, "good oral, written, and interpersonal communication skills were reported among the most notable deficiencies observed in new college graduates" (Scheetz, 1995). Interpersonal skills are considered a "key career advantage for finance professionals in the next century" (Messmer, 1999). In studies in the health care industry, communication skills likewise figure prominently, both enabling nurses to rise in the corporate hierarchy and building patient trust (Nordhaus-Bike, 1999; Titlow, Rackoff, & Emanuel, 1999). Researchers have also identified interpersonal skills as one of six areas that define the professional competence of physicians and trainees (Epstein & Hundert, 2002). And a study focusing on the education of hotel and restaurant administrators concluded that the area of "communication and interpersonal skills" was one of the three vitally important subjects that need to be emphasized (Dittman, 1997). The importance of interpersonal communication skills seems to extend over the entire spectrum of professions.

This book, in short, is about improving your interpersonal skills so that you'll be more effective in a wide variety of interpersonal communication situations: with your family; with supervisors, coworkers, and subordinates; and with acquaintances, friends, and lovers. A website devoted specifically to this textbook and offering lots of useful information on a wide variety of interpersonal communication issues—including the connection between interpersonal communication and the media—is available at www.ablongman.com/devito. The home page for this website is shown on page 4.

Before beginning your study of this exciting and practical area, examine your own beliefs about interpersonal communication by taking the self-test below.

> The secret of success is constancy to purpose.
>
> —Benjamin Disraeli

Test Yourself

What Do You Believe about Interpersonal Communication?

Respond to each of the following statements with T (true) if you believe the statement is usually true or F (false) if you believe the statement is usually false.

_____ ❶ Good communicators are born, not made.

_____ ❷ The more you communicate, the better at communicating you will be.

_____ ❸ In your interpersonal communications, a good guide to follow is to be as open, empathic, and supportive as you can be.

_____ ④ The best guide to follow when communicating with someone from another culture is to ignore the differences and treat the other person just as you'd treat members of your own culture.

_____ ⑤ Fear of speaking is detrimental, and to be an effective speaker you must eliminate it.

_____ ⑥ When there is conflict, your relationship is in trouble.

HOW DID YOU DO? As you probably figured out, all six statements are generally false. As you read this text, you'll discover not only why these beliefs are false but also the trouble you can get into when you assume they're true. For now, and in brief, here are some of the reasons why each statement is (generally) false: (1) Effective communication is learned; all of us can improve our abilities and become more effective communicators. (2) It isn't the amount of communication that matters, it's the quality. If you practice bad habits, you're more likely to grow less effective than more effective. (3) Because each interpersonal situation is unique, the type of communication appropriate in one situation may not be appropriate in another. (4) Ignoring differences will often merely create problems; people from different cultures may, for example, follow different rules for what is and what is not appropriate in interpersonal communication. (5) Most speakers are nervous; managing, not eliminating, the fear will enable you to become more effective regardless of your current level of apprehension. (6) All meaningful relationships experience conflict; the trick is to manage it effectively.

WHAT WILL YOU DO? This is a good place to start practicing the critical thinking skill of questioning commonly held assumptions—about communication and about yourself as a communicator. Do you hold beliefs that may limit your thinking about communication? For example, do you believe that certain kinds of communication are beyond your capabilities? Do you impose limits on how you see yourself as a communicator?

❝ If people knew how hard I worked to get my mastery, it wouldn't seem so wonderful after all. ❞

—Michaelangelo

Allyn & Bacon Companion Website
Messages: Building Interpersonal Communication Skills, 6/e

Welcome to the Companion Website for *Messages: Building Interpersonal Communication Skills, Sixth Edition*

Joseph A. DeVito
Diana Murphy

To get started make a selection from the drop down menu above.

To learn more about this book, including ordering information, visit its catalog page.

Browser Tuneup

SKILLS VIEWPOINT

Researchers have found that 80 percent of young women consider a spouse who can communicate his feelings more desirable than a spouse who earns a good living (**www.gallup.com/poll/releases/pr010627b.asp**, accessed June 27, 2001). How important, compared to all the other factors you might take into consideration in choosing a partner, is the ability to communicate? What specific communication skills would you consider "extremely important" in a life partner?

What Is Interpersonal Communication?

Interpersonal communication is communication that occurs between persons who have a connection or relationship. **Communication** occurs when you send or receive messages and when you assign meaning to such messages. Interpersonal communication is always distorted by "noise," occurs within a context, and involves some opportunity for feedback.

Interpersonal communicators are conscious of each other and of their connection with each other. They're interdependent; what one person thinks and says impacts on what the other thinks and says. Interpersonal communication includes the conversations that take place between an interviewer and a potential employee, between a son and his father, between two sisters, between a teacher and a student, or between two lovers or two friends. Even the stranger asking for directions from a local resident has a relationship with that person.

Some early theories viewed the communication process as linear. In this *linear* view of communication, the speaker spoke and the listener listened; after the speaker finished speaking, the listener would speak. Communication was seen as proceeding in a relatively straight line. Speaking and listening were seen as taking place at different times—when you spoke, you didn't listen; and when you listened, you didn't speak (Figure 1.1).

This linear **model,** or representation of the process, soon gave way to an *interactional* view in which the speaker and the listener were seen as exchanging turns at speaking and listening. For example, A spoke while B listened and then B (exchanging the listener's role for the speaker's role) spoke in response to what A said and A listened (see Figure 1.2 on page 6). Speaking and listening were still viewed as separate acts that did not overlap and that were not performed at the same time by the same person.

A more satisfying view, and the one currently held, sees communication as a *transactional* process in which each person serves simultaneously as speaker and listener. According to the **transactional view,** at the same time that you send messages, you're also receiving messages from your own communications and from the reactions of the other person (see Figure 1.3 on page 6). And at the same time that you're listening, you're also sending messages. In a transactional view, each person is seen as both speaker and listener, as simultaneously communicating and receiving messages

> **If your lips would keep from slips,**
> **Five things observe with care;**
> **To whom you speak, of whom you speak,**
> **And how, and when, and where.**
>
> —W. E. Norris

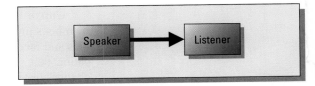

Figure 1.1

The Linear View of Human Communication
Communication researchers (Pearson, Nelson, Titsworth, & Harter, 2003) suggest that you think of the speaker as passing a ball to the listener, who either catches the ball or fumbles it. Can you think of another analogy or metaphor for this linear view of communication?

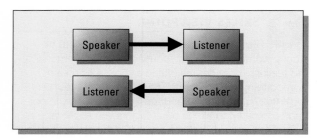

Figure 1.2

The Interactional View

In this view, continuing with the ball-throwing analogy, the speaker would pass the ball to the listener, who would then pass the ball back or fumble it (Pearson, Nelson, Titsworth, & Harter, 2003). What other analogy would work here?

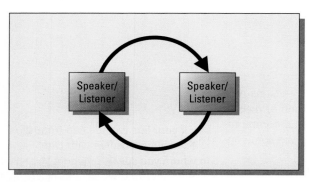

Figure 1.3

The Transactional View

In this view, a complex ball game is under way in which each player could send and receive any number of balls at any time. Players would be able to throw and catch balls at the very same time (Pearson, Nelson, Titsworth, & Harter, 2003). Can you think of any other analogies for this transactional view of communication?

(Watzlawick, Beavin, & Jackson, 1967; Watzlawick, 1977, 1978; Barnlund, 1970; Wilmot, 1987).

Also, in a transactional view the elements of communication are seen as *inter*dependent (never *in*dependent). Each exists in relation to the others. A change in any one element of this **process** produces changes in the other elements. For example, suppose you're talking with a group of your friends and your mother enters the group. This change in "audience" will lead to other changes; perhaps you'll change what you say or how you say it. Regardless of what change occurs, other changes will follow as a result.

Often, of course, interpersonal communication takes place face-to-face; and this is the type of interaction that probably comes to mind when you think of conversation. But, especially today, much conversation takes place online. Online communications are a part of people's experience throughout the world. Such communications are important personally, socially, and professionally. Let's look at three major online types of conversation and the ways in which they differ from one another and from face-to-face interaction: e-mail, the mailing list group, and the chat group.

In *e-mail*, you usually type your letter in an e-mail program and send it (along with other documents you may wish to attach) from your computer to your server (the computer at your school or at some commercial organization like America Online), which relays your message through a series of computer hookups and eventually to the server of the person you're addressing. Unlike face-to-face communication, e-mail does not take place in real time. You may send your message today, but the receiver may not read it for a week and may take another week to respond. Much of the spontaneity created by real-time communication is missing. You may, for example, be very enthusiastic about a topic when you send your e-mail but practically forget it by the time someone responds.

The *mailing list group* (or listserv) consists of a group of people interested in a particular topic who communicate with one another through e-mail. Generally, you subscribe to a list and communicate with all other members by addressing your mail to the group e-mail address. Any message you send to this address will be sent to each member who subscribes to the list. Your message is sent to all members at the same time; there are no asides to the person sitting next to you, as in face-to-face groups. A useful site for mailing lists, www.topica.com, contains thousands of mailing lists and discussion groups.

Chat groups have proliferated across the Internet. These groups enable members to converse in real time in discussion groups called channels. At any one time there are thousands of channels, so your chances of finding a topic you're interested in is high.

Unlike mailing lists, chat communication takes place in real time. You see a member's message as it's being sent; there's virtually no delay. As with both mailing lists and face-to-face conversation, the purposes of chat groups vary from communication that simply maintains connection with others (what many would call "idle chatter" or "phatic communication") to extremely significant discussions in science, education, health, politics, and just about any field you can name. The same is true with instant messaging (IM). Although most instant messaging seems to involve maintaining a connection with others, people use instant messaging to serve any and all communication functions that can be accomplished with few words.

Communication in a chat group resembles the conversation you'd observe at a large party. The guests divide into small groups varying from two people on up, and

5 Ways to Cautious Computer Communication

As a result of the differences between the evanescence of face-to-face communication and the permanency of electronic communication, you may wish to be cautious in your e-mail messages, newsgroup postings, and website messages.

1. Electronic messages are difficult to destroy. E-mails that you delete may remain on servers and be retrieved by a clever hacker.
2. Electronic messages may easily be made public; the ease of forwarding e-mails or newsgroup postings makes it especially important to consider that unintended receivers may read your messages.
3. Electronic messages are not privileged communication and can easily be used against you, especially in the workplace. Criticism of others may one day return to haunt you in accusations of discrimination.
4. Electronic messages provide permanent records. It is hard to argue, for example, that "That's not exactly what I said" if it is exactly what you said.
5. Electronic message files can be accessed by a nosy colleague or a visiting neighbor, who may then forward them to others.

Applying Interpersonal Skills/Then and Now

Have you (or has someone you know) ever written an e-mail or newsgroup post that got into the wrong hands? What happened? What might you do differently now?

each group discusses its own topic or version of a general topic. For example, in a group about travel, five people may be discussing the difficulties of traveling to Communist countries, three people may be discussing airport security systems, and two people may be discussing bargain rates for cruises to Mexico—all on this one channel. Chat groups also allow you to "whisper": to communicate with one other person without giving access to your message to other participants. So, although you may be communicating in one primary group (say, dealing with airport security), you also have your eye trained to pick up something particularly interesting in another group, much as you do at a party. Such groups also notify you when someone new comes into the group and when someone leaves. Like mailing lists, chat groups enable you to communicate with people you would never meet and interact with otherwise. Because such groups are international, they provide excellent exposure to other cultures, other ideas, and other ways of communicating.

In face-to-face conversation you're expected to contribute to the ongoing discussion. In chat groups you can simply observe; in fact, you're encouraged to "lurk"—to observe the participants' interaction before you say anything yourself. In this way, you'll be able to learn the cultural rules and norms of the group.

Another obvious difference between face-to-face and computer communication is that in face-to-face interaction the individuals are clearly identified—at least usually. In computer-mediated communication, however, you may remain anonymous. You may also pose as someone you're not: as a person of another sex or race, for example, or even as someone who is significantly older or younger than you really are, or of significantly different status (Saunders, Robey, & Vaverek, 1994). In face-to-face communication your physical self—the way you look, the way you're dressed—

"I loved your E-mail, but I thought you'd be older."

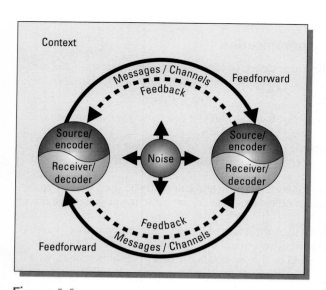

Figure 1.4

The Process of Interpersonal Communication
This model puts into visual form the various elements of the interpersonal communication process. How would you diagram the interpersonal communication process?

greatly influences the way your messages will be interpreted. In computer-mediated communication you reveal your physical self through your own descriptions. Although you may send photos of yourself via computer, you can also send photos of others and claim they're of yourself. There is, in short, much greater opportunity for presenting yourself as you want to present yourself when communicating via computer.

Given the basic definition of interpersonal communication, the transactional perspective, and an understanding that interpersonal communication occurs in many different forms, let's expand our model as in Figure 1.4 and look at each of the essential elements in interpersonal communication: source–receiver, messages, feedback, feedforward, channel, noise, context, and competence. Along with this discussion you may wish to visit the websites of some of the major communication organizations to see how they discuss communication. See, for example, **www.natcom.org** and **www.icahdq.org** for the two major academic associations in communication.

Source–Receiver

Interpersonal communication involves at least two persons. Each functions as a **source** (formulates and sends messages) and operates as a **receiver** (receives and understands messages). The linked term *source–receiver* emphasizes that each person is both source and receiver.

By putting your meanings into sound waves (or gestures, facial expressions, or postural adjustments), you're putting your thoughts and feelings into a **code,** or a set of symbols—a process called *en*coding. By translating sound (and light) waves into ideas, you're taking them out of the code they're in, a process called *de*coding. So we can call speakers (or, more generally, senders) **encoders:** those who put their meanings *into* a code. And we can call listeners (or, more generally, receivers) **decoders:** those who take meanings *out of* a code. Since encoding and decoding activities are combined in each person, the term *encoding–decoding* is used to emphasize this inevitable dual function.

Usually you encode an idea into a code that the other person understands; for example, you use words and gestures for which both you and the other person have similar meanings. At times, however, you may want to exclude others; so, for example, you might speak in a language that only one of your listeners knows or use jargon to prevent others from understanding. At other times, you may assume incorrectly that the other person knows your code and, for example, unknowingly use words or gestures the other person simply doesn't understand.

For interpersonal communication to occur, then, meanings must be encoded and decoded. If Jamie has his eyes closed and is wearing stereo headphones as his dad is speaking to him, interpersonal communication is not taking place—simply because the messages, both verbal and nonverbal, are not being received.

Messages

For interpersonal communication to exist, **messages** that express your thoughts and feelings must be sent and received. Interpersonal communication may be verbal or nonverbal, but it's usually a combination of both. You communicate interpersonally with words as well as with gestures and touch, for example. Even the clothes you wear communicate, as do the way you walk and the way you shake hands, comb your hair, sit, smile, or frown. Everything about you has the potential to send interpersonal messages, and every message has an **effect,** or outcome.

In face-to-face communication your messages are both verbal and nonverbal; you supplement your words with facial expressions, body movements, and variations in vocal volume and rate, for example. When you communicate through a keyboard, your message is communicated basically with words. This does not mean that you cannot communicate emotional meanings; in fact, some researchers have argued that diagrams, pictures, and varied typefaces enable you to communicate messages that are rich in emotional meaning (Lea & Spears, 1995). Similarly, you can use emoticons. But basically a keyboarded or written message is communicated with words. Because of this, sarcasm, for example, is difficult to convey unambiguously—whereas in face-to-face communication you might wink or smile to indicate that your message should not be taken seriously or literally.

Message Overload   Message overload (often called information overload in business) is one of the greatest obstacles to communication efficiency and may even lead to health problems in corporate managers (Lee, 2000). The ease with which people can copy or forward e-mail and Internet messages has obviously contributed to message overload, as has the junk e-mail and spam that seems to grow every day. Invariably, you must select certain messages to attend to and other messages to ignore. Today, for example, the American worker is exposed to more messages in one year than a person living in 1900 was in his or her entire life. The average employee now receives more than 50 e-mails daily. And in one day the average manager sends and receives more than 100 documents.

One of the problems message overload creates is that it absorbs an enormous amount of time. The more messages you have to deal with, the less time you have for the most important messages or tasks. Similarly, errors are more likely under conditions of message overload, simply because you cannot devote the needed time to any one item. The more rushed you are, the more likely you are to make mistakes.

Another problem is that the overabundance of messages may make it difficult for you to determine efficiently which messages need immediate attention and which don't, which messages may be discarded and which must be retained. Consider your own ways of dealing with message overload (Uris, 1986). Do you

- *think before passing on messages, realizing that not all messages must be passed on—that not everyone needs to know everything?*
- *use the messages as they come to you and then throw them out? For example, do you write the relevant dates for a meeting on your calendar and then throw out the announcement or delete the e-mail?*
- *organize your messages? Have you created folders to help you store and retrieve the information you need quickly?*
- *get rid of extra copies? When you receive multiple copies, do you get rid of all but the one you need?*
- *distinguish between messages that you should save and messages that are only cluttering up your space?*

Feedback   **Feedback** is a special type of message. When you send a spoken or written message to another person, you get feedback from your own message: You hear what you say, you feel the way you move, you see what you write. On the basis of this information, you may correct yourself, rephrase something, or perhaps smile at a clever turn of phrase. This is self-feedback.

You also get feedback from others. The person with whom you're communicating is constantly sending you messages that indicate how he or she is receiving and responding to your messages. Nods of agreement, smiles, puzzled looks, and questions asking for clarification are all examples of feedback.

Message Skills

Message Overload: Combat message overload by using and disposing of messages as they come to you, organizing, getting rid of extra copies, and distinguishing between messages to save and messages to throw away.

Message Skills

Feedback: Listen to both verbal and nonverbal feedback—from yourself and from others—and use these cues to help you adjust your messages.

Giving Effective Feedback

Here are three situations in which you might want to give feedback. For each situation *(a)* indicate the kind of feedback that you would consider appropriate (positive or negative? person focused or message focused? immediate or delayed? low in monitoring or high in monitoring? supportive or critical?), and *(b)* write one or two sentences in which you express feedback that has the qualities you identified in *(a)*.

For example, let's say a friend, someone you like but don't have romantic feelings for, asks for a date. You might decide to give feedback that is positive, person focused, immediate, low-monitored, and supportive, saying something like "Pat, I'm really flattered and truly appreciate your invitation. But I really can't accept. I'm seeing someone and I think it could get serious. So I have to decline."

1. A colleague persists in talking explicitly about sex despite your previous and frequent objections.
2. A telemarketer—the fifth this evening—asks you to change your long-distance carrier.
3. A homeless person smiles at you on the street and asks for some change.

Feedback comes in a variety of styles and serves a variety of purposes. Use it and read it; it's a significant part of the interpersonal interaction.

> " I am not sure I have learned anything else as important. I have been able to realize what a prime role what I have come to call 'feedforward' has in all our doings. "
>
> —I. A. Richards

Notice that in face-to-face communication you can monitor the feedback of the other person as you're speaking. In computer-mediated communication that feedback will come much later and thus is likely to be more clearly thought out and perhaps more closely monitored.

Feedforward   Much as feedback contains information about messages already sent, **feedforward** conveys information about messages before you send them. Opening comments such as "Wait until you hear this" or "I'm not sure of this, but . . ." or "Don't get me wrong, but . . ." are examples of feedforward. These messages tell the listener something about the messages to come or about the way you'd like the listener to respond. Nonverbally, you give feedforward by, for example, your facial expressions, eye contact, and physical posture; with these nonverbal messages you tell the other person something about the messages you'll be sending. A smile may signal a pleasant message; eye avoidance may signal that the message to come is difficult and perhaps uncomfortable to express. A book's table of contents, its preface, and (usually) its first chapter are also examples of feedforward.

Channel

The communication **channel** is the medium through which message signals pass. The channel works like a bridge connecting source and receiver. Normally two, three, or four channels are used simultaneously. Thus, for example, in face-to-face **speech** interactions, you speak and listen, using the vocal–auditory channel. You also, however, make gestures and receive these signals visually, using the visual channel. Similarly, you emit odors and smell those of others (chemical channel). Often you touch one another, and this too communicates (tactile channel).

Another way to classify channels is by the means of communication. Thus, face-to-face contact, telephones, e-mail, movies, television, smoke signals, and telegraph would be types of channels. Of most relevance today, of course, is the difference between face-to-face and computer-mediated interpersonal communication: interaction through e-mail, chat groups, instant messaging, news postings, film, television, radio, fax, or smoke signals.

Message Skills

Feedforward: Use feedforward when you feel your listener needs background or when you want to ease into a particular topic, such as bad news.

Giving Effective Feedforward

For each of the following situations, you may feel there's a need to preface your remarks with some kind of feedforward—some kind of prefatory comments before stating your main or primary message. For each situation *(a)* identify the specific purpose you hope to achieve with your feedforward and *(b)* write a brief feedforward message that helps you achieve the purposes you identified in *(a)*.

1. You see an attractive person in one of your classes and would like to get to know the person a bit more with the possible objective of a date.
2. You just saw the posted grades for the midterm; your close friend failed, but you did extremely well. In the cafeteria you meet your friend, who asks, "How'd I do on the midterm?"
3. You have a reputation for injecting outlandish ideas into otherwise formal and boring discussions. This time, however, you want to offer a proposal that you fear will seem to be one of your standard outlandish comments but is actually an idea that you think could work. You want to assure your group that this idea is worthy of their undivided attention.

Feedforward can help set a favorable mood or give listeners needed information—paving the way for greater interpersonal effectiveness.

At times one or more channels may be damaged. For example, in the case of people who are blind, the visual channel is impaired and so adjustments have to be made. Table 1.1 on page 12 gives you an idea of how such adjustments between blind and sighted persons can make interpersonal communication more effective.

Message Skills

Channel: Assess your channel options (for example, face-to-face, e-mail, leaving a voicemail message) before communicating important messages.

Noise

Noise is anything that interferes with your receiving a message someone is sending or with their receiving your message. Noise may be physical (loud talking, honking cars, illegible handwriting, "garbage" on your computer screen), physiological (hearing or visual impairment, articulation disorders), psychological (preconceived ideas, wandering thoughts), or semantic (misunderstood meanings). Technically, noise is anything that distorts or gets in the way of the message.

A useful concept in understanding noise and its importance in communication is **signal-to-noise ratio.** In this phrase the term *signal* refers to information that you'd find useful; *noise* refers to information that is useless (to you). So, for example, mailing lists or newsgroups that contained lots of useful information would be high on signal and low on noise; those that contained lots of useless information would be high on noise and low on signal.

Because messages may be visual as well as spoken, noise too may be visual. Thus, sunglasses that prevent someone from seeing the nonverbal messages from your eyes would be considered noise, as would blurred type on a printed page. Table 1.2 on page 13 identifies the four major types of noise in more detail.

All communications contain noise. Noise cannot be totally eliminated, but its effects can be reduced. Making your language more precise, sharpening your skills for sending and receiving nonverbal messages, and improving your listening and feedback skills are some ways to combat the influence of noise.

Message Skills

Noise Management: Reduce physical, physiological, psychological, and semantic noise as best you can; use repetition and restatement and, when in doubt, ask if you're clear.

Context

Communication always takes place within a context: an environment that influences the form and the content of communication. At times this context is so natural that you ignore it, like street noise. At other times the context stands out, and the ways in which

TABLE 1.1 *Interpersonal Communication Tips*

BETWEEN BLIND AND SIGHTED PEOPLE

People vary greatly in their visual abilities; some are totally blind, some are partially sighted, and some have unimpaired vision. Ninety percent of people who are "legally blind" have some vision. All, however, have the same need for communication and information. Here are some tips for making communication between blind and sighted people more effective.

If you're the sighted person and are talking with a blind person:

1. Identify yourself; don't assume the blind person will recognize your voice.
2. Face the blind person; you'll be easier to hear. At the same time, don't shout. People who are visually impaired are not hearing impaired. Speak at your normal volume.
3. Because your gestures, eye movements, and facial expressions cannot be seen, encode into speech all the meanings you wish to communicate.
4. Use audible turn-taking cues. When you pass the role of speaker to a person who's visually impaired, don't rely on nonverbal cues; instead, say something like "Do you agree with that, Joe?"
5. Use normal vocabulary and discuss topics that you'd discuss with sighted people. Don't avoid terms like *see* or *look* or even *blind*. Don't avoid discussing a television show or a painting or the way your new car looks; these are normal conversational topics for all people.
6. In guiding a person who is blind, follow these simple suggestions:
   a. If you want to offer assistance, ask first ("Would you like me to hold your arm as we go upstairs?") instead of just grabbing the person.
   b. Identify obstacles before reaching them: "There are three steps coming up."
   c. When you have to leave, make sure the blind person is comfortable where he or she is. For example, ask if the person would like to sit while you get the coffee.

If you're the blind person and are interacting with a sighted person:

1. Help the sighted person meet your special communication needs. If you want your surroundings described, ask. If you want the person to read the road signs, ask.
2. Be patient with the sighted person. Many people are nervous talking with people who are blind for fear of offending. Put them at ease in a way that also makes you more comfortable.

Sources: These suggestions were drawn from the Cincinnati Association for the Blind, http://www.cincyblind.org, and the Royal National Institute of the Blind, http://www.rnib.org, both accessed April 5, 2002.

it restricts or stimulates your communications are obvious. Think, for example, of the different ways you'd talk at a funeral, in a quiet restaurant, and at a rock concert.

The **context of communication** has at least four dimensions: physical, cultural, social–psychological, and temporal. The room, workplace, or outdoor space in which communication takes place—the tangible or concrete environment—is the *physical dimension*. When you communicate face-to-face you're both in essentially the same physical environment. In computer-mediated communication you may both be in drastically different environments; one of you may be on a beach in San Juan while another is in a Wall Street office.

The *cultural dimension* consists of the rules, norms, beliefs, and attitudes of the people communicating that are passed from one generation to another. For example, in some cultures it's considered polite to talk to strangers; in others it's something to be avoided.

The *social–psychological* dimension includes, for example, the status relationships among the participants: distinctions such as who is the employer and who the employee, who is the salesperson and who the store owner. The formality or informality, the friendliness or hostility, the cooperativeness or competitiveness of the interaction are also part of the social–psychological dimension.

TABLE 1.2   Four Types of Noise

One of the most important skills in communication is to recognize the types of noise and to develop ways to combat them. For example, what kinds of noise occur in the classroom? What kinds of noise occur in your family communications? What kinds occur at work? What can you do to combat these kinds of noise?

TYPE OF NOISE	DEFINITION	EXAMPLE
Physical	Interference that is external to both speaker and listener; interferes with the physical transmission of the signal or message	Screeching of passing cars, hum of computer, sunglasses
Physiological	Physical barriers within the speaker or listener	Visual impairments, hearing loss, articulation problems, memory loss
Psychological	Cognitive or mental interference	Biases and prejudices in senders and receivers, closed-mindedness, inaccurate expectations, extreme emotionalism (anger, hate, love, grief)
Semantic	Different meanings assigned by speaker and listener	Language differences, use of jargon or overly complex terms not understood by listener, dialectical differences in meaning

The *temporal* or *time dimension* has to do with where a particular message fits into a sequence of communication events. For example, if you tell a joke about sickness immediately after your friend tells you she is sick, the joke will be perceived differently from the same joke told as one of a series of similar jokes to your friends in the locker room of the gym.

Interpersonal Competence

Your ability to communicate effectively is your **interpersonal competence** (Spitzberg & Cupach, 1989; Wilson & Sabee, 2003). A major goal of this text (and your course) is to expand and enlarge your competence so you'll have a greater arsenal of communication options at your disposal. It's much like learning vocabulary: The more words you know, the more ways you'll have to express yourself. The greater your interpersonal competence, the more options you'll have for communicating with friends, lovers, and family; with colleagues on the job; and in just about any situation in which you'll talk with another person. The greater your competence, the greater your own power to accomplish successfully what you want to accomplish—to ask for a raise or a date; establish temporary work relationships, long-term friendships, or romantic relationships; communicate empathy and support; or gain compliance or resist the compliance tactics of others. Whatever your interpersonal goal, increased competence will help you accomplish it more effectively.

In short, interpersonal competence includes knowing how interpersonal communication works and how to best achieve your purposes by adjusting your messages according to the context of the interaction, the person with whom you're interacting, and a host of other factors discussed throughout this text. The process goes like this: knowledge of interpersonal communication *leads to* greater interpersonal ability *leads to* a greater number of available choices or options for interacting *leads to* greater likelihood of interpersonal effectiveness.

Interpersonal competence consists largely of understanding the way interpersonal communication works and mastering its **skills** (including **power** and the often neglected skills of **listening**). These skills depend on **critical thinking,** are specific to a given **culture,** and rest on an **ethical foundation.** Understanding the nature of these six themes of competence and how they are highlighted in this text will enable you to gain most from studying and working with this material (see Figure 1.5 on page 14).

Figure 1.5

The Competent Interpersonal Communicator

Indicate how competent you feel you are in each of these six areas right now, give yourself scores from 1 (little competence) to 10 (a great deal of competence). Return to this figure periodically to rerate yourself. By the end of the course, you should have increased all of your scores significantly.

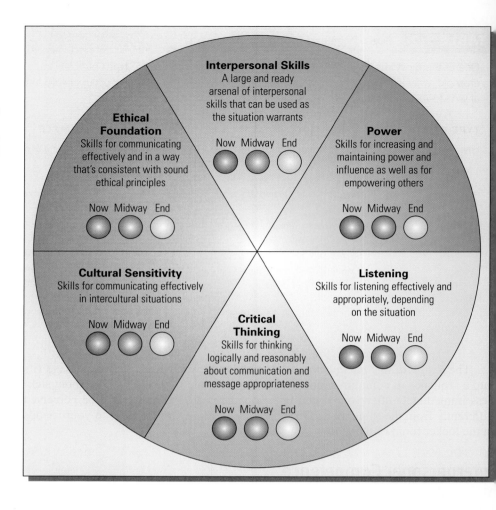

Interpersonal Skills
A large and ready arsenal of interpersonal skills that can be used as the situation warrants
Now Midway End

Ethical Foundation
Skills for communicating effectively and in a way that's consistent with sound ethical principles
Now Midway End

Power
Skills for increasing and maintaining power and influence as well as for empowering others
Now Midway End

Cultural Sensitivity
Skills for communicating effectively in intercultural situations
Now Midway End

Critical Thinking
Skills for thinking logically and reasonably about communication and message appropriateness
Now Midway End

Listening
Skills for listening effectively and appropriately, depending on the situation
Now Midway End

> " Important principles may and must be flexible. "
>
> —Abraham Lincoln

Competence and Interpersonal Skills   This text explains the theory and research in interpersonal communication in order to provide you with a solid understanding of how interpersonal communication works. With that understanding as a firm foundation, you'll be better able to develop and master the very practical skills of interpersonal communication. In addition to discussing the skills and their relevant theory throughout the text, the book highlights interpersonal communication skills in three other main ways. (1) *Message Skills* notes appear in the margins throughout the text to highlight and summarize selected skills. (2) *Skill Building Exercises* appear throughout the text, giving you opportunities to practice some of the skills discussed in the text; for example, to practice reducing apprehension, communicating your emotions (even negative ones), formulating excuses, and confronting intercultural difficulties. (3) *Skills Toolboxes* (one per chapter) identify clusters of interpersonal skills that are useful in specific situations; for example, ways to empower apprehensives, to network more effectively, and to deal with complaints.

In learning the skills of interpersonal communication (or any set of skills), you'll probably at first sense an awkwardness and self-consciousness; the new behaviors may not seem to fit comfortably. As you develop more understanding and use the skills more, this awkwardness will gradually fade and the new behaviors will begin to feel comfortable and natural. You'll facilitate your progress toward mastery if you follow a logical system of steps. Here's one possible system, called STEP (Skill, Theory, Example, Practice):

1. Get a clear understanding of what the *skill* is.

2. Understand the *theory;* if you understand the reasons for the suggestions offered, it will help make the skill more logical.

3. Develop *examples,* especially your own; this will help to make the material covered here a more integral part of communication behavior.

4. *Practice* with the Skill Building Exercises included in this text as well as with those on the website; practice alone at first, then with supportive friends, and then in general day-to-day interactions.

Competence and Power   Communication skills and power are integrally related. If you have strong interpersonal communication skills, you're likely to have power and influence—socially, at school, in your close relationships, at work, or just about any place where people interact. If you have poor interpersonal skills, you're likely to have much less power and influence.

Because of this close connection, power concepts are integrated throughout the text. And Chapter 12, "Power and Interpersonal Communication," focuses specifically on skills for increasing personal and interpersonal power. As stated in the introduction, the aim of this text is to make you a more powerful and a more empowering interpersonal communicator.

Competence and Listening   Often we tend to think of competence in interpersonal communication as "speaking effectiveness," paying little attention to listening. But listening is an integral part of interpersonal communication; you cannot be a competent communicator if you're a poor listener. Listening, therefore, is emphasized in this text in two major ways: (1) *Chapter 4 is devoted to listening* and covers the nature and importance of listening, the steps you go through in listening, the role of culture and gender in listening, and ways to increase your listening effectiveness. (2) *Twelve "Listen to This" boxes are positioned throughout the text* to illustrate how

> ❝ The new source of power is not money in the hands of a few but information in the hands of many. ❞
>
> —John Naisbitt

Listening to New Ideas

Because you'll be listening to lots of new ideas in this course and in this text, it's appropriate to begin these "Listen to This" boxes with a useful technique for listening to new ideas. The technique is called PIP'N and derives from Carl Rogers's (1970; Kramer, 1997) work on paraphrase as a means for ensuring understanding and from Edward deBono's (1976) PMI (plus, minus, interesting) technique. You can use this technique silently, as in thinking about something you hear, or aloud, as you might in conversation. PIP'N involves four steps that follow the acronym:

P = *Paraphrase.* Put in your own words what you think the speaker is saying. In conversation this will ensure that you and the speaker have the same general understanding. Your paraphrase will also provide the speaker with the opportunity to elaborate or clarify his or her ideas.

I = *Interesting.* Identify something interesting that you find in the idea under discussion. Think of why this idea might be interesting to you, to others, to the organization.

P = *Positive.* Identify what is positive about the idea. What's good about it? How might it solve a problem or make a situation better?

N = *Negative.* Identify any negatives that you think the idea might entail. Might it prove expensive? Will it be difficult to implement? Is it directed at insignificant issues?

Applying Listening Skills

How might you use PIP'N? For practice, you may want to try PIP'N on the PIP'N technique itself: (1) Paraphrase the PIP'N technique, (2) say why the technique is interesting, (3) say something positive about it, and (4) say something negative about it.

listening relates to the topic of each chapter and to provide a variety of specific listening skills. Among the topics of these boxes are the importance of listening to yourself, the role of gender differences, and ways to listen during conflict.

Competence and Critical Thinking   Without critical thinking there can be no competent exchange of ideas, no competent communication. Critical thinking is logical thinking; it's thinking that is well reasoned, unbiased, and clear. It involves thinking intelligently, carefully, and with as much clarity as possible. It's the opposite of what you'd call sloppy, illogical, or careless thinking. It's "the process of examining information and reaching a judgment or decision" (Wade & Tavris, 1990). And, not surprisingly, according to one study of corporate executives, critical thinking is one of the stepping stones to effective management (Miller, 1997, p. 71).

Critical thinking is universal across all areas of knowledge and experience. Although this book focuses on probably the most important form of all human behavior, interpersonal communication, critical thinking will prove of value in the arts and humanities, the social sciences, and the sciences, as well as in just about any situation in which you find yourself.

Because of its central importance, critical thinking is integrated throughout the text. In addition, each of the boxed features require the application of critical thinking principles.

Competence and Culture   The term *culture* refers to the lifestyle of a group of people. A group's culture consists of their values, beliefs, artifacts, ways of behaving, and ways of communicating. Culture includes all that members of a social group have produced and developed—their language, ways of thinking, art, laws, and religion. Culture is transmitted from one generation to another not through genes but through communication and learning; especially through the teachings of parents, peer groups, schools, religious institutions, and government agencies. Because most cultures teach women and men different attitudes and ways of communicating, many of the gender differences we observe may be considered cultural. So, while not minimizing the biological differences between men and women, most people agree that gender differences are, in part, cultural.

Competence is sometimes culture specific; communications that prove effective in one culture will not necessarily prove effective in another. For example, giving a birthday gift to a close friend would be appreciated by members of many cultures and in some cases would be expected. But Jehovah's Witnesses frown on this practice, because they don't celebrate birthdays (Dresser, 1996, 1999). Because of the vast range of cultural differences that affect interpersonal communication, every chapter discusses the role of culture.

Competence and Ethics   Interpersonal communication also involves questions of *ethics*. There is a moral dimension to any interpersonal communication act (Jaksa & Pritchard, 1994; Bok, 1978). For example, although it might be effective to lie in selling a product, it would not be ethical. The decisions you make concerning communication need to be guided by what you consider right as well as by what you consider effective.

Ethical dimensions of interpersonal communication are presented throughout the text in "Ethical Messages" features. Woven through these discussions of ethics are two overriding questions that will influence all your ethical decisions: Are ethical principles objective or subjective? and Does the end justify the means?

In an *objective* view, you'd argue that the rightness or wrongness of an act is absolute and exists apart from the values or beliefs of any individual or culture. With this view, you'd hold that there are standards that apply to all people in all situations at all times. If lying, false advertising, using illegally obtained evidence, or revealing secrets you've promised to keep were considered unethical, then they would be unethical regardless of circumstances or of cultural values and beliefs. In an objective view the end can never justify the means; an unethical act is never justified regardless of how good or beneficial its results (or ends) might be.

The Ethics of Communicating in Cyberspace

Because of the explosion in computer communication, "nethics" (the ethics of Internet communication) has become an important part of ethical communication generally. Of course, the same principles that govern ethical face-to-face interaction should also prevail when you communicate online. Here, however, are a few principles with special relevance to computer communication. It's unethical to:

1. Invade the privacy of others. Reading the files of another person or breaking into files that you're not authorized to read is unethical, just as it would be to read a person's diary or personal letters.
2. Harm others or their property. Creating computer viruses, publishing instructions for making bombs, or creating websites that promote sexism, racism, heterosexism, or ageism is unethical.
3. Spread falsehoods. Lying on the Internet—about other people, about the powers of medical or herbal treatment, or about yourself (in, say, misrepresenting yourself in chat groups) is unethical.
4. Plagiarize. Appropriating the work of another as your own—whether the original work appeared on the Internet or in a book or journal—is unethical.
5. Steal passwords, PIN numbers, or authorization codes that belong to others. It's similar to stealing and using another person's credit card.
6. Copy software programs that you haven't paid for.

What Would You Do?

As an experiment you develop a computer virus that can destroy websites. Recently you've come across various websites that you feel promote child pornography. You wonder if you can ethically destroy these websites. And, further, you wonder if not destroying them can actually be more unethical than using your newly developed virus.

In a *subjective* view of ethics, you'd argue that absolute statements about right and wrong are too rigid and that the ethics of a message depends on the culture's values and beliefs as well as on the particular circumstances. Thus, a subjective position would claim that lying might be wrong to win votes or sell cigarettes, but that it might be quite ethical if good would result from it—as when we try to make friends feel better by telling them that they look great or that they'll get well soon. In a subjective view a good end would often justify the use of means that would in other situations be considered unethical.

As you read the Ethical Messages boxes and respond to the ethical issues raised, ask yourself to what extent your responses reflect an objective or a subjective view of ethics and to what extent you believe that the end may justify the means.

These six themes of competence are not separate and distinct from one another but rather interact and overlap. For example, as already noted, critical thinking pervades the entire interpersonal communication process, but it also serves as a foundation for your cultural awareness, listening effectiveness, and skill development. Similarly, an awareness of cultural differences will make you more effective as a listener, more discerning in using skills, and more conscious of the ethical dimension of interpersonal communication. So, as you read the text and work actively with the concepts, remember that everything in it—including the regular text, the Message Skills notes, the boxed features, the material in the margins, and the summaries and vocabulary tests at the end of the chapters—is designed to contribute to one overarching aim: to increase your interpersonal communication competence.

Principles of Interpersonal Communication

Another way to define interpersonal communication is to consider its major principles. These principles are significant in terms of explaining theory and also, as you'll see, have very practical applications.

Interpersonal Communication Is a Package of Signals

Communication behaviors, whether they involve verbal messages, gestures, or some combination thereof, usually occur in "packages" (Pittenger, Hockett, & Danehy, 1960). Usually, verbal and nonverbal behaviors reinforce or support each other. All parts of a message system normally work together to communicate a particular meaning. You don't express fear with words while the rest of your body is relaxed. You don't express anger through your posture while your face smiles. Your entire body works together—verbally and nonverbally—to express your thoughts and feelings.

With any form of communication, whether interpersonal messages, small group communication, public speaking, or mass media, you probably pay little attention to its "packaged" nature. It goes unnoticed. But when there's an incongruity—when the chilly handshake belies the verbal greeting, when the nervous posture belies the focused stare, when the constant preening belies the expressions of being comfortable and at ease—you take notice. Invariably you begin to question the credibility, the sincerity, and the honesty of the individual.

Often contradictory messages are sent over a period of time. Note, for example, that in the following interaction the employee is being given two directives: (1) Use initiative, and (2) Don't use initiative. Regardless of what he or she does, rejection will follow.

Employer: You've got to learn to take more initiative. You never seem to take charge, to take control.
Employee: (Takes the initiative, makes decisions.)
Employer: You've got to learn to follow the chain of command and not do things just because you want to.
Employee: (Goes back to old ways, not taking any initiative.)
Employer: Well, I told you. We expect more initiative from you.

Contradictory messages are particularly damaging when children are involved. Children can neither escape from such situations nor communicate about the communications. They can't talk about the lack of correspondence between one set of messages and another set. They can't ask their parents, for example, why they don't hold them or hug them when they say they love them.

Contradictory messages may be the result of the desire to communicate two different emotions or feelings. For example, you may like a person and want to communicate a positive feeling, but you may also feel resentment toward this person and want to communicate a negative feeling as well. The result is that you communicate both feelings; for example, you say that you're happy to see the person, but your facial expression and body posture communicate your negative feelings (Beier, 1974). In this example, and in many similar cases, the socially acceptable message is usually communicated verbally, whereas the less socially acceptable message is communicated nonverbally.

Interpersonal Communication Involves Content *and* Relationship Messages

Interpersonal messages combine **content and relationship dimensions.** That is, they refer to the real world, to something external to both speaker and listener; and at the same time they also refer to the relationship between the parties. For example, a supervisor may say to a trainee, "See me after the meeting." This simple message has a content message that tells the trainee to see the supervisor after the meeting. It also contains a **relationship message** that says something about the connection between the supervisor and the trainee. Even the use of the simple command shows there is a status difference that allows the supervisor to command the trainee. You can appreciate this most clearly if you visualize this command being made by the trainee to the supervisor. It appears awkward and out of place, because it violates the normal relationship between supervisor and trainee.

Many conflicts arise because people misunderstand relationship messages and cannot clarify them. Other problems arise when people fail to see the difference between content messages and relationship messages. A good example occurred when my mother came to stay for a week at a summer place I had. On the first day she swept the kitchen floor six times. I had repeatedly told her that it did not need sweeping, that I would be tracking in dirt and mud from the outside. She persisted in sweeping, however, saying that the floor was dirty. On the content level, we were talking about the value of sweeping the kitchen floor. On the relationship level, however, we were talking about something quite different. We were each saying, "This is my house." When I realized this, I stopped complaining about the relative usefulness of sweeping a floor that did not need sweeping. Not surprisingly, she stopped sweeping.

"It's not about the story. It's about Daddy taking time out of his busy day to read you the story."

Ignoring Relationship Messages   Examine the following interchange and note how relationship considerations are ignored:

Messages	Comments
Paul: I'm going bowling tomorrow. The guys at the plant are starting a team.	He focuses on the content and ignores any relationship implications of the message.
Judy: Why can't we ever do anything together?	She responds primarily on a relationship level, ignoring the content implications of the message and expressing her displeasure at being ignored in his decision.
Paul: We can do something together anytime; tomorrow's the day they're organizing the team.	Again, he focuses almost exclusively on the content.

This example reflects research findings that show that men focus more on content messages, whereas women focus more on relationship messages (Wood, 1994). Once you recognize this gender difference, you can increase your sensitivity to the opposite sex.

Acknowledging Relationship Messages   Here is essentially the same situation but with added sensitivity to relationship messages and to gender differences.

Messages	Comments
Paul: The guys at the plant are organizing a bowling team. I'd sure like to be on the team. I'd like to go to the organizational meeting tomorrow. Okay?	Although he focuses on content, he shows awareness of the relationship dimensions by asking if this would be okay and by expressing his desire rather than his decision to attend this meeting.
Judy: That sounds great, but I'd really like to do something together tomorrow.	She focuses on the relationship dimension but also acknowledges his content orientation. Note too that she does not respond defensively, as if she has to defend herself or her emphasis on relationship aspects.
Paul: How about your meeting me at Luigi's and we can have dinner after the organizational meeting?	He responds to the relationship aspect —without abandoning his desire to join the bowling team—and seeks to incorporate it into his

Messages	Comments
	communications. He tries to negotiate a solution that will meet both Judy's and his needs.
Judy: That sounds great. I'm dying for spaghetti and meatballs.	She responds to both messages, approving of both his joining the team and their meeting for dinner.

Arguments over the content dimension—such as what happened in a movie—are relatively easy to resolve. You may, for example, simply ask a third person what took place or see the movie again. Arguments on the relationship level, however, are much more difficult to resolve, in part because people seldom recognize that the argument is about relationship messages.

Interpersonal Communication Is a Process of Adjustment

The principle of **adjustment** states that interpersonal communication can take place only to the extent that the people talking share the same communication system. We can easily understand this when dealing with speakers of two different languages; much miscommunication is likely to occur. The principle, however, takes on particular relevance when you realize that no two people share identical communication systems. Parents and children, for example, not only have very different vocabularies but also, more importantly, have different meanings for some of the terms they have in common. (Consider, for example, the differences between parents' and children's understanding of such terms as *music, success,* and *family.*) Different cultures and social groups, even when they share a common language, also have different nonverbal communication systems. To the extent that these systems differ, communication will be hindered.

Part of the art of interpersonal communication is learning the other person's signals, how they're used, and what they mean. People in close relationships—either as intimate friends or as romantic partners—realize that learning the other person's signals takes a long time and, often, great patience. If you want to understand what another person means—by smiling, by saying "I love you," by arguing about trivial matters, by making self-deprecating comments—you have to learn that person's system of signals. Furthermore, you have to share your own system of signals with others so that they can better understand you. Although some people may know what you mean by your silence or by your avoidance of eye contact, others may not. You cannot expect others to decode your behaviors accurately without help.

This principle is especially important in intercultural communication, largely because people from different cultures use different signals and sometimes the same signals to signify quite different things. In much of the United States, focused eye contact means honesty and openness. But in Japan and in many Hispanic cultures, that same behavior may signify arrogance or disrespect if engaged in by, say, a youngster with someone significantly older.

Communication Accommodation An interesting theory largely revolving around adjustment is communication accommodation theory. This theory holds that speakers will adjust to or accommodate to the speaking style of their listeners so as to gain, for example, social approval and greater communication efficiency (Giles, Mulac, Bradac, & Johnson, 1987). For example, when two people have a similar speech rate, they seem to be attracted to each other more than to those with dissimilar rates (Buller, LePoire, Aune, & Eloy, 1992). Speech rate similarity has also been associated with greater sociability and intimacy (Buller & Aune, 1992). Also, the speaker who uses language intensity similar to that of listeners is judged to have greater credibility than the speaker who uses intensity different from that of listeners (Aune & Kikuchi, 1993). Still another study found that roommates who had similar

Message Skills

Content and Relationship: Listen to both the content and the relationship aspects of messages, distinguish between them, and respond to both.

Message Skills

Context Adjustment: Adjust your messages to the physical, cultural, social–psychological, and temporal context.

communication attitudes (both were high in communication competence and willingness to communicate, and low in verbal aggressiveness) were highest in roommate liking and satisfaction (Martin & Anderson, 1995). Although this theory has not been tested on computer communication, it would make the prediction that styles of written communication in e-mail or chat rooms would also evidence accommodation.

As illustrated throughout this text, communication characteristics are influenced greatly by culture (Albert & Nelson, 1993). Thus, the communication similarities that lead to attraction and more positive perceptions are more likely to be present in *intra*cultural communication than in *inter*cultural encounters. This may present an important (but not insurmountable) obstacle to intercultural communication.

Interpersonal Communication Is Ambiguous

All messages are ambiguous to some degree. An ambiguous message is a communication that can be interpreted as having more than one meaning. Sometimes ambiguity results when we use words that can be interpreted differently. Informal time terms offer good examples; different people may interpret terms such as *soon, right away, in a minute, early,* and *late* very differently. The terms themselves are ambiguous. A more interesting type of ambiguity is grammatical ambiguity. You can get a feel for this type of ambiguity by trying to paraphrase—rephrase in your own words—the following sentences:

- *What has the cat in its paws?*
- *Visiting neighbors can be boring.*
- *They are frying chickens.*

Each of these ambiguous sentences can be interpreted and paraphrased in at least two different ways:

- *What monster has the cat in its paws? What does the cat have in its paws?*
- *To visit neighbors is boring. Neighbors who visit are boring.*
- *Those people are frying chickens. Those chickens are for frying.*

Although these examples are particularly striking, some degree of ambiguity exists in all interpersonal communication. When you express an idea, you never communicate your meaning exactly and totally; rather, you communicate your meaning with some reasonable accuracy—enough to give the other person a reasonably clear idea of what you mean. Sometimes, of course, you're less accurate than you anticipated and your listener "gets the wrong idea," or "gets offended" when you only meant to be humorous, or "misunderstands your emotional meaning." Because of this inevitable uncertainty, you may qualify what you're saying, give an example, or ask, "Do you know what I mean?" These clarifying tactics help the other person understand your meaning and reduce uncertainty (to some degree).

Similarly, all relationships contain uncertainty. Consider a close interpersonal relationship of your own, and ask yourself the following questions. Answer each question according to a six-point scale on which 1 means "completely or almost completely uncertain" and 6 means "completely or almost completely certain." How certain are you about these questions?

- *What can and can't you and your partner say to each other in this relationship?*
- *Do you and your partner feel the same way about each other?*
- *How would you and your partner describe this relationship?*
- *What is the future of the relationship?*

Very likely you were not able to respond with "6" for all four questions. And it's equally likely that your relationship partner would be unable to respond to every question with a 6. These questions—taken from a relationship uncertainty scale (Knoblock & Solomon, 1999)—and similar others illustrate that you probably experience some degree of uncertainty about the norms that govern your relationship communication (Question 1), the degree to which the two of you see the relationship in similar ways (Question 2), the definition of the relationship (Question 3), and the relationship's future (Question 4).

The skills of interpersonal communication presented throughout this text can give you tools for appropriately reducing ambiguity and making your meaning as unambiguous as possible.

Interpersonal Communication Is Inevitable, Irreversible, and Unrepeatable

Three characteristics often considered together are interpersonal communication's *inevitability, irreversibility,* and *unrepeatability.*

Communication Is Inevitable Often communication is intentional, purposeful, and consciously motivated. Sometimes, however, you are communicating even though you may not think you are, or may not even want to. Take, for example, the student sitting in the back of the room with an "expressionless" face, perhaps staring out the window. The student may think that she or he is not communicating with the teacher or with the other students. On closer inspection, however, you can see that the student *is* communicating something—perhaps lack of interest or simply anxiety about a private problem. In any event, the student is communicating whether she or he wishes to or not—demonstrating the principle of **inevitability.** You cannot *not* communicate. In the same way, you cannot *not* influence the person you interact with (Watzlawick, 1978). Persuasion, like communication, is also inevitable. The issue, then, is not whether you will or will not persuade or influence another; rather, it's how you'll exert your influence.

SKILLS VIEWPOINT

With very good intentions, you write a close friend in an e-mail: "I guess you'll just never learn how to talk to professional people." To your surprise, your friend becomes extremely offended. Although you know you can't take the statement back (communication really is irreversible), you want to lessen its negative tone and its effect on your friendship. What might you say?

Communication Is Irreversible Notice that only some processes can be reversed. For example, you can turn water into ice and then reverse the process by turning the ice back into water. Other processes, however, are irreversible. You can, for example, turn grapes into wine, but you cannot reverse the process and turn wine into grapes. Interpersonal communication is an irreversible process. Although you may try to qualify, deny, or somehow reduce the effects of your message, you cannot withdraw the message you have conveyed. Similarly, once you press the send key, your e-mail is in cyberspace and impossible to reverse. Because of **irreversibility,** be careful not to say things you may wish to withdraw later. Similarly, monitor carefully messages of commitment, messages sent in anger, or messages of insult or derision. Otherwise you run the risk of saying something you'll be uncomfortable with later.

Communication Is Unrepeatable The reason for communication's unrepeatability is simple: Everyone and everything are constantly changing. As a result, you never can recapture the exact same situation, frame of mind, or relationship dynamics that defined a previous interpersonal act. For example, you never can repeat meeting someone for the first time, comforting a grieving friend, or resolving a specific conflict.

You can, of course, try again; you can say, "I'm sorry I came off so pushy, can we try again?" Notice, however, that even when you say this, you have not erased the initial (and perhaps negative) impression. Instead, you try to counteract this impression by going through the motions again. In doing so, you hope to create a more positive impact that will lessen the original negative effect.

Face-to-face communication is evanescent; it fades after you have spoken. There is no trace of your communications outside of the memories of the parties involved or of those who overheard your conversation. In computer-mediated communication, however, the messages are written and may be saved, stored, and printed. Both face-to-face and computer-mediated messages may be kept confidential or revealed publicly. But computer messages can be made public more easily and spread more quickly than face-to-face messages. And, of course, in the case of written messages there is clear evidence of what you said and when you said it.

Interpersonal Communication Is Purposeful

Interpersonal communication can be used to accomplish a variety of purposes (see Figure 1.6). Understanding how interpersonal communication serves these varied purposes will help you more effectively achieve your own interpersonal purposes. Interpersonal communication enables you to *learn,* to better understand the external world—the world of objects, events, and other people. Although a great deal of information comes from the media, you probably discuss and ultimately "learn" or internalize information through interpersonal interactions. In fact, your beliefs, attitudes, and values are probably influenced more by interpersonal encounters than by the

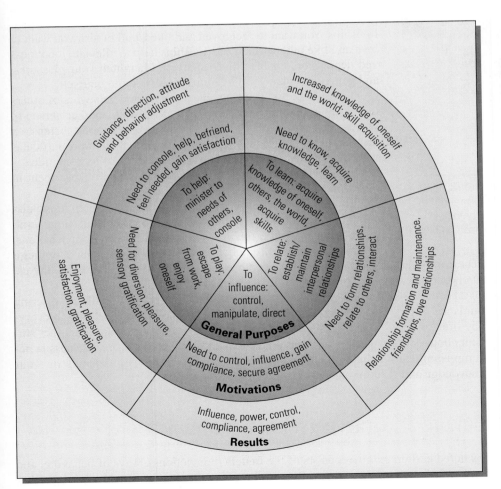

Figure 1.6

Why You Engage in Interpersonal Communication

This figure illustrates the five purposes of interpersonal communication discussed in the text and relates these purposes to the motives you have for engaging in interpersonal communication and the results you want to achieve. The innermost circle contains the general purposes, the middle circle the motivations, and the outer circle the results that you might hope to achieve by engaging in interpersonal communication. A similar typology of purposes comes from research on motives for communicating. In a series of studies Rubin and her colleagues (Rubin, Fernandez-Collado, & Hernandez-Sampieri, 1992; Rubin & Martin, 1994; Rubin, Perse, & Barbato, 1998; Rubin & Rubin, 1992; Graham, 1994; Graham, Barbato, & Perse, 1993) have identified six primary motives for communication: pleasure, affection, inclusion, escape, relaxation, and control. How do these compare to the five general purposes shown here?

media or even by formal education. Through interpersonal communication you also learn about yourself. By talking about yourself with others, you gain valuable feedback on your feelings, thoughts, and behaviors. Through these communications you also learn how you appear to others—who likes you, who dislikes you, and why.

Interpersonal communication helps you *relate*. One of the greatest needs people have is to establish and maintain close relationships. You want to feel loved and liked, and in turn you want to love and like others. Such relationships help to alleviate loneliness and depression, enable you to share and heighten your pleasures, and generally make you feel more positive about yourself.

Very likely, you *influence* the attitudes and behaviors of others in your interpersonal encounters. You may wish another person to vote a particular way, try a new diet, buy a new book, listen to a record, see a movie, take a specific course, think in a particular way, believe that something is true or false, or value some idea—the list is endless. A good deal of your time is probably spent in interpersonal persuasion.

Talking with friends about your weekend activities, discussing sports or dates, telling stories and jokes, and, in general, just passing the time fulfill a *play* function. Far from frivolous, this purpose is an extremely important one. It gives our activities a necessary balance and our mind a needed break from all the seriousness around us. Everyone has an inner child, and that child needs time to play.

Therapists of various kinds serve a helping function professionally by offering guidance through interpersonal interaction. But everyone interacts to *help* in everyday life: You console a friend who has broken off a love affair, counsel another student about courses to take, or offer advice to a colleague about work. Success in accomplishing this helping function, professionally or otherwise, depends on your knowledge and skill in interpersonal communication.

Culture and Interpersonal Communication

As noted earlier, *culture* consists of the **beliefs** (convictions), ways of behaving, and artifacts of a group that are transmitted through communication and learning rather than through genes. Gender is considered a cultural variable, at least in part, because cultures teach boys and girls different attitudes, beliefs, values, and ways of communicating and relating to one another. This does not, of course, deny that biological differences also play a role in the differences between male and female behavior. In fact, recent research continues to uncover biological roots of traits we once thought were entirely learned, such as happiness and shyness (McCroskey, 1998).

Because your interpersonal communications are heavily influenced by the culture in which you were raised, culture is given a prominent place in this text. This section explains the relevance of culture to interpersonal communication and the aims and benefits of a cultural perspective.

A walk through any large U.S. city or through many small towns, through schools and colleges, or into this country's business and manufacturing centers will convince you that the United States is largely a collection of lots of different cultures. These cultures coexist somewhat separately but also with each influencing the others. This coexistence has led some researchers to refer to these cultures as cocultures (Shuter, 1990; Samovar & Porter, 1991; Jandt, 2000). And consider these facts (*The New York Times Almanac, 2002; The World Almanac and Book of Facts, 2002):* The foreign-born population of the United States is increasing dramatically. In 1980 the foreign-born population was 14 million (about 6.2 percent of the total population), in 1990 it was 19.8 million (7.9 percent), and in 2000 it was 28.4 million (10.4 percent). Increasingly frequent communication in a multicultural context is inevitable (see Figure 1.7).

In your more immediate environment, consider the number of foreign students who come to the United States to continue their education. For the years 2000–2001, China led the list with 59,939 students. India was next with 54,664. Other countries with large numbers of students in the United States were Japan (46,497), South Korea

> In addition to their shared values, beliefs, and behaviors, the members of a particular culture share a common history. Any culture's past inextricably binds it to the present and guides its future.
>
> —James W. Neuliep

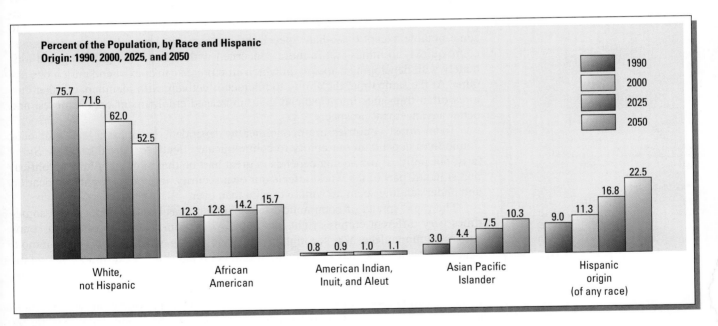

Figure 1.7

The Faces of the Nation

This figure shows percentages of the U.S. population by race and Hispanic origin for the years 1990 and 2000 and the projections for the years 2025 and 2050. It's important to realize that within each group there are also wide cultural variations. Whites from Sweden are culturally quite different from whites from Greece or Russia, and Asians from Japan are culturally quite different from those from China or Korea. To complicate matters even further, not all Japanese or all Chinese or all Koreans are culturally similar. There are wide variations within each country, just as there are cultural differences between whites from, say, Manhattan and those from rural Tennessee.

(46,000), Taiwan (28,566), Canada (25,279), Indonesia (11,625), Thailand (11,187), Turkey (10,983), and Mexico (10,670) (*New York Times,* Education Life, Section 4A, January 13, 2002). Frequent intercultural communication is simply a part of college life today.

U.S. corporations, too, are becoming more and more intercultural. Increasingly you see large and small corporations announcing that future growth will depend on expansion into foreign countries. Manufacturing, media, information technology, and farming interests depend on foreign markets. Business opportunities, therefore, have an increasingly international dimension, making cultural awareness and intercultural communication competence essential skills for professional success.

In addition, we're living in a time of great gender changes. Many men, for example, are doing a great deal more in caring for their children; the term *househusband* is becoming increasingly common and perhaps a little less negative in connotation. More obvious, perhaps, is that women are becoming more visible in fields once occupied exclusively by men—politics, law enforcement, the military, and the clergy are some examples. And, of course, women are increasingly entering corporate executive ranks; the glass ceiling may not have disappeared, but it is cracked.

The Importance of Culture

There are lots of reasons for the cultural emphasis you'll find in this book. Most obvious, perhaps, are the vast demographic changes taking place throughout the United States. With these changes have come different interpersonal customs and the need to understand and adapt to new ways of looking at communication.

As a people we've become increasingly sensitive to cultural differences. U.S. society has moved from a perspective that endorsed **cultural assimilation** (people should leave their native culture behind and adapt to their new culture) to a view that values cultural diversity (people should retain their native cultural ways). And with some notable exceptions—hate speech, racism, sexism, homophobia, and classism come quickly to mind—we're more concerned with saying the right thing and ultimately with developing a society in which all cultures can coexist and enrich one another. At the same time, the ability to interact effectively with members of other cultures often translates into financial gain, increased employment opportunities, and better advancement prospects.

Today most countries are economically dependent on one another. Our economic lives depend on our ability to communicate effectively across cultures. Similarly, our political well-being depends in great part on that of other cultures. Political unrest in any part of the world affects our own security. Intercultural communication and understanding seem now more crucial than ever.

The rapid spread of communication technology has brought foreign and sometimes very different cultures right into your living room. News from foreign countries is commonplace. You see nightly—in vivid color—what is going on in remote countries. Technology has made intercultural communication easy, practical, and inevitable. Daily the media bombard you with evidence of racial tensions, religious disagreements, sexual bias—in general, of the problems caused when intercultural communication fails. And, of course, the Internet has made intercultural communication as easy as writing a note on your computer. You can now communicate by e-mail just as easily with someone in Europe or Asia, for example, as with someone in another city or state.

Still another reason for the importance of cultural awareness is that interpersonal competence is specific to a given culture; what proves effective in one culture may prove ineffective in another. For example, in the United States corporate executives get down to business during the first several minutes of a meeting. In Japan, however, business executives interact socially for an extended period and try to find out something about one another. Thus, the communication principle influenced by U.S. culture would advise participants to tackle the meeting's agenda during the first five minutes.

> ❝ I am not an Athenian or a Greek, but a citizen of the world. ❞
>
> —Socrates

The principle influenced by Japanese culture would advise participants to avoid dealing with business until everyone has socialized sufficiently and feels well enough acquainted to begin negotiations. Neither principle is right and neither is wrong. Each is effective within its own culture, and ineffective outside its own culture.

The Aim of a Cultural Perspective

Because culture permeates all forms of communication, it's necessary to understand its influences if you're to understand how interpersonal communication works and master interpersonal communication skills. As illustrated throughout this text, culture influences communications of all types (Moon, 1996). It influences what you say to yourself and how you talk with friends, lovers, and family in everyday conversation. It influences how you interact in groups and how much importance you place on the group versus the individual. It influences the topics you talk about and the strategies you use in communicating information or in persuading. And it influences how you use the media and the credibility you attribute to them.

A cultural emphasis helps distinguish what is universal (true for all people) from what is relative (true for people in one culture and not true for people in other cultures) (Matsumoto, 1994). The principles for communicating information and for changing listeners' attitudes, for example, will vary from one culture to another. If you're to understand communication, you need to know how its principles vary and how the principles must be qualified and adjusted on the basis of cultural differences.

And of course you need cultural understanding in order to communicate effectively in a wide variety of intercultural situations. Success in interpersonal communication—on your job and in your social life—will depend on your ability to communicate effectively with persons who are culturally different from yourself.

This emphasis on culture does not imply that you should accept all cultural practices or that all cultural practices are equal (Hatfield & Rapson, 1996). For example, cockfighting, foxhunting, and bullfighting are parts of the culture of some Latin American countries, England, and Spain, respectively; but you need not find these activities acceptable or equal to a cultural practice in which animals are treated kindly. Further, a cultural emphasis does not imply that you have to accept or follow even the practices of your own culture. For example, even if the majority in your culture find cockfighting acceptable, you need not agree with or follow the practice. Similarly, you may reject your culture's values and beliefs; its religion or political system; or its attitudes toward the homeless, the handicapped, or the culturally different. Of course, going against your culture's traditions and values is often very difficult. But it's important to realize that culture only influences; it does not determine your values or behavior. Often, for example, personality factors (such as your degree of assertiveness, extroversion, or optimism) will prove more influential than culture (Hatfield & Rapson, 1996).

As demonstrated throughout this text, cultural differences exist across the interpersonal communication spectrum—from the way you use eye contact to the way you develop or dissolve a relationship (Chang & Holt, 1996). But these differences should not blind you to the great number of similarities existing among even the most widely separated cultures. Close interpersonal relationships, for example, are common in all cultures, even though people in different cultures enter into them for very different reasons. Further, remember that differences are usually matters of degree. For example, most cultures value honesty, although not all value it to the same degree. Also, the advances in media and technology and the widespread use of the Internet are influencing cultures and cultural change and are perhaps homogenizing different cultures to some degree, lessening differences and increasing similarities.

? SKILLS VIEWPOINT

Three different work colleagues who you've become friendly with have developed chain e-mail lists, and you're on all of them. Your mailbox overflows with long and detailed missives, websites your colleagues find interesting, and photos, all of which take forever to download on your old computer. You want to get off these chain lists. What do you say?

> ❝ As inhabitants of the twenty-first century, you no longer have a choice about whether to live and communicate in a world of many cultures. ❞
>
> —Myron W. Lustig and Jolene Koester

Summary of Concepts

This chapter explored the nature of interpersonal communication, looked at several principles of interpersonal communication, and explained the centrality of culture.

1. Interpersonal communication is a transactional process that takes place between two or more people who have a relationship.
2. Essential to an understanding of interpersonal communication are the following elements: source–receiver, encoding–decoding, messages (including message overload, feedback, and feedforward), channel, noise (physical, physiological, psychological, and semantic), context (physical, cultural, social–psychological, and temporal), and competence.
3. Interpersonal communication is:
   - a package of signals that usually reinforce but may also contradict one another
   - both content and relationship messages; we communicate about objects and events in the world but simultaneously about the relationship between the sources–receivers
   - a process of adjustment by which we each accommodate the specialized communication system of the other
   - ambiguous to some extent
   - inevitable (communication will occur whether we want it to or not), irreversible (once something is received, it remains communicated and cannot be erased from a listener's memory), and unrepeatable (no communication act can ever be repeated exactly)
   - purposeful; through interpersonal communication we learn, relate, influence, play, and help
4. Interpersonal communication is heavily influenced by culture—by the beliefs, attitudes, and values cultures teach and practice.

Vocabulary Quiz: The Language of Interpersonal Communication

Match the terms of interpersonal communication with their definitions. Record the number of the definition next to the appropriate term.

_____ interpersonal communication

_____ encoding

_____ feedback

_____ ambiguity

_____ cultural context

_____ feedforward

_____ relationship messages

_____ source–receiver

_____ signal-to-noise ratio

_____ communication as a transactional process

1. Messages sent back to the source in response to the source's messages.
2. Each person in the interpersonal communication act.
3. Information about messages that are yet to be sent.
4. Having more than one meaning.
5. The rules and norms, beliefs and attitudes of the people communicating.
6. Communication as an ongoing process in which each part depends on each other part.
7. Communication that takes place between persons who have a relationship.
8. Messages referring to the connection between the two people communicating.
9. A measure of meaningful message compared to interference.
10. The process of sending messages; for example, in speaking or writing.

Four for Discussion

1. The popularity of American media and America's domination of the Internet, some researchers point out, foster an Americanization of different cultures. Some people find this an unpleasant prospect and see it as the loss of diversity; others may see it as inevitable and as the result of a democratic process whereby people select the values and customs they wish to adopt. How do you feel about this Americanization?

2. The "feedback theory of relationships" holds that in satisfying interpersonal relationships feedback is positive, person focused, immediate, low in monitoring, and supportive—and that in unsatisfying relationships feedback is negative, self-focused, nonimmediate, high in monitoring, and critical. How effective do you find this theory in explaining relationships with which you're familiar?

3. What characters in television sitcoms or dramas demonstrate superior interpersonal competence? What characters demonstrate obvious interpersonal incompetence?

4. Using the principles of interpersonal communication discussed in this chapter, describe what is going on in these several cases and offer any suggestions you think would help.

   • Karla's fiancé, Tom, did not speak up in defense of her proposal at a company for which both work. Karla feels that Tom created a negative attitude and encouraged others to reject her ideas. Tom says that he felt he could not defend her proposal because others in the room would have seen his defense as motivated by their relationship. So he thought it was best to say nothing.

   • A couple have been together for 20 years but are arguing about seemingly insignificant things—who takes out the garbage, who does the dishes, who decides where to eat, and on and on. The arguments are so frequent and so unsettling that the pair are seriously considering separating.

   • Pat and Chris have been online friends for the last two years, communicating with each other at least once a day. Recently Pat wrote several things that Chris interpreted as insulting and as ridiculing Chris's feelings and dreams. Chris wrote back that these last messages were greatly resented and then stopped writing. Pat has written every day for the last two weeks to try to patch things up, but Chris won't respond.

Web Explorations

Explore our text website at **www.ablongman.com/devito** to find:

Exercises and Self-Tests

A variety of exercises relevant to the content of this chapter include (1) Models of Interpersonal Communication, (2) Ethics in Interpersonal Communication, (3) How Can You Respond to Contradictory Messages? (4) I'd Prefer to Be, (5) Applying the Axioms, and (6) Analyzing an Interaction. Two self-tests will enable you to explore your (7) Cultural Beliefs and Values and (8) What You Know about Research.

Writing Resources and Assignments

A guide to writing about interpersonal communication is available to you containing suggestions for writing papers in communication in general and suggestions for writing specific papers of personal experience, concept or principle explanation, review, and research. Suggestions for each of these kinds of papers, focusing on the contents of this chapter, are also available at the website.

Explore our research resources at **www.researchnavigator.com** and

Read an article.

Read a popular or scholarly article on the nature, elements, or principles of interpersonal communication. On the basis of this article, what can you add to the discussion presented here?

Investigate key terms.

Investigate one of the key terms discussed in this chapter (for example, encoding, decoding, competence, messages, feedback, feedforward, channel, noise, context, purpose, or ethics). What additional insights can you provide?

Find answers.

Try finding answers to any one of the following questions. If you can't find answers—after all, research hasn't provided answers to all interesting questions—then try designing a research study that would help you answer the question.

1. Are interpersonal communication skills related to success as a friend, lover, or parent?
2. How is interpersonal communication applicable to your own profession?
3. How do men and women differ in their interpersonal communication patterns?

The Self in Interpersonal Communication

Self-Concept and Self-Awareness

Self-Disclosure

Interpersonal Apprehension

> Aesop, the great writer of fables, tells the story of Mercury, one of the gods of Ancient Rome. Although only a lesser god, Mercury aspired to be more. So one day, disguised as an ordinary man, he entered a sculptor's studio, where he saw statues of the gods and goddesses for sale. Eyeing a statue of Jupiter, one of the major gods, Mercury asked the price. "A crown," the sculptor said. Mercury laughed, for he thought that was such a low price; maybe Jupiter was not so important after all. Then he asked the price of a statue of Juno, a major goddess. "Half a crown," said the sculptor. This seemed to please Mercury, who thought that surely his likeness would command a much higher price. So, pointing to a statue of himself, he proudly asked its price. "Oh, that; I'll give you that one free if you buy the other two."

In comparing his reputation to the reputations of others, Mercury was engaging in **social comparison,** a way of gaining insight into self-concept and increasing self-awareness. Through this comparison Mercury got a good idea of his own *relative* importance. In this chapter we look at self-concept and self-awareness, and particularly at how you develop your image of yourself and how you can increase your own self-awareness. With this as a foundation, we then look at self-disclosure, the process of revealing yourself to another person; and we consider speaker apprehension and some ways to reduce your own fear of communication.

Self-Concept and Self-Awareness

Central to all forms of interpersonal communication is your self-concept—the image you have of yourself—and how that image is formed. Equally significant is your self-awareness, the degree to which you know yourself. Let's look first at self-concept.

Self-Concept

Your **self-concept** is your image of who you are. It's how you perceive yourself: your feelings and thoughts about your strengths and weaknesses and your abilities and limitations. Self-concept develops from the image that others have of you; the comparisons you draw between yourself and others; your cultural experiences in the realms of race, ethnicity, gender, and gender roles; and your evaluation of your own thoughts and behaviors (Figure 2.1).

Others' Images of You   If you wished to see the way your hair looked, you'd probably look in a mirror. But what would you do if you wanted to see how friendly or how assertive you are? According to the concept of the *looking-glass self* (Cooley, 1922), you would look at the image of yourself that others reveal to you through their behaviors, and especially through the way they treat you and react to you.

You don't want to seek such information from just anyone, however. People who are overly negative, who have personal agendas, or who know you only slightly are generally poor sources for seeking self-insight. Rather, you would look to those who are most significant in your life—to your *significant others*. As a child, for example, you would look to your parents and then to your elementary school teachers. As an adult you might look to your friends and romantic partners. If these significant others think highly of you, you will see a positive self-image reflected in their behaviors; if they think little of you, you will see a more negative image.

Social Comparisons   Another way you develop self-concept is to compare yourself with others, to engage in what are called social comparisons (Festinger, 1954).

> " Even when we are quite alone, how often do we think with pleasure or pain of what others think of us—of their imagined approbation or disapprobation. "
>
> —Charles Darwin

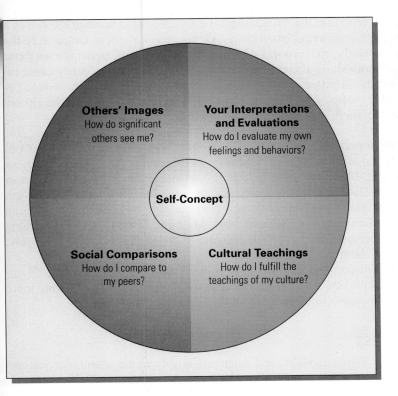

Figure 2.1

The Sources of Self-Concept
This diagram depicts the four sources of self-concept, the four contributors to how you see yourself. As you read about self-concept, consider the influence of each of these four factors throughout your life. For example, which factor influenced you most as a preteen? Which influences you the most now? Which will influence you the most 20 years from now?

Within the diagram:

Others' Images
How do significant others see me?

Your Interpretations and Evaluations
How do I evaluate my own feelings and behaviors?

Self-Concept

Social Comparisons
How do I compare to my peers?

Cultural Teachings
How do I fulfill the teachings of my culture?

Again, you don't choose just anyone. Rather, when you want to gain insight into who you are and how effective or competent you are, you look to your peers. For example, after an examination you probably want to know how you performed relative to the other students in your class. This gives you a clearer idea as to how effectively you performed. If you play on a baseball team, it's important to know your batting averages in comparison with the batting averages of others on the team. Your absolute score on the exam or your batting average may be helpful in telling you something about your performance, but you gain a different perspective when you see your scores in comparison with those of your peers.

Cultural Teachings   Through your parents, teachers, and the media, your culture instills in you a variety of beliefs, values, and attitudes—about matters such as success (how you should define and achieve it); the relevance of religion, race, or nationality; and the ethical principles you should follow in business and in your personal life. These teachings provide benchmarks against which you can measure yourself. For example, your ability to achieve what your culture defines as success will contribute to a positive self-concept. Your failure to achieve what your culture values (for example, not being married by the time you're 30) may contribute to a negative self-concept.

When you demonstrate the qualities that your culture (or organization, because organizations are much like cultures) teaches, you will see yourself as a cultural success and will be rewarded by other members of the culture (or organization). Seeing yourself as culturally successful and getting rewarded by others will contribute positively to your self-concept. When you fail to demonstrate such qualities, you're more likely to see yourself as a cultural failure and to be punished by other members of the culture, contributing to a more negative self-concept.

Because you belong to a variety of cultures and because each of these cultures exerts influence on your attitudes and beliefs, you may find that some of these influences contradict one another. Thus, for example, you may have been taught that it's important to be financially successful—but that money is the root of all evil or,

" However much we guard against it, we tend to shape ourselves in the image others have of us. "

—Eric Hoffer

recalling religious scripture, that "it's easier for a camel to pass through the eye of a needle than for a rich man to get into heaven." Or you may have been taught to be the best in your field but also to be cooperative and helpful to others, perhaps even those you find yourself competing against. Such contradictory beliefs may easily cause intrapersonal conflicts. In extreme cases you may decide to reject the attitudes and beliefs of one culture—often the "old-world" culture—in favor of those of the culture with which you feel more comfortable.

Your Own Observations, Interpretations, and Evaluations   You also observe, interpret, and evaluate your own behavior. For example, let's say you believe that lying is wrong. If you lie, you will probably evaluate this behavior in terms of your internalized beliefs about lying and will react negatively to your own behavior. You may, for example, experience guilt as a result of your behavior's contradicting your beliefs. On the other hand, let's say that you pull someone out of a burning building at great personal risk. You will probably evaluate this behavior positively; you will feel good about this behavior and, as a result, about yourself.

The more you understand why you view yourself as you do, the better you'll understand who you are. You can gain additional insight into yourself by looking more closely at self-awareness—and especially at the Johari model of the self.

Self-Awareness

Because you control your thoughts and behaviors largely to the extent that you understand who you are, it's crucial to increase your self-awareness. **Self-awareness** will also help you identify your strengths and weaknesses so that you can capitalize on your strengths and direct your energies to correcting your weaknesses. The **Johari window,** a model of four selves, is particularly helpful in explaining the self and in offering suggestions on how to increase self-awareness (Figure 2.2).

Your Four Selves   Assume that the model in Figure 2.2 represents you. The model is divided into quadrants, each of which contains a different self. Visualize the entire Johari window as of constant size but each section as variable: sometimes small, sometimes large. That is, changes in one quadrant will cause changes in the other quadrants. For example, if you enlarge the open self, then another self must get smaller.

The Johari model emphasizes that the several aspects of the self are not separate and distinct pieces. Rather, they're parts of a whole that interact with one another.

Figure 2.2

The Johari Window
This diagram is a tool commonly used for examining what you know and don't know about yourself. It will also prove an effective way of explaining the nature of self-disclosure, covered later in this chapter. The window gets its name from its inventors, *Jo*seph Luft and *Har*ry Ingham. When interacting with your peers, which self is your largest? Your smallest?

Source: From *Group Processes: An Introduction to Group Dynamics,* 3rd ed., by Joseph Luft. Copyright © 1984 by Mayfield Publishing. Reprinted with permission of The McGraw-Hill Companies.

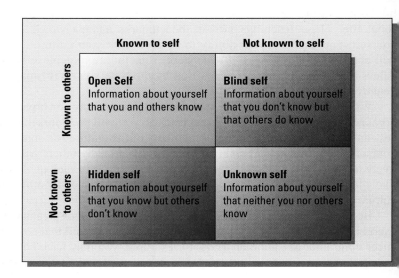

Like the model of interpersonal communication, this model of the self is transactional: Each part is dependent on each other part.

Your *open self* represents all the information, behaviors, attitudes, feelings, desires, motivations, and ideas that characterize you. The type of information included here might vary from your name and sex to your age, religious affiliation, and batting average. The size of your open self changes depending on the situation and the individuals you're interacting with. Some people probably make you feel comfortable and support you. To them, you may open yourself wide. To others you might prefer to leave most of yourself closed or unknown.

Your *blind self* represents all the things about yourself that others know but that you do not. These include, for example, your habit of rubbing your nose when you get angry, your defense mechanisms, and your repressed experiences. Interpersonal communication depends on both parties' sharing the same basic information about each other. Where blind areas exist, communication will be more difficult. Yet blind areas always exist. You can shrink your blind area, but you can never totally eliminate it.

Your *hidden self* contains all that you know of yourself but that you keep to yourself. This area includes all your successfully kept secrets. In any interaction, this area includes everything you have not revealed and perhaps seek actively to conceal. When you move information from this area to the open area—as in, say, telling someone a secret—you're self-disclosing, a process examined later in this chapter.

Your *unknown self* represents truths that exist but that neither you nor others know. We infer the existence of this unknown self from dreams, psychological tests, or therapy. For example, through therapy you might become aware of your high need for acceptance and of how this influences the way you allow people to take advantage of you. With this insight, this information moves from the unknown self to the hidden self and perhaps to the open self.

Increasing Self-Awareness Embedded in the discussion of the Johari window were suggestions on how to increase your own self-awareness. Let's look at those suggestions in more detail.

Listen to Others. You can learn a great deal about yourself from *listening to others* and seeing yourself as others do. Conveniently, others are constantly giving you the very feedback you need to increase self-awareness. In every interpersonal interaction, people comment on you in some way—on what you do, what you say, how you look. Sometimes these comments are explicit: "Loosen up," "Don't take things so hard," "You seem angry." Often, however, they're hidden in the way others look at you or in what they talk about. Pay close attention to this kind of information (both explicit and hidden) and use it to increase your own self-awareness.

Increase Your Open Self. Revealing yourself to others will help increase your self-awareness. At the very least, you will bring into focus what you may have buried within. As you discuss yourself, you may see connections that you had previously missed. With feedback from others, you may gain still more insight. Also, by increasing your open self, you increase the chances that others will reveal what they know about you.

Seek Out Information to Reduce Your Blind Self. Encouraging people to reveal what they know about you will further help increase your awareness. You need not be so blatant as to say, "Tell me about myself" or "What do you think of me?" You can, however, use some situations that arise every day to gain self-information. "Do you think I came down too hard on the kids today?" "Do you think I was

? SKILLS VIEWPOINT

You're going to an interview for the job of a lifetime. You really need feedback on your strengths and weaknesses. You need to increase your self-awareness—fast. You have friends and work colleagues who know you very well and are likely to give you honest feedback. What do you say to encourage them to give you the positive *and negative* feedback you need?

Listening to Yourself

Self-talk is important because it influences the way you feel about yourself. Listen carefully to both self-destructive and self-affirming statements.

Self-destructive statements damage self-esteem and prevent you from building meaningful and productive relationships. They may be about yourself ("I'm boring"), your world ("They'll never offer me this job"), or your relationships ("All the good people are already in relationships"). Recognizing that you may have internalized such beliefs is a first step toward eliminating them. A second step involves recognizing that these beliefs are unrealistic and self-defeating and substituting more realistic ones (Ellis, 1988).

Self-affirming statements, on the other hand, are positive and supportive. They remind you of your successes and focus on your good deeds, positive qualities, strengths, and virtues. These statements concentrate on your potential, not your limitations (Brody, 1991). Here is just a small sampling of self-affirmations that you may wish to try to say to yourself and most important listen to: "I'm a competent person"; "I'm worth loving and having as a friend"; "I'm a good team player"; "I'm empathic and supportive"; "I facilitate open communication"; "I can accept my past but can also let it go"; "I'm an effective and valuable worker"; "I'm open-minded and listen fairly to others"; "I can apologize"; "I'm flexible and can adjust to different situations."

Applying Listening Skills

Sally's 10-year-old son has low self-esteem that prevents him from trying to do things that he's probably capable of doing. For example, he refuses to play baseball because he thinks he can't; he refuses to answer questions in class because he thinks he'll be wrong. What would you suggest that Sally do to help her son listen to and perhaps change his self-talk?

"It may surprise you to know that, contrary to your experience, you're actually very happily married."

assertive enough when asking for a raise?" But use this route to self-awareness in moderation. If you do it too often, your friends will soon look for someone else to talk with.

Another way to seek out information about yourself is to visualize how you're seen by your parents, teachers, friends, the stranger on the bus, your neighbor's child. Recognize that each of these people sees you differently; to each you're a different person. Yet you're really *all* those persons. The experience will surely give you new and valuable perspectives on yourself. It will convince you that you're actually a different person, depending on the person you're interacting with. For example, my colleagues see me as serious and always doing a hundred things at the same time. My students, however, see me as humorous and laid back.

Self-Disclosure

When you move information from the hidden self into the open self, you're self-disclosing; you're revealing information about yourself to others. You can self-disclose through overt statements as well as through slips of the tongue and unconscious nonverbal movements. **Self-disclosure** may involve information that you tell others freely or information that you normally keep hidden. It may supply information ("I earn $45,000") or reveal feelings ("I'm feeling really depressed"). Self-disclosure can vary from the insignificant ("I'm a Sagittarius") to the highly revealing ("I'm currently in an abusive relationship," "I'm always depressed").

Only new knowledge represents "disclosure." To tell someone something about yourself that he or she already knows is not self-disclosure. And self-disclosure involves at least one other individual. It cannot be *intra*personal communication (communication with yourself). Nor may you "disclose" in a way that makes the message impossible for another person to understand. For a communication to be self-disclosure, someone must receive and understand the information.

Factors Influencing Self-Disclosure

Many factors influence whether or not you disclose, what you disclose, and to whom you disclose. Among the most important factors are who you are, your culture, your gender, who your listeners are, and what your topic is.

Who You Are   Highly sociable and extroverted people self-disclose more than those who are less sociable and more introverted. People who are apprehensive about talking in general also self-disclose less than those who are more comfortable in communicating.

Competent people engage in self-disclosure more than less competent people. Perhaps competent people have greater self-confidence and more positive things to reveal. Similarly, their self-confidence may make them more willing to risk possible negative reactions (McCroskey & Wheeless, 1976).

Your Culture   Different cultures view self-disclosure differently. People in the United States, for example, disclose more than those in Great Britain, Germany, Japan, or Puerto Rico (Gudykunst, 1983). American students also disclose more than students from most Middle East countries (Jourard, 1971). Similarly, American students self-disclose more about controversial issues and to different types of people than do Chinese students (Chen, 1992). Chinese Singaporean students consider more topics to be taboo and inappropriate for self-disclosure than their British peers (Goodwin & Lee, 1994). Among the Kabre of Togo, secrecy is a major part of everyday interaction (Piot, 1993).

Ethical messages

Outing

An interesting variation on self-disclosure occurs when someone else takes information from your hidden self and makes it public. Although this third-party disclosure can concern any aspect of a person's hidden self—for example, an athlete's prison record or drug habit, a movie star's ill health or alcoholism, or a politician's friends or financial dealings—the media have made a special case out of revealing a person's affectional orientation; the process is called **outing** (Gross, 1991; Signorile, 1993; Johansson & Percy, 1994).

Those against outing argue that people have a right to privacy and say no one else should take that right from them. Because outing can lead to severe consequences—for example, loss of a job, expulsion from the military, or social and physical harassment—no one but the individual himself or herself has the right to reveal such information. Those in favor of outing argue that it's an expedient political and social weapon to silence gay men and lesbians who support homophobic policies.

What Would You Do?

An excellent staff reporter and regular contributor to the college newspaper brings the editor a story revealing that a particular professor is a lesbian. This professor has repeatedly voted against adding any gay or lesbian courses to the curriculum. She is also an advisor to an exclusive sorority that has repeatedly refused admission to lesbian students. What would be the ethically responsible thing for this editor to do? What would you do in this situation, if you were the editor and final judge as to whether to publish the article?

In some cultures—for example, Mexican—there's a strong emphasis on discussing all matters in a positive mode, and this undoubtedly influences the way Mexicans approach self-disclosure as well. Negative self-disclosures, for example, are usually made only to close intimates and then only after considerable time has elapsed in a relationship. This reluctance to disclose negative information extends to people's HIV-positive status and thus is creating serious problems in Mexico's efforts to prevent and treat HIV infection (Szapocznik, 1995).

These differences aside, there are also important similarities across cultures. For example, people from Great Britain, Germany, the United States, and Puerto Rico are all more apt to disclose certain kinds of personal information—such as details about hobbies, interests, attitudes, and opinions on politics and religion—than to discuss finances, sex, personality, and interpersonal relationships (Jourard, 1971). Similarly, one study showed self-disclosure patterns between American males to be virtually identical to those between Korean males (Won-Doornink, 1991).

Your Gender   The popular stereotype of gender differences in self-disclosure emphasizes the male's reluctance to speak about himself. For the most part, research supports this view and shows that women disclose more than men. This is especially true in same-sex dyads (two-person groups); women disclose more intimately (and with more emotion) when talking with other women than with men (Shaffer, Pegalis, & Bazzini, 1996). Men and women, however, make negative disclosures nearly equally (Naifeh & Smith, 1984).

More specifically, women disclose more than men about their previous romantic relationships, their feelings about their closest same-sex friends, their greatest fears, and what they don't like about their partners (Sprecher, 1987). Women also seem to increase the depth of their self-disclosures as the relationship becomes more intimate, while men seem not to change their self-disclosure levels. Finally, women even self-disclose more to members of the extended family than men do (Komarovsky, 1964; Argyle & Henderson, 1985; Moghaddam, Taylor, & Wright, 1993). One notable exception occurs in initial encounters. Here men will disclose more intimately than women, perhaps "in order to control the relationship's development" (Derlega, Winstead, Wong, & Hunter, 1985).

Although to some extent men and women give different reasons for avoiding self-disclosure (Rosenfeld, 1979), both genders share this reason: "If I disclose, I might project an image I do not want to project." In a society in which image is so important—in which a person's image is often the basis for success or failure—this explanation is not surprising.

Your Listeners   Self-disclosure occurs more readily in small groups than in large groups. Dyads, or groups of two people, are the most hospitable setting for self-disclosure. With one listener, you can attend to the responses carefully. You can monitor the disclosures, continuing if there is support from your listener and stopping if there is not. With more than one listener, such monitoring becomes difficult, because the listeners' responses are sure to vary.

Because you disclose, generally at least, on the basis of support you receive, you probably disclose to people you like (Derlega, Winstead, Wong, & Greenspan, 1987; Collins & Miller, 1994), to people you trust (Wheeless & Grotz, 1977), to people who show you concern and affection (Roberts & Aruguete, 2000), and to people you feel understand you (Martin, Anderson, & Mottet, 1999). You probably also come to like those to whom you disclose (Berg & Archer, 1983; Collins & Miller, 1994).

At times self-disclosure occurs more in temporary than in permanent relationships—for example, between strangers on a train or plane, a kind of "in-flight intimacy" (McGill, 1985). In this kind of situation, two people set up an intimate self-disclosing relationship during a brief travel period, but they don't pursue it beyond that point. In a similar way, you might set up a relationship with one or several people on the Internet and engage in significant disclosure. Perhaps knowing that you'll never see these other people and that they will never know where you live or work or what you look like makes it a bit easier. You're also more likely to disclose information you received from a low-level intimate (say a casual acquaintance) to a higher-level intimate (say a best friend) than you are to disclose information you received from a high-level intimate to a low-level intimate. This is a specific instance of the more general principle that you're more likely to communicate important information upward (to those of greater intimacy) than downward (to those of less intimacy) (Yovetich & Drigotas, 1999).

You're more likely to disclose when the person you're with discloses. This **dyadic effect** (what one person does, the other person does likewise) probably leads you to feel more secure and reinforces your own self-disclosing behavior. Disclosures are also more intimate when they're made in response to the disclosures of others (Berg & Archer, 1983). Research finds, too, that reciprocal self-disclosure occurs more quickly and at higher levels online than it does in face-to-face interactions (Levine, 2000; Joinson, 2001).

Your Topic   You're also more likely to disclose about some topics than others. For example, as mentioned earlier, you're probably more likely to self-disclose information about your job or hobbies than about your sex life or financial situation (Jourard, 1968, 1971). You're also more likely to disclose favorable information than unfavorable information. And dating couples are more likely to disclose information about nonsexual topics than about sexual ones (Byers & Demmons, 1999). Generally, the more personal and negative the topic, the less likely people are to self-disclose. Consider your own willingness to self-disclose. How willing would you be to disclose such topics as the following to, say, members of this class?

- *your attitudes toward different nationalities and races*
- *your feelings about your parents*
- *your sexual fantasies*
- *your past sexual experiences*
- *your ideal mate*
- *your drinking and/or drug-taking behavior*
- *your personal goals*
- *your unfulfilled desires*
- *your major weaknesses*
- *your feelings about the people in the class*

The Rewards and Dangers of Self-Disclosure

Like other forms of interpersonal communication, self-disclosure entails both potential rewards and potential dangers. Let's look first at the rewards.

Rewards of Self-Disclosure   Research shows that self-disclosure helps to increase self-knowledge, communication and relationship effectiveness, and physiological well-being.

Self-Knowledge.   One reward of self-disclosure is that you gain a new perspective on yourself, a deeper understanding of your own behavior. Through self-disclosure you may bring to consciousness a great deal that you might otherwise keep from conscious analysis. For example, as Tony talks about the difficulties he had living with an alcoholic father, he may remember details of his early life or entertain new feelings.

Even **self-acceptance** is difficult without self-disclosure. You accept yourself largely through the eyes of others. Through self-disclosure and subsequent support,

> Let others confide in you. It may not help you, but it surely will help them.
>
> —Roger G. Imhoff

you may be in a better position to see the positive responses to you. And you're more likely to respond by developing a more positive self-concept.

Communication Effectiveness. You understand the messages of another person largely to the extent that you understand the person. For example, you can tell when a friend is serious or joking, when someone you know well is being sarcastic out of fear and when out of resentment. Self-disclosure is an essential condition for getting to know another individual.

Couples who engage in significant self-disclosure are found to remain together longer than couples who do not (Sprecher, 1987). Self-disclosure helps us achieve a closer relationship with the person to whom we self-disclose (Schmidt & Cornelius, 1987). Within a sexual relationship self-disclosure increases sexual rewards and general relationship satisfaction. These two benefits in turn increase sexual satisfaction (Byers & Demmons, 1999). Without self-disclosure, meaningful relationships seem impossible to develop. Interestingly enough, we also come to increase our affection for our partner when we self-disclose.

Physiological Health. People who self-disclose are less vulnerable to illnesses and less likely to feel depressed (Pennebacker, 1991). For example, bereavement over the death of someone very close is linked to physical illness for those who bear this alone and in silence. But it's unrelated to any physical problems for those who share their grief with others. Similarly, women who suffer sexual trauma normally experience a variety of illnesses (among them headaches and stomach problems). Women who keep these experiences to themselves, however, suffer these illnesses to a much greater extent than those who talk with others about these traumas. The physiological effort required to keep your burdens to yourself seems to interact with the effects of the trauma to create a combined stress that can lead to physical illness.

Dangers of Self-Disclosure There are risks to self-disclosure, however. The more you reveal about yourself to others, the more areas of your life you expose to possible attack. Especially in the competitive contexts of work or romance, the more others know about you, the more they'll be able to use against you. This simple fact has prompted power watcher Michael Korda (1975, p. 302) to advise that you "never reveal all of yourself to other people, hold something back in reserve so that people are never quite sure if they really know you." This advice is not necessarily to suggest that you be secretive; rather, Korda is advocating "remaining slightly mysterious, as if [you] were always capable of doing something surprising and unexpected."

As you weigh decisions whether to self-disclose or not, keep Korda's advice in mind. Let's consider some of the potential personal, relational, and professional risks to self-disclosure.

Personal Risks. If you self-disclose certain aspects of your life, you may face rejection from even the closest friends and family members. Those who disclose that they have thoughts of suicide, bouts of depression, or dishonest activities, for example, may find that their friends and family no longer want to be quite as close as before.

Relationship Risks. Even in close and long-lasting relationships, self-disclosure can cause problems. Total self-disclosure may prove threatening to a relationship by decreasing trust. Self-

? SKILLS VIEWPOINT

You've met a wonderful person who seems to self-disclose easily, fully, and warmly. You, on the other hand, have trouble revealing your feelings and talking about your past. Your problem is that your reluctance to disclose is causing problems; your partner is putting pressure on you to talk more about yourself. You just aren't ready to do so with this person at this time. What do you say?

disclosures concerning infidelity, romantic fantasies, past indiscretions or crimes, lies, or hidden weaknesses and fears could easily have such negative effects.

Professional Risks.   Revealing political views or attitudes toward different religious or racial groups may create problems on the job—as may disclosing health problems, such as HIV-positive status (Fesko, 2001). Teachers who disclose former or current drug use or cohabitation with students may find themselves being denied tenure, teaching at undesirable hours, and eventually falling victim to "budget cuts." Teachers or students who, in the supportive atmosphere of their interpersonal communication course, disclose details about their sex life or financial condition or reveal self-doubts, anxieties, or fantasies may find some less-than-sympathetic listeners later using that information against them. Openly gay and lesbian personnel in the military—as well as in education, fire departments, law enforcement, or health care agencies, to cite just a few examples—may find themselves confined to desk jobs, barred from further advancement, or even charged with criminal behavior and fired.

Message Skills

Deciding to Self-Disclose:
Consider the potential benefits (for example, self-knowledge, increased communication effectiveness, and physiological health) as well as the potential personal, relationship, and professional risks.

Guidelines for Self-Disclosure

Because self-disclosure is an important type of interpersonal communication with the potential for great rewards and great dangers, here are some guidelines, first for making self-disclosures and second for responding to the disclosures of others.

Guidelines for Making Self-Disclosures   Should you disclose? Consider the following questions.

What Is Your Motivation for Self-Disclosing?   Self-disclose out of a concern for the relationship, for the others involved, and for yourself. Some people self-disclose out of a desire to hurt the listener rather than from a desire to improve the relationship—as when children tell their parents that they never loved them or when a person informs a relationship partner that he or she stifled emotional development. However, let's say that you feel ignored and unimportant because your partner devotes all available time to professional advancement. Instead of letting these feelings smolder and turn into resentment, it might be helpful to the relationship to disclose them.

Is This Self-Disclosure Appropriate?   Appropriate self-disclosures include honest expressions of feelings ("I feel uncomfortable when you criticize me in front of my friends"), past behaviors that another has a right to know ("I was married when I was 17; we divorced two years later"), or personal abilities or lack of them that affect others ("I've never hung wallpaper before but I'll do my best"). Self-disclose in an atmosphere in which your listener can give open and honest responses. Don't wait until you're boarding the bus to say to your friend, "I got some really bad news today. I'll tell you about it later."

? SKILLS VIEWPOINT
A casual friend of yours meets you at a shopping mall and almost immediately begins to disclose about family, finances, sexual problems, and so on. You really don't want to hear this now or ever. At the same time, however, you don't want to hurt this friend by expressing indifference. But, the sad fact is that you don't want to listen to these disclosures. What do you say?

Is the Other Person Also Disclosing?   During your disclosures, give the other person a chance to reciprocate with his or her own disclosures. If the other person does not do so, then reassess your own self-disclosures. The lack of reciprocity may signal that this person, at this time and in this context, does not welcome your disclosures. Therefore, disclose gradually and in small increments so that you can retreat if the responses are not positive enough. Lack of reciprocity may also be due to cultural differences; in some cultures, significant self-disclosure takes place only after an extremely long acquaintanceship or may be considered inappropriate among, say, opposite-sex friends.

Message Skills

Appropriateness of Self-Disclosure: When thinking of disclosing, consider the legitimacy of your motives, the appropriateness of the disclosure, the listener's responses (is the dyadic effect operating?), and the potential burdens such disclosures might impose.

Will This Self-Disclosure Impose Burdens? Carefully weigh the potential problems that the self-disclosure may cause. Could you, if you were to disclose your previous prison record, afford to lose your job? If you were to disclose your previous failed romantic relationships, would you be willing to risk discouraging your present relational partner?

Ask yourself whether you're making unreasonable demands on the listener. For example, consider the person who discloses in confidence to his or her own mother-in-law an affair with a neighbor. This type of situation places an unfair burden on the mother-in-law. She is now in a bind: Should she break her promise of secrecy or allow her own child to believe a lie? Often such disclosures do not make the relationship a better one. Instead they may simply add tension and friction.

In making your choice between disclosing and not disclosing, keep in mind—besides the advantages and dangers already noted—the irreversible nature of communication discussed in Chapter 1. No matter how many times you may try to qualify something or take it back, once you have said something, you cannot withdraw it. You cannot erase the conclusions and inferences listeners have made on the basis of your disclosures.

Guidelines for Responding to Disclosures When someone discloses to you, it's usually a sign of trust and affection. In serving this most important receiver function, keep the following in mind.

Practice the Skills of Effective and Active Listening. The skills of effective listening are discussed in detail in Chapter 4. These are especially important when listening to self-disclosures. Listen with empathy. Listen with an open mind. Repeat in your own words what you think the speaker has said so you can be sure you understand both the thoughts and the feelings. Express an understanding of the speaker's feelings to allow the speaker the opportunity to see these through the eyes of another individual. Ask questions to ensure your own understanding and to signal your own interest and attention.

Skill building exercise

Self-Disclosing Appropriately

Whether you should self-disclose is one of the most difficult decisions you have to make in interpersonal communication. Here are several instances of impending self-disclosure. For each situation, indicate: *(a)* the channel of communication you'd recommend (for example, face-to-face, e-mail), *(b)* the context you'd suggest the person arrange to self-disclose in, and *(c)* a few sentences that you'd recommend the speaker might say in effectively self-disclosing

1. Tom is engaged to Cathy. But over the past few months he has fallen in love with another woman. He now wants to end his relationship with Cathy. Tom wants to break his engagement and disclose his new relationship. What should Tom say?
2. Sam has been living in a romantic relationship with another man for the past several years. Sam wants to tell his parents, with whom he has been very close throughout his life. What should Sam say?
3. Kathy and Kelley have been friends since grade school and are currently seniors in college. The problem is that Kathy has been secretly dating Kelley's boyfriend, Hogan. Kathy plans to disclose this affair and to tell Kelley that she and Hogan are getting engaged. What should Kathy say?

Self-disclosure is a complex communication process with significant advantages and disadvantages. Disclose only after mindfully considering the potential effects.

3 Ways to Resist Pressure to Self-Disclose

You may, on occasion, find yourself in a situation in which a friend, colleague, or romantic partner is pressuring you to self-disclose. In such cases you may wish to weigh the pros and cons of self-disclosure and then make your decision as to whether and what you'll disclose. If your decision is not to disclose and you're still being pressured, then you need to say something. Here are a few suggestions for dealing with these situations.

1. Don't be pushed. Although there may be certain legal or ethical reasons for disclosing, generally, if you don't want to disclose, you don't have to. Don't be pushed into disclosing because others are doing it or because you're asked to. Realize that you're in control of what you reveal and to whom and when you reveal it. Remember that self-disclosure has significant consequences. If you're not sure you want to reveal something, at least not until you've had additional time to think about it, then don't.
2. Be assertive in your refusal to disclose. Say, very directly, "I'd rather not talk about that now" or "Now is not the time for this type of discussion." Chapter 12 offers more specific guidelines for communicating assertiveness.
3. Alternatively, be indirect and move to another topic. Avoid the request to disclose and change the subject. This is often a polite way of saying "I'm not talking about it" and may be the preferred choice in certain situations and with certain people. Most often people will get the hint and understand your refusal to disclose. If they don't, then you may need to use the more direct and assertive approach.

Applying Interpersonal Skills/Then and Now
Have you ever been pressured to self-disclose? What happened? Would you do anything differently now?

Support the Discloser. Express support for the person during and after the disclosures. Try to avoid making judgments. Concentrate on **affirmation**—understanding and empathizing with the discloser. Make your supportiveness clear to the discloser through your verbal and nonverbal responses. Nod your head to show you understand and echo the person's feelings and thoughts. Maintain eye contact and otherwise show your positive attitudes toward the discloser and the act of disclosing.

Keep the Disclosures Confidential. When a person discloses to you, it's because she or he wants you to know these feelings and thoughts. If the discloser wishes others to share these, then it's up to her or him to disclose to them. If you reveal these disclosures to others, it will probably inhibit this person's future disclosures. As a result, your relationship will suffer. In addition to keeping the disclosures confidential, avoid using them against the person at some later time. Many self-disclosures expose a vulnerability, a weakness. If you later turn around and use these against the person, you betray the confidence and trust invested in you.

It's interesting to note that one of the netiquette rules of e-mail is that you shouldn't forward mail to third parties without the writer's permission. This rule is a useful one for self-disclosure generally: Maintain confidentiality; don't pass on to others disclosures made to you without the person's permission.

Message Skills
Responding to Others' Disclosures: Listen actively, support the discloser, and keep the disclosures confidential.

Interpersonal Apprehension

You'll profit most from this discussion if you first take the self-test on the next page. This test measures your communication **apprehension,** or fear or anxiety in interpersonal communication situations.

Revealing Yourself in Interpersonal Relationships

At what stage in a relationship—if any—do you have an obligation to reveal the information listed in the first column below? Record your answers for romantic relationships in the second column and for friendship relationships in the third column. Use numbers from 1 to 10, visualizing relationships on a continuum on which 1 is initial contact and 10 is extreme intimacy. If you feel you would never have an obligation to reveal this information, use 0.

Information	Romantic Relationship	Friendship Relationship
HIV status		
Past sexual experiences		
Annual salary and net worth		
Affectional orientation		
Race, nationality, and religious beliefs		
Social and political beliefs and attitudes		

In which type of relationship—romantic or friendship—do you incur the greater obligation to reveal yourself? In which type of relationship do you have less of an obligation to reveal such information (the 0s in your responses)? In which type of relationship does the obligation to reveal yourself come earlier? Try formulating in one sentence the obligation you have as a friend or as a romantic partner to reveal information about yourself.

You don't have to reveal everything about yourself, but there may be obligations to reveal some information to certain relationship partners.

Test Yourself

How Apprehensive Are You?

INSTRUCTIONS: This questionnaire consists of six statements concerning your feelings about communication with other people. Please indicate in the space provided the degree to which each statement applies to you by marking whether you (1) strongly agree, (2) agree, (3) are undecided, (4) disagree, or (5) strongly disagree with each statement. There are no right or wrong answers. Work quickly; record your first impression.

_____ ❶ While participating in a conversation with a new acquaintance, I feel very nervous.

_____ ❷ I have no fear of speaking up in conversations.

_____ ❸ Ordinarily I am very tense and nervous in conversations.

_____ ❹ Ordinarily I am very calm and relaxed in conversations.

_____ ❺ While conversing with a new acquaintance, I feel very relaxed.

_____ ❻ I'm afraid to speak up in conversations.

HOW DID YOU DO? Compute your score as follows:

_____ ❶ Begin with the number 18; it's used as a base so that you won't wind up with negative numbers.

_____ **②** To 18, add your scores for items 2, 4, and 5.

_____ **③** Subtract your scores for items 1, 3, and 6 from your step 2 total.

_____ **④** The result (which should be somewhere between 6 and 30) is your apprehension score for interpersonal conversations. The higher the score, the greater your apprehension. A score above 18 indicates some degree of apprehension.

WHAT WILL YOU DO? Try first to identify those interpersonal situations that create the greatest communication apprehension for you. What factors can you identify that contribute to apprehension? What can you do to reduce the impact of those factors?

Source: From James C. McCroskey, *An Introduction to Rhetorical Communication,* 7/e. Published by Allyn & Bacon, Boston, MA. Copyright © 1997 by Pearson Education. Adapted by permission of the publisher.

Fear and anxiety cause some people to develop negative feelings about communication and therefore to expect the worst of themselves when they're called on to speak. To those who feel high anxiety in such circumstances, it just doesn't seem worthwhile to try. This is not to say that apprehensives are ineffective or unhappy people. Most of them have learned or can learn to deal with their communication anxiety or fear.

"Communication apprehension," researchers note, "is probably the most common handicap . . . suffered by people in contemporary American society" (McCroskey & Wheeless, 1976). According to surveys of college students, between 10 and 20 percent suffer "severe, debilitating communication apprehension"; another 20 percent suffer from "communication apprehension to a degree substantial enough to interfere to some extent with their normal functioning."

Apprehensive Behaviors

We can also look at apprehension in more behavioral terms (Richmond & McCroskey, 1996). Generally, apprehension causes a decrease in the frequency, strength, and likelihood of engaging in communication transactions. High apprehensives avoid communication situations; when forced to participate, they do so as little as possible. This reluctance to communicate shows itself in a variety of forms. For example, in small group situations, apprehensives not only will talk less but also will avoid the "seats of influence" in the group leader's direct line of sight. Even in classrooms high-apprehension individuals avoid seats where they can easily be called on, and they maintain little direct eye contact with the instructor, especially when a question is likely to be asked. Closely related to this behavior is the finding that apprehensives have more negative attitudes toward school, earn poorer grades, and are more likely to drop out of college (McCroskey, Booth-Butterfield, & Payne, 1989).

Apprehensives disclose little and avoid occupations with heavy communication demands (for example, teaching or public relations). Within their occupations, they're less desirous of advancement than others, largely because with advancement comes an increase in the need to communicate. High apprehensives are even less likely to get job interviews.

Apprehensives also engage more in steady dating, a finding that is not unexpected. One of the most difficult communication situations is asking for a date—especially a first date—and developing a new relationship. Consequently, once a dating relationship

SKILLS VIEWPOINT

Research finds that in the classroom, increased instructor clarity and immediacy (language that creates a connection between sender and receiver) helps to reduce *receiver apprehension*—people's fear that they won't be able to understand the message to which they're listening (Chesebro & McCroskey, 1998). Assuming that these findings would also apply to the health care context, what specifically might health care professionals do to help reduce apprehension among patients?

has been established, the apprehensive is reluctant to give this up and go through the anxiety of another first date and another get-acquainted period.

Your level of communication apprehension will even influence your satisfaction with dating (Powers & Love, 2000). Ask yourself if the following statements are basically true (yes) or basically false (no) about your own feelings about communicating with your dating partner:

- *I am comfortable in developing intimate conversations with my partner.*
- *I feel I am an open communicator with my partner.*
- *I am hesitant to develop a "deep" conversation with my partner.*
- *Even in casual conversations with my partner, I feel I must guard what I say.*

If you said yes to the first two statements and no to the last two, then, research shows, you're more likely to experience interpersonal communication satisfaction. If, on the other hand, you said no to the first two and yes to the last two, then you're likely to experience a lack of satisfaction.

Culture and Apprehension

Interacting with members of cultures different from your own can create uncertainty, fear, and anxiety, all of which contribute to apprehension (Stephan & Stephan, 1992).

When you're speaking with people from cultures very different from your own, you're likely to be more uncertain about the situation and about your hearers' possible responses (Gudykunst & Nishida, 1984; Gudykunst, Yang, & Nishida, 1985). When you're sure of a situation and can predict what will happen, you're more likely to feel comfortable and at ease. But when you cannot predict what will happen, you're likely to become more apprehensive (Gudykunst & Kim, 1992).

Such situations can also engender fear. You might, for example, have a greater fear of saying something that might prove offensive or of revealing your own prejudices. The fear is easily transformed into apprehension. These situations can also

Skill building *exercise*

Reducing Apprehension

This approach to reducing apprehension, called *performance visualization,* is designed to reduce your outward signs of nervousness and also to reduce negative thinking (Ayres & Hopf, 1993, 1995). Try reducing your own communication apprehension by following these simple suggestions.

1. The first part of performance visualization is to develop a positive attitude and a positive self-perception. So visualize yourself as an effective speaker. Imagine yourself communicating as a fully and totally confident individual. Look at your listeners and speak. Throughout your conversation, see yourself as fully in control of the situation. See your listeners in rapt attention from the time you begin to the time you stop. Throughout this visualization, avoid all negative thoughts. As you visualize yourself as an effective speaker, take special note of how you walk, look at your listeners, and respond to questions, and especially of how you feel about the whole experience.
2. The second part of performance visualization can help you model your performance on that of an especially effective speaker. View a particularly competent speaker and make a mental "movie" of what happens. Try also selecting a video you can replay several times. As you review the actual video and the mental movie, begin to shift yourself into the role of speaker. Become this effective speaker.

Apprehension can't be eliminated, but it can be managed and in many cases reduced.

create anxiety. For example, if your prior relationships with members of a culturally different group were few, or if they were unpleasant, then you're likely to experience greater anxiety when dealing with other members of that group than if your prior experiences were numerous and positive (Stephan & Stephan, 1985, 1992).

Your thoughts and feelings about the other people will also influence your apprehension. For example, if you hold stereotypes and prejudices, or if you feel that you're very different from these other people, you're likely to experience more apprehension than if you saw them as similar to you.

Managing Apprehension

Although most of us suffer from some communication apprehension, we can successfully manage it and control it—at least to some degree. Here are some suggestions (Beatty, 1988; McCroskey, 1997; Richmond & McCroskey, 1996).

Acquire Communication Skills and Experience   If you lack skills in typing, you can hardly expect to type very well. Yet we rarely assume that a lack of interpersonal skills and experience can cause difficulty with communication and create apprehension. It can. After all, if you had never asked for a date and had no idea how to do it, it would be natural to feel apprehension in doing so. In this course you're gaining the skills of effective interpersonal interaction. Engage in experiences—even if they prove difficult at first—to help you acquire the skills you need most. The more preparation and practice you put into something, the more comfortable you will feel with it.

"How will you ever know whether you're a flying squirrel if you don't give it a shot?"

Focus on Success   The more you perceive a situation as one in which others will evaluate you, the greater your apprehension will be (Beatty, 1988). Employment interviews and asking for a date, for example, are anxiety-provoking largely because they're highly evaluative. Your prior history in similar situations also influences the way you respond to new ones. Prior success generally (though not always) reduces apprehension. Prior failure generally (though not always) increases apprehension. If you see yourself succeeding, you'll stand a good chance of doing just that. So think positively. Concentrate your energies on doing the best job you can in any situation you find yourself in. You now have new skills and new experiences, and these will increase your chances for success. Do be careful, however, that your focus on success does not translate into the need to appear perfect, an attitude that is likely to increase your interpersonal apprehension (Saboonchi, Lundh, & Oest, 1999).

Reduce Unpredictability   The more unpredictable the situation, the greater your apprehension is likely to be. Ambiguous situations and new situations are unpredictable. Therefore, you naturally become anxious. In managing apprehension, therefore, try to reduce any unpredictability. When you're familiar with the situation and with what is expected of you, you're better able to predict what will happen. This will reduce the ambiguity and perceived newness of the situation. So, for example, if you're going to ask the boss for a raise, become familiar with as much of the situation as you can. If possible, sit in the chair you will sit in; then rehearse your statement of the reasons you deserve the raise and the way in which you'll present them.

Put Apprehension in Perspective   Whenever you engage in a communication experience, remember that the world won't end if you don't succeed. Also remember that other people are not able to perceive your apprehension as sharply as you do. You may feel a dryness in your throat and a rapid heartbeat; however, no one knows this but you.

" I am only one,
But still I am one.
I cannot do everything.
But still I can do something;
And because I cannot do everything
I will not refuse to do the
    something that I can do. "

—Edward Everett

Empowering Apprehensives

At the same time that you want to manage and perhaps lessen your own apprehension, consider the values and means of empowering others to manage and better control their own apprehension. Here are some suggestions, based largely on the insights of shyness and apprehension researchers (Carducci & Zimbardo, 1996; Richmond & McCroskey, 1998).

Message Skills

Communication Apprehension Management: To reduce anxiety acquire necessary communication skills and experiences, focus on prior successes, reduce unpredictability, and put apprehension in perspective.

- Don't overprotect the shy person, especially the shy child. If you constantly rush to a child's aid every time he or she experiences social anxiety, the child will never learn how to cope with it. Instead, be supportive (indirectly). Nudge, instead of push, a child or an adult to try out new communication situations. In this way you can help the shy person to interact in small doses and eventually to develop the self-confidence needed for more extended interaction.

- Demonstrate your understanding and empathy for apprehensives' shyness. Don't minimize their fear of communication situations—something those with little apprehension often do. Practice active listening, should you sense they wish to discuss their anxiety and shyness.

- Avoid making shy people the center of attention. That is exactly what they don't want. And never make their shyness the topic of a group conversation. Saying, "Oh, James; he's so bright, but he's so shy" only makes it more difficult for James to open his mouth. At the same time, make sure that you give shy people opportunities to speak and that you don't monopolize the conversation. For example, ask their opinions; when appropriate, try to steer the conversation in the direction of a shy person's expertise and area of competence.

Summary of Concepts

This chapter explored the self in interpersonal communication, looking first at self-concept and self-awareness along with ways to increase self-awareness; second at the process of self-disclosure along with some of its advantages and disadvantages; and third at apprehension, including what causes it and how you can manage it.

1. The self-concept is the image that you have of yourself. It develops from the images of you that others have and that they reveal to you, the comparisons you make between yourself and others, and the ways you interpret and evaluate your own thoughts and behaviors.

2. The four selves are the open self (what we and others know about us), the blind self (what others know but we do not know), the hidden self (what we know but keep hidden from others), and the unknown self (what neither we nor others know).

3. We may increase self-awareness by asking ourselves about ourselves, listening to others, actively seeking information about ourselves, seeing ourselves from different perspectives, and increasing our open selves.

4. Self-disclosure is a type of communication in which we reveal information about ourselves to others.

5. Self-disclosure is generally reciprocal; the self-disclosures of one person stimulate the self-disclosures of the other person.

6. Both men and women avoid self-disclosure for fear of projecting a negative image.

7. Through self-disclosure you may gain self-knowledge, increase communication effectiveness, enhance the meaningfulness of your interpersonal relationships, and promote physical health.

8. There are also serious dangers in self-disclosing. Your interpersonal, social, and business relationships may suffer if your self-disclosures are not positively received.

9. Communication apprehension is a feeling of fear or anxiety about interpersonal communication situations.

10. Persons with high apprehension behave differently from persons with low apprehension. High apprehensives communicate less and avoid situations and occupations that demand lots of communication. High apprehensives have more negative attitudes toward school, are more likely to drop out of college, are less likely to advance in their jobs, and tend to engage more in steady dating.

11. Techniques for managing communication apprehension include acquiring communication skills and experience, focusing on success, reducing unpredictability, and becoming familiar with the situation.

Vocabulary Quiz: The Language of the Self

Match the terms listed here with their definitions. Record the number of the definition next to the appropriate term.

_____ Johari window

_____ the open self

_____ the blind self

_____ the hidden self

_____ the unknown self

_____ self-awareness

_____ self-disclosure

_____ the dyadic effect

_____ communication apprehension

_____ gender and culture

1. Fear or anxiety in interpersonal communication situations.
2. The part of the self that contains information known to others but unknown to yourself.
3. The tendency for the behaviors of one person to stimulate similar behaviors in the other person.
4. The part of the self that contains information known to yourself and to others.
5. The part of the self that contains information known to yourself but unknown to others.
6. A model of the four selves.
7. Self-knowledge.
8. The process of revealing something significant about yourself to another individual or to a group.
9. The part of the self that contains information unknown to both yourself and to others.
10. Two of the factors influencing self-disclosure.

Four for Discussion

1. Some people engage primarily in downward social comparison; they compare themselves to those they know are worse off than they are on a particular quality. Others engage primarily in upward social comparison; they compare themselves to those who are better looking, more successful, smarter, and so on (Aspinwall & Taylor, 1993). What do you see as the advantages and disadvantages of each type of comparison?

2. As a parent, would you share with your children your financial and personal worries? The answer would probably depend at least in part on your socioeconomic status and on whether you were a single parent or one of two parents (McLoyd & Wilson, 1992). Research finds that members of middle-class two-parent families are reluctant to share financial problems with their children, preferring to shelter them from some of life's harsher realities. Low-income single mothers, however, feel that sharing problems with their children will protect them, because they will know how difficult life is and what they're up against. The researchers argue that disclosing such worries actually creates problems for the child, such as aggressiveness, difficulties in concentrating on learning in school, and anxiety disorders. What would your general advice be to parents?

3. Shyness researchers have argued that the people we single out as heroes are those who call attention to themselves, such as rock stars and media personalities; "people who are most likely to be successful are those who are able to obtain attention and feel comfortable with it" (Carducci & Zimbardo, 1996, p. 66). Who are your heroes? Are they the people who call attention to themselves? Are any of your heroes high communication apprehensives or shy individuals?

4. Much has been written about the unwillingness of men to reveal their feelings and to self-disclose on intimate levels. Do you find that men and women disclose differently? Do men and women expect the same level of self-disclosure from their partners?

Web Explorations

Explore our text website at
www.ablongman.com/devito
to find:

Exercises and Self-Tests

A variety of exercises relevant to the content of this chapter include (1) Disclosing Your Hidden Self, (2) Weighing the Rewards and Dangers of Self-Disclosure (additional cases), (3) Time for Self-Disclosure, (4) Facilitating Self-Disclosure, and (5) Reducing Apprehension with Systematic Desensitization. Self-tests include (6) How Willing to Disclose Are You? (7) What Do You Have a Right to Know? (8) How Shy Are You? (9) How Apprehensive Are You in Employment Interviews? (10) How Apprehensive Are You in Group Discussions? and (11) How Apprehensive Are You in Public Speaking?

Writing Resources and Assignments

Suggestions for writing papers of personal experience (for example, your experience with self-disclosure), concept or principle explanation (for example, self-concept, apprehension), review (for example, gender differences in self-disclosure), and research on interpersonal communication and the self (for example, the relationship between self-disclosure and self-awareness) are available.

Explore our research resources at
www.researchnavigator.com
and

Read an article.

Read a popular or scholarly article on the self (for example, self-concept, self-esteem, self-awareness), self-disclosure, or communication apprehension. On the basis of this article, what can you add to the discussion presented here?

Investigate key terms.

Investigate one of the key terms discussed in this chapter (for example, self-concept, self-awareness, social comparison, self-awareness, self-disclosure, communication apprehension, self-esteem, dyadic effect). What additional insights can you provide?

Find answers.

Try finding answers to one of the following questions or designing a research study to answer it.

1. Do people change their self-concept as they age?
2. How do children and adults differ in self-disclosure to friends?
3. Are shyness and communication apprehension hereditary? Learned?

Perception in Interpersonal Communication

The Stages of Perception

The Processes of Perception

Increasing Accuracy in Interpersonal Perception

> An ant in search of food came across a chrysalis, a butterfly in the pupa stage, that was very close to changing into a butterfly. "What a poor, pitiful animal you are," said the ant. "I can walk and run as I please; I can climb the tallest tree. But you are here imprisoned in your shell, barely able to move your tail." The chrysalis heard the ant but said nothing. A few days later, when the ant passed again, he saw only the shell and wondered what had become of the chrysalis. But then he saw the most beautiful winged creature flying above him. "It is I," said the butterfly, "the animal you pitied while you boasted of your own abilities." And with that the butterfly took flight and was soon out of sight.

In this fable told by Aesop, the ant learned that appearances are often deceptive and that what you think you see may not be the entire story—a lesson that will prove useful as you perceive people and messages, the topic of this chapter.

The Stages of Perception

Perception is the process by which you become aware of objects, events, and especially people through your senses: sight, smell, taste, touch, and hearing. Perception is an active, not a passive process. Your perceptions result from what exists in the outside world *and* from your own experiences, desires, needs and wants, loves and hatreds. One of the reasons why perception is so important in interpersonal communication is that it influences your communication choices. The messages you send and listen to will depend on how you see the world, on how you size up specific situations, on what you think of the people with whom you interact.

Interpersonal perception is a continuous series of processes that blend into one another. *For convenience of discussion* we can separate these processes into five stages: (1) You sense, you pick up some kind of stimulation; (2) you organize the stimuli in some way; (3) you interpret and evaluate what you perceive; (4) you store your perception in memory; and (5) you retrieve it when needed.

Stage One: Stimulation

At this first stage, your sense organs encounter a **stimulus**—you hear a new CD, you see a friend, you smell someone's perfume, you taste an orange, you feel another's sweaty palm. Naturally, you don't perceive everything; rather, you engage in **selective perception.** This general term includes selective attention and selective exposure. In **selective attention,** you attend to those things that you anticipate will fulfill your needs or will prove enjoyable. For example, when daydreaming in class, you don't hear what the instructor is saying until your name is called. Your selective attention mechanism focuses your senses on your name.

Through **selective exposure** you expose yourself to people or messages that will confirm your existing beliefs, that will contribute to your objectives, or that will prove satisfying in some way. For example, after you buy a car, you're more apt to read and listen to advertisements for the car you just bought, because these messages tell you that you made the right decision. At the same time, you will tend to avoid advertisements for the cars that you considered but eventually rejected, because these messages would tell you that you made the wrong decision.

You're also more likely to perceive stimuli that are greater in intensity than surrounding stimuli and those that have novelty value. For example, television commercials normally play at a greater intensity than regular programming to ensure that you take special notice. You're also more likely to notice the coworker who dresses in a novel way than you are to notice the one who dresses like everyone else. You will quickly perceive someone who shows up in class wearing a tuxedo or at a formal party in shorts.

Stage Two: Organization

At the second stage, you organize the information your senses pick up. Three interesting ways in which people organize their perceptions are by rules, by schemata, and by scripts. Let's look at each briefly.

Organization by Rules   One frequently used rule is that of *proximity* or physical closeness. The rule, simply stated, would say: Things that are physically close together constitute a unit. Thus, using this rule, you would perceive people who are often together, or messages spoken one immediately after the other, as units—as belonging together. You also assume that verbal and nonverbal signals sent at about the same time are related and constitute a unified whole; you assume they follow a *temporal rule*, which says that things occurring together in time belong together.

Another rule is *similarity:* Things that are physically similar, things that look alike, belong together and form a unit. This principle of similarity would lead you to see people who dress alike as belonging together. Similarly, you might assume that people who work at the same jobs, who are of the same religion, who live in the same building, or who talk with the same accent belong together.

You use the principle of *contrast* when you note that some items (people or messages, for example) don't belong together—that they are too different from each other to be part of the same perceptual organization. So, for example, in a conversation or a public speech, listeners will focus their attention on changes in intensity or rate, because these contrast with the rest of the message.

Organization by Schemata   Another way you organize material is by creating **schemata,** mental templates or structures that help you organize the millions of items of information you come into contact with every day as well as those you already have in memory. Schemata may thus be viewed as general ideas about people (e.g., Pat and Chris, Japanese people, Baptists, New Yorkers), about yourself (your qualities, abilities, and even liabilities), or about social roles (e.g., the characteristics of a police officer, a professor, or a multibillionaire CEO). (The word *schemata* is the plural of *schema* and is preferred to the alternative plural *schemas*.)

You develop schemata from your own experience—from actual experiences as well as from television, reading, and hearsay. Thus, for example, you might have a schema for college athletes; it might include perceptions that athletes are physically strong, ambitious, academically weak, and egocentric. And, of course, you've probably developed schemata for different religious, racial, and national groups; for men and women; and for people of different affectional orientations. Each group with which you have some familiarity will be represented in your mind in some kind of schema. Schemata help you organize your perceptions by allowing you to classify millions of people into a manageable number of categories or classes. As we'll see below, however, schemata can also create problems—they can lead you to see what is not there or to miss seeing what is there.

Organization by Scripts   A script is a type of schema; but because it's a special type, it's given a different name. Like a schema, a **script** is also an organized body of information—but instead of being about people, it's about some action, event, or procedure. It's a general idea of how some event should play out or unfold; it's the rules governing events and their sequence. For example, you probably have a script for eating in a restaurant with the actions organized into a pattern something like this: Enter, take a seat, review the menu, order from the menu, eat your food, ask for the bill, leave a tip, pay the bill, exit the restaurant. Similarly, you probably have scripts for how you do laundry, conduct an interview, introduce someone to someone else, or ask for a date.

Stage Three: Interpretation–Evaluation

The interpretation–evaluation stage of perception (the two processes cannot be separated) is inevitably subjective and is greatly influenced by your experiences, needs, wants, values, beliefs about the way things are or should be, expectations, physical and emotional state, and so on. Your interpretation–evaluation will be influenced by your rules, schemata, and scripts as well as by your gender; for example, women have been found to view others more positively than men (Winquist, Mohr, & Kenny, 1998).

For example, upon meeting a new person who is introduced to you as a college football player, you will tend to apply your schema to this person and view him as physically strong, ambitious, academically weak, and egocentric. You will, in other words, see this person through the filter of your schema and evaluate him according to your schema for college athletes. Similarly, when viewing someone performing some series of actions (say, eating in a restaurant), you apply your script to this event and view the event through the script. You interpret the actions of the diner as appropriate or inappropriate depending on your script for this behavior and the ways in which the diner performs the sequence of actions.

Stage Four: Memory

Your perceptions and their interpretations–evaluations are put into memory; they're stored so that you may ultimately retrieve them at some later time. So, for example, you have in memory your schema for college athletes and the fact that Ben Williams is a football player. Ben Williams is then stored in memory with "cognitive tags" that tell you that he's strong, ambitious, academically weak, and egocentric. Now, despite the fact that you've not witnessed Ben's strength or ambitions and have no idea of his academic record or his psychological profile, you still may store your memory of Ben along with the qualities that make up your schema for "college athletes."

Now let's say that at different times you hear that Ben failed Spanish I (normally an A or B course at your school), that Ben got an A in chemistry (normally a tough course), and that Ben is transferring to Harvard as a theoretical physics major. Schemas act as filters or gatekeepers; they allow certain information to get stored in relatively objective form, much as you heard or read it, but may distort or prevent other information from getting stored. As a result, these three items of information about Ben may get stored very differently in your memory along with your schema for college athletes.

For example, you may readily store the information that Ben failed Spanish, because it's consistent with your schema; it fits neatly into the template you have for college athletes. Information that's consistent with your schema—such as in this example—will strengthen your schema and make it more resistant to change (Aronson, Wilson, & Akert, 1999). Depending on the strength of your schema, you may also store in memory, even though you didn't hear it, a perception that Ben did poorly in other courses as well. The information that Ben got an A in chemistry, because it contradicts your schema (it just doesn't seem right), may easily be distorted or lost. The information that Ben is transferring to Harvard, however, is a bit different. This information is also inconsistent with your schema; but it is so drastically inconsistent that you may begin to look at this mindfully and may even begin to question your schema, or perhaps to view Ben as an exception to the general rule. In either case, you're going to etch Ben's transferring to Harvard very clearly in your mind.

Stage Five: Recall

At some later date, you may want to recall or access the information you have stored in memory. Let's say you want to retrieve your information about Ben because he's a topic of conversation among you and a few friends. As we'll see in our discussion of listening in Chapter 4, memory isn't reproductive; you don't simply reproduce what you've heard or seen. Rather, you reconstruct what you've heard or seen into a whole that is meaningful to you—depending in great part on your schemata and scripts—and it's this reconstruction that you store in memory. Now, when you want to retrieve this information from memory, you may recall it with a variety of inaccuracies. Specifically, you're likely to

- recall information that is consistent with your schema; in fact, you may not even be recalling the specific information (say about Ben) but may actually be recalling your schema (which contains the information about college athletes and, because of this, also about Ben)

- fail to recall information that is inconsistent with your schema; you have no place to put that information and so you easily lose it or forget it

- recall information that drastically contradicts your schema, because it forces you to think (and perhaps rethink) about your schema and its accuracy; it may even force you to revise your schema for college athletes in general

Reflections on the Model of Perception

Before moving on to the more specific processes involved in interpersonal perception, let's spell out some of the implications of this five-stage model for your own interpersonal perceptions:

1. Everyone relies heavily on shortcuts; rules, schemata, and scripts, for example, are all useful shortcuts that simplify your understanding, remembering, and recalling information about people and events. If you didn't have these shortcuts, then you'd have to treat every person, role, or action differently from each other person, role, or action. This would make every experience a new one totally unrelated to anything you already know. If you didn't use these shortcuts, you'd be unable to generalize, draw connections, or otherwise profit from previously acquired knowledge.

2. Shortcuts, however, may mislead you; they may contribute to your remembering things that are consistent with your schemata even if they didn't occur, and to your distorting or forgetting information that is inconsistent.

3. What you remember about a person or an event isn't an objective recollection but is more likely heavily influenced by your preconceptions or your schemata about what belongs and what doesn't belong, what fits neatly into the templates in your brain and what doesn't fit. Your reconstruction of an event or person contains a lot of information that was not in the original sensory experience and may omit a lot that was in the experience.

4. Judgments about members of other cultures are often ethnocentric; because your schemata and scripts are created on the basis of your own cultural beliefs and experiences, you can easily (but inappropriately) apply these to members of other cultures. So it's easy to infer that when members of other cultures do things that conform to your scripts, they're right, and when they do things that contradict your scripts, they're wrong—a classic example of ethnocentric thinking. As you can appreciate, this tendency can easily contribute to intercultural misunderstandings.

5. A similar problem arises when you base your scripts for different cultural groups on stereotypes you may have derived from television or movies. For example, you may have scripts for religious Muslims that you derived from stereotypes presented in the media, and which you then apply to all Muslims,

Message Skills

Perceptual Shortcuts: Be mindful of your perceptual shortcuts so that they don't mislead you and result in inaccurate perceptions.

© 1991 Mark Stivers. Reprinted by permission.

Taking Another's Perspective

Taking the perspective of the other person and looking at the world through this perspective, this point of view, rather than through your own is crucial in achieving mutual understanding. For each of the specific behaviors listed below, identify specific circumstances that would lead to a *positive perception* and specific circumstances that might lead to a *negative perception*.

For example, let's say that you observe Grace giving a beggar in the street a 20-dollar bill. Specific circumstances leading to a positive perception might be, for example: *Grace once had to beg to get money for food. She now shares all she has with those who are going through the same experience.* Specific circumstances leading to a negative perception might be, for example: *Grace grew up in luxury. She just wants to show people that she has so much money she can afford to give $20 to a total stranger.*

1. A passerby ignoring a homeless person who asks for money.
2. A middle-aged man walking down the street with his arms around a teen-age girl.
3. A mother refusing to admit her teen-age son back into her house.

To understand the perspective of another person, try to understand the reasons for their behaviors and resist defining these reasons from your own perspective.

seeing what conforms to your script and failing to see or distorting what does not conform to your script.

6. Memory is especially unreliable when the information is ambiguous—when it can be interpreted in different ways. Thus, for example, consider the statement, "Ben didn't do as well in his other courses as he would have liked." If your schema of Ben was "brilliant" then you might "remember" that Ben got B's. But if, as in our example, your schema was of the academically weak athlete, you might "remember" that Ben got D's. Conveniently, but unreliably, schemata reduce ambiguity.

> " We must always tell what we see. Above all, and this is more difficult, we must always see what we see. "
>
> —Charles Peguy

The Processes of Perception

Before reading about the specific processes that you use in perceiving other people, examine your own perception strategies by taking the self-test below.

 Test Yourself

How Accurate Are You at People Perception?

Respond to each of the following statements with T (true) if the statement is usually or generally accurate in describing your behavior, or with F (false) if the statement is usually or generally inaccurate in describing your behavior.

_____ ❶ When I know some things about another person, I can pretty easily fill in what I don't know.

_____ ❷ I make predictions about people's behaviors that generally prove to be true.

_____ ❸ Generally my expectations are borne out by what I actually see; that is, my initial expectations usually match my eventual perceptions.

_____ ❹ I base most of my impressions of people on the first few minutes of our meeting.

_____ ⑤ I generally find that people I like possess positive characteristics and people I don't like possess negative characteristics.

_____ ⑥ I have clear ideas of what people of different national, racial, and religious groups are really like.

_____ ⑦ I generally attribute people's attitudes and behaviors to their most obvious physical or psychological characteristic.

_____ ⑧ I believe that the world is basically just, that good things happen to good people and bad things happen to bad people.

HOW DID YOU DO? This test was designed to preview issues to be considered in this chapter. All statements refer to perceptual processes that you may use but that can lead you to form inaccurate impressions. The first six statements refer to processes we'll explore in detail: implicit personality theory (question 1), self-fulfilling prophecy (2), perceptual accentuation (3), primary–recency (4), consistency (5), and stereotyping (6). Statements 7 and 8 refer to two mistakes we may make in attributing motives to other people's—and even our own—behaviors: overattribution (7) and the self-serving bias (8), which often involves a belief that the world is fundamentally just. Ideally, you would have responded with "false" to all of these statements, indicating that you regularly avoid falling into these potential traps.

WHAT WILL YOU DO? As you read this chapter, think about these processes and consider how you might use them to make your perceptions of people more accurate. At the same time, recognize that situations vary widely and that the suggestions offered will prove useful most but not all of the time.

Implicit Personality Theories

Each person has a subconscious or implicit system of rules—an **implicit personality theory**—that says which characteristics of an individual go with other character-

Ethical messages

Censoring Messages and Interactions

A gatekeeper is a person or institution that regulates what information gets through from a source to a receiver. Television programmers, for example, are gatekeepers in determining which programs people will see. Teachers, authors, newsgroup moderators, and parents are also gatekeepers—passing on certain information and preventing other information from getting through.

Similarly, relational gatekeepers encourage certain relationships and discourage or even prevent other relationships. Parents, for example, often encourage their children to play with and become friends with children from the same racial or national group and religion; they may discourage friendships with children from different cultures. Your friends may exert pressure on you to date one person and not another, to associate with some people but not others.

What Would You Do?

Jennifer and Colleen have been friends all through college. Recently, John has been interested in Colleen and so approaches Jennifer to ask what his chances are. John's been charged with physically abusing a former girlfriend, and rumor has it that he's still married. Colleen, on the other hand, is extremely vulnerable and would probably be tempted by John's fast talk. Jennifer is convinced that John would be bad for Colleen and so tells John that Colleen is not interested in him. Jennifer also decides not to tell Colleen anything about John's interest. Is Jennifer ethical in lying to John? Is she ethical in concealing John's expression of interest? If you were Colleen's best friend, what would you do in this situation?

istics. Consider, for example, the following brief statements. What word in parentheses do you think best completes each sentence?

- *Carlo is energetic, eager, and (intelligent, stupid).*
- *Kim is bold, defiant, and (extroverted, introverted).*
- *Joe is bright, lively, and (thin, heavy).*
- *Ava is attractive, intelligent, and (likable, unlikable).*
- *Susan is cheerful, positive, and (outgoing, shy).*
- *Angel is handsome, tall, and (friendly, unfriendly).*

What makes some of these choices seem right and others wrong is your implicit personality theory. Your theory may, for example, have told you that a person who is energetic and eager is also intelligent, not stupid—even though there is no logical reason why a stupid person could not be energetic and eager.

The well-documented **halo effect** is a function of the implicit personality theory (Dion, Berscheid, & Walster, 1972; Riggio, 1987). If you believe a person has some positive qualities, you're likely to infer that she or he also possesses other positive qualities. There is also a *reverse halo effect:* If you know a person possesses several negative qualities, you're more likely to infer that the person also has other negative qualities.

In using implicit personality theories, apply them carefully and critically so as to avoid perceiving qualities in an individual that your theory tells you should be present when they really aren't. Similarly, be careful of ignoring or distorting qualities that don't conform to your theory but that are actually present in the individual.

As might be expected, the implicit personality theories that people hold differ from culture to culture, from group to group, and even from person to person. For example, the Chinese have a concept called *shi gu* that refers to "someone who is worldly, devoted to his or her family, socially skillful, and somewhat reserved" (Aronson, Wilson, & Akert, 1999, p. 117). This concept isn't easily encoded in English. English, on the other hand, has a concept of the "artistic type," a generalization that seems absent in Chinese. Thus, although it is easy for speakers of English or Chinese to refer to specific concepts—as in describing someone as socially skilled or creative—each language creates its own generalized categories. In Chinese the qualities that make up *shi gu* are seen as going together more easily than they might be for an English speaker; they're part of the implicit personality theory of more Chinese speakers than English speakers.

The Self-Fulfilling Prophecy

A **self-fulfilling prophecy** occurs when you make a prediction that comes true because you act on it as if it were true; you act on your schema as if it were true and in doing so make it true (Merton, 1957). There are four basic steps in the self-fulfilling prophecy:

1. You make a prediction or formulate a belief about a person or a situation. For example, you predict that Pat is friendly in interpersonal encounters.
2. You act toward that person or situation as if that prediction or belief were true. For example, you act as if Pat were a friendly person.
3. Because you act as if the belief were true, it becomes true. For example, because of the way you act toward Pat, Pat becomes comfortable and friendly.
4. You observe *your* effect on the person or the resulting situation, and what you see strengthens your beliefs. For example, you observe Pat's friendliness, and this reinforces your belief that Pat is in fact friendly.

The self-fulfilling prophecy can also be seen when you make predictions about yourself and fulfill them. Perhaps you enter a group situation convinced that the

Message Skills

Implicit Personality Theory: Bring your implicit personality theory to your mindful state to subject your perceptions and conclusions to logical analysis.

❝ Of all the self-fulfilling prophecies in our culture, the assumption that aging means decline and poor health is probably the deadliest. ❞

—Marilyn Ferguson

other members will dislike you. Almost invariably you'll be proved right; the other members will appear to you to dislike you. What you may be doing is acting in a way that encourages the group to respond to you negatively. In this way you fulfill your prophecies about yourself.

A widely known example of the self-fulfilling prophecy is the **Pygmalion effect.** In a well-known study, teachers were told that certain pupils were expected to do exceptionally well, although they were late bloomers. The names of these students were actually selected at random by the experimenters. The results, however, were not random. The students whose names were given to the teachers actually performed at a higher level than others. In fact, these students' IQ scores even improved more than did the other students'. The teachers' expectations probably prompted them to give extra attention to the selected students, thereby positively affecting their performance (Rosenthal & Jacobson, 1968; Insel & Jacobson, 1975). Studies have found the same general effect in military training and business setting; trainees and workers performed better when their supervisors were given positive information about them (McNatt, 2001). In fact, researchers have identified the Pygmalion effect in contexts as varied as leadership, athletic coaching, and effective stepfamilies (Eden, 1992; Solomon et al., 1996; Einstein, 1995; McNatt, 2001).

Self-fulfilling prophecies can short-circuit critical thinking and influence another person's behavior (or your own) so that it conforms to your prophecy. As a result, they can lead you to see what you predicted rather than what is really there—for example, to perceive yourself as a failure because you have predicted it rather than because of any actual failures.

SKILLS VIEWPOINT

You tend to make self-fulfilling predictions about yourself. Perhaps you make the prediction that people don't like you and so you don't extend yourself to others. Or perhaps you assume that others will like you; in that case, you're more likely to approach them with a positive attitude and demeanor. In what ways might you use the self-fulfilling prophecy to increase your interpersonal effectiveness?

Primacy–Recency

Assume for a moment that you're enrolled in a course in which half the classes are extremely dull and half extremely exciting. At the end of the semester, you evaluate the course and the instructor. Will your evaluation be more favorable if the dull classes occurred in the first half of the semester and the exciting classes in the second? Or will it be more favorable if the order were reversed? If what comes first exerts the most influence, you have a *primacy effect*. If what comes last (or most recently) exerts the most influence, you have a *recency effect*.

In the classic study on the effects of **primacy and recency** in interpersonal perception, college students perceived a person who was described as "intelligent, industrious, impulsive, critical, stubborn, and envious" more positively than a person described as "envious, stubborn, critical, impulsive, industrious, and intelligent" (Asch, 1946). Clearly, there's a tendency to use early information to get a general idea about a person and to use later information to make this impression more specific. The initial information helps you form a schema for the person. Once that schema is formed, you're likely to resist information that contradicts it.

One interesting practical implication of primacy–recency is that the first impression you make on others is likely to be the most important. The reason for this is that the schema that others form of you functions as a filter to admit or block additional information about you. If the initial impression or schema is positive, others are likely to readily remember additional positive information, because it confirms this original positive image or schema. Similarly, they are likely to forget or distort negative information, because it contradicts this original positive schema. They are also more likely to place a positive interpretation on information that is really ambiguous. If the initial impression is positive, then, you win all three ways.

Message Skills

Self-Fulfilling Prophecy: Take a second look at your perceptions when they correspond very closely to your initial expectations; the self-fulfilling prophecy may be at work.

" Manage every second of a first meeting. Do not delude yourself that a bad impression can be easily corrected. Putting things right is a lot harder than getting them right the first time. "

—David Lewis

The tendency to give greater weight to early information and to interpret later information in light of early impressions can lead you to formulate a total picture of an individual on the basis of initial impressions that may not be typical or accurate. For example, if you judge a job applicant as generally nervous when he or she may simply be showing normal nervousness at being interviewed for a much needed job, you will have misperceived this individual.

Similarly, this tendency can lead you to discount or distort subsequent perceptions so as not to disrupt your initial impression or upset your original schema. For example, you may fail to see signs of deceitfulness in someone you like because of your early impression that this person is good and honest.

Consistency

The tendency to maintain balance among perceptions or attitudes is called **consistency** (McBroom & Reed, 1992). You expect certain things to go together and other things not to go together. On a purely intuitive basis, for example, respond to the following sentences by noting your *expected* response:

- *I expect a person I like to (like, dislike) me.*
- *I expect a person I dislike to (like, dislike) me.*
- *I expect my friend to (like, dislike) my friend.*
- *I expect my friend to (like, dislike) my enemy.*
- *I expect my enemy to (like, dislike) my friend.*
- *I expect my enemy to (like, dislike) my enemy.*

❓ SKILLS VIEWPOINT

You and your business partner are in the process of interviewing web designers. Unfortunately, however, your partner forms initial impressions that cannot be changed no matter what you say. As soon as a potential designer walks in, the partner forms an impression and makes a decision. The problem is that this has been going on for weeks and you still don't have a designer. What do you say?

According to most consistency theories, your expectations would be as follows: You would expect a person you liked to like you (1) and a person you disliked to dislike you (2). You would expect a friend to like a friend (3) and to dislike an enemy (4). You would expect your enemy to dislike your friend (5) and to like your other enemy (6). All these expectations are intuitively satisfying.

Further, you would expect someone you liked to possess characteristics you like or admire. And you would expect your enemies not to possess characteristics you like or admire. Conversely, you would expect people you liked to lack unpleasant characteristics and those you disliked to possess unpleasant characteristics.

Uncritically assuming that an individual is consistent can lead you to ignore or distort your perceptions of behaviors that are inconsistent with your picture of the whole person. For example, you may misinterpret Kim's basic shyness because your image of Kim is "bold, defiant, and extroverted." Consistency can also lead you to see certain behaviors as positive if you interpreted other behaviors positively (the halo effect) or as negative if you interpreted other behaviors negatively (the reverse halo effect).

Stereotyping

One of the most common shortcuts in interpersonal perception is stereotyping. A sociological or psychological **stereotype** is a fixed impression of a group of people; it's a schema. We all have attitudinal stereotypes—of national, religious, sexual, or racial groups, or perhaps of criminals, prostitutes, teachers, or plumbers. If you have these fixed impressions, you will, on meeting a member of a particular group, often see that person primarily as a member of that group and apply to him or her all the characteristics you assign to

Listening to Other Perspectives

"Galileo and the Ghosts" is a technique for altering your perception of a problem or person or situation by seeing it through the eyes of a particular group of people (DeVito, 1996). It involves setting up a mental "ghostthinking" team, much the way executives and politicians hire ghostwriters to write their speeches or corporations and research institutes maintain think tanks. In this ghostthinking technique, you select a team of four to eight "people" you admire; for example, historical figures like Aristotle or Picasso, fictional figures like Wonder Woman or Batman, contemporary figures like Oprah Winfrey or Jerry Springer, or persons from other cultures or of a different gender or affectional orientation.

You pose a problem or question and then ask yourself how this team of ghosts would perceive the problem or answer the question, allowing yourself to listen to their perceptions. Of course, you're really listening to yourself—but to yourself taking the role of another person. The technique forces you to step outside your normal role and to consider the perspective of someone totally different from you. As a result, your own perception of the problem will change. You can also use this technique to appreciate—and ultimately empathize with—the perspective of your romantic partner, friend, parent, or child.

Applying Listening Skills

Pat and Chris, a couple in their 40s who have been together for the last 15 years, have been having tremendous difficulty communicating; each claims the other doesn't understand and doesn't empathize. What suggestions would you offer to help them listen more effectively to other perspectives?

that group. If you meet someone who is a prostitute, for example, there is a host of characteristics for prostitutes that you may apply to this one person. To complicate matters further, you will often "see" in this person's behavior the manifestation of characteristics that you would not "see" if you didn't know that this person was a prostitute. In online communication, because there are few visual and auditory cues, it's not surprising to find that people rely heavily on stereotypes in forming impressions of online communication partners (Jacobson, 1999).

Stereotypes can easily distort accurate perception and prevent you from seeing an individual as an individual rather than as a member of a group. And this tendency to group people and to respond to individuals primarily as members of groups can lead you to perceive an individual as possessing those qualities (usually negative) that you believe characterize his or her group (for example, "All Mexicans are . . ." or "All Baptists are . . .")—and therefore to fail to appreciate the multifaceted nature of

Message Skills

Stereotypes: Focus on the individual rather than on the individual's membership in one group or another.

? SKILLS VIEWPOINT

Your life partner is a great person—except for a habit of thinking and talking in stereotypes, especially about the opposite sex. This drives you crazy, and you want to show that this type of behavior is illogical and hurtful. What do you say?

all individuals and groups. Stereotyping can also lead you to ignore each person's unique characteristics and therefore to fail to benefit from the special contributions each individual can bring to an encounter.

Attribution

Attribution is the process by which we try to explain the motivation for a person's behavior. Perhaps the major way we do this is to ask ourselves if the person was in control of the behavior. If people are in control of their own behavior, then we feel justified in praising them for positive behaviors and blaming them for negative behaviors. You probably make similar judgments based on controllability in many situations. Consider, for example, how you would respond to situations such as Doris's failing her history exam or Sidney's having his car repossessed because he failed to keep up the payments.

Very likely you would be sympathetic to Doris and Sidney if you feel that they were *not* in control of what happened; for example, if the examination was unfair or if Sidney couldn't make his car payments because he lost his job as a result of discrimination. On the other hand, you probably would not be sympathetic or might blame these people for their problems if you felt that they were in control of what happened; for example, if Doris partied instead of studying or if Sidney gambled his payments away.

Generally, research shows that if we feel people are in control of negative behaviors, we will come to dislike them. If we feel people are not in control of negative behaviors, we will not blame them for their negative circumstances.

Three major attribution problems can interfere with the accuracy of your interpersonal perceptions: the self-serving bias, overattribution, and the fundamental attribution error.

After getting a poor performance evaluation, you may well attribute it to the difficulty of the job or to unfairness on the part of the supervisor (that is, to uncontrollable factors). After getting an extremely positive evaluation, however, you're more likely to attribute it to your ability or hard work (that is, to controllable factors). This tendency is the **self-serving bias,** our tendency to take credit for the positive and deny responsibility for the negative (Bernstein, Stephan, & Avis, 1979). To prevent the self-serving bias from distorting your attributions, consider the potential influences of both internal and external factors on both your positive and negative behaviors. Ask yourself to what extent your negative behaviors may be due to internal (controllable) factors and your positive behaviors to external (uncontrollable) factors. Just asking the question will prevent you from mindlessly falling into the self-serving bias trap.

If someone you work with had alcoholic parents or is blind or was born into great wealth, there's often a tendency to attribute everything that person does to such factors. And so you might say, "Sally has difficulty working on a team because she grew up in a home of alcoholics," "Alex overeats because he's blind," or "Lillian lacks ambition because she always got whatever she wanted without working for it." This is called **overattribution**—the tendency to single out one or two obvious characteristics and attribute everything a person does to these one or two characteristics. To prevent overattribution, recognize that most behaviors result from a lot of factors and that you almost always make a mistake when you select one factor and attribute everything to it. When you make a judgment, ask yourself if other factors that might be creating the behaviors that seem at first glance to stem solely from one factor.

When Pat is late for a meeting, you're more likely to conclude that Pat is inconsiderate or irresponsible or "scatterbrained" than to attribute the lateness to a bus breakdown or a traffic accident. This tendency to conclude that people do what they do because that's the kind of people they are, not because of the situation they're in, is known as the **fundamental attribution error.** When you commit this error, you overvalue the contribution of internal factors and undervalue the influence of exter-

Message Skills

Self-Serving Bias: Become mindful of giving too much weight to internal factors (when explaining your positives) and too little weight to external factors (when explaining your negatives).

Message Skills

Overattribution: Avoid overattribution; rarely is any one factor an accurate explanation of complex human behavior.

Perceiving Differences

Examine each of the following situations and indicate how each of the persons identified might view the situation.

1. Pat, a single parent, has two small children (ages 7 and 12) who often lack some of the important things children their age should have—such as school supplies, sneakers, and toys—because Pat can't afford them. Yet Pat smokes two packs of cigarettes a day.

   Pat sees . . .
   The 12-year-old daughter sees . . .
   The children's teacher sees . . .

2. Chris has extremely high standards and feels that getting all A's in college is an absolute necessity; Chris would be devastated by receiving even one B. In fear of earning that first B (after three and a half years of college), Chris cheats on an examination in a course on family communication and gets caught by the instructor.

   Chris sees . . .
   The instructor sees . . .
   The average B− student sees . . .

3. Pat, a supervisor in an automobile factory, has been ordered to increase production or be fired. In desperation Pat gives a really tough message to the workers—many of whom are greatly insulted and, as a result, slow down rather than increase their efforts.

   Pat sees . . .
   The average worker sees . . . .
   Pat's supervisor sees . . .

Each person perceives the world differently. For effective communication to take place, each person needs to understand the perceptions of the other.

nal factors. To avoid making this error, ask yourself if you're giving undue emphasis to internal factors, and consider what external factors might have accounted for another's behavior. Interestingly enough, this tendency may be culture specific, not universal as previously thought (Goode, 2000). For example, research finds that Asians are less likely to commit this fundamental attribution error than Americans. In one study researchers presented American and Korean students with a speech endorsing a particular position and told them that the writer had been instructed to write this and really had no choice. Americans were more likely to decide that the speaker believed in the position endorsed; they concluded that the speech expressed what the speaker really believed (and not the external circumstances of being forced to write the speech). Korean students, on the other hand, were less likely to believe in the sincerity of the speaker and gave greater weight to the external factor that the speaker was forced to write the speech.

Message Skills

Fundamental Attribution Error:
Avoid the fundamental attribution error, whereby you attribute someone's behavior solely to internal factors while minimizing or ignoring situational forces.

Increasing Accuracy in Interpersonal Perception

Your effectiveness in interpersonal communication depends largely on the accuracy of your perceptions. Here are four suggestions to help you perceive other people more accurately.

Analyze Your Perceptions

When you become aware of your perceptions, you'll be able to subject them to logical and critical analysis. Here are some suggestions.

CURTIS © 1993 Ray Billingsley. Reprinted with special permission of King Features Syndicate.

- Recognize your own role in perception. Your emotional and physiological state will influence the meaning you give to your perceptions. A movie may seem hysterically funny when you're in a good mood but just plain stupid if you're in a bad mood or preoccupied with family problems. Know when your perceptual evaluations are unduly influenced by your own biases; for example, by a tendency to perceive only the positive in people you like and only the negative in people you don't like. Even your gender will influence your perceptions. Women consistently evaluate other people more positively than do men on such factors as agreeableness, conscientiousness, and emotional stability (Winquist, Mohr, & Kenny, 1998).

- Avoid early conclusions. On the basis of your observations, formulate hypotheses to test against additional information and evidence rather than drawing conclusions you then look to confirm.

- Look for a variety of cues before making a judgment. For example, in making a judgment about a place to work, you'd logically use a variety of cues—salary, opportunity for advancement, benefits package, the working environment, and probably lots of other factors as well. After examining these cues, you'd make a judgment about the suitability of this job. In a similar way, it's useful to use a variety of cues when making judgments of people.

- Be alert to any *confirmation bias*—a tendency to seek out and believe information that supports your position or bias. Conversely, a *disconfirmation bias* may lead you to avoid any information that would contradict your position or bias.

5 Ways to Talk on the Phone

Talking on the telephone is much like talking in person, except that you can't see each other. As a result, the facial and eye cues that normally accompany face-to-face interaction are missing. Here are some suggestions for improving your telephone skills.

1. Use "continuity sounds" to confirm that you're listening and understanding (Walker, 1998).
2. Repeat important information to confirm that your understanding is accurate.
3. Open and close your conversation on a positive note.
4. Use regular conversational techniques, as needed. For example, speak in relatively short exchanges, summarizing as appropriate, asking questions, and so on.
5. If you call, ask the person if this is a convenient time to talk. Unlike e-mail, which can be accessed and responded to when you want to, a phone call might interrupt something important; it's important to check first before launching into your message.

Applying Interpersonal Skills/Then and Now

Have you ever experienced a really unpleasant phone conversation? What happened? What would you do differently now?

When evaluating information, ask yourself if you're being influenced by either of these biases. Bringing this possibility to consciousness will help you think more critically about the information (Edwards & Smith, 1996; Kuhn, Weinstock, & Flaton, 1994).

Check Your Perceptions

Perception checking is another way to reduce uncertainty and to make your perceptions more accurate. The goal of perception checking is to explore further the thoughts and feelings of the other person, not to prove that your initial perception is correct. With this simple technique, you lessen your chances of misinterpreting another's feelings. At the same time, you give the other person an opportunity to elabo-

? SKILLS VIEWPOINT

Try using perception checking in such situations as these: *(a)* Your friend says he wants to drop out of college; *(b)* a neighbor expresses fear of being robbed; *(c)* your cousin hasn't called you in several months, though you've called her at least six times. What do you say?

rate on his or her thoughts and feelings. In its most basic form, perception checking consists of two steps:

- Describe what you see or hear, recognizing that even descriptions are not really objective but are heavily influenced by who you are, your emotional state, and so on. At the same time, you may wish to describe what you think is happening. Again, try to do this as descriptively (not evaluatively) as you can. Sometimes you may wish to offer several possibilities: "You've called me from work a lot this week. You seem concerned that everything is all right at home." Or, "You've not wanted to talk with me all week. You say that my work is fine but you don't seem to want to give me the same responsibilities that other editorial assistants have."

- Seek confirmation. Ask the other person if your description is accurate. Be careful that your request for confirmation does not sound as though you already know the answer; ask for confirmation in as supportive a way as possible, for example, "Are you worried about me or the kids?" or "Are you displeased with my work? Is there anything I can do to improve my job performance?"

Reduce Your Uncertainty

Reducing uncertainty enables you to achieve greater accuracy in perception. In large part people learn about uncertainty and how to deal with it from their culture. In some cultures people do little to avoid uncertainty and have little anxiety about not knowing what will happen next; uncertainty is a normal part of life, and people accept it as it comes. Members of these cultures don't feel threatened by unknown situations. Examples of such low-anxiety cultures include Singapore, Jamaica, Denmark, Sweden, Hong Kong, Ireland, Great Britain, Malaysia, India, Philippines, and the United States. Members of other cultures do much to avoid uncertainty and have a great deal of anxiety about not knowing what will happen next; they see uncertainty as threatening and as something that must be counteracted. Examples of such high-anxiety cultures include Greece, Portugal, Guatemala, Uruguay, Belgium, El Salvador, Japan, Yugoslavia, Peru, France, Chile, Spain, and Costa Rica (Hofstede, 1997).

Because weak-uncertainty-avoidance cultures have great tolerance for ambiguity and uncertainty, they minimize the importance of rules governing communication and relationships (Hofstede, 1997; Lustig & Koester, 1999). People in these cultures readily tolerate individuals who don't follow the same rules as the cultural majority. Cultures with weak uncertainty avoidance may even encourage different approaches and perspectives. Strong-uncertainty-avoidance cultures, in contrast, create very clear-cut rules for communication that must not be broken.

Students from weak-uncertainty-avoidance cultures appreciate freedom in education and prefer vague assignments without specific timetables. These students want to be rewarded for creativity and readily accept an instructor's lack of knowledge. Students from strong-uncertainty-avoidance cultures prefer highly structured experiences with little ambiguity; they prefer specific objectives, detailed instructions, and definite timetables. These students expect to be judged on the basis of the right answers and expect the instructor to have all the answers all the time (Hofstede, 1997).

A variety of strategies can help reduce uncertainty (Berger & Bradac, 1982; Gudykunst, 1994):

- Observing another person while he or she is engaged in an active task, preferably interacting with others in relatively informal social situations, will often reveal a great deal about the person. The reason is that in informal situations people are less apt to monitor their behaviors and more likely to reveal their true selves.

- You can manipulate situations to observe people in more revealing contexts. Employment interviews, theatrical auditions, and student teaching are typical situations designed to reveal how people act and react—and thus to help reduce uncertainty.

- When you log on to a chat group for the first time and you lurk, reading the exchanges between the other group members before saying anything yourself, you're learning about the people in the group and about the group itself and thus reducing uncertainty. When uncertainty is reduced, you're more likely to make contributions that will be appropriate to the group and less likely to violate any of the group's norms; in short, you're more likely to communicate effectively.

- Another way to reduce uncertainty is to collect information by asking others about a person. For example, you might ask a colleague if a third person finds you interesting and might like to have dinner with you.

- And of course you can interact with the individual. For example, you can ask questions: "Do you enjoy sports?" "What did you think of that computer science course?" "What would you do if you got fired?" You also gain knowledge of another by disclosing information about yourself. Your disclosures will help create an environment that encourages disclosures from the person about whom you wish to learn more.

Message Skills
Reducing Uncertainty: Use passive, active, and interactive strategies to reduce uncertainty.

Increase Your Cultural Sensitivity

Recognizing and being sensitive to cultural differences will help increase your accuracy in perception. For example, Russian or Chinese artists such as ballet dancers will often applaud their audience by clapping. Americans seeing this may easily interpret the behavior as egotistical. Similarly, a German man will enter a restaurant before the woman in order to see if the place is respectable enough for the woman to enter. This simple custom can easily seem rude to members of cultures in which courtesy means allowing the woman to enter first (Axtell, 1993).

Within every cultural group there are wide and important differences. As not all Americans are alike, neither are all Indonesians, Greeks, Mexicans, and so on. When you make assumptions that all people of a certain culture are alike, you're thinking in stereotypes. Recognizing not only the differences between another culture and your own but also the differences among members of any given culture will help you perceive situations more accurately.

Cultural sensitivity will help counteract the considerable difficulty most people have in understanding the nonverbal messages of people from other cultures. For example, its easier to decode the emotions communicated facially by members of your own culture than to read facial expressions in members of other cultures (Weathers, Frank, & Spell, 2002). This "in-group advantage" can assist your perceptional accuracy with members of your own culture but will often hinder your accuracy with members of other cultures (Elfenbein & Ambady, 2002).

Message Skills
Culture and Perception: Increase accuracy in perception by learning as much as you can about the cultures of those with whom you interact.

Summary of Concepts

This chapter discussed how perception works, the processes that influence perception, and how you can make your perceptions more accurate.

1. Perception is the process by which you become aware of the many stimuli impinging on your senses. It occurs in five stages: sensory stimulation occurs, sensory stimulation is organized, sensory stimulation is interpreted and evaluated, sensory stimulation is held in memory, and sensory stimulation is recalled.
2. Processes that influence perception include: (1) implicit personality theories, (2) self-fulfilling prophecy, (3) primacy–recency, (4) consistency, (5) stereotyping, and (6) attribution.
3. Implicit personality theories are the private personality theories people hold, which influence how they perceive other people.
4. The self-fulfilling prophecy occurs when you make a prediction or formulate a belief that comes true because you have made the prediction and acted as if it were true.
5. Primacy–recency has to do with the relative influence of stimuli as a result of their order. If what occurs first exerts greater influence, you have a primacy effect. If what occurs last exerts greater influence, you have a recency effect.
6. Consistency influences you to see what is consistent with your expectations and not to see what is inconsistent.
7. Stereotyping is the tendency to develop and maintain fixed, unchanging perceptions of groups of people and to use these perceptions to evaluate individuals, ignoring their unique particular characteristics.
8. Attribution is the process through which you try to understand the behaviors of others (and your own, in self-attribution)—particularly the reasons or motivations for these behaviors. Perceptions of controllability often influence attributions. Errors of attribution include the self-serving bias, overattribution, and the fundamental attribution error.
9. To increase the accuracy of your interpersonal perceptions: (1) Critically analyze your perceptions; formulate hypotheses rather than conclusions, look for a variety of cues (especially contradictory ones), and be aware of your own biases. (2) Check your perceptions, describing what you see or hear and asking for confirmation. (3) Reduce uncertainty by, for example, lurking before joining a group or interacting with the person. (4) Be culturally sensitive, recognizing the differences between your own and other cultures and also differences among members of any specific culture.

Vocabulary Quiz: The Language of Interpersonal Perception

Match the terms dealing with interpersonal perception with their definitions. Record the number of the definition next to the appropriate term.

_____ script

_____ implicit personality theory

_____ stereotype

_____ proximity

_____ the fundamental attribution error

_____ self-fulfilling prophecy

_____ halo effect

_____ perception checking

_____ self-serving bias

_____ schemata

1. Overvaluing internal factors and undervaluing external factors in explaining behavior.
2. Increasing accuracy in perception by describing what you think is going on and asking for confirmation.
3. A theory about people that you have and through which you perceive others.
4. The tendency to see things that are physically close to each other as belonging together, as forming a unit.
5. An organized mental template for the way an action, or procedure should take place.
6. A fixed impression of a group of people.
7. The mental templates or structures that help you organize information in memory.
8. The situation in which we make a prediction and then act in a way that makes the prediction come true.
9. A tendency to take credit for positive outcomes and to deny responsibility for negative events.
10. The tendency to generalize a person's virtue or expertise from one area to another.

Four for Discussion

1. In making evaluations of other people, we tend to assume that we first think about the situation and then make the evaluation. Some research claims, however, that we really don't think before assigning any perception a positive or negative value. This research argues that all perceptions have a positive or negative value attached to them and that these evaluations are most often automatic, involving no conscious thought. Immediately upon perceiving a person, idea, or thing, we attach a positive or negative value (*New York Times,* August 8, 1995, C1, C10). What do you think of this claim? Can you think of examples from your own experience that would support or contradict this view?

2. Although most of the research on the self-fulfilling prophecy illustrates its distorting effect on behavior, it's been argued that organizations could use the self-fulfilling prophecy to stimulate higher performance (Eden, 1992; Field, 1989). For example, managers could be told that employees had extremely high capabilities; managers would then act as if this were true and thus promote high-level performance in the workers. Consider how you might go about using the self-fulfilling prophecy to encourage behaviors you wanted to increase in strength and frequency. For example, what might you do to encourage persons who are high in communication apprehension to speak up with greater confidence or to encourage people who are reluctant to self-disclose to reveal more of their inner selves? How might this strategy be used in the college classroom or in parenting?

3. Writers to advice columnists generally attribute their problems to external sources (argumentative in-laws, a negative climate at work). The columnists' responses, however, more often focus on internal sources (the writer's temper, an unwillingness to compromise). The columnists' advice, therefore, is usually directed at the writer (you shouldn't have done that; apologize; get out of the relationship) (Schoeneman & Rubanowitz, 1985). Do you find that this happens when people discuss their problems with you, whether face-to-face, in letters, or in e-mails? Do you generally respond as the columnists do?

4. What stereotypes do you think men entertain about women? What stereotypes do you think women entertain about men? How might these stereotypes influence their interpersonal interactions?

Web Explorations

Explore our text website at
www.ablongman.com/devito
to find:

Explore our research resources at
www.researchnavigator.com
and

Exercises and Self-Tests

Exercises relevant to perception include (1) Perceiving My Selves, (2) How Do You Make Attributions? (3) Barriers to Accurate Perception, and (4) What Are Your Cultural Perceptions?

Writing Resources and Assignments

You'll find suggestions for writing papers of personal experience (for example, overcoming your own perceptual biases), concept or principle explanation (for example, stereotypes), review (for example, the uncertainty reduction), or research (for example, the status of self-fulfilling prophecy research) on perception in interpersonal communication.

Read an article.

Read a popular or academic article on perception, how it works, or how it can be made more effective. On the basis of this article, what can you add to the discussion presented here?

Investigate key terms.

Investigate one of the key terms discussed in this chapter (for example, perception, self-fulfilling prophecy, primacy and recency, script, schemata, stereotype, or attribution). What additional insights can you provide?

Find answers.

Try finding answers to one of the following questions, or design a research study to answer it.

1. Are people who attribute controllability to the homeless more negative in their evaluation of homelessness than those who attribute a lack of controllability?
2. Are men and women equally accurate in interpersonal perception?
3. What is the current status of research on the halo effect?

Listening in Interpersonal Communication

4

The Stages of Listening

Styles of Listening Effectively

Listening, Culture, and Gender

> In an advertisement to encourage mentoring, the Harvard Mentoring Project and the Partnership for a Drug-Free America (www.mentoring.org) list three steps:

- • Step 1: Listen.
- • Step 2: Share what you know.
- • Step 3: Repeat Step 1.

The ad continues, "It can be that easy to turn a kid's life around" (*New York Times,* January 5, 2003, p. 30).

As you'll soon see, and despite the mentoring proponents' optimistic language, Steps 1 and 3 are actually quite difficult. Listening is a lot more than hearing—it depends on a cluster of communication skills, which you'll read about in this chapter.

Regardless of what you do, listening will prove a crucial communication component. For example, one study concluded that in this era of technological transformation, employees' interpersonal skills are especially significant; workers' advancement will depend on their ability to speak and write effectively, to display proper etiquette, and to listen attentively. And in a survey of 40 CEOs of Asian and Western multinational companies, respondents cited a lack of listening skills as the major shortcoming of top executives (Witcher, 1999).

If you measured the importance of every activity by the time you spent on that activity, then—according to the research studies available—listening would be your most important communication activity. Studies conducted from 1929 to 1980 showed that listening was the most often used form of communication, followed by speaking, reading, and writing (Rankin, 1929; Werner, 1975; Barker, Edwards, Gaines, Gladney, & Holley, 1980; Steil, Barker, & Watson, 1983; Wolvin & Coakley, 1996). This was true of high school and college students as well as of adults from a wide variety of fields. Today, of course, these studies are dated and their findings of limited value. Your communication patterns are very different from those of someone raised and educated before widespread use of home computers. However, anecdotal evidence, although certainly not conclusive in any way, suggests that listening probably is still the most used communication activity. Just think of how you spend your day; listening probably occupies a considerable amount of time.

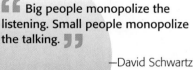

" Big people monopolize the listening. Small people monopolize the talking. "

—David Schwartz

Another way to look at the importance of listening is to consider the numerous benefits or payoffs that accrue to the effective listener. For example, the effective listener is more likely to emerge as a group leader and in general is a more effective, adaptive seller—of ideas as well as things (Johnson & Bechler, 1998; Kramer, 1997; Castleberry & Shepherd, 1993). Table 4.1 describes additional benefits and purposes of listening. Not surprisingly, as the table shows, the purposes are the same as those identified for interpersonal communication in Chapter 1: to learn, relate, influence, play, and help.

This chapter examines the listening process; the varied styles of listening you might use in different situations; and some cultural and gender differences in listening, together with the implications of these differences for effective interpersonal listening.

The Stages of Listening

" The first duty of love is to listen. "

—Paul Tillich

With perception as a foundation we can now examine the stages of listening—essentially the process of message perception. This unique type of perception that we call listening, as you'll see, is best understood as an extension of perception, relying on many of the same principles but demonstrating additional principles that are unique to listening.

Listening can be described as a series of five steps: *receiving, understanding, remembering, evaluating,* and *responding*. The process is visualized in Figure 4.1 on

TABLE 4.1 | Effective Listening: Purposes and Payoffs

This table identifies the major purposes and payoffs of effective listening. Can you identify other purposes and payoffs?

PURPOSES AND PAYOFFS	EXAMPLES
Learn: Acquire knowledge of others, the world, and yourself, so as to avoid problems and make more reasonable decisions.	Listening to Peter telling about his travels to Cuba will help you understand more about Peter as well as about life in a communist country; listening to the difficulties your sales staff has may help you improve sales training.
Relate: Form and maintain friendships and love relationships on the basis of social acceptance and popularity because people come to like those who are attentive and supportive.	Others will increase their liking for you once they feel you have genuine concern for them.
Influence: Have an effect on the attitudes and behaviors of others because people are more likely to respect and follow those who they feel have listened to and understood them.	Workers are more likely to follow your advice once they feel you have truly listened to and heard their points of view, concerns, and insights.
Play: Know when to suspend critical and evaluative thinking and when to simply engage in passive and accepting listening.	Listening to the stories and anecdotes of coworkers will allow you to gain a more comfortable balance between the world of work and the world of play and perhaps to see humor in a world of seriousness.
Help: Be able to assist other people because you hear more, empathize more, and come to understand others more deeply.	Listening to your child's complaints about her teacher (instead of responding "What did you do wrong?") will put you in a better position to help your child cope with school and with her teacher.

page 73. Both this model and the suggestions for listening improvement throughout this chapter, draw on theories and models that numerous listening researchers have developed (e.g., Nichols & Stevens, 1957; Nichols, 1961; Barker & Gaut, 2002; Steil, Barker, & Watson, 1983; Brownell, 1987; Alessandra, 1986; Nichols, 1995). Note that the listening process is a circular one. The responses of person A serve as the stimuli for person B, whose responses, in turn, serve as the stimuli for person A, and so on.

Each of these stages involves principles that need to be followed as you make your way from receiving to responding.

Receiving

Listening is a much more extensive process than hearing. Hearing is essentially the first stage of listening: receiving. Listening begins, but does not end, with receiving messages the speaker sends. These messages are both verbal and nonverbal; they consist not only of words but also of gestures, facial expressions, and the like. At this stage you note what is said (verbally and nonverbally) and also what is omitted. For example, you receive not only your friend's request for a loan, but also the omission of any stated intention to pay you back in a reasonable time. The following suggestions should help you receive messages more effectively. Analyze your own receiving. Do you

- *focus your attention on the speaker's verbal and nonverbal messages, on what is said and not said?*
- *avoid distractions in the environment; if necessary, shut off the stereo or tell your assistant to hold all calls?*
- *focus your attention on the speaker, not on what you'll say next?*
- *maintain your role as listener; avoid interrupting the speaker until she or he is finished?*
- *avoid assuming you understand what the speaker is going to say before he or she actually says it?*

Message Skills

Receiving: Focus attention on both the verbal and the nonverbal messages; both communicate essential parts of the total meaning.

Figure 4.1

The Five Stages of Listening
This model depicts the stages involved in listening. Note that receiving or hearing is not the same thing as listening but is in fact only the first step in a five-step process. How would you further distinguish between hearing and listening? Can you identify people you know who "hear" but don't "listen"?

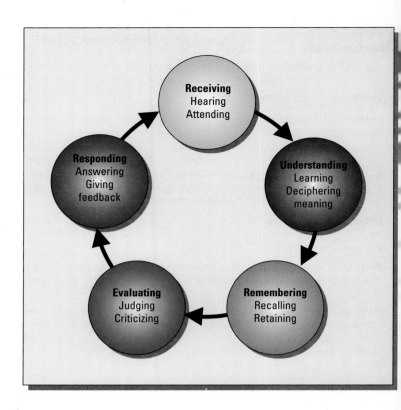

In this brief discussion of receiving—and, in fact, in this entire chapter on listening—the unstated assumption is that both individuals can receive auditory signals without difficulty. For the many people who have hearing impairments, however, listening presents a variety of problems. Table 4.2 provides tips for communication between deaf and hearing people.

Understanding

Understanding occurs when you learn what the speaker means. Understanding includes both the thoughts that are expressed and the emotional tone that accompanies them; for example, the urgency or the joy or sorrow expressed in the message. When you understand what a person says, you also and at the same time interpret what the person means; the two processes go on simultaneously and cannot be separated.

In understanding, do you

- *relate the speaker's new information to what you already know? (E.g., how will this new proposal change our present health care?)*
- *see the speaker's messages from the speaker's point of view; avoid judging the message until it's fully understood as the speaker intended it?*
- *ask questions for clarification, if necessary; ask for additional details or examples if needed?*
- *rephrase (paraphrase) the speaker's ideas to check on your understanding of the speaker's thoughts and feelings?*

Remembering

Messages that you receive and understand need to be retained for at least some period of time. In some small group and public speaking situations you can augment your memory by taking notes or by taping the messages. In most interpersonal communi-

Message Skills

Understanding: Relate new information to what you already know, ask questions, and paraphrase what you think the speaker said to make sure you understand.

TABLE 4.2 *Interpersonal Communication Tips*

BETWEEN DEAF AND HEARING PEOPLE

People differ greatly in their hearing ability; some are totally deaf and can hear nothing, others have some hearing loss and can hear some sounds, and still others have impaired hearing but can hear most speech. Although many people with profound hearing loss can speak, their speech may seem labored and less clear than the speech of those with unimpaired hearing. Here are some suggestions to help deaf and hearing people communicate more effectively.

If you have unimpaired hearing:

1. Set up a comfortable context. Reduce the distance between yourself and the person with a hearing impairment. Reduce the background noise. Turn off the television and even the air conditioner.

2. Face the person and avoid any interference with the visual cues from your speech; for example, avoid smoking, chewing gum, or holding your hand over your mouth. Make sure the lighting is adequate.

3. Speak with an adequate volume, but don't shout. Shouting can distort your speech and may insult the person. Be especially careful to avoid reducing volume at the ends of your sentences.

4. Because some words are easier to lip-read than others, it often helps if you can rephrase your ideas in different ways.

5. In group situations only one person should speak at a time. Similarly, avoid the tendency to talk to a person with hearing loss through a third party. Elementary school teachers, for example, have been found to direct fewer comments to deaf children than to hearing students (Cawthon, 2001). So direct your comments to the person himself or herself.

6. Ask the person if there is anything you can do to make it easier for him or her to understand you.

7. Don't avoid terms like *hear, listen, music,* or *deaf* when they're relevant to the conversation. Trying to avoid these common terms will make your speech sound artificial.

8. Use nonverbal cues that help communicate your meaning; gestures indicating size or location and facial expressions indicating emotions and feelings are often helpful.

If you have impaired hearing:

1. Do your best to eliminate background noise.

2. Move closer to the speaker if this helps. Alert the other person that this closer distance will help you hear better.

3. If you feel the speaker can make adjustments that will make it easier for you to understand, ask. For example, ask the speaker to repeat a message, to speak more slowly or more distinctly, or to increase his or her volume.

4. If you hear better in one ear than another, position yourself accordingly and, if necessary, clue the other person in to this fact.

5. If necessary, ask the person to write down certain information, such as phone numbers or website addresses. Carrying a pad and pencil will prove helpful, both for this purpose and in the event that you wish to write something down for others.

Sources: These suggestions were drawn from a variety of sources: *Tips for Communicating with Deaf People* (Rochester Institute of Technology, National Technical Institute for the Deaf, Division of Public Affairs); **http://www.his.com/~lola/deaf.html**; **http://www.zak.co.il/deaf-info/old/ comm_strategies.html**; and **http://www.agbell.org/information/brochures_communication.cfm**. All websites accessed April 5, 2002.

---

cation situations, however, such note taking would be considered inappropriate—although you often do write down a phone number or an appointment or directions.

What you remember is not what was actually said, but what you think (or remember) was said. Memory for speech is reconstructive, not reproductive. In other words, you don't simply reproduce in your memory what the speaker said; rather, as noted in the discussion of perception in Chapter 3, you reconstruct the messages you hear into a system that makes sense to you.

In remembering, do you

- *identify the central ideas and the major support advanced?*
- *summarize the message in an easier-to-retain form, but not ignore crucial details or qualifications?*
- *repeat names and key concepts to yourself silently or, if appropriate, aloud?*
- *(if this is a formal talk) identify the message's structure and use it (see it in your mind) to organize what the speaker is saying?*

Message Skills

Remembering: Identify the central ideas, summarize the message in an easier-to-retain form, and repeat ideas (aloud or to yourself) to help you remember.

Evaluating

Evaluating: Try first to understand fully what the speaker means and then look to identify any biases or self-interests that might lead the speaker to give an unfair presentation.

Evaluating consists of judging the messages. At times you may try to evaluate the speaker's underlying intent, often without much conscious awareness. For example, Elaine tells you she is up for a promotion and is really excited about it. You may then try to judge her intention. Does she want you to use your influence with the company president? Is she preoccupied with the possible promotion, thus telling everyone? Is she looking for a pat on the back? Generally, if you know the person well, you will be able to identify the intention and respond appropriately.

In other situations **evaluation** is more in the nature of a critical analysis. For example, while listening to proposals advanced in a business meeting, you would evaluate them. Are they practical? Will they increase productivity? What is the evidence? Are there more practical alternative proposals?

In evaluating, do you

- *resist evaluation until you fully understand the speaker's point of view?*
- *assume that the speaker is a person of goodwill, and give the speaker the benefit of any doubt by asking for clarification on issues you object to? (For example, are there any other reasons for accepting this new proposal?)*
- *distinguish facts from opinions and personal interpretations on the part of the speaker?*
- *identify any biases, self-interests, or prejudices that may lead the speaker to slant information unfairly?*

Responding

Message Skills

Responding occurs in two phases: (1) the responses you make while the speaker is talking and (2) the responses you make after the speaker has stopped talking. Responses made while the speaker is talking should be supportive and should acknowledge that you're listening. These include what nonverbal researchers call *backchanneling cues:* responses such as "I see," "yes," and "uh-huh," which let the speaker know you're paying attention (more on this in Chapter 8).

Responses after the speaker has stopped talking are generally more elaborate. Examples include expressing empathy ("I know how you must feel"); asking for clarification ("Do you mean this new health plan will replace the old one? Or will it be just a supplement?"); challenging ("I think your evidence is weak"); and agreeing ("You're absolutely right, and I'll support your proposal when it comes up for a vote").

In responding, do you

- *express support for the speaker throughout the talk by using varied backchanneling cues?*
- *express support for the speaker in your final responses?*
- *own your own responses; that is, state your thoughts and feelings as your own, using "I-messages"? For example, say, "I think the new proposal will entail greater expense than you outlined" rather than "everyone will object to the plan's cost."*

> **"** Listening is not merely not talking, though even that is beyond most of our powers, it means taking a vigorous, human interest in what is being told us. **"**
>
> —Alice Duer Miller

Message Skills

Responding: Express support for the speaker using I-messages instead of you-messages.

Reflections on the Model of Listening

A few general comments should round out the presentation of the five steps in listening.

1. Listening is a collection of skills involving attention and concentration (receiving), learning (understanding), memory (remembering), critical thinking (evaluation), and feedback (responding). Listening can go wrong at any stage; by the same token, you can enhance your listening ability by strengthening the skills needed for each step of the process.

Listen to this

Listening Ethically

As a listener you have ethical obligations. First, you owe the speaker an *honest hearing*. Avoid pre-judging the speaker. Try to put aside prejudices and preconceptions so you can evaluate the speaker's message fairly. At the same time, try to empathize with the speaker. You don't have to agree with the speaker, but try to understand emotionally as well as intellectually what the speaker means. Then accept or reject the speaker's ideas on the basis of the information offered, not on the basis of some bias or incomplete understanding.

Second, you owe the speaker *honest responses*. Just as you should be honest with the listener when speaking, you should be honest with the speaker when listening. This means giving open and honest feedback. It also means reflecting honestly on the questions that the speaker raises. Much as the listener has a right to expect an active speaker, the speaker has the right to expect an active listener. The speaker has a right to expect a listener who will actively deal with, rather than just passively hear, the message.

Applying Listening Skills

You're in conversation with a friend and your friend's friend (who you're meeting for the first time). During the conversation this individual states political and social beliefs that you personally find reprehensible. How do you adjust your listening to give this person both an honest hearing and honest responses?

2. All five stages overlap. When you listen, you're performing all five processes at essentially the same time. For example, when listening in conversation, you're not only paying attention to what other people are saying, but also critically evaluating what they just said and perhaps giving feedback.

3. Listening is never perfect. There are lapses in attention, misunderstandings, lapses in memory, inadequate critical thinking, and inappropriate responding. The goal is to minimize these glitches as best you can.

4. Listening is situational; in other words, your style of listening should vary with the situation. You listen differently depending on your purpose, your conversational partner, and the type of message. For example, in some cases you'll need to be especially critical and in others especially supportive. The next section elaborates on this concept, explaining the major styles of listening and how you might use them most effectively depending on the situation.

"Of course I'm paying attention—I've pressed the mute button."

The New Yorker Collection 2003 Barbara Smaller from cartoonbank.com. All rights reserved.

Before reading about the styles and principles of effective listening, examine your own listening habits and tendencies by taking the accompanying self-test. Even though the "desirable" answers will be obvious, try to give responses that are true for you in most of your listening experiences.

Test Yourself

How Do You Listen?

INSTRUCTIONS: Respond to each statement using the following scale: 1 = always, 2 = frequently, 3 = sometimes, 4 = seldom, and 5 = never.

_____ ❶ I listen actively, communicate acceptance of the speaker, and prompt the speaker to further explore his or her thoughts.

Reducing Barriers to Listening

Visualize yourself ready to talk in one or two of the following situations. For each situation, *(a)* identify at least two potential barriers to listening (from any stage—receiving, understanding, remembering, evaluating, or responding) that might arise in each encounter, and *(b)* for each potential barrier identify a corresponding remedy or corrective action you might take to reduce or eliminate the barrier.

1. One of your best friends tells you he's HIV positive.
2. A romantic partner of several years suggests a trial separation.
3. An instructor's lecture demeans some of your most cherished and valued religious beliefs, calling them "rubbish" and "primitive."
4. A doctor, reviewing the results of an extensive battery of tests, gives you bad news.
5. At a department meeting at work, your proposal—which you thought was brilliant and which you worked on for two months—is severely criticized and rejected by the group.

Listening obstacles are all around us, making effective listening a much more difficult task than most people realize.

_____ ❷ I listen to what the speaker is saying and feeling; I try to feel what the speaker feels.

_____ ❸ I listen without judging the speaker.

_____ ❹ I listen to the literal meanings that a speaker communicates; I don't look too deeply into hidden meanings.

_____ ❺ I listen without active involvement; I generally remain silent and take in what the other person is saying.

_____ ❻ I listen objectively; I focus on the logic of the ideas rather than on the emotional meaning of the message.

_____ ❼ I listen critically, evaluating the speaker and what the speaker is saying.

_____ ❽ I look for the hidden meanings; the meanings that are revealed by subtle verbal or nonverbal cues.

HOW DID YOU DO? These statements focus on the ways of listening discussed in this chapter. All of these ways are appropriate at some times but not at other times. It depends. So the only responses that are really inappropriate are "always" and "never." Effective listening is listening that is tailored to the specific communication situation.

WHAT WILL YOU DO? Consider how you might use these statements to begin to improve your listening effectiveness. A good way to begin doing this is to review these statements, trying to identify situations in which each statement would be appropriate and situations in which each statement would be inappropriate.

> " Listening, not imitation, may be the sincerest form of flattery. "
>
> —Joyce Brothers

Styles of Listening Effectively

Listening is situational (Brownell, 2002). As we've seen, the way you listen should depend on the situation you are in. You don't listen to a State of the Union address in the same way that you listen to Jay Leno's monologue or to a proposal for a date. At the least you need to adjust your listening on the basis of (1) your purposes (are you listening to learn? To give comfort?) and (2) your knowledge of and relationship to

SKILLS VIEWPOINT

Would it be more difficult to empathize with someone who was overjoyed because of winning a $7-million lottery or with someone who was overcome with sadness because of a death of a loved one? How easy or difficult would it be for you to empathize with someone who was depressed because an expected $40,000 raise turned out to be only $25,000? In general, how can you improve your empathizing skills when dealing with both the negative and the positive feelings of others?

the other person (does this person exaggerate or lie? or need support or perhaps a reality check?). The following discussion will provide specific suggestions for how to adjust your listening style and how you can avoid the pitfalls and barriers to ineffective listening.

Empathic and Objective Listening

If you're to understand what a person means and what a person is feeling, you need to listen with some degree of empathy (Rogers, 1970; Rogers & Farson, 1981). To *empathize* with others is to feel with them, to see the world as they see it, to feel what they feel. Only when you achieve this can you fully understand another person's meaning. Empathic listening will also help you enhance your relationships (Barrett & Godfrey, 1988; Snyder, 1992).

Although for most communication situations empathic listening is the preferred mode of responding, there are times when you need to go beyond it and to measure the speaker's meanings and feelings against some objective reality. It's important to listen to Peter tell you how the entire world hates him and to understand how Peter feels and why he feels this way. But then you need to look a bit more objectively at the situation and perhaps see Peter's paranoia or self-hatred. Sometimes you have to put your empathic responses aside and listen with objectivity and detachment.

In adjusting your empathic and objective listening focus, keep the following recommendations in mind.

- Punctuate from the speaker's point of view (Chapter 1). That is, see the sequence of events as the speaker does and try to figure out how this perspective can influence what the speaker says and does.
- Engage in equal, two-way conversation. To encourage openness and empathy, try to eliminate any physical or psychological barriers to equality; for example, step from behind the large desk separating you from your employees. Avoid interrupting the speaker—a sign that what you have to say is more important.
- Seek to understand both thoughts and feelings. Don't consider your listening task finished until you've understood what the speaker is feeling as well as what he or she is thinking.

Message Skills

Empathic and Objective Listening: Punctuate the interaction from the speaker's point of view, engage in dialogue, and seek to understand the speaker's thoughts and feelings.

Ethical messages

A Question of Choice

One way of looking at interpersonal communication ethics is from the perspective of choice. The assumption made in this view is that people have a right to make their own choices. Interpersonal communications are ethical to the extent that they facilitate a person's freedom of choice by presenting that person with accurate information. Communications are unethical to the extent that they interfere with people's freedom of choice by preventing them from securing information relevant to the choices they will make. The ethical communicator provides others with the kind of information they need in making their own choices.

You have the right to information about yourself that others possess and that influences the choices you'll make. Thus, for example, you have the right to face your accusers, to know what witnesses will be called to testify against you, to see your credit ratings, and to know what Social Security benefits you'll receive. On the other hand, you don't have the right to information about others; for example, information about whether your neighbors are happy or what they argue about or how much money they have.

At the same time, you also have the obligation to reveal information that you possess that bears on the choices of your society. Thus, for example, you have an obligation to identify wrongdoing that you witness, to identify someone in a police lineup, to report criminal activity, and to testify at a trial when you possess pertinent information. This information is essential for society to accomplish its purposes and to make its legitimate choices.

What Would You Do?

Pat and Chris are weekend pot smokers and smoke only when the children are out of the house. Their teenager, however, has heard rumors about the smoking and asks them if they smoke pot. Will it be ethical for Pat and Chris to lie and say they don't smoke? Will it be ethical for them to tell the truth and say they do smoke? If you were one of the parents, what would you do in this situation?

- Avoid "offensive listening"—the tendency to listen to bits and pieces of information that will enable you to attack the speaker or find fault with something the speaker has said (Floyd, 1985).
- Strive especially to be objective when listening to friends or foes alike. Your attitudes may lead you to distort messages—to block out positive messages about a foe or negative messages about a friend. Guard against "expectancy hearing," in which you fail to hear what the speaker is really saying and instead hear what you expect.

Nonjudgmental and Critical Listening

Effective listening includes both nonjudgmental and critical responses. You need to listen nonjudgmentally—with an open mind and with a view toward understanding. But you also need to listen critically—with a view toward making some kind of evaluation or judgment. Clearly, it's important to listen first for understanding while suspending judgment. Only after you've fully understood the relevant messages should you evaluate or judge.

Supplement open-minded listening with critical listening. Listening with an open mind will help you understand the messages better; listening with a critical mind will help you analyze and evaluate the messages. In adjusting your nonjudgmental and critical listening, focus on the following guidelines:

- Keep an open mind. Avoid prejudging. Delay your judgments until you fully understand both the content and the intention the speaker is communicating. Avoid either positive or negative evaluation until you have a reasonably complete understanding.
- Avoid filtering out or oversimplifying complex messages. Similarly, avoid filtering out undesirable messages. Clearly, you don't want to hear that something

> ❝ Listen long enough and the person will generally come up with an adequate solution. ❞
>
> —Mary Kay Ash

you believe is untrue, that people you care for are unkind, or that ideals you hold are self-destructive. Yet it's important that you reexamine your beliefs by listening to these messages.

- Recognize your own biases. These may interfere with accurate listening and cause you to distort message reception through a process of assimilation—the tendency to integrate and interpret what you hear or think you hear in keeping with your own biases, prejudices, and expectations. For example, are your ethnic, national, or religious biases preventing you from appreciating a speaker's point of view?

- Avoid uncritical listening when you need to make evaluations and judgments.

- Recognize and combat the normal tendency to sharpen—a process in which we tend to highlight, emphasize, and perhaps embellish one or two aspects of a message. Often the concepts that are sharpened are incidental remarks that somehow stand out from the rest of the message.

- Recognize popular but fallacious forms of reasoning, such as the following (Lee & Lee, 1972, 1995; Pratkanis & Aronson, 1991):

  - *Name-calling* involves giving an idea, a group of people, or a political philosophy a bad name ("atheist," "neo-Nazi," "cult"). In the opposite of name-calling, the speaker tries to make you accept some idea by associating it with things you value highly ("democracy," "free speech," "academic freedom"). Remember that although labels can be useful, they also can obscure the actual person or idea. Listen first to evidence and argument; never take labels as evidence or reasons for judgment.

  - The *testimonial* approach involves using the image associated with some person to gain your approval (if you respect the person) or your rejection (if you don't respect the person). This is the technique of advertisers who dress people up to look like doctors or plumbers or chefs to sell their products. Listen carefully to the person's credentials; be suspicious when you hear such phrases as "experts agree," "scientists say," "good cooks know," or "dentists advise." Ask yourself exactly who these experts are and what the source of their expertise is.

  - The *bandwagon* technique tries to persuade you to accept or reject an idea or proposal because "everybody is doing it." The goal is to get you to "jump on the bandwagon." You'll hear this technique used frequently during election time, when campaigns trumpet poll results to entice you to join the group and vote for one person or another. Again, listen to the evidence; 50,000 Frenchmen—as the saying goes—can be wrong.

  - *Agenda-setting* involves claiming that a particular issue is crucial and all others are unimportant and insignificant. Agenda-setting crops up frequently in interpersonal conflict situations: Each person may claim that her or his viewpoint is the accurate and important one and that the other person's is less accurate and less important. But in almost all situations, and especially in cases of interpersonal conflict, there are many issues—and many sides to each issue.

  - In *attack* one person accuses another person (usually an opponent) of serious wrongdoing, with the result that the issue under discussion never gets examined. An example is a remark such as "How can I ever believe you after you lied?" Although a person's personal reputation and past behavior are often relevant, listen most carefully to the issue at hand. When personal attack draws attention away from other issues, then it becomes fallacious.

? SKILLS VIEWPOINT

You overhear a group of younger students trying to help another student, but you know their advice is not going to work and may actually make the problem worse. What types of listening will help you to best understand the younger students' interaction and enable you to respond most effectively to them?

Message Skills

Nonjudgmental and Critical Listening: Keep an open mind, avoid filtering out difficult messages, and recognize your own biases. When listening to make judgments, listen extra carefully, ask questions when in doubt, and check your perceptions before criticizing.

Surface and Depth Listening

In Shakespeare's *Julius Caesar*, Marc Antony, in giving the funeral oration for Caesar, says: "I come to bury Caesar, not to praise him. / The evil that men do lives after them; / The good is oft interred with their bones." And later: "For Brutus is an honourable man; / So are they all, all honourable men." But Antony, as we know, did come to praise Caesar and to convince the crowd that Brutus was not an honorable man.

In most messages there's an obvious meaning that you can derive from a literal reading of the words and sentences. But in reality, most messages have more than one level of meaning. Sometimes, as in *Julius Caesar,* the other level is the opposite of the literal meaning; at other times it seems totally unrelated. Consider some frequently heard types of messages. Carol asks you how you like her new haircut. On one level, the meaning is clear: Do you like the haircut? But there's also another and perhaps more important level: Carol is asking you to say something positive about her appearance. In the same way, the parent who complains about working hard at the office or in the home may, on a deeper level, be asking for an expression of appreciation. The child who talks about the unfairness of the other children in the playground may be asking for comfort and love, for some expression of caring.

To appreciate these other meanings, you need to engage in depth listening. If you respond only to the surface-level communication (the literal meaning), you miss the opportunity to make meaningful contact with the other person's feelings and needs. If you say to the parent, "You're always complaining. I bet you really love working so hard," you fail to respond to this call for understanding and appreciation. In regulating your surface and depth listening, consider the following guidelines:

- Focus on both verbal and nonverbal messages. Recognize both consistent and inconsistent "packages" of messages and use these as guides for drawing inferences about the speaker's meaning. Ask questions when in doubt. Listen also to what is omitted. Remember that speakers communicate by what they leave out as well as by what they include.

- Listen for both content and relational messages. The student who constantly challenges the teacher is on one level communicating disagreement over content. However, on another level—the relationship level—the student may be voicing objections to the instructor's authority or authoritarianism. The instructor needs to listen and respond to both types of messages.

- Make special note of statements that refer back to the speaker. Remember that people inevitably talk about themselves. Whatever a person says is, in part, a function of who that person is. Attend carefully to those personal, self-referential messages.

- Don't, however, disregard the literal meaning of interpersonal messages in trying to uncover the more hidden meanings. Balance your listening between surface and underlying meanings. Respond to the different levels of meaning in the messages of others as you would like others to respond to yours—sensitively but not obsessively, readily but not overambitiously.

Active and Inactive Listening

One of the most important communication skills you can learn is that of active listening (Gordon, 1975). Consider the following interaction. You're disappointed that you have to redo your entire budget report, and you say, "I can't believe I have to redo this entire report. I really worked hard on this project and now I have to do it all over again." To this you get three different responses:

Apollo: That's not so bad; most people find they have to redo their first reports. That's the norm here.

Most of the successful people I've known are the ones who do more listening than talking.

—Bernard Baruch

Message Skills

Surface and Depth Listening: Focus on both verbal and nonverbal messages, on both content and relationship messages, and on statements that refer back to the speaker. At the same time, do not avoid the surface or literal meaning.

Athena: You should be pleased that all you have to do is a simple rewrite. Peggy and Michael both had to completely redo their entire projects.

Diana: You have to rewrite that report you've worked on for the last three weeks? You sound really angry and frustrated.

All three listeners are probably trying to make you feel better. But they go about it in very different ways and, we can be sure, with very different results. Apollo tries to lessen the significance of the rewrite. This type of well-intended response is extremely common but does little to promote meaningful communication and understanding. Athena tries to give the situation a positive spin. With these responses, however, both these listeners are also suggesting that you should not be feeling the way you do. They're also implying that your feelings are not legitimate and should be replaced with more logical feelings.

Diana's response, however, is different from the others. Diana uses active listening. **Active listening** owes its development to Thomas Gordon (1975), who made it a cornerstone of his P-E-T (Parent Effectiveness Training) technique; it is a process of sending back to the speaker what you as a listener think the speaker meant—both in content and in feelings. Active listening, then is not merely repeating the speaker's exact words, but rather putting together into some meaningful whole your understanding of the speaker's total message.

Active listening serves several important functions. First, it helps you as a listener check your understanding of what the speaker said and, more important, what he or she meant. Reflecting back perceived meanings to the speaker gives the speaker an opportunity to offer clarification and correct any misunderstandings.

Second, through active listening you let the speaker know that you acknowledge and accept his or her feelings. In the sample responses given, the first two listeners challenged your feelings. Diana, the active listener, who reflected back to you what she thought you meant, accepted what you were feeling. In addition, she also explicitly identified your emotions; she commented that you sounded "angry and frustrated," allowing you an opportunity to correct her interpretation if necessary. A word of caution, however: In understanding the other person and in communicating this understanding back to the person, be especially careful to avoid sending what Gordon (1975) calls "solution messages." Solution messages tell the person how he or she *should* feel or what he or she *should* do. The four types of messages that send solutions and that you'll want to avoid in your active listening are:

- ordering messages—*Do this . . . , Don't touch that . . .*
- warning and threatening messages—*If you don't do this, you'll . . . , If you do this, you'll . . .*
- preaching and moralizing messages—*People should all . . . , We all have responsibilities . . .*
- advising messages—*Why don't you . . . , What I'd do is . . .*

Third, active listening stimulates the speaker to explore feelings and thoughts. Diana's response encourages you to elaborate on your feelings. This opportunity to elaborate also helps you deal with your feelings by talking them through.

Three simple techniques may help you succeed in active listening: Paraphrase the speaker's meaning, express understanding, and ask questions.

- *Paraphrase the speaker's meaning.* Stating in your own words what you think the speaker means and feels can help ensure understanding and also shows interest in the speaker. Paraphrasing gives the speaker a chance to extend what was originally said. Thus, when Diana echoes your thoughts, you're given the opportunity to elaborate on why rewriting the budget report is so daunting to you.

  But in paraphrasing, be objective; be especially careful not to lead the speaker in the direction you think he or she should go. Also, be careful that you don't overdo paraphrase; only a very small percentage of statements need para-

> " The opposite of talking isn't listening. The opposite of talking is waiting. "
>
> —Fran Lebowitz

> " There is only one cardinal rule: one must always listen to the patient. "
>
> —Oliver Sacks

Paraphrasing to Ensure Understanding

Here are a few situations in which you might want to use paraphrasing to ensure that you understand the speaker's thoughts and feelings. For each situation, *(a)* identify the thoughts you feel the speaker is expressing, *(b)* identify the feelings you think the speaker is experiencing, and *(c)* put these thoughts and feelings into a paraphrase.

1. Did you hear I got engaged to Jerry? Our racial and religious differences are really going to cause difficulties for both of us. But we'll work it through.
2. I got a C on that paper. That's the worst grade I've ever received. I just can't believe that I got a C. This is my major. What am I going to do?
3. That rotten, inconsiderate pig just up and left. He never even said goodbye. We were together for six months and after one small argument he leaves without a word.
4. I'm just not sure what to do. I really love Sofia. But she really wants to get married. I do too, and yet I don't want to make such a commitment. I really don't need that kind of pressure.

Paraphrasing helps you check your understanding of the speaker and also helps reinforce and support the speaker.

❓ SKILLS VIEWPOINT

Your best friend just broke up his newest relationship and comes to you in the hope that—as with all the other breakups—you'll listen to his tale of woe. It seems like this happens at least once a week, and you're fed up; you're determined not to spend the next three hours listening to him. What do you say?

phrasing. Paraphrase when you feel there's a chance for misunderstanding or when you want to express support for the other person and keep the conversation going.

- *Express understanding of the speaker's feelings.* In addition to paraphrasing the content, echo the feelings the speaker expressed or implied ("You must have felt horrible"). This expression of feelings will help you further check your perception of the speaker's feelings. This also will allow the speaker to see his or her feelings more objectively—especially helpful when they're feelings of anger, hurt, or depression—and to elaborate on these feelings.

- *Ask questions.* Asking questions strengthens your own understanding of the speaker's thoughts and feelings and elicits additional information ("How did you feel when you read your job appraisal report?"). Ask questions to provide just enough stimulation and support so the speaker will feel he or she can elaborate on these thoughts and feelings. These questions should further confirm your interest and concern for the speaker but not pry into unrelated areas or challenge the speaker in any way.

Consider this dialogue and note the active listening techniques used throughout:

Pat: That jerk demoted me. He told me I wasn't an effective manager. I can't believe he did that, after all I've done for this place.

Chris: I'm with you. You've been manager for three or four months now, haven't you?

Pat: A little over three months. I know it was probationary, but I thought I was doing a good job.

Chris: Can you get another chance?

Pat: Yes, he said I could try again in a few months. But I feel like a failure.

Chris: I know what you mean. It sucks. What else did he say?

Listening Actively

Here are a few situations in which you might want to listen actively. For each situation, write an active listening response in which you *(a)* paraphrase the speaker's meaning, *(b)* express understanding of the speaker's meaning, and *(c)* ask questions to clarify any potential misunderstandings.

1. Your friend Phil has just broken up a love affair and is telling you about it. "I can't seem to get Lee out of my mind," he says. "All I do is daydream about what we used to do and all the fun we used to have."
2. A young nephew tells you that he cannot talk with his parents. No matter how hard he tries, they just don't listen. "I tried to tell them that I can't and don't want to play baseball. But they ignore me and tell me that all I need is practice."
3. Your mother has been having a difficult time at work. She was recently passed up for a promotion and received one of the lowest merit raises given in the company. "I'm not sure what I did wrong," she tells you. "Maybe I should just quit."

Active listening allows you to connect with another person by demonstrating your understanding and support.

Pat: He said I had trouble getting the paperwork done on time.
Chris: You've been late filing the reports?
Pat: A few times.
Chris: Is there a way to delegate the paperwork?
Pat: No, but I think I know now what needs to be done.
Chris: You sound as though you're ready to give that manager's position another try.
Pat: Yes, I think I am, and I'm going to let him know that I intend to apply in the next few months.

Even in this brief interaction, Pat has moved from unproductive anger and feelings of failure to a determination to correct an unpleasant situation. Note, too, that Chris didn't offer solutions but "simply" listened actively.

As stressed throughout this discussion, listening is situational; the type of listening that is appropriate varies with the situation. You can visualize a listening situation as one in which you have to make choices among at least the four styles of effective listening just discussed. Each listening situation should call for a somewhat different configuration of listening responses; the art of effective listening is largely one of making appropriate choices along these four dimensions.

"I can't get off the phone, he won't stop listening!"
Reprinted by permission of Jerry Marcus.

Listening, Culture, and Gender

Listening is difficult in part because of the inevitable differences in communication systems between speakers and listeners. Because each person has had a unique set of experiences, each person's communication and meaning system is going to be different from each other person's. When speaker and listener come from different cultures or are of different genders, the differences and their effects are naturally so much greater. Let's look first at culture.

Message Skills

Active and Inactive Listening: Be an active listener: Paraphrase the speaker's meaning, express understanding of the speaker's feelings, and ask questions when necessary.

Listening and Culture

The culture in which you were raised will influence your listening in a variety of ways. Here we look at some of these: language and speech, direct and indirect styles, nonverbal differences, and feedback.

Even when speaker and listener speak the same language, they speak it with different meanings and different accents. No two speakers speak exactly the same language. Every speaker speaks an *idiolect:* a unique variation of the language (King & DiMichael, 1992). Speakers of the same language will, at the very least, have different meanings for the same terms because they have had different experiences.

Speakers and listeners who have different native languages and who may have learned English as a second language will have even greater differences in meaning. Translations are never precise and never fully capture the meaning in the other language. If you learned your meaning for *house* in a culture in which everyone lived in their own house with lots of land around it, then communicating with someone whose meaning was learned in a neighborhood of high-rise tenements is going to be difficult. Although each of you will hear the word *house,* the meanings you'll develop will be drastically different. In adjusting your listening—especially when in an intercultural setting—understand that the speaker's meanings may be very different from yours even though you're speaking the same language.

Some cultures—those of Western Europe and the United States, for example—favor **direct speech** in communication; they advise us to "say what you mean and mean what you say." Many Asian cultures, on the other hand, favor **indirect speech;** they emphasize politeness and maintaining a positive public image rather than literal truth. Listen carefully to persons with different styles of directness. Consider the possibility that the meanings the speaker wishes to communicate with, say, indirectness, may be very different from the meanings you would communicate with indirectness.

Another area of difference is that of accents. In many classrooms throughout the United States, there will be a wide range of accents. Those whose native language is a tonal one such as Chinese (in which differences in pitch signal important meaning differences) may speak English with variations in pitch that may be puzzling to others. Those whose native language is Japanese may have trouble distinguishing *l* from *r,* because Japanese does not include this distinction. The native language acts as a filter and influences the accent given to the second language.

? SKILLS VIEWPOINT

What changes would you like to see in the listening behavior of the men in your family? What changes would you like to see in the listening behavior of women in your family? More generally, what listening skills would you like to see men learn? What listening skills would you like to see women learn?

Speakers from different cultures also have different *display rules:* cultural rules that govern which nonverbal behaviors are appropriate and which are inappropriate in a public setting. As you listen to other people, you also "listen" to their nonverbals. If these are drastically different from what you expect on the basis of the verbal message, you may perceive a kind of noise or interference or even contradictory messages. Also, of course, different cultures may give very different meanings to the same nonverbal gesture, a topic considered in detail in Chapter 6.

Variations in directness are often especially clear when people give feedback. Members of some cultures tend to give direct and honest feedback. Speakers from these cultures—the United States is a good example—expect feedback to be an honest reflection of what their listeners are feeling. In other cultures—Japan and Korea are good examples—it's more important to be positive than to be truthful; listeners may respond with positive feedback (say, in commenting on a business colleague's proposal) even though they don't feel positive. Listen to feedback, as you would all messages, with a full recognition that various cultures view feedback very differently.

Message Skills

Cultural Differences in Listening: Be especially flexible when listening in a multicultural setting, realizing that people from other cultures give different listening cues and may operate with different rules for listening.

Listening and Gender

Deborah Tannen opened her chapter on listening in her best-selling *You Just Don't Understand: Women and Men in Conversation* (1990) with several anecdotes illustrating that when men and women talk, men lecture and women listen. The lecturer is positioned as the superior—as the teacher, the expert. The listener is positioned as the inferior—as the student, the nonexpert.

Women, according to Tannen, seek to build rapport and establish a closer relationship and so use listening to achieve these ends. For example, women use more listening cues that let the other person know they are paying attention and are interested. Men not only use fewer listening cues but interrupt more; and they will often

Skills toolbox

5 Ways to Deal with Difficult Listeners

Walt Whitman once said, "To have great poets, there must be great audiences too." The same is true of interpersonal interaction: To have great interpersonal communication, there must be great listeners as well as great talkers. Here are a few types of difficult listeners and brief suggestions for dealing with them.

1. The static listener gives no feedback, remains relatively motionless, reveals no expression. *Ask questions. Pause to allow him or her to say something. Ask for agreement with your facial expressions.*
2. The monotonous feedback giver seems responsive, but the responses never vary; regardless of what you say, the response is the same. *Comment on the feedback, saying, for example, "So, you agree?" or "Am I making sense?"*
3. The overly expressive listener reacts to just about everything with extreme responses. Even though you're saying nothing provocative, the reaction is intense. *Some people are just more expressive than others; take pleasure that you're having such an effect.*
4. The eye avoider looks all around the room and at others but never at you. *Maintain eye contact as much as possible, and ask questions to try to involve the other person in what you're saying.*
5. The preoccupied listener listens to other things at the same time, often on headphones with the sound so loud that it interferes with your own thinking. *If what you're saying requires total concentration, then ask for it, saying something like "This is really important" or "I really need your total concentration."*

Applying Interpersonal Skills/Then and Now

Have you ever been confronted by one of these listeners? What did you do to get the person to listen more effectively? What would you do if this happened today?

change the topic to one they know more about or one that is less relational or people oriented or more factual, such as sports statistics, economic developments, or political problems. Men, research shows, play up their expertise, emphasize it, and use it in dominating the conversation. Women play down their expertise.

Now you might be tempted to conclude from this that women play fair in conversation and that men don't; for example, that men consistently seek to put themselves in a position superior to women. But that may be too simple an explanation. Research shows that men communicate this way not only with women but also with other men. Men are not showing disrespect for their female conversational partners but are simply communicating as they normally do. Women, too, communicate as they do not only with men but also with other women.

Tannen argues that the goal of a man in conversation is to be accorded respect; so a man seeks to display his knowledge and expertise even if he has to change the topic to one he knows a great deal about. Women, on the other hand, seek to be liked; so a woman expresses interest, rarely interrupts a man to take her turn as speaker, and gives lots of cues (verbally and nonverbally) to indicate that she is listening.

Men and women also show that they are listening in different ways. A woman is more apt to give lots of listening cues, such as interjecting "yeah" or "uh-huh," nodding in agreement, and smiling. Women also make more eye contact when listening than do men, who are more apt to look around and often away from the speaker (Brownell, 2002). A man is more likely to listen quietly without giving lots of listening cues as feedback. Tannen also argues, however, that men do listen less to women than women listen to men. The reason, says Tannen, is that listening places the person in an inferior position, whereas speaking places the person in a superior position.

There is no evidence to show that these differences represent any negative motives—desires on the part of men to prove themselves superior or on the part of women to ingratiate themselves. Rather, these differences in listening are largely the result of the way in which men and women have been socialized.

Message Skills

Gender Differences in Listening: Understand that in general, women give more cues that they're listening and appear more supportive in their listening than men.

Summary of Concepts

This chapter first defined listening, explored its five stages, and identified some of the reasons you listen; then discussed the types of listening and how best to adjust your listening to achieve maximum effectiveness; and, last, looked at the wide cultural and gender differences in listening.

1. *Listening* may be viewed as a five-step process: receiving, understanding, remembering, evaluating, and responding. Listening difficulties and obstacles exist at each of these stages.
2. We listen for a variety of reasons: to learn, to relate, to influence, to play, and to help.

3. Effective listening depends on finding appropriate balances among empathic and objective, nonjudgmental and critical, surface and depth, and active and inactive listening.
4. Cultural differences in accents, in nonverbal behaviors, in directness, and in the feedback people give and expect may create listening difficulties.
5. Men and women seem to listen with different purposes in mind and with different behaviors.

Vocabulary Quiz: The Language of Listening

Match these terms about listening with their definitions. Record the number of the definition next to the appropriate term.

_____ listening

_____ offensive listening

_____ name-calling

_____ empathic listening

_____ supportive listening

_____ testimonial

_____ active listening

_____ memory

_____ paraphrase

_____ evaluating

1. A reconstructive (not a reproductive) process.
2. A process of sending back to the speaker what the listener thinks the speaker means.
3. A technique of associating the image of some respected person with an idea so as to promote the idea.
4. A stage in the listening process in which you make judgments about a message.
5. A restatement of something said in your own words.
6. Listening for ideas to attack.
7. A process of receiving, understanding, remembering, evaluating, and responding to messages.
8. Placing yourself in the position of the speaker so that you feel as the speaker feels.
9. Associating an idea with a negatively evaluated name to discredit the idea.
10. Listening without judgment or evaluation; listening for understanding.

Four for Discussion

1. The term *false memory syndrome* refers to the tendency to "remember" past experiences that never actually occurred. Most of the studies on false memory syndrome have centered on beliefs of abuse and other traumatic experiences. Often these false memories are implanted by therapists and interviewers whose persistent questioning over a period of time creates such a realistic scenario that the individual comes to believe these things actually occurred (Porter, Brit, Yuille, & Lehman, 2000). In what other, less dramatic ways can false memory syndrome occur?

2. Although empathy has an almost universally positive image, some evidence suggests that it also has a negative side. For example, people are most empathic with those who are similar—racially and ethnically as well as in appearance and social status. The more empathy you feel toward your own group, the less empathy—and possibly even the more hostility—you feel toward other groups. The same empathy that increases your understanding of your own group decreases your understanding of other groups. So although empathy may encourage group cohesiveness and identification, it can also create dividing lines between your group and "them" (Angier, 1995). Have you ever experienced or witnessed these negative effects of empathy?

3. The popular belief is that men listen the way they do to prove themselves superior and that women listen as they do to ingratiate themselves. Although there is no evidence to support this belief, it persists in the assumptions people make about the opposite sex. What do you believe accounts for the differences in the way men and women listen?

4. What types of listening would you use (and which types would you not use) in each of the following situations? *(a)* Your steady dating partner for the last five years tells you that spells of depression are becoming more frequent. *(b)* An instructor lectures on the contributions of ancient China to modern civilization. *(c)* A physician discusses your recent physical tests and recommendations. *(d)* A salesperson tells you the benefits of the new computer. *(e)* A gossip columnist details the life of your favorite celebrity.

Web Explorations

Explore our text website at
www.ablongman.com/devito
to find:

Explore our research resources at
www.researchnavigator.com
and

Exercises and Self-Tests

A variety of exercises and self-tests on listening include (1) Experiencing Active Listening, (2) Regulating Your Listening Perspective (additional cases), (3) Sequential Communication, (4) Reducing Barriers to Listening, (5) Typical Man, Typical Woman, (6) Paraphrasing to Ensure Understanding (additional cases), and (7) How Can You Express Empathy?

While you're online, you may also want to check out the International Listening Association to get an overview of a professional academic organization devoted to listening; visit **www.listen.org**.

Writing Resources and Assignments

Suggestions are available on writing about listening in personal experience (for example, your own listening successes and failures), principle or concept explanation (for example, false memory syndrome), review (for example, the importance of listening in the workplace), or research (for example, whether men and women listen differently).

Read an article.

Read an academic or popular article on listening, styles or types of listening, or culture or gender differences in listening. On the basis of this article, what can you add to the discussion presented here?

Investigate key terms.

Investigate one of the key terms discussed in this chapter (for example, listening, direct and indirect styles, false memory syndrome, critical listening, feedback, empathy, active listening). What additional insights can you provide?

Find answers.

Try finding answers to one of the following questions, or design a research study to answer it.

1. Do women and men listen equally effectively?
2. What do experts in your own field say about listening?
3. Do men or women differ in their empathic abilities? In their empathic behaviors?

Verbal
Messages

5

Principles of Verbal Messages

Confirmation and Disconfirmation

Using Verbal Messages Effectively and Critically

On the second night of their honeymoon, a newly married husband and wife are sitting at a hotel bar. The woman strikes up a conversation with the couple next to her. The husband refuses to communicate with the couple and becomes antagonistic toward his wife and the couple. The wife then grows angry because he has created such an awkward and unpleasant situation. Each becomes increasingly disturbed, and the evening ends in a bitter conflict, each spouse convinced of the other's lack of consideration. Eight years later, the couple analyze this argument. Apparently the word *honeymoon* had meant different things to each of them. To the husband it meant a golden opportunity to ignore the rest of the world and simply explore each other. He felt his wife's interaction with the other couple implied there was something lacking in him. To the wife her honeymoon meant an opportunity to try out her new role as wife. "I had never had a conversation with another couple as a wife before," she says. "Previous to this I had always been a 'girlfriend' or 'fiancée' or 'daughter' or 'sister.'"

This example—taken from Ronald D. Laing, H. Phillipson, and A. Russell Lee in *Interpersonal Perception* (1966; also Watzlawick, 1977)—illustrates the confusion that can result when you look for meaning in the words and not in the person. This confusion is one of the ways that verbal messages, the topic of this chapter, can fail to communicate their intended meaning.

Principles of Verbal Messages

In interpersonal communication you use two major signal systems—the verbal and the nonverbal. This chapter focuses on the *verbal* system and covers the principles of verbal messages, the ways in which you use **language** to confirm or to disconfirm another person, and ways to make your verbal messages more effective.

Messages Are Denotative and Connotative

Two general types of meaning are essential to identify: denotation and connotation. The term **denotation** refers to the meaning you'd find in a dictionary; it's the meaning that members of the culture assign to a word. **Connotation** is the emotional meaning that specific speakers/listeners give to a word. Take as an example the word *death*. To a doctor this word might mean (denote) the time when the heart stops. This is an objective description of a particular event. On the other hand, to a mother who is informed of her son's death, the word means (connotes) much more. It recalls her son's youth, ambitions, family, illness, and so on. To her *death* is a highly emotional, subjective, and personal word. These emotional, subjective, or personal associations are the word's connotative meaning. The denotation of a word is its objective definition. The connotation of a word is its subjective or emotional meaning.

Semanticist S. I. Hayakawa (Hayakawa & Hayakawa, 1989) coined the terms "snarl words" and "purr words" to further clarify the distinction between denotative and connotative meaning. Snarl words are highly negative ("She's an idiot," "He's a pig," "They're a bunch of losers"). Sexist, racist, heterosexist, and ageist language, and hate speech generally, provide lots of other examples. Purr words are highly positive ("She's a real sweetheart," "He's a dream," "They're the greatest").

"Since the food you serve is not organically grown, is it safe to assume that the meat is laced with antibiotics and the salad is chockful of pesticides?"

Message Skills

Connotative Meanings: Clarify your connotative meanings if you have any doubts that your listeners might misunderstand you; as a listener, ask questions if you have doubts about the speaker's connotations.

Snarl and purr words, although they may sometimes seem to have denotative meaning and to refer to the "real world," are actually connotative in meaning. These terms do not describe people or events in the real world but rather the speaker's feelings about these people or events.

Messages Vary in Directness

Consider your own tendency to be direct or indirect. Imagine you're talking with a friend. Of the seven paired sentences below, how many would you use from the Indirect column? How many from the Direct column?

Indirect Messages	Direct Messages
Would you like to watch The Sopranos?	*I'd like to watch* The Sopranos.
I'd really like some ice cream.	*Would you get me a plate of ice cream?*
Isn't it chilly in here?	*Jenny, please close the window.*
It must have been expensive.	*How much did you pay?*
I really need to find someone to mind the dog for the weekend.	*Would you mind watching my dog next weekend?*
Doing anything this weekend?	*I'd like to go to the movies; want to come?*
Phone's ringing.	*Would you please answer the phone?*

The messages in the Indirect column are, in large part, attempts to get the listener to say or do something without committing the speaker. The messages in the Direct column, on the other hand, express the speaker's preferences clearly and/or ask the listener to do or say something. Direct and indirect messages can also be nonverbal. For example, to communicate that it's late, you might use an indirect message such as glancing at your watch; or you might use a more direct message such as getting up and putting on your jacket.

Advantages and Disadvantages of Indirect Messages

Indirect messages have both advantages and disadvantages. On the positive side, indirect messages allow you to express a thought without insulting or offending anyone; they allow you to observe the rules of polite interaction. So instead of saying, "I'm bored with this group," you say, "It's getting late, and I have to get up early tomorrow." Instead of saying, "This food tastes like cardboard," you say, "I just started my diet" or "I just ate." In each instance you're stating a preference indirectly so as to avoid offending someone. Not all direct messages, however, should be considered impolite. In one study of Spanish and English speakers, for example, no evidence was found to support the assumption that politeness and directness were incompatible (Mir, 1993).

Sometimes indirect messages allow you to ask for compliments in a socially acceptable manner. A person who says, "I was thinking of getting a nose job" may hope to get the response, "A nose job? You? Your nose is perfect."

Indirect messages, however, also have disadvantages and can also create problems. Consider the following dialogue:

Pat: You wouldn't like to have my parents over for dinner this weekend, would you?

Chris: I really wanted to go to the shore and just relax.

Pat: Well, if you feel you have to go to the shore, I'll make the dinner myself. You go to the shore. I really hate having them over and doing all the work myself. It's such a drag shopping, cooking, and cleaning all by myself.

Given this situation, Chris has two basic alternatives. One is to stick with the plans to go to the shore and relax. In this case Pat is going to be upset and Chris is going to be made to feel guilty for not helping with the dinner. A second alternative is to give in to Pat, help with the dinner, and not go to the shore. In this case Chris is going to have to give up a much desired plan and is likely to resent Pat's "manipulative" tactics. Regardless of which decision is made, this "win–lose" strategy creates resentment, competition, and often an "I'll get even" attitude. With direct requests, this type of situation is much less likely to develop. Consider:

Pat: I'd like to have my parents over for dinner this weekend. What do you think?

Chris: Well, I really wanted to go to the shore and just relax.

Regardless of what develops next, both individuals are starting out on relatively equal footing. Each has clearly and directly stated a preference. Although at first these preferences seem mutually exclusive, it may be possible to meet both persons' needs. For example, Chris might say, "How about going to the shore this weekend and having your parents over next weekend? I'm really exhausted; I could use the rest." Here is a direct response to a direct request. Unless there is some pressing need to have Pat's parents over for dinner this weekend, this response may enable each to meet the other's needs.

Gender and Cultural Differences in Directness A popular stereotype in much of the United States holds that women are indirect in making requests and in giving orders—and that this indirectness communicates powerlessness, a discomfort with authority. Men, the stereotype continues, are direct, sometimes to the point of being blunt or rude. This directness communicates men's power and comfort with their own authority.

Deborah Tannen (1994b) provides an interesting perspective on these stereotypes. Women are, it seems, more indirect in giving orders; they are more likely to say, for example, "It would be great if these letters could go out today" rather than "Have these letters out by three." But Tannen (1994b, p. 84) argues that "issuing orders indirectly can be the prerogative of those in power" and in no way shows powerlessness. Power, to Tannen, is the ability to choose your own style of communication.

Men, however, are also indirect but in different situations (Rundquist, 1992). According to Tannen men are more likely to use indirectness when they express weakness, reveal a problem, or admit an error. Men are more likely to speak indirectly in expressing emotions other than anger. Men are also more indirect when they shrink from expressions of increased romantic intimacy. Men are thus indirect, the theory goes, when they're saying something that goes against the masculine stereotype.

Many Asian and Latin American cultures stress the values of indirectness, largely because indirectness enables a person to avoid appearing criticized or contradicted and thereby losing face. An example of a somewhat different kind of indirectness is the greater use of intermediaries to resolve conflict among the Chinese than among North Americans (Ma, 1992). In most of the United States, however, you're taught that directness is the preferred style. "Be up-front" and "Tell it like it is" are commonly heard communication guidelines. Contrast these with the following two Japanese principles of indirectness (Tannen, 1994b):

omoiyari, a concept close to empathy, says that a listener needs to understand the speaker without the speaker's being specific or direct. This style obviously places a much greater demand on the listener than would a direct speaking style.

Message Skills

Indirect Messages: Use indirect messages when a more direct style might prove insulting or offensive, but be aware that they may create misunderstanding.

? SKILLS VIEWPOINT

You're a mentor to several foreign students at your university. They want you to help them fit in with the majority. What would you teach them about the cultural rules operating in your college classrooms?

sassuru advises listeners to anticipate a speaker's meanings and use subtle cues from the speaker to infer his or her total meaning.

In thinking about direct and indirect messages, it's important to be aware of the ease with which misunderstandings can occur. For example, a person who uses an indirect style of speech may be doing so to be polite and may have been taught this style by his or her culture. If you assume, because of your own culture, that the person is using indirectness to be manipulative, then miscommunication is inevitable.

Messages Vary in Abstraction

Consider the following list of terms:

- entertainment
- film
- American film
- classic American suspense film
- *Rear Window*

At the top is the general or abstract word *entertainment*. Note that entertainment includes all the other items on the list plus various other items—television, novels, drama, comics, and so on. *Film* is more specific and concrete. It includes all of the items below it as well as various other items such as Indian film or Russian film. It excludes, however, all entertainment that is not film. *American film* is again more specific than film and excludes all films that are not American. *Classic American suspense film* further limits American film to a time period. *Rear Window* specifies concretely the one item to which reference is made.

The most general term—in this case, *entertainment*—conjures up many different images. One person may focus on television, another on music, another on comic books, and still another on radio. To some, *film* may bring to mind the early silent films. To others, it brings to mind high-tech special effects. To still others, it recalls Disney's animated cartoons. *Rear Window* guides the listener still further—in this case, to one film. But, note that even though *Rear Window* identifies one film, differ-

> ❝ Whatever we call a thing, whatever we say it is, it is not. For whatever we say is words, and words are words and not things. The words are maps, and the map is not the territory. ❞
> —Harry Weinberg

Skill building exercise

Climbing the Abstraction Ladder

For each of the terms listed below, indicate at least four possible terms that indicate increasing specificity. The first example is provided as an illustration.

Level 1	Level 2 (more specific than 1)	Level 3 (more specific than 2)	Level 4 (more specific than 3)	Level 5 (more specific than 4)
House	*mansion*	*brick mansion*	*large brick mansion*	*governor's mansion*
Entertainment				
Transportation				
Toy				
Sports				

Words exist at different levels of abstraction. As you get more specific, you more clearly communicate your own meanings and more easily direct the listener's attention to what you wish.

Figure 5.1

The Abstraction Ladder

As you go up in abstraction, you get more general; as you go down in abstraction, you get more specific. How would you arrange the following terms in order of abstraction, from most specific to most general: vegetation, tree, elm tree, thing, organic thing, blooming elm tree?

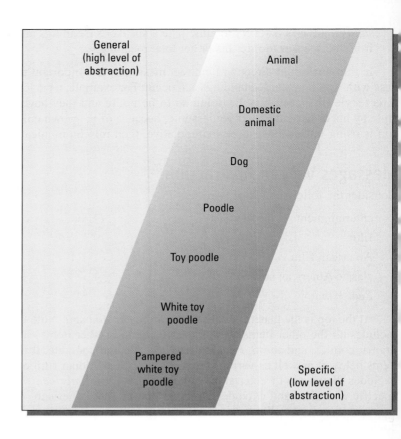

Message Skills

Abstractions: Use both abstract and specific terms when describing or explaining.

ent listeners are likely to focus on different aspects of the film: perhaps its theme, perhaps the acting, perhaps its financial success. So, as you get more specific—less abstract—you more effectively guide the images that come to your listeners' minds.

Effective verbal messages include words that range widely in abstractness (Figure 5.1). At times a general term may suit your needs best; at other times a more specific term may serve better. The general suggestion for effective communication is to use abstractions sparingly and to express your meanings specifically with words that are low in abstraction. However, are there situations in which terms high in abstraction would be more effective than specific terms? How would you describe advertisements for cosmetics in terms of high and low abstraction? Advertisements for cereals? Advertisements for cat and dog food? How would you describe a political campaign speech in terms of abstraction?

Message Meanings Are in People

If you wanted to know the meaning of the word *love*, you'd probably turn to a dictionary. There you'd find, according to *Webster's:* "the attraction, desire, or affection felt for a person who arouses delight or admiration or elicits tenderness, sympathetic interest, or benevolence." This is the denotative meaning.

But where would you turn if you wanted to know what Pedro means when he says, "I'm in love"? Of course, you'd turn to Pedro to discover his meaning. It's in this sense that meanings are not in words but in people. Consequently, to uncover meaning, you need to look into people and not merely into words.

Message Skills

Meanings in People: When deciphering meaning, the best source is the person; meanings are in people. When in doubt, find out—from the source.

Also recognize that as you change, you also change the meanings you created out of past messages. Thus, although the message sent may not have changed, the meanings you created from it yesterday and the meanings you create today may be quite different. Yesterday, when a special someone said, "I love you," you created certain meanings. But today, when you learn that the same "I love you" was said to three other people or when you fall in love with someone else, you drastically change the meanings you draw from those three words.

Message Meanings Depend on Context

Both verbal and nonverbal communications exist in a context, and that context to a large extent determines the meaning of any verbal or nonverbal behavior. In terms of verbal messages, the same words may have totally different meanings when they occur in different contexts. For example, the greeting, "How are you?" means "Hello" to someone you pass regularly on the street but means "Is your health improving?" when said to a friend in the hospital. Similarly, the meaning of a given message depends on the other behavior it accompanies or is close to in time. Saying "That stinks" in reaction to the behavior of a politician means something quite different from that same comment in reaction to a piece of overripe cheese. Divorced from the context, it's often impossible to tell what meaning the words are intended to convey.

Especially important is the cultural context, a context emphasized throughout this text. The cultural context will influence not only the meaning assigned to speech but whether your meaning is friendly, offensive, lacking in respect, condescending, sensitive, and so on.

Messages Vary in Inclusion

Some messages are inclusive; they include all people present and they acknowledge the relevance of others. Other messages exclude specific people and in some cases entire cultural groups.

You see messages of exclusion in the use of in-group language in the presence of an out-group member. When doctors get together and discuss medicine, there's no problem. But when they get together with someone who isn't a doctor, they often fail to adjust to this new person. Instead, they simply continue with discussions of anatomy, symptoms, medication, and other topics that exclude others present. When the "others" are patients, you have serious communication problems.

Another form of excluding talk is using the terms of one's own cultural group as universal, as applying to everyone. The problem is that the use of such terms excludes others. For example, *church* refers to a place of worship for specific religions but not for all religions. Similarly, *Bible* refers to the Christian religious scriptures and is not a general term for "religious scriptures." Nor does *Judeo–Christian tradition* include the religious traditions of everyone. Similarly, the terms *marriage, husband,* and *wife* refer to some heterosexual relationships and exclude others; they also exclude gay and lesbian relationships.

When you're in a group, instead of using language that excludes one or more members, consider the principle of **inclusion.** Regardless of the type of communication situation you're in, try to find ways to include everyone in the interaction. Even if job-related issues have to be discussed in the presence of someone who is not a fellow employee, you can include that person by, for example, seeking his or her perspective or drawing an analogy from his or her field.

Another way to practice inclusion in a group discussion is to fill in relevant details for those who may be unaware of them. When people, places, or events are mentioned, briefly identify them, as in "Margo—she's Jeff's daughter—loved San Francisco State."

Also, consider the vast array of alternative terms that are inclusive rather than exclusive. For example, the Association of American University Presses (Schwartz, 1995) recommends using *place of worship* instead of *church, temple,* or *mosque* when you wish to talk about religious houses of worship in general. Similarly, *committed relationship* is more inclusive than *marriage, couples therapy* is more inclusive than *marriage counseling,* and *life partner* is more inclusive than *husband* or *wife. Religious scriptures* is more inclusive than *Bible.* Of course, if you're referring

Message Skills

Meanings Depend on Context: Look at the context for cues as to how you should interpret the meanings of messages.

> **ff** No more fiendish punishment could be devised, even if such a thing were physically possible, than that one should be turned loose in society and remain absolutely unnoticed by all the members thereof. **JJ**
>
> —William James

to, say a specific Baptist church or specific married heterosexual couples, then the terms *church* and *marriage* are appropriate.

For a related but somewhat different perspective on inclusion and exclusion, let's turn to the communication behaviors known as confirmation and disconfirmation.

Confirmation and Disconfirmation

Before reading about confirmation and disconfirmation, take the self-test below to examine your own communication behavior.

 Test Yourself

How Confirming Are You?

In your typical communications, how likely are you to display the following behaviors? Use the following scale in responding to each statement: 5 = always, 4 = often, 3 = sometimes, 2 = rarely, and 1 = never.

_____ ❶ I acknowledge the contributions of the other person by, for example, supporting or taking issue with what the person says.

_____ ❷ I communicate as both speaker and listener, with involvement, and with a concern and respect for the other person.

_____ ❸ I signal my understanding of the other person both verbally and nonverbally.

_____ ❹ I ask questions as appropriate concerning the other person's thoughts and feelings.

_____ ❺ I respond to the other person's requests, by, for example, returning phone calls and answering letters within a reasonable time.

_____ ❻ I encourage the other person to express his or her thoughts and feelings.

HOW DID YOU DO? All six statements are phrased so that they express confirming behaviors. Therefore, high scores (say, above 20) reflect a strong tendency to engage in confirmation. Low scores (say, below 15) reflect a strong tendency to engage in disconfirmation. Don't assume, however, that all situations call for confirmation and that only insensitive people are disconfirming. You may wish to consider situations in which disconfirmation would be, if not an effective response, at least a legitimate one.

WHAT WILL YOU DO? Because most people want to become more confirming, the text offers suggestions for increasing your own confirming behaviors. Treating the statements in the self-test as suggestions for increasing confirmation is a good way to start.

> **ff** It is not only true that the language we use puts words in our mouths; it also puts notions in our heads. **JJ**
>
> —Wendell Johnson

The terms confirmation and disconfirmation—as illustrated in the self-test—refer to the extent to which you acknowledge another person. Consider this situation. You've been living with someone for the last six months and you arrive home late one night. Your partner, let's say Pat, is angry and complains about your being so late. Which of the following is most likely to be your response?

- Stop screaming. I'm not interested in what you're babbling about. I'll do what I want, when I want. I'm going to bed.

- What are you so angry about? Didn't you get in three hours late last Thursday when you went to that office party? So knock it off.

- You have a right to be angry. I should have called to tell you I was going to be late, but I got involved in an argument at work, and I couldn't leave until it was resolved.

In the first response, you dismiss Pat's anger and even indicate dismissal of Pat as a person. In the second response, you reject the validity of Pat's reasons for being angry but do not dismiss either Pat's feelings of anger or Pat as a person. In the third response, you acknowledge Pat's anger and the reasons for it. In addition, you provide some kind of explanation and, in doing so, show that both Pat's feelings and Pat as a person are important and that Pat has the right to know what happened. The first response is an example of disconfirmation, the second of rejection, and the third of confirmation.

Disconfirmation is a communication pattern in which you ignore someone's presence as well as that person's communications. You say, in effect, that this person and what this person has to say are not worth serious attention or effort; that this person and this person's contributions are so unimportant or insignificant that there is no reason to concern yourself with them.

Note that disconfirmation is not the same as **rejection.** In rejection you disagree with the person; you indicate your unwillingness to accept something the other person says or does. In disconfirming someone, however, you deny that person's significance; you claim that what this person says or does simply does not count.

Confirmation is the opposite communication pattern. In confirmation you not only acknowledge the presence of the other person but also indicate your acceptance of this person, of this person's self-definition, and of your relationship as defined or viewed by this other person.

You can gain insight into a wide variety of offensive language practices by viewing them as types of disconfirmation, as language that alienates and separates. Four obvious practices are sexism, heterosexism, racism, and ageism.

Message Skills

Confirmation: When you wish to be confirming, acknowledge (verbally and/or nonverbally) others in your group and their contributions.

Skill building exercise

Confirming, Rejecting, and Disconfirming

Here are three practice situations. For each situation, (1) write the three potential responses as indicated; then (2), after completing all three situations, indicate what effects each type of response is likely to generate.

1. Enrique receives this semester's grades in the mail; they're a lot better than previous semesters' grades but are still not great. After opening the letter, Enrique says: "I really tried hard to get my grades up this semester." Enrique's parents respond:

   With disconfirmation
   With rejection
   With confirmation

2. Pat, who has been out of work for the past several weeks, says: " I feel like such a failure; I just can't seem to find a job. I've been pounding the pavement for the last five weeks and still nothing." Pat's friend responds:

   With disconfirmation
   With rejection
   With confirmation

3. Judy's colleague at work comes to her, overjoyed, and tells her that she has just been promoted to vice president of marketing, skipping three steps in the hierarchy and tripling her salary. Judy responds:

   With disconfirmation
   With rejection
   With confirmation

Although each type of response serves a different purpose, confirming responses seem most likely to promote communication satisfaction.

SKILLS VIEWPOINT

When asked what they would like to change about the communication of the opposite sex, men said they wanted women to be more direct and women said they wanted men to stop interrupting and offering advice (Noble, 1994). What one change would you like to see in the communication style of the opposite sex? Of your own sex?

❝ Language exerts hidden power, like a moon on the tides. ❞

—Rita Mae Brown

Sexism

One widespread expression of sexism is **sexist language:** language that puts down someone because of his or her gender (a term usually used to refer to language derogatory toward women). The National Council of Teachers of English has proposed guidelines for nonsexist (gender-free, gender-neutral, or sex-fair) language. These guidelines concern the use of the generic word *man*, the use of generic *he* and *his*, and sex role stereotyping (Penfield, 1987).

Generic *Man* The word *man* refers most clearly to an adult male. To use the term to refer to both men and women emphasizes maleness at the expense of femaleness. Similarly, the terms *mankind* or *the common man* or even *cavemen* imply a primary focus on adult males. Gender-neutral terms can easily be substituted. Instead of *mankind,* you can say *humanity, people,* or *human beings.* Instead of the *common man,* you can say *the average person* or *ordinary people.* Instead of *cavemen,* you can say *prehistoric people* or *cave dwellers.*

Similarly, the use of terms such as *policeman* or *fireman* and other terms that presume maleness as the norm—and femaleness as a deviation from this norm—are clear and common examples of sexist language. Consider using nonsexist alternatives for these and similar terms; make these alternatives (for example, *police officer* and *firefighter*) a part of your active vocabulary. Try coming up with alternatives for each of these terms: *man, mankind, countryman, manmade, the common man, manpower, repairman, doorman, fireman, stewardess, waitress, salesman, mailman, web master,* and *actress.*

Generic *He* and *His* The use of the masculine pronoun to refer to any individual regardless of sex is certainly declining. But as recently as 1975 all college textbooks, for example, used the masculine pronoun as generic. There seems to be no legitimate reason why the feminine pronoun cannot alternate with the masculine pronoun to refer to hypothetical individuals, or why terms such as *he and she* or *her and him* cannot be used instead of just *he* or *him.* Alternatively, you can restructure your sentences to eliminate any reference to gender. For example, the NCTE Guidelines (Penfield, 1987) suggest that instead of saying, "The average student is worried about his grades," you say, "The average student is worried about grades." Instead of saying, "Ask that each student hand in his work as soon as he is finished," say, "Ask students to hand in their work as soon as they're finished."

Sex Role Stereotyping The words you use often reflect a sex role bias—the assumption that certain roles or professions belong to men and others belong to women. To eliminate sex role stereotyping from verbal communication, avoid, for example, making the hypothetical elementary school teacher female and the college professor male. Avoid referring to doctors as male and nurses as female. Avoid noting the sex of a professional with terms such as "female doctor" or "male nurse." When you're referring to a specific doctor or nurse, the person's gender will become clear when you use the appropriate pronoun: "Dr. Smith wrote the prescription for her new patient" or "The nurse recorded the patient's temperature himself."

Heterosexism

A close relative of sexism is heterosexism—a relatively new addition to the list of linguistic prejudices. As the term implies, *heterosexism* refers to attitudes, behaviors, and language that disparage gay men and lesbians. As with racist language, **heterosexist language** includes derogatory terms used for lesbians and gay men. For

Listening to Gender Differences

The best way to start thinking about gender differences in language is to think aobut your own beliefs. These beliefs influence what you hear (or think you hear) and the interpretations you give to what you hear. Here are 10 phrases that have been used to describe "women's speech." Which do you think are true?

1. emotional rather than logical
2. vague and ambiguous
3. sprawling, tending to jump from one idea to another
4. highly personal and unbusinesslike
5. more polite than men's speech
6. weak (for example, uses weak intensifiers like *so* and *such* and few exclamations)
7. oriented toward seeking permission by, for example, using tag questions (as in "Let's meet at ten o'clock, *OK*?")
8. more euphemistic than men's speech (containing more polite words as substitutes for taboo or potentially offensive terms) and using less slang and swear terms
9. less effective than men's speech generally
10. less forceful and less in control than men's speech

These 10 characteristics were drawn from the research of Cheris Kramarae (1974a, 1974b, 1977, 1981; also see Coates & Cameron, 1989, and Gamble & Gamble, 2003; Stewart, Cooper, Stewart, with Friedley, 2003). There is some evidence to support " true" for numbers 5, 7, and 8; women's speech often is more polite and does contain more "tag" questions. The other phrases are likely more stereotypes than actual descriptions.

Applying Listening Skills

James is convinced that women's speech is exactly as described in these 10 statements and admits that because of this he has tremendous difficulty listening fairly and openly to women, both on the job and in his personal interactions. What listening skills would you suggest James learn?

---

example, surveys in the military showed that 80 percent of those surveyed heard "offensive speech, derogatory names, jokes or remarks about gays" and that 85 percent believed that such derogatory speech was "tolerated" (*New York Times,* March 25, 2000, p. A12). You also see heterosexism in more subtle forms of language usage; for example, when you qualify a professional—as in "gay athlete" or "lesbian doctor"—and, in effect, say that athletes and doctors are not normally gay or lesbian. Further, this kind of expression highlights the affectional orientation of the athlete or the doctor in a context where it may have no relevance. This practice, of course, is the same as qualifying by gender, already noted.

Still another instance of heterosexism—and perhaps the most difficult to deal with—is the presumption of heterosexuality. Usually, people assume the person they're talking to or about is heterosexual. And usually they're correct, because most people are heterosexual. At the same time, however, note that this presumption denies the lesbian or gay identity a certain legitimacy. The practice is very similar to the presumptions of whiteness and maleness that we have made significant inroads in eliminating. Here are a few additional suggestions for avoiding heterosexist or what some call homophobic language. Do you

- *avoid offensive nonverbal mannerisms that parody stereotypes when talking about gay men and lesbians?*
- *avoid "complimenting" gay men and lesbians by saying that*

? SKILLS VIEWPOINT

After years of thinking about it, you've decided to come out of the closet. But you're not sure how to go about it. You suspect that some people know, but nothing has ever been said. What do you say, and to whom?

they "don't look it". To gay men and lesbians, this is not a compliment. Similarly, expressing disappointment that a person is gay—often thought to be a compliment, as in comments such as "What a waste!"—is not really a compliment.

- *avoid making the assumption that every gay or lesbian knows what every other gay or lesbian is thinking? It's very similar to asking a Japanese person why Sony is investing heavily in the United States or, as one comic put it, asking an African American, "What do you think Jesse Jackson meant by that last speech?"*
- *avoid denying individual differences? Saying things like "Lesbians are so loyal" or "Gay men are so open with their feelings," which ignore the reality of wide differences within any group, are potentially insulting to all groups.*
- *avoid overattribution, the tendency to attribute just about everything a person does, says, and believes to the fact that the person is gay or lesbian? This tendency helps to activate and perpetuate stereotypes.*
- *remember that relationship milestones are important to all people? Ignoring anniversaries or birthdays of, say, a relative's partner is resented by everyone.*

Racism

According to Andrea Rich (1974), "any language that, through a conscious or unconscious attempt by the user, places a particular racial or ethnic group in an inferior position is racist." **Racist language** expresses racist attitudes. It also, however, contributes to the development of racist attitudes in those who use or hear the language. Even when racism is subtle, unintentional, or even unconscious, its effects are systematically damaging (Dovidio, Gaertner, Kawakami, & Hodson, 2002).

Racist terms are used by members of one culture to disparage members of other cultures, their customs, or their accomplishments. Racist language emphasizes differences rather than similarities and separates rather than unites members of different cultures. Generally, racist language is used by the dominant group to establish and maintain power over other groups. The social consequences of racist language in terms of employment, education, housing opportunities, and general community acceptance are well known.

Many people feel that it's permissible for members of a culture to refer to themselves in racist terms. That is, Asians may use the negative terms referring to Asians, Italians may use the negative terms referring to Italians, and so on. This issue is seen clearly in rap music, in which performers use derogatory racial terms (*New York Times,* January 24, 1993, 1, 31). The reasoning seems to be that groups should be able to laugh at themselves.

It's interesting to note that terms denoting some of the major movements in art—for example, *impressionism* and *cubism*—were originally applied negatively. The terms were then adopted by the artists themselves and eventually became positive. A parallel can be seen in the use of the word *queer* by some lesbian and gay organizations. The purpose of these groups in using the term is to cause it to lose its negative connotation.

One possible problem, though, is that such terms may not lose their negative connotations and may simply reinforce the negative stereotypes that society has already assigned to certain groups. By using these terms, members may come to accept the labels with their negative connotations and thus contribute to their own stereotyping.

It has often been pointed out (Ossie Davis, 1973; Bosmajian, 1974) that there are aspects of language that may be inherently racist. For example, one examination of English found 134 synonyms for *white*. Of these, 44 had positive connotations (for example, "clean," "chaste," and "unblemished"), and only 10 had negative connotations (for example, "whitewash" and "pale"). The remaining were relatively neu-

> **"** Racism is the dogma that one ethnic group is condemned by nature to congenital inferiority and another group is destined to congenital superiority. **"**
>
> —Ruth Benedict

tral. Of the 120 synonyms for *black*, 60 had unfavorable connotations ("unclean," "foreboding," and "deadly"), and none had positive connotations.

Ageism

Ageism is discrimination based on age. One researcher offers a more comprehensive definition: "any attitude, action, or institutional structure which subordinates a person or group because of age or any assignment of roles in society purely on the basis of age" (Traxler, 1980, p. 14). In the United States and throughout much of the industrialized world, ageism signifies discrimination against the old and against aging in general. But ageism can also refer to prejudice against other age groups. For example, if you describe all teenagers as selfish and undependable, you're discriminating against a group purely because of their age and thus are ageist in your statements. In some cultures—some Asian and some African cultures, for example—the old are revered and respected. Younger people seek them out for advice on economic, ethical, and relationship issues.

Popular language is replete with examples of ageist phrases; *little old lady, old hag, old-timer, over the hill, old coot,* and *old fogy* are just some examples. As with sexism, qualifying a description of someone in terms of his or her age demonstrates ageism. For example, if you refer to "a quick-witted 75-year-old" or "an agile 65-year-old" or "a responsible teenager," you are implying that these qualities are unusual in people of these ages and thus need special mention. You're saying that "quick-wittedness" and "being 75" do not normally go together; you imply the same abnormality for "agility" and "being 65" and for "responsibility" and "being a teenager." The problem with this kind of stereotyping is that it's simply wrong. There are many 75-year-olds who are extremely quick witted (and many 30-year-olds who aren't).

You also communicate ageism when you speak to older people in overly simple words or explain things that don't need explaining. Nonverbally, you demonstrate ageist communication when, for example, you avoid touching an older person but touch others, or when you avoid making direct eye contact with the older person but readily do so with others. Also, it's a mistake to speak to an older person at an overly high volume; this suggests that all older people have hearing difficulties, and it tends to draw attention to the fact that you are talking down to the older person.

Of course, the media perpetuate ageist stereotypes by depicting older people as unproductive, complaining, and unromantic. Rarely, for example, do television or films show older people working productively, being cooperative and pleasant, and engaging in romantic and sexual relationships.

One useful way to avoid ageism is to recognize and avoid the illogical stereotypes that ageist language is based on. Do you

- *avoid talking down to a person because he or she is older? Older people are not mentally slow; most people remain mentally alert well into old age.*
- *refrain from refreshing an older person's memory each time you see the person? Older people can and do remember things.*
- *avoid implying that relationships are no longer important? Older people continue to be interested in relationships.*
- *speak at a normal volume and maintain a normal physical distance? Being older does not mean being hard of hearing or being unable to see; most older people hear and see quite well, sometimes with hearing aids or glasses.*
- *engage older people in conversation as you would wish to be engaged? Older people are interested in the world around them.*

Even though you want to avoid ageist communication, there are times when you may wish to make adjustments when talking with someone who does have language or communication difficulties. The American Speech and Hearing Association offers several useful suggestions (http://www.asha.org, accessed January 31, 2003):

- Reduce as much background noise as you can.
- Ease into the conversation by beginning with casual topics and then moving into more familiar topics. Stay with each topic for a while; avoid jumping too quickly from one topic to another.
- Speak in relatively short sentences and questions.
- Give the person added time to respond. Some older people react more slowly and need extra time.
- Listen actively. Practice the skills of active listening discussed in the previous chapter.

Cultural Identifiers

Perhaps the best way to avoid sexism, heterosexism, racism, and ageism in language is to examine the preferred cultural identifiers to use (and not to use) in talking about members of different groups. As always, when in doubt, find out. The preferences and many of the specific examples identified here are drawn largely from the findings of the Task Force on Bias-Free Language of the Association of American University Presses (Schwartz, 1995). Do realize that not everyone would agree with these recommendations; they're presented here—in the words of the Task Force—"to encourage sensitivity to usages that may be imprecise, misleading, and needlessly offensive" (Schwartz, 1995, p. ix). They're not presented so that you can "catch" someone being "politically incorrect" or label someone "culturally insensitive."

Generally: The term *girl* should be used only to refer to a very young female and is equivalent to *boy*. Neither term should be used for people older than say 13 or 14. *Girl* is never used to refer to a grown woman; nor is *boy* used to refer to persons in blue-collar positions, as it once was. *Lady* is negatively evaluated by many, because it connotes the stereotype of the prim and proper woman. *Woman* or *young woman* is preferred. *Older person* is preferred to *elder, elderly, senior,* or *senior citizen* (technically, someone older than 65).

Generally: *Gay* is the preferred term to refer to a man who has an affectional preference for other men, and *lesbian* is the preferred term for a woman who has an affectional preference for other women. (*Lesbian* means "homosexual woman," so the phrase *lesbian woman* is redundant.) This preference for the term *lesbian* is not universal among homosexual women, however; in one survey, for example, 58 percent preferred *lesbian*, but 34 percent preferred *gay* (Lever, 1995). *Homosexual* refers to both gay men and lesbians but more often merely denotes a sexual orientation to members of a person's own sex. *Gay* and *lesbian* refer to a lifestyle and not simply to sexual orientation. *Gay* as a noun, although widely used, may prove offensive in some contexts; for example, "We have two gays on the team." Although used within the gay community in an effort to remove the negative stigma through frequent usage, the term *queer*—as in "queer power"—is often resented when used by outsiders. Because most scientific thinking holds that one's sexuality is genetically determined rather than being a matter of choice, the term *sexual orientation* rather than *sexual preference* or *sexual status* (which is also vague) is preferred.

Generally: Most African Americans prefer *African American* to *black* (Hecht, Collier, & Ribeau, 1993), though *black* is often used with *white* and is used in a variety of other contexts (for example, Department of Black and Puerto Rican Studies, *Journal of Black History,* and Black History Month). The American Psychological Association recommends that both terms be capitalized, but *The Chicago Manual of*

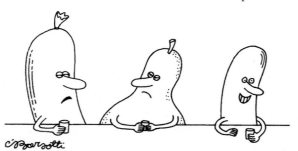

"It doesn't have a damn thing to do with political correctness, pal. I'm a sausage, and that guy's a wienie."

Style (a manual used by most newspapers and publishing houses) recommends using lowercase. The terms *Negro* and *colored*, although used in the names of some organizations (for example, the United Negro College Fund and the National Association for the Advancement of Colored People), are not used outside of these contexts.

Generally: *White* is used to refer to those whose roots are in European cultures, but not to Hispanics. A parallel to *African American* is the phrase *European American*. Few European Americans, however, would want to be called that; most would prefer to specify their national origins; for example, to use *German American* or *Greek American*. This preference may well change as Europe becomes a more cohesive and united entity. *People of color*—a somewhat literary-sounding term appropriate perhaps to public speaking but awkward to use in most conversations—is preferred to *nonwhites,* which implies that whiteness is the norm and *nonwhiteness* is a deviation from that norm. The same is true of the term *non-Christian.*

Generally: The term *Hispanic* refers to anyone who identifies himself or herself as belonging to a Spanish-speaking culture. People born in Spain prefer to be called *Spanish* rather than *Hispanic. Latina* (female) and *Latino* (male) refer to persons whose roots are in one of the Latin American countries, such as the Dominican Republic, Nicaragua, or Guatemala. *Hispanic American* refers to United States residents from Spanish-speaking cultures and includes people from Mexico, the Caribbean, and Central and South America. In emphasizing a Spanish heritage, however, the term is really inaccurate, because of the large numbers in the Caribbean and in South America whose origins and languages are French or Portuguese. *Chicana* (female) and *Chicano* (male) refer to persons with roots in Mexico, though these terms often connote a nationalist attitude (Jandt, 2000) and are considered offensive by many Mexican Americans. *Mexican American* is preferred.

> " For me, words are a form of action, capable of influencing change. "
>
> —Ingrid Bengis

6 Ways to Effective Business E-Mail

Netiquette is the system of rules for communicating politely over the Internet or over an intranet. These rules, as you'll see, are especially applicable to business e-mail; but they apply generally to all computer-mediated communication.

1. Don't shout. WRITING IN CAPS IS PERCEIVED AS SHOUTING. It's okay to use caps occasionally to achieve emphasis. If you wish to give emphasis, underline, _like this_, or use asterisks *like this*.
2. If your e-mail system has a spell-checker or grammar checker, use it. There's little sense in sending e-mails that may be read by those making decisions about promotions and work assignments, only to show that you're careless in spelling or grammar.
3. Respond to e-mails promptly. Even if you have to give a more extended response than you now have time for, reply as soon as possible; for example, "Thanks for your e-mail. I'll need a few days to track down the information you want. I'll be back to you asap." It takes almost no time to do this but assures the sender that his or her message reached the right person and will get a response.
4. Be brief. Follow the maxim of quantity by communicating only the information that is needed; follow the maxim of manner by communicating clearly, briefly, and in an organized way.
5. When sending e-mail to a group of people, consider the value of not disclosing each person's e-mail address and instead consider addressing it to "undisclosed recipients" or to "colleagues."
6. Resist the tendency to clog the e-mail systems of colleagues with baby photos, long drawn-out stories, or attachments that they probably don't want.

Applying Interpersonal Skills/Then and Now

Have you ever communicated impolitely over the Net? What specifically did you do? What would you do differently now?

Inuk (plural, *Inuit*) was officially adopted at the Inuit Circumpolar Conference to refer to the indigenous peoples of Alaska, Northern Canada, Greenland, and Eastern Siberia. *Inuk* is preferred to *Eskimo* (a term the U.S. Census Bureau uses), which was applied to the indigenous peoples of Alaska by Europeans and derives from a word that means "raw meat eaters" (Maggio, 1997).

The word *Indian* technically refers only to someone from India, not to members of other Asian countries or to the indigenous peoples of North America. *American Indian* or *Native American* is preferred, even though many Native Americans do refer to themselves as *Indians* and *Indian people*. The term *native American* (with a lowercase *n*) is most often used to refer to persons born in the United States. Although the term technically could refer to anyone born in North or South America, people outside the United States generally prefer more specific designations such as *Argentinean, Cuban*, or *Canadian*. The term *native* means an indigenous inhabitant; it's not used to mean "member of a less developed culture."

Muslim is the preferred form (rather than the older *Moslem*) to refer to a person who adheres to the religious teachings of Islam. *Quran* (rather than *Koran*) is the preferred term for the scriptures of Islam. The terms "Mohammedan" or "Mohammedanism" are not considered appropriate; they imply worship of Muhammad, the prophet, which is "considered by Muslims to be a blasphemy against the absolute oneness of God" (Maggio, 1997, p. 277).

Although there is no universal agreement, *Jewish people* is often preferred to *Jews;* and *Jewess* (a Jewish female) is considered derogatory. *Jew* should be used only as a noun and is never correctly used as a verb or an adjective (Maggio, 1997).

When history was being written with a European perspective, Europe was taken as the focal point and the rest of the world was defined in terms of its location relative to that continent. Thus, Asia became the East or the Orient, and Asians became *Orientals*—a term that is today considered inappropriate or "Eurocentric." People from Asia are *Asians,* just as people from Africa are *Africans* and people from Europe are *Europeans*.

Message Skills

Cultural Identifiers: Use cultural identifiers that are sensitive to the desires of others; when appropriate, make clear the cultural identifiers you prefer.

? SKILLS VIEWPOINT

You come upon a group of students from your communication class and join in the conversation. During the conversation you observe that all of the other people are of the same race and are using negative self-reference terms. Trying to be one of the group, you too use these terms. Immediately all the students' facial expressions tell you that you've been extremely culturally insensitive. You really meant no offense, but you now realize that the linguistic privilege possessed by insiders does not apply to outsiders. You need to explain yourself. What do you say?

Using Verbal Messages Effectively and Critically

A chief concern in using verbal messages is to recognize what critical thinking theorists call "conceptual distortions": mental mistakes, misinterpretations, or reasoning fallacies. Avoiding these distortions and substituting a more critical, more realistic analysis is probably the best way to improve your own use of verbal messages.

Messages Symbolize Reality (Partially)

Language symbolizes reality; it's not the reality itself. Of course, this is obvious. But consider: Have you ever reacted to the way something was labeled or described rather than to the actual item? Have you ever bought something because of its name rather than because of the actual object? If so, you were probably responding as if language were reality, a distortion called intensional orientation.

Intensional Orientation **Intensional orientation** (the *s* in *intensional* is intentional) refers to our tendency to view people, objects, and events in the way they're talked about—the way they're labeled. For example, if Sally were labeled "uninteresting," you would, responding intensionally, evaluate her as uninteresting even before listening to what she had to say. You'd see Sally through a filter imposed by the label "uninteresting." **Extensional orientation,** on the other hand, is the tendency to look first at the actual people, objects, and events and only afterwards at their labels. In this case, it would mean looking at Sally without any preconceived labels, guided by what she says and does, not by the words used to label her.

The way to avoid intensional orientation is to extensionalize. Recognize that language provides labels for things and should never be given greater attention than the actual thing. Give your main attention to the people, things, and events in the world as you see them and not as they're presented in words. For example, when you meet Jack and Jill, observe and interact with them. Then form your impressions. Don't re-

> " Words can destroy. What we call each other ultimately becomes what we think of each other, and it matters. "
>
> —Jeanne J. Kirkpatrick

> " My doctor is wonderful. Once, in 1955, when I couldn't afford an operation, he touched up the x-rays. "
>
> —Joey Bishop

Skill building exercise

Thinking and Talking in E-Prime

The term **E-Prime (E')** refers to normal English without the verb *to be* (Bourland, 1965–66; Wilson, 1989). Statements in E-prime can be more accurate and descriptive than conventional sentences. For example, the statement "The movie was great" implies that "greatness" is in the movie rather than in your perception of the movie. E-prime versions (for example, "I loved the movie" or "The movie kept my interest throughout the two hours") make it clear that you're talking about how you perceived the movie and not about something that is in the movie. When you say "The movie was great" you also imply that everyone will see it in the same way. On the other hand, when you say "I loved the movie" you leave open the possibility for differences of opinion. To appreciate the difference between statements that use the verb *to be* and those that do not, (1) in the second column rewrite the following sentences without using the verb *to be* in any of its forms—*is, are, am, was,* and so on. Then (2), in the third column, indicate the differences in meaning between the statements using *to be* and the E-prime rewrites.

Regular "to be" form	E-prime rewrite	Differences in meaning
a. I'm a poor student.		
b. They're inconsiderate.		
c. Is this valuable?		

The verb *to be* suggests that qualities are in the person or thing rather than in the observer. The verb *to be* also implies a permanence that is not true of the world in which you live.

Chapter 5 Verbal Messages

Message Skills

Intensional Orientation: Avoid intensional orientation. Look to people and things first and to labels second.

Message Skills

Allness: Avoid allness statements; they invariably misstate the reality and will often offend the other person.

spond to them as "greedy, money-grubbing landlords" simply because Harry labeled them this way. Don't respond to Carmen as "lazy and inconsiderate" because Elaine told you she was.

Allness   A related distortion is to forget that language symbolizes only a portion of reality, never the whole. When you assume that you can know all or say all about anything, you're into a pattern of behavior called **allness.** You never see all of anything. You never experience anything fully. You see a part, then conclude what the whole is like. You have to draw conclusions on the basis of insufficient evidence (because you always have insufficient evidence). A useful **extensional device** to help combat the tendency to think that all can or has been said about anything is to end each statement mentally with **et cetera**—a reminder that there is more to learn, more to know, and more to say; that every statement is inevitably incomplete (Korzybski, 1933). To be sure, some people overuse "et cetera." They use it not as a mental reminder but as a substitute for being specific. This obviously is to be avoided and merely adds to the distortions in communication.

To achieve **nonallness,** recognize that language symbolizes only a part of reality, never the whole. Whatever someone says—regardless of what it is or how extensive it is—is only part of the story.

Messages Express Facts and Inferences

We sometimes construct statements of both facts and inferences without making any linguistic distinction between the two. Similarly, when we articulate or listen to such statements, we often don't make a clear distinction between statements of facts and statements of inference. Yet there are great differences between the two. Barriers to clear thinking can be created when inferences are treated as facts, a tendency called **fact–inference confusion.**

Ethical messages

Lying

Lying occurs when "one person intends to mislead another, doing so deliberately, without prior notification of this purpose, and without having been explicitly asked to do so by the target [the person the liar intends to mislead]" (Ekman, 1985b, p. 28). As this definition makes clear, a person can lie by omission as well as by commission. If you omit something relevant, and if this omission causes others to be misled, you've lied just as surely as if you had made a false statement (Bok, 1978).

Similarly, although most lies are verbal, some are nonverbal—and most seem to involve at least some nonverbal elements. Common examples of nonverbal lying include the innocent facial expression and focused eye contact despite the consciousness of unethical behavior and the knowing nod despite the inner awareness of ignorance.

What Would You Do?

On the basis of your own ethical beliefs about lying, which probably are greatly influenced by your culture, what would you do in the following situations? Would you

- *lie to make another person feel good? For example, would you tell someone that he or she looked great or had a great sense of humor?*
- *lie to enable another person to save face? For example, would you voice agreement with an idea you found foolish, say you enjoyed meeting a person when you didn't, or compliment another person when it was totally undeserved?*
- *lie to get what you deserved but couldn't get any other way? For example, would you lie to get a well-earned promotion or raise or another chance with your relationship partner?*
- *lie to get yourself out of an unpleasant situation? For example, would you lie to get out of an unwanted date, an extra office chore, or a boring conversation?*

For example, you can say, "She's wearing a blue jacket," and you can say, "He's harboring an illogical hatred." Although the sentences have similar structures, they're different. You can observe the jacket and the blue color, but how do you observe "illogical hatred"? Obviously, this is not a **factual statement** but an **inferential statement.** It's one you make on the basis not only of what you observe, but of what you infer. For a statement to be considered factual, it must be made by the observer after observation and must be limited to what is observed (Weinberg, 1959).

There is nothing wrong with making inferential statements. You must make them to talk about much that is meaningful to you. The problem arises when you act as if those inferential statements are factual. You may test your ability to distinguish facts from inferences by taking the self-test below (based on tests constructed by Haney, 1973).

 Test Yourself

Can You Distinguish Facts from Inferences?

INSTRUCTIONS: Carefully read the following report and the observations based on it. Indicate whether you think, on the basis of the information presented in the report, that the observations are true, false, or doubtful. Write T if the observation is definitely true, F if the observation is definitely false, and ? if the observation may be either true or false. Judge the observations in order. Do not reread the observations after you have indicated your judgment, and do not change any of your answers.

A well-liked college teacher had just completed making up the final examinations and had turned off the lights in the office. Just then a tall, broad figure with dark glasses appeared and demanded the examination. The professor opened the drawer. Everything in the drawer was picked up and the individual ran down the corridor. The dean was notified immediately.

_____ ❶ The thief was tall and broad and wore dark glasses.

_____ ❷ The professor turned off the lights.

_____ ❸ A tall figure demanded the examination.

_____ ❹ The examination was picked up by someone.

_____ ❺ The examination was picked up by the professor.

_____ ❻ A tall, broad figure appeared after the professor turned off the lights in the office.

_____ ❼ The man who opened the drawer was the professor.

_____ ❽ The professor ran down the corridor.

_____ ❾ The drawer was never actually opened.

_____ ❿ Three persons are referred to in this report.

HOW DID YOU DO? After you answer all 10 questions, form small groups of five or six and discuss the answers. Look at each statement from each member's point of view. For each statement, ask yourself, "How can you be absolutely certain that the statement is true or false?" You should find that only one statement can be clearly identified as true and only one as false; eight should be marked "?".

WHAT WILL YOU DO? As you read this chapter, try to formulate specific guidelines that will help you distinguish facts from inferences.

To avoid fact–inference confusion, phrase your own inferential statements as tentative and leave open the possibility of being proved wrong. For example, treat the statement "Our biology teacher was fired for poor teaching" as the inferential statement it is; this allows you to consider other explanations and psychologically prepares you to be proved wrong.

This distinction is equally important when you are listening. Most talk is inferential, so beware of the speaker who presents everything as fact. Analyze closely and you'll uncover a world of inferences.

Messages Can Obscure Distinctions

Messages can obscure distinctions, both by generalizing about people or events that are covered by the same label but are really quite different (indiscrimination) and by making it easy to focus on extremes rather than on the vast middle ground (polarization).

Indiscrimination   Each word in the language can refer to lots of things; most general terms refer to a wide variety of individuals. Words such as *teacher* or *textbook* or *computer program* refer to lots of specific people and things. When you allow the general term to obscure the specific differences (say, among teachers or textbooks), you're into a pattern called indiscrimination.

Indiscrimination is the failure to distinguish between similar but different people, objects or events. It occurs when you focus on classes and fail to see that each phenomenon is unique and needs to be looked at individually.

Everything is unlike everything else. Our language, however, provides you with common nouns such as *teacher, student, friend, enemy, war, politician,* and *liberal.* Such terms lead you to focus on similarities—to group together all teachers, all students, all politicians. At the same time, the terms divert attention away from the uniqueness of each person, each object, and each event.

This kind of misevaluation is at the heart of stereotyping on the basis of nationality, race, religion, gender, age, or affectional orientation. A stereotype, you'll remember from previous discussions, is a fixed mental picture of a group that is applied to each individual in the group without regard to his or her unique qualities.

Most stereotypes are negative and denigrate the group to which they refer. Some, however, are positive. A particularly glaring example is the popular stereotype of Asian American students as successful, intelligent, and hardworking.

Whether stereotypes are positive or negative, they create the same problem: They provide you with shortcuts that are often inappropriate. For instance, when you meet a particular person, your first reaction may be to pigeonhole him or her into some category—perhaps religious, national, or academic. Then you assign to this person all the qualities that are part of your stereotype ("She's a typical academic: never thinks of the real world"). Regardless of the category you use or the specific qualities you're ready to assign, you fail to give sufficient attention to the individual's unique characteristics. Two people may both be Christian, Asian, and lesbian, for example, but each will be different from the other. Indiscrimination is a denial of another's uniqueness.

A useful antidote to indiscrimination (and stereotyping) is the **index.** This mental subscript identifies each individual as an individual even though both may be covered by the same label. Thus, politician$_1$ is not politician$_2$; teacher$_1$ is not teacher$_2$. The index helps you to discriminate among without discriminating against. Although a label ("politician," for example) covers all politicians, the index makes sure that each politician is thought about as an individual.

Polarization   Language also obscures differences because it has lots of terms to denote extremes and few terms to denote middle ground, a situation that often leads to **polarization.** You can appreciate the role language plays in fostering polarization by trying to identify the opposites of the following terms: *happy, long, wealth, life, healthy, up, left, legal, heavy, strong*. This should be relatively easy; you probably can identify the opposites very quickly. Now, however, identify the middle terms, the terms referring to the middle ground between the italicized terms and the opposites. These terms should be more difficult to come up with and should take you more time and effort. Further, if you compare your responses with those of others, you'll find that most people agree on the opposites; most people would have said *unhappy, short, poverty*, and so on. But when it comes to the middle terms, the degree of agreement will be much less. Thus, language makes it easy to focus on opposites and relatively difficult to talk about the middle areas.

Polarization, then, is the tendency to look at the world in terms of opposites and to describe it in extremes—good or bad, positive or negative, healthy or sick, intelligent or stupid. Polarization is often referred to as the fallacy of "either/or" or "black and white." Most of life exists somewhere between the extremes. Yet there's a strong tendency to view only the extremes and to categorize people, objects, and events in terms of these polar opposites.

Problems are created when opposites are used in inappropriate situations. For example, "The politician is either for us or against us." These two options do not include all possibilities. The politician may be for us in some things and against us in other things, or may be neutral.

To correct this polarizing tendency, beware of implying (and believing) that two extreme classes include all possible classes—that an individual must be one or the other, with no alternatives ("Are you pro-abortion or pro-life?"). Most people, most events, most qualities exist between polar extremes. When others imply that there are only two sides or two alternatives, look for the middle ground.

Static Evaluation   Another distinction language often obscures is that of change. Language changes only very slowly, especially when compared to the rapid pace at which people and things change. The statements you make about an event or person need to change as quickly and as dramatically as people and events change. When you retain an evaluation (most often in the form of an internalized message), despite the changes in the person or thing, you're engaging in **static evaluation.**

It's important to act in accordance with the notion of change, not merely to accept it intellectually. If you failed at something once, that does not necessarily mean that you'll fail again. If you were rejected once, that does not mean you'll be rejected again. You've changed since the first failure and the first rejection. You're a different person now, and you need to make new evaluations and initiate new efforts.

The mental **date** is a useful device for keeping language (and thinking) up to date and for guarding against static evaluation. Date your statements and especially your evaluations; remember that Pat Smith$_{1999}$ is not Pat Smith$_{2005}$, that academic abilities$_{2001}$ are not academic abilities$_{2005}$. In talking and in listening, look carefully at messages that claim that what was true still is. It may or may not be. Look for change; be suspicious of the implication of nonchange.

> A word is not a crystal, transparent and unchanged, it is the skin of a living thought and may vary greatly in color and content according to the circumstances and the time in which it is used.
>
> —Oliver Wendell Holmes

Message Skills

Dating Statements: Date your statements to avoid thinking of the world as static and unchanging. Reflect the inevitability of change in your messages.

Summary of Concepts

This chapter looked at verbal messages: the nature of language and the ways in which language works; the concept of disconfirmation and how it relates to sexism, heterosexism, and racist language; and the ways in which you can use language more effectively.

1. Verbal messages are both denotative (objective and generally easily agreed upon) and connotative (subjective and generally highly individual in meaning).
2. Verbal messages vary in directness; they can state exactly what you mean, or they can hedge and state your meaning very indirectly.

3. Verbal messages vary in abstraction; they can vary from extremely general to extremely specific.
4. Message meanings are in people, not in things.
5. Meanings are context-based; the same message in a different context will likely mean something different.
6. Messages vary in inclusion and exclusion.
7. Disconfirmation is the process of ignoring the presence and the communications of others. Confirmation means accepting, supporting, and acknowledging the importance of the other person.
8. Sexist, heterosexist, racist, and ageist language unfairly puts down and negatively evaluates groups.

9. Using language effectively involves eliminating conceptual distortions and substituting more accurate assumptions about language, the most important of which are:
   - Language symbolizes reality; it's not the reality itself.
   - Language can express both facts and inferences, and distinctions need to be made between them.
   - Language can obscure distinctions in its use of general terms that lead us to ignore differences (indiscrimination), in its emphasis on extreme rather than middle terms (polarization), and in its emphasis on nonchange (static evaluation).

Vocabulary Quiz: The Language of Language

Match these terms about language with their definitions. Record the number of the definition next to the appropriate term.

_____ polarization

_____ intensional orientation

_____ connotative meaning

_____ fact–inference confusion

_____ confirmation

_____ static evaluation

_____ indiscrimination

_____ ageism

_____ level of abstraction

_____ netiquette

1. Treating inferences as if they were facts.
2. The denial of change in language and in thinking.
3. The emotional, subjective aspect of meaning.
4. A communication pattern of acknowledgement and acceptance.
5. The rules for polite communication on the Internet.
6. The degree of generality or specificity of a term.
7. Discrimination based on age.
8. The failure to see the differences among people or things covered by the same label.
9. A focus on the way things are talked about rather than on the way they exist.
10. A focus on extremes to the neglect of the middle.

Four for Discussion

1. Visualize yourself seated with a packet of photographs before you. You're asked to scratch out the eyes in each photograph. You're further told that this is simply an experiment and that the individuals (all strangers) whose pictures you have will not be aware of anything that has happened here. As you progress through the pictures, scratching out the eyes, you come upon a photograph of your mother. What do you do? Are you able to scratch out the eyes as you have done with the pictures of the strangers? Are you responding intensionally or extensionally? Can you identify other examples of how you or those you know act intensionally instead of extensionally?

2. One of your instructors persists in calling the female students girls, refers to gay men and lesbians as queers, and refers to various racial groups in ways that most people would consider inappropriate. When told that these terms are offensive, the instructor claims the right to free speech and argues that a restriction on free speech would be a far greater wrong than being culturally or politically incorrect. How would you comment on this argument?

3. Using a good search engine such as Google (www.google.com), Vivisimo (www.vivisimo.com), or AskJeeves (www.ask.com), look up "hate speech" and campus codes on hate speech. After reading about hate speech and the codes that have been developed, formulate your own position on campus codes for hate speech. Are you in favor of or opposed to such codes? What reasons can you offer in support of your position? If you're in favor of codes, how would you write such a code of conduct?

4. Ethnocentrism gives you pride in your culture and its achievements and contributes to your willingness to sacrifice for the culture. At the same time, however, it may lead you to see other cultures and members of other cultures as inferior and to be unwilling to profit from the insights and contributions of other cultures. How would you describe your ethnocentrism? What are some of the good things and some of the not-so-good things about your ethnocentrism?

Web Explorations

 Explore our text website at **www.ablongman.com/devito** to find:

Exercises and Self-Tests

A variety of exercises will help you work actively with the concepts discussed in this chapter: (1) Integrating Verbal and Nonverbal Messages, (2) Using the Abstraction Ladder as a Creative Thinking Tool, (3) How Can You Vary Directness for Greatest Effectiveness? (4) How Can You Rephrase Clichés? (5) Identifying the Barriers to Communication, (6) How Do You Talk? As a Woman? As a Man? (7) How Do You Talk about the Middle? and (8) "Must Lie" Situations. Two self-tests will help you examine some of your own language skills: (9) How Direct Are You? and (10) Can You Distinguish between Commonly Confused Words?

Writing Resources and Assignments

You will find suggestions for writing papers of personal experience (for example, your own use of direct and indirect language), concept or principle explanation (for example, ageism, hate speech), review (for example, online dictionaries, gender differences in verbal messages), or research on verbal messages (for example, how do businesses deal with sexism in the workplace).

 Explore our research resources at **www.researchnavigator.com** and

Read an article.

Read an academic or popular article on meaning or messages; for example, on message directness, language, confirmation or disconfirmation, sexism, heterosexism, ageism, racism, hate speech, or the relationship of language and culture. On the basis of this article, what can you add to the discussion presented here?

Investigate key terms.

Investigate one of the key terms discussed in this chapter (for example, meaning, message, abstraction, denotation and connotation, directness, intensional orientation, allness, polarization, language, symbol, disconfirmation, racism, sexism, heterosexism, or hate speech). What additional insights can you provide?

Find answers.

Try finding answers to one of the following questions, or design a research study to answer it.

1. Do men and women follow different rules for politeness in, say, conversation? In business?
2. How is politically incorrect language dealt with in the workplace?
3. How is disconfirmation used in Internet communication?
4. What are the effects of using racist, sexist, heterosexist, and ageist language on campus?

Nonverbal Messages

6

The Functions of Nonverbal Messages

The Channels of Nonverbal Messages

Culture and Nonverbal Messages

▶ Bob leaves his apartment at 8:15 A.M. and stops at the corner drugstore for breakfast. Before he can speak, the counterman says, "The usual?" Bob nods yes. While he savors his danish, an overweight man pushes onto the adjoining stool and overflows into his space. Bob scowls and the man pulls himself in as much as he can. Bob has sent two messages without speaking a syllable.

▶ George is talking to Charley's wife at a party. Their conversation is entirely trivial, yet Charley glares at them suspiciously. Their physical proximity and the movements of their eyes reveal that they are powerfully attracted to each other.

▶ Jose Ybarra and Sir Edmund Jones are at the same party and it is important for them to establish a cordial relationship for business reasons. Each is trying to be warm and friendly yet they will part with mutual distrust, and their business transaction will probably fall through. Jose, in Latin fashion, moved closer and closer to Sir Edmund as they spoke, and this movement was miscommunicated as pushiness to Sir Edmund, who kept backing away from this intimacy, and this was miscommunicated to Jose as coldness. The silent languages of Latin and English cultures are more difficult to learn than their spoken languages.

In these three examples, supplied by researchers Edward and Mildred Hall (1971), you see the powerful messages communicated without words. In this chapter we look at these nonverbal messages—the ways they function in interaction with verbal messages, the types or channels of nonverbal messages, and the cultural variations in nonverbal communication.

Nonverbal communication is communication without words. You communicate nonverbally when you gesture, smile or frown, widen your eyes, move your chair closer to someone, wear jewelry, touch someone, raise your vocal volume, or even say nothing. The crucial aspect is that the message you send is in some way received by one or more other people. If you gesture while you are alone in your room and no one is there to see you, then, most theorists would argue, communication has not taken place. The same is true of verbal messages, of course; if you recite a speech and no one hears it, then communication has not taken place.

Competence in nonverbal communication can yield two principal benefits (Burgoon & Hoobler, 2002). First, the greater your ability to encode and decode nonverbal signals, the higher your popularity and psychosocial well-being are likely to be. (Not surprisingly, encoding and decoding abilities are highly correlated; if you're good at expressing yourself nonverbally, then you're likely to also be good at reading the nonverbal cues of others.) This relationship is likely part of a more general relationship: Research indicates that people who are high in interpersonal skills generally are perceived to be high on such positive qualities as expressiveness, self-esteem, outgoingness, social comfort, sociability, and gregariousness. Interpersonal skills really do matter. Second, the greater your nonverbal skills, the more successful you're likely to be at influencing and deceiving others. Skilled nonverbal communicators are highly persuasive. This persuasive power can be used to help or support another, or it can be used to deceive and fool.

Directly related to these advantages are research findings showing that women are the better encoders and decoders of nonverbal messages (Hall, 1998; Burgoon & Hoobler, 2002). Although this superiority does not hold in all contexts, it does apply in most. For example, in a review of 21 research studies on encoding, 71 percent found women to be superior senders of nonverbal messages. And in a review of 61 studies on decoding, 84 percent found women to be superior receivers (Hall, 1998).

As you begin your study of nonverbal communication, keep the following suggestions in mind.

❝ I have noticed that nothing I have never said ever did me any harm. ❞

—Calvin Coolidge

- Analyze your own nonverbal communication patterns. If you're to use this material in any meaningful way to change some of your behaviors, for example, then self-analysis is essential.
- Observe. Observe. Observe. Observe the behaviors of those around you and your own. See in everyday behavior what you read about here and discuss in class.
- Resist the temptation to draw conclusions from nonverbal behaviors. Instead, develop hypotheses (educated guesses) about what is going on, and test the validity of your hypotheses on the basis of other evidence.
- Connect and relate. Although textbooks (like this one) must present the areas of nonverbal communication separately, the various elements all work together in actual communication situations.
- Nonverbal messages may be used alone; may function as the primary channel of communication, with the verbal message in a secondary role; or may serve in a secondary role (Burgoon & Hoobler, 2002).

The Functions of Nonverbal Messages

To appreciate the many functions of nonverbal communication, let's look at (1) the ways in which nonverbal communication messages are integrated with verbal messages and (2) the functions that researchers have focused on most extensively (Burgoon & Hoobler, 2002; Burgoon & Bacue, 2003).

Integrating Nonverbal and Verbal Messages

In face-to-face communication you blend verbal and nonverbal messages to best convey your meanings. Here are six ways in which nonverbal messages are used with verbal messages; these will help to highlight the important interaction and integration of nonverbal and verbal messages (Knapp & Hall, 1996).

- Nonverbal communication often serves to *accent* or emphasize some part of the verbal message. You might, for example, raise your voice to underscore a particular word or phrase, bang your fist on the desk to stress your commitment, or look longingly into someone's eyes when saying "I love you."
- Nonverbal communication may *complement* or add nuances of meaning not communicated by your verbal message. Thus, you might smile when telling a story (to suggest that you find it humorous) or frown and shake your head when recounting someone's deceit (to suggest your disapproval).
- You may deliberately *contradict* your verbal messages with nonverbal movements—for example, by crossing your fingers or winking to indicate that you're lying.
- Movements may serve to *regulate*—to control, or indicate your desire to control, the flow of verbal messages, as when you purse your lips, lean forward, or make hand gestures to indicate that you want to speak. You might also put up your hand or vocalize your pauses (for example, with "um" or "ah") to indicate that you have not finished and are not ready to relinquish the floor to the next speaker.
- You can *repeat* or restate the verbal message nonverbally. You can, for example, follow your verbal "Is that all right?" with raised eyebrows and a questioning look, or motion with your head or hand to repeat your verbal "Let's go."
- You may also use nonverbal communication to *substitute* or take the place of verbal messages. For instance, you can signal "OK" with a hand gesture. You can nod your head to indicate yes or shake your head to indicate no.

Researching Nonverbal Communication Functions

Although nonverbal communication serves the same functions as verbal communication, nonverbal researchers have singled out several functions in which nonverbal messages play particularly important roles (Burgoon, Buller, & Woodall, 1996; Burgoon & Hoobler, 2002).

Forming and Managing Impressions   It is largely through the nonverbal communications of others that you form impressions of them. Based on a person's body size, skin color, and dress, as well as on the way the person smiles, maintains eye contact, and expresses himself or herself facially, you form impressions—you judge who the person is. One nonverbal researcher groups these impressions into four categories (Leathers, 1997): credibility (how competent and believable you find the person), likeability (how much you like or dislike the person), attractiveness (how attractive you find the person), and dominance (how dominant the individual is).

Of course, you reveal yourself to others largely through the same nonverbal signals you use to size up others. But not only do you communicate your true self nonverbally; you also manage the impression that you give to others. Impression management may, for example, mean appearing brave when you're really scared or happy when you're really sad.

Forming and Defining Relationships   Much of your relationship life is lived nonverbally. Largely through nonverbal signals, you communicate the nature of your relationship to another person; and you and that person communicate nonverbally with each other. Holding hands, looking longingly into each other's eyes, and even dressing alike are ways in which you communicate closeness in your interpersonal relationships.

You also use nonverbal signals to communicate your relationship dominance and status (Knapp & Hall, 1996). The large corner office with the huge desk communicates high status just as the basement cubicle communicates low status.

Structuring Conversation and Social Interaction   When you're in conversation, you give and receive cues—signals that you're ready to speak, to listen, to comment on what the speaker just said—that regulate and structure the interaction. These turn-taking cues may be verbal (as when you say, "What do you think?"), but most often they're nonverbal: A nod of the head in the direction of someone else signals that you're ready to give up your speaking turn and want this other person to say something. You also show that you're listening and that you want the conversation to continue (or that you're not listening and want the conversation to end) largely through nonverbal signals.

Influence and Deception   You can influence others not only through what you say but also through your nonverbal signals. A focused glance that says you're committed; gestures that further explain what you're saying; appropriate dress that says, "I'll easily fit in with this organization"—these are a few examples of ways in which you can exert nonverbal influence.

And with the ability to influence, of course, comes the ability to deceive—to lie, to mislead another person into thinking something is true when it's false or that something is false when it's true. One common example of nonverbal deception is using your eyes and facial expressions to communicate a liking for other people, when you're really interested only in gaining their support in some endeavor. Not surprisingly, you also use nonverbal signals to detect deception in others. For example, you may well suspect a person of lying if he or she avoids eye contact, fidgets, and conveys verbal and nonverbal messages that are inconsistent.

Emotional Expression   Although people often explain and reveal emotions verbally, nonverbal expressions probably communicate more about emotional experi-

Integrating Verbal and Nonverbal Messages

Try reading each of the following aloud in two ways—first to communicate the statement's literal meaning, then to communicate a meaning opposite to the literal one. As you go along, try to identify the nonverbal differences between the literal and the opposite-meaning renditions. Look specifically at *(a)* how you read the statements in terms of rate, pauses, and volume; *(b)* how your facial and eye expressions differed; and *(c)* how your gestures or body posture differed.

1. Yes, I have the job of a lifetime.
2. I can't wait to receive my test results.
3. Wow! I had some fantastic date last night.
4. Did you see him pitch that great game last night?
5. Did you see the way she decorated her apartment—real style, don't you think?

You cannot speak a sentence without using nonverbal signals, and these signals influence the meaning the receiver gets.

ence. For example, you reveal your level of happiness or sadness or confusion largely through facial expressions. Of course, you also reveal your feelings by posture (for example, whether tense or relaxed), gestures, eye movements, and even the dilation of your pupils.

Nonverbal messages often help people communicate unpleasant messages, messages they might feel uncomfortable putting into words (Infante, Rancer, & Womack, 2002). For example, you might avoid eye contact and maintain large distances between yourself and someone with whom you didn't want to interact or with whom you wanted to decrease the intensity of your relationship.

The Channels of Nonverbal Messages

Nonverbal communication is probably most easily explained in terms of the various channels through which messages pass. Here we'll survey 10 channels: body, face, eye, space, artifactual, touch, paralanguage, silence, time, and smell.

Body Messages

Two aspects of the body are especially important in communicating messages: first, the movements you make with your body, and second, the general appearance of your body.

Body Movements   Nonverbal researchers identify five major types of body movements: emblems, illustrators, affect displays, regulators, and adaptors (Ekman & Friesen, 1969; Knapp & Hall, 1996).

Emblems are body gestures that directly translate into words or phrases; for example, the OK sign, the thumbs-up for "good job," and the V for victory. You use these consciously and purposely to communicate the same meaning as the words. But emblems are culture specific, so be careful when using your culture's emblems in other cultures. For example, when President Nixon visited Latin America and gestured with the OK sign, intending to communicate something positive, he was quickly informed that this gesture was not universal. In Latin America the gesture has a far more negative meaning. Here are a few cultural differences in the emblems you may commonly use (Axtell, 1993):

> " The body says what words cannot. "
>
> —Martha Graham

- In the United States, to say "hello" you wave with your whole hand moving from side to side but in a large part of Europe that same signal means "no." In Greece such a gesture would be considered insulting to the person to whom you're waving.

- The V for victory is common throughout much of the world; but if you make this gesture in England with the palm facing your face, it's as insulting as the raised middle finger is in the United States.

- In Texas the raised fist with little finger and index finger raised is a positive expression of support, because it represents the Texas longhorn steer. But in Italy it's an insult that means "Your spouse is having an affair with someone else." In parts of South America it's a gesture to ward off evil, and in parts of Africa it's a curse: "May you experience bad times."

- In the United States and in much of Asia, hugs are rarely exchanged among acquaintances; but among Latins and Southern Europeans hugging is a common greeting gesture, and failing to hug someone may communicate unfriendliness.

Illustrators enhance (literally "illustrate") the verbal messages they accompany. For example, when referring to something to the left, you might gesture toward the left. Most often you illustrate with your hands, but you can also illustrate with head and general body movements. You might, for example, turn your head or your entire body toward the left. You might also use illustrators to communicate the shape or size of objects you're talking about.

Research points to still another advantage of illustrators—namely, that they increase your ability to remember. In one study people who illustrated their verbal messages with gestures remembered some 20 percent more than those who didn't gesture (Goldin-Meadow, Nusbaum, Kelly, & Wagner, 2001).

Affect displays include movements of the face (smiling or frowning, for example) as well as of the hands and general body (body tension or relaxation, for example) that communicate emotional meaning. You use affect displays to accompany and reinforce your verbal messages but also as substitutes for words; for example, you might smile while saying how happy you are to see your friend, or you might simply smile. Or you might rush to greet someone with open arms. Because affect displays are centered primarily in the facial area, we'll consider these in more detail in the "Facial Messages" section beginning on page 121. Affect displays are often unconscious; frequently, for example, you smile or frown without awareness. At other times, however, you may smile with awareness, consciously trying to convey pleasure or friendliness.

Regulators are behaviors that monitor, control, coordinate, or maintain the speaking of another individual. When you nod your head, for example, you tell the speaker to keep on speaking; when you lean forward and open your mouth, you tell the speaker that you would like to say something.

Adaptors are gestures that satisfy some personal need. **Self-adaptors** are self-touching movements; for example, rubbing your nose, scratching to relieve an itch, or moving your hair out of your eyes. **Alter-adaptors** are movements directed at the person with whom you're speaking, such as removing lint from a person's jacket, straightening a person's tie, or folding your arms in front of you to keep others a comfortable distance from you. **Object-adaptors** are gestures focused on objects; for example, doodling on or shredding a Styrofoam coffee cup.

Table 6.1 summarizes these five types of body movements.

Body Appearance   Your general body appearance also communicates. Height, for example, has been shown to be significant in a wide variety of situations. Tall presidential candidates have a much better record of winning elections than do their shorter opponents. Tall people seem to be paid more and are favored by personnel interviewers over shorter job applicants (Keyes, 1980; Guerrero, DeVito & Hecht, 1999; Knapp & Hall, 1996; Jackson & Ervin, 1992).

Message Skills

Body Movements: Use body and hand gestures to reinforce your communication purposes.

TABLE 6.1	Five Body Movements	

Can you give at least one additional example of each of these five body movements?

	NAME AND FUNCTION	EXAMPLES
	EMBLEMS directly translate words or phrases	"OK" sign, "come here" wave, hitchhiker's sign
	ILLUSTRATORS accompany and literally "illustrate" verbal messages	Circular hand movements when talking of a circle; hands far apart when talking of something large
	AFFECT DISPLAYS communicate emotional meaning	Expressions of happiness, surprise, fear, anger, sadness, disgust/contempt
	REGULATORS monitor, maintain, or control the speaking of another	Facial expressions and hand gestures indicating "keep going," "slow down," or "what else happened?"
	ADAPTORS satisfy some need	Scratching head

Your body also reveals your race (through skin color and tone) and may even give clues as to your specific nationality. Your weight in proportion to your height will also communicate messages to others, as will the length, color, and style of your hair.

Your general **attractiveness,** which includes both visual appeal and pleasantness of personality, is also a part of body communication. Attractive people have the advantage in just about every activity you can name. They get better grades in school, are more valued as friends and lovers, and are preferred as coworkers (Burgoon, Buller, & Woodall, 1996). Although we normally think of attractiveness as culturally determined—and to some degree it is—research seems to suggest that definitions of attractiveness are becoming universal (Brody, 1994). A person rated as attractive in one culture is likely to be rated as attractive in other cultures, even in cultures whose people are widely different in appearance.

Facial Messages

Throughout your interpersonal interactions, your face communicates many things, especially your emotions. Facial movements alone seem to communicate messages about pleasantness, agreement, and sympathy; the rest of the body doesn't provide any additional information in those realms. But for other emotional messages—for example, the intensity with which an emotion is felt—both facial and bodily cues enter in (Graham, Bitti, & Argyle, 1975; Graham & Argyle, 1975).

Some researchers in nonverbal communication claim that facial movements may express at least the following eight emotions: happiness, surprise, fear, anger, sadness, disgust, contempt, and interest (Ekman, Friesen, & Ellsworth, 1972). Others propose that in addition, facial movements may also communicate bewilderment and determination (Leathers, 1997).

Try to express surprise using only facial movements. Do this in front of a mirror and try to describe in as much detail as possible the specific movements of the face that make up a look of surprise. If you signal surprise like most people, you probably use raised and curved eyebrows, long horizontal forehead wrinkles, wide-open eyes, a dropped-open mouth, and lips parted with no tension. Even if there were differences from one person to another—and clearly there would be—you probably could recognize the movements listed here as indicative of surprise.

Of course, some emotions are easier to communicate and to decode than others. For example, in one study, participants judged happiness with 55 to 100 percent

Listening with Power

Much as you can communicate power and authority with words and nonverbal expressions, you can also communicate power through listening. Here are some suggestions:

- Respond visibly but in moderation—an occasional nod or a facial expression that says "that's interesting" is usually sufficient. Too little response says you aren't listening; too much says you aren't listening critically.

- Avoid adaptors such as playing with your hair or a pencil or doodling. These signal that you're uncomfortable and hence that you lack power.

- Maintain an open posture. Resist covering your face, chest, or stomach with your hands. These gestures may communicate defensiveness and vulnerability and hence powerlessness.

- Avoid interrupting the speaker. The reason is simple: Not interrupting is one of the rules of business communication that powerful people follow and powerless people don't.

- You can also signal power through "visual dominance behavior" (Exline, Ellyson, & Long, 1975). For example, the average speaker maintains lots of eye contact while listening and less while speaking. When you want to signal dominance, you might reverse this pattern and maintain lots of eye contact while talking but much less while listening.

Applying Listening Skills

Marco is a new project director at a conservative advertising company. Normally an extremely expressive individual, Marco wonders if he should curb his effusiveness while listening, say at company meetings. Or should he be his regular self, even though that would violate many of the suggestions given above? What listening advice would you give Marco?

accuracy, surprise with 38 to 86 percent accuracy, and sadness with 19 to 88 percent accuracy (Ekman, Friesen, & Ellsworth, 1972). Research finds that women and girls are more accurate judges of facial emotional expression than men and boys (Hall, 1984; Argyle, 1988).

As you've probably experienced, you may interpret the same facial expression differently depending on the context in which it occurs. For example, in a classic study, when researchers showed participants a smiling face looking at a glum face, the participants judged the smiling face to be vicious and taunting. But when presented with the same smiling face looking at a frowning face, they saw it as peaceful and friendly (Cline, 1956).

Another factor influencing facial expressions is culture. Members of different cultures use facial expressions very differently, largely because cultures have different rules for displays of emotional expression. For example, in one study Japanese and American students watched a film of an operation (Ekman, 1985a, b). Experimenters videotaped the students in two situations: alone while watching the film and in an interview situation about the film. When alone, the students showed very similar reactions. In the interview, however, the American students displayed facial expressions indicating displeasure, whereas the Japanese students didn't show any great emotion. Similarly, Japanese women aren't supposed to reveal broad smiles and so will hide their smiles, sometimes with their hands (cf. Ma, 1996). Women in the United States, on the other hand, have no such restrictions and are more likely to smile openly. Thus, many differences in facial expression and in the meanings attributed to such expressions seem to depend on **cultural display rules**—rules for appropriate emotional display—and not on the way different cultures express emotions (cf. Matsumoto, 1991).

Similarly, cultural differences exist in decoding the meaning of a facial expression. For example, researchers asked American and Japanese students to judge the meanings of smiling and neutral facial expressions. The Americans rated the smiling face as more attractive, more intelligent, and more sociable than the neutral face. The

SKILLS VIEWPOINT

No matter what Shasta says, she smiles and expresses herself in a lilting tone that leads most people to feel she is pleased. She hopes to become a hospital administrator, however, and this tendency may create problems and work against her candidacy. What would you teach Shasta about facial expression?

Japanese, however, rated the smiling face as more sociable but not as more attractive, and they rated the neutral face as the more intelligent (Matsumoto & Kudoh, 1993).

Facial Management   As each of us learns our culture's nonverbal system of communication, we also learn certain **facial management techniques;** for example, ways to hide certain emotions and to emphasize others. Consider your own use of such facial management techniques. As you do so, think about the types of interpersonal situations in which you would use each technique (Malandro, Barker, & Barker, 1989). When might you

- intensify, *or exaggerate a feeling?*
- deintensify, *or underplay or minimize a feeling?*
- neutralize, *or cover up or hide a feeling?*
- mask, *or replace or substitute the expression of one emotion for another?*

These facial management techniques help you display emotions in a socially acceptable way. For example, if someone gets bad news in which you secretly take pleasure, the display rule dictates that you frown and otherwise nonverbally signal displeasure. If you place first in a race and your best friend barely finishes, the display rule requires that you minimize your expression of happiness and certainly avoid any signs of gloating. If you violate these display rules, you'll appear insensitive. So, although facial management techniques may be deceptive, they're expected and even required by the rules for polite interaction.

Facial Feedback   The **facial feedback hypothesis** holds that your facial expressions influence physiological arousal (Lanzetta, Cartwright-Smith, & Kleck, 1976; Zuckerman, Klorman, Larrance, & Spiegel, 1981). In one study, for example, participants held a pen in their teeth to simulate a sad expression and then rated a series of photographs. Results showed that mimicking sad expressions actually increased the degree of sadness the participants reported feeling when viewing the photographs (Larsen, Kasimatis, & Frey, 1992).

Further support for this hypothesis comes from a study that compared (1) participants who felt emotions such as happiness and anger with (2) those who both felt and expressed these emotions. In support of the facial feedback hypothesis, partici-

> **Without wearing any mask we are conscious of, we have a special face for each friend.**
>
> —Oliver Wendell Holmes

Message Skills

Facial Messages: Use facial expressions to communicate involvement. In listening, look to the facial expressions of others as cues to their emotions and meaning.

pants who felt and expressed the emotions became emotionally aroused faster than did those who only felt the emotion (Hess, Kappas, McHugo, Lanzetta, et al., 1992).

Generally, research finds that facial expressions can produce or heighten feelings of sadness, fear, disgust, and anger. But this effect does not occur with all emotions; smiling, for example, doesn't seem to make us feel happier (Burgoon, Buller, & Woodall, 1996). Further, it has not been demonstrated that facial expressions can eliminate one feeling and replace it with another. So if you're feeling sad, smiling will not eliminate the sadness and replace it with gladness. A reasonable conclusion seems to be that your facial expressions can influence some feelings but not all (Burgoon, Buller, & Woodall, 1996; Cappella, 1993).

Eye Messages

From Ben Jonson's poetic exhortation "Drink to me only with thine eyes, / And I will pledge with mine" to the scientific observations of modern researchers (Hess, 1975; Marshall, 1983), the eyes have long been regarded as the most important nonverbal message system.

Research on communication via the eyes (a study known technically as oculesis) shows that these messages vary depending on the duration, direction, and quality of the eye behavior. For example, in every culture there are strict, though unstated, rules for the proper duration for eye contact. In our culture the average length of gaze is 2.95 seconds. The average length of mutual gaze (two persons gazing at each other) is 1.18 seconds (Argyle & Ingham, 1972; Argyle, 1988). When eye contact falls short of this amount, you may think the person is uninterested, shy, or preoccupied. When the appropriate amount of time is exceeded, you may perceive the person as showing unusually high interest.

The direction of the eye glance also communicates. In much of the United States, you're expected to glance alternately at the other person's face, then away, then again at the face, and so on. The rule for the public speaker is to scan the entire audience, not focusing for too long on or ignoring any one area of the audience. When you break these directional rules, you communicate different meanings—abnormally high or low interest, self-consciousness, nervousness over the interaction, and so on. The quality of eye behavior—how wide or how narrow your eyes get during interaction—also communicates meaning, especially interest level and such emotions as surprise, fear, and disgust.

Eye Contact   With eye contact you send a variety of messages. One such message is a request for feedback. In talking with someone, we look at her or him intently, as if to say, "Well, what do you think?" As you might predict, listeners gaze at speakers more than speakers gaze at listeners. In public speaking, you may scan hundreds of people to secure this feedback.

Another type of message informs the other person that the channel of communication is open and that he or she should now speak. You see this regularly in conversation, when one person asks a question or finishes a thought and then looks to you for a response.

Eye contact may also send messages about the nature of the relationship. For example, if you engage in prolonged eye contact coupled with a smile, you'll signal a positive relationship. If you stare or glare at the person while frowning, you'll signal a negative relationship.

Eye contact messages enable you to psychologically lessen the physical distance between yourself and another person. When you catch someone's eye at a party, for example, you become psychologically close though physically far apart.

Eye Avoidance   The eyes are "great intruders," observed sociologist Erving Goffman (1967). When you avoid eye contact or avert your glance, you help others to maintain their privacy. You may do this when you see a couple arguing in public: You

> *An eye can threaten like a loaded and leveled gun, or it can insult like hissing or kicking; or, in its altered mood, by beams of kindness, it can make the heart dance for joy.*
>
> —Ralph Waldo Emerson

turn your eyes away (though your eyes may be wide open) as if to say, "I don't mean to intrude; I respect your privacy." Goffman refers to this behavior as **civil inattention.**

Eye avoidance can also signal lack of interest—in a person, a conversation, or some visual stimulus. At times you may hide your eyes to block off unpleasant stimuli (a particularly gory or violent scene in a movie, for example) or close your eyes to block out visual stimuli and thus heighten other senses. For example, you may listen to music with your eyes closed. Lovers often close their eyes while kissing, and many prefer to make love in a dark or dimly lit room.

Spatial Messages

Space is an especially important factor in nonverbal interpersonal communication, although we seldom think about it. Edward T. Hall (1959, 1963, 1966), who has pioneered the study of spatial communication, called this study **proxemics.** We can examine this broad area by looking at the messages communicated by distance and territory.

Proxemic Distances   Four proxemic distances correspond closely to the major types of relationships: intimate, personal, social, and public (see Table 6.2).

In **intimate distance,** ranging from actual touching to 18 inches, the presence of the other individual is unmistakable. Each person experiences the sound, smell, and feel of the other's breath. You use intimate distance for lovemaking, comforting, and protecting. This distance is so short that most people do not consider it proper in public.

Personal distance refers to the protective "bubble" that defines your personal space, ranging from 18 inches to 4 feet. This imaginary bubble keeps you protected and untouched by others. You can still hold or grasp another person at this distance, but only by extending your arms; this allows you to take certain individuals such as loved ones into your protective bubble. At the outer limit of personal distance, you can touch

TABLE 6.2   Relationships and Proxemic Distances

These four distances can be further divided into close and far phases; the far phase of one level (say, personal) blends into the close phase of the next level (social). Do your relationships also blend into one another? Or are, say, your personal relationships totally separated from your social relationships?

RELATIONSHIP		DISTANCE
	Intimate Relationship	Intimate Distance 0 _____ 18 inches close phase far phase
	Personal Relationship	Personal Distance 1½ _____ 4 feet close phase far phase
	Social Relationship	Social Distance 4 _____ 12 feet close phase far phase
	Public Relationship	Public Distance 12 _____ 25+ feet close phase far phase

another person only if both of you extend your arms. At this distance you conduct much of your interpersonal interactions; for example, talking with friends and family.

At **social distance,** ranging from 4 to 12 feet, you lose the visual detail you have at personal distance. You conduct impersonal business and interact at a social gathering at this social distance. The more distance you maintain in your interactions, the more formal they appear. In offices of high officials, the desks are positioned so the official is assured of at least this distance from clients.

Public distance, from 12 to 25 feet or more, protects you. At this distance you could take defensive action if threatened. On a public bus or train, for example, you might try to keep at least this distance from a drunken passenger. Although at this distance you lose fine details of the face and eyes, you're still close enough to see what is happening.

The specific distances that you maintain between yourself and other individuals depend on a wide variety of factors (Burgoon, Buller, & Woodall, 1996). Among the most significant factors are *gender* (women in same-sex dyads sit and stand closer to each other than do men, and people approach women more closely than they approach men); *age* (people maintain closer distances with similarly aged others than they do with those much older or much younger); and *personality* (introverts and highly anxious people maintain greater distances than do extroverts). Not surprisingly, you'll tend to maintain shorter distances with people you're familiar with than with strangers, and with people you like than with those you don't like.

Territoriality   Another type of communication having to do with space is **territoriality,** a possessive reaction to an area or to particular objects. You interact basically in three types of territories (Altman, 1975):

- **Primary territories** are areas that you might call your own; these areas are your exclusive preserve. Primary territories might include your room, your desk, or your office.

- **Secondary territories** are areas that don't belong to you but which you have occupied and with which you're associated. They might include your usual table in the cafeteria, your regular seat in the classroom, or your neighborhood turf.

- **Public territories** are areas that are open to all people; they may be owned by some person or organization, but they are used by everyone. They are places such as movie houses, restaurants, and shopping malls.

Skill building exercise

Sitting at the Company Meeting

The graphic here represents a meeting table with 12 chairs, one of which is already occupied by the boss. Below are listed four messages you might want to communicate if you were present at such a meeting. For each of these messages, indicate *(a)* where you would sit to communicate the desired message and *(b)* any other possible messages that your choice of seat would likely communicate.

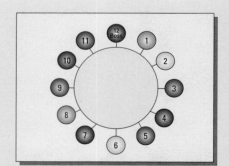

1. You want to polish the apple and ingratiate yourself with your boss.
2. You aren't prepared and want to be ignored.
3. You want to challenge your boss on a certain policy that will come up for a vote.
4. You want to be accepted as a new (but important) member of the company.

Nonverbal choices (such as the seat you select or the clothes you wear) have an impact on communication and on your image as a communicator.

When you operate in your own primary territory, you have an interpersonal advantage, often called the **home field advantage.** In their own home or office, people take on a kind of leadership role: They initiate conversations, fill in silences, assume relaxed and comfortable postures, and maintain their positions with greater conviction. Because the territorial owner is dominant, you stand a better chance of getting your raise approved, your point accepted, or a contract resolved in your favor if you're in your own territory (your office, your home) rather than in someone else's (your supervisor's office, for example) (Marsh, 1988).

Like animals, humans mark both their primary and secondary territories to signal ownership. Humans use three types of **markers:** central markers, boundary markers, and earmarkers (Goffman, 1971). **Central markers** are items you place in a territory to reserve it for you—for example, a drink at the bar, books on your desk, or a sweater over a library chair.

Boundary markers serve to divide your territory from that of others. In the supermarket checkout line, the bar placed between your groceries and those of the person behind you is a boundary marker, as are fences, armrests that separate your chair from those on either side, and the contours of the molded plastic seats on a bus.

Earmarkers—a term taken from the practice of branding animals on their ears—are identifying marks that indicate your possession of a territory or object. Trademarks, nameplates, and initials on a shirt or attaché case are all examples of earmarkers.

Markers are also important in giving you a feeling of belonging. For example, one study found that students who marked their college dorm rooms by displaying personal items stayed in school longer than did those who didn't personalize their spaces (Marsh, 1988).

**"Never let her catch you in her garden . . .
Humans are *very* territorial."**

© 2001. Reprinted courtesy of Bunny Hoest and *Parade* magazine.

Again, like animals, humans use territory to signal their status. For example, the size and location of your territory (your home or office, say) indicates something about your status. Status is also signaled by the unwritten law governing the right of invasion. Higher-status individuals have a "right" to invade the territory of lower-status persons, but the reverse is not true. The boss of a large company, for example, can barge into the office of a junior executive, but the reverse would be unthinkable. Similarly, a teacher may invade a student's personal space by looking over her or his shoulder as the student writes, but the student cannot do the same to the teacher.

Artifactual Messages

Artifactual messages are messages conveyed through objects or arrangements made by human hands—such as color, clothing, jewelry, and the decoration of space. Let's look at each of these briefly.

Color   There is some evidence that colors affect us physiologically. For example, respiratory movements increase with red light and decrease with blue light. Similarly, eye blinks increase in frequency when eyes are exposed to red light and decrease when exposed to blue. This seems consistent with our intuitive feelings that blue is more soothing and red more arousing. When a school changed the color of its walls from orange and white to blue, the blood pressure of the students decreased and their academic performance increased (Malandro, Barker, & Barker, 1989).

Color communication also influences perceptions and behaviors (Kanner, 1989). People's acceptance of a product, for example, can be largely determined by its packaging, especially its color. In one study participants described the very same coffee taken from a yellow can as weak, from a dark brown can as too strong, from a red can as rich, and from a blue can as mild. Even your acceptance of a person may depend on the colors the person wears. Consider, for example, the comments of one

Message Skills

Artifactual Communication: Use artifacts (for example, color, clothing, body adornment, space decoration) to communicate desired messages.

color expert (Kanner, 1989): "If you have to pick the wardrobe for your defense lawyer heading into court and choose anything but blue, you deserve to lose the case. . . ." Black is so powerful it could work against the lawyer with the jury. Brown lacks sufficient authority. Green would probably elicit a negative response.

Clothing and Body Adornment

People make inferences about who you are, at least in part, from the way you dress. Whether accurate or not, these inferences will affect what people think of you and how they react to you. Your socioeconomic class, your seriousness, your attitudes (for example, whether you're conservative or liberal), your concern for convention, your sense of style, and perhaps even your creativity will all be judged in part by the way you dress (Molloy, 1977; Burgoon, Buller, & Woodall, 1995; Knapp & Hall, 1996). Similarly, college students tend to perceive an instructor dressed informally as friendly, fair, enthusiastic, and flexible and the same instructor dressed formally as prepared, knowledgeable, and organized (Malandro, Barker, & Barker, 1989).

Body adornment also communicates about aspects of who you are—from a concern about being up to date, to a desire to shock, to perhaps a lack of interest in appearances. Your jewelry, too, sends messages about you. Some jewelry is a form of **cultural display,** indicating a particular cultural or religious affiliation. Wedding and engagement rings are obvious examples that communicate specific messages. College rings and political buttons likewise convey messages. If you wear a Rolex watch or large precious stones, others are likely to infer that you're rich. Men who wear earrings will be judged differently from men who don't. What judgments people make will depend, of course, on who the receiver is, on the communication context, and on all the other factors identified throughout this text.

Body piercings have become increasingly popular, especially among the young. Nose and nipple rings and tongue and belly-button jewelry send a variety of messages. Although people wearing such jewelry may wish to communicate different meanings, those interpreting the messages of body piercings seem to infer that the wearers are communicating an unwillingness to conform to social norms and a willingness to take greater risks than those without such piercings (Forbes, 2001). It's worth noting that in a study of employers' perceptions, employers rated and ranked applicants with eyebrow piercings significantly lower than those without such piercings (Acor, 2001).

Tattoos—whether temporary or permanent—likewise communicate a variety of messages, often the name of a loved one or some symbol of allegiance or affiliation. Tattoos also communicate to the wearers themselves. For example, tattooed students see themselves (and perhaps others do as well) as more adventurous, creative, individualistic, and risk prone than those without tattoos (Drews, Allison, & Probst, 2000).

SKILLS VIEWPOINT

One of your colleagues and friends has been passed over for promotion several times. You think you know the reason—namely, that your friend dresses totally inappropriately in light of company standards. You feel an obligation to help your friend by speaking candidly. What do you say?

Space Decoration

The way you decorate your private spaces speaks about you. The office with a mahogany desk and bookcases and oriental rugs communicates your importance and status within the organization, just as a metal desk and bare floor indicate a worker much farther down in the hierarchy.

Similarly, people will make inferences about you based on the way you decorate your home. The expensiveness of the furnishings may communicate your status and wealth; their coordination, your sense of style. The magazines you choose may reflect your interests, and the arrangement of chairs around a television set may reveal how important watching television is to you. The contents of bookcases lining the walls reveal the importance of reading in your life. In fact, there is probably little in your home that would not send messages from which others would draw inferences about you. Computers, wide-screen televisions, well-equipped kitchens, and oil paintings of great grandparents, for example, all say something about the people who live in the home.

Similarly, the absence of certain items will communicate something about you. Consider what messages you would get from a home where no television, phone, or books could be seen.

Touch Messages

Touch communication, or **tactile communication,** is perhaps the most primitive form of communication (Montagu, 1971). Touch develops before the other senses; even in the womb the child is stimulated by touch. Soon after birth the child is fondled, caressed, patted, and stroked. In turn, the child explores its world through touch and quickly learns to communicate a variety of meanings through touch.

The Meanings of Touch   Researchers in the field of **haptics**—the study of touch—have identified the major meanings of touch (Jones & Yarbrough, 1985):

- *Positive emotion.* Touch may communicate such positive feelings as support, appreciation, inclusion, sexual interest or intent, or affection.
- *Playfulness.* Touch often communicates our intention to play, either affectionately or aggressively.
- *Control.* Touch may direct the behaviors, attitudes, or feelings of the other person. To get attention, for example, you may touch a person as if to say, "Look at me" or "Look over here."
- *Ritual.* Ritualistic touching centers on greetings and departures; for example, shaking hands to say hello or goodbye or hugging, kissing, or putting your arm around another's shoulder when greeting or saying farewell.
- *Task-relatedness.* Task-related touching occurs while you're performing some function, such as removing a speck of dust from another person's face or helping someone out of a car.

Do recognize that different cultures will view these types of touching differently. For example, some task-related touching, viewed as acceptable in much of the United States, would be viewed negatively in some cultures. Among Koreans, for example, it's considered disrespectful for a storekeeper to touch a customer in, say, handing back change; it's considered too intimate a gesture. But members of other cultures, expecting some touching, may consider the Koreans' behavior cold and insulting.

Touch Avoidance   Much as we touch and are touched, we also avoid touch from certain people and in certain circumstances. Researchers in nonverbal communication have found some interesting relationships between **touch avoidance** and other significant communication variables (Andersen & Leibowitz, 1978; Hall, 1996). Among research findings, for example, is the fact that touch avoidance is positively related to communication apprehension; those who fear oral communication also score high on touch avoidance. Touch avoidance is also high with those who self-disclose little. Both touch and self-disclosure are intimate forms of communication; thus, people who are reluctant to get close to another person by self-disclosing also seem reluctant to get close by touching.

Older people have higher touch-avoidance scores for opposite-sex persons than do younger people. As we get older we're touched less by members of the opposite sex, and this decreased frequency may lead us to avoid touching.

Males score higher on same-sex touch avoidance than do females, a finding that confirms popular stereotypes. Men avoid touching other men, but women may and do touch other women. On the other hand, women have higher touch-avoidance scores for opposite-sex touching than do men.

> "There is a very simple rule about touching," the manager continued. "*When you touch, don't take.* Touch the people you manage only when you are *giving* them something—reassurance, support, encouragement, whatever."
>
> —Kenneth Blanchard and Spencer Johnson

Message Skills
Touch and Touch Avoidance: Respect the touch-avoidance tendencies of others; pay special attention to cultural and gender differences in touch preferences.

Paralanguage Messages

The term **paralanguage** refers to the vocal but nonverbal dimensions of speech. It refers to how you say something, not what you say. A traditional exercise students use to increase their ability to express different emotions, feelings, and attitudes is to repeat a sentence while accenting or stressing different words. One popular sentence is "Is this the face that launched a thousand ships?" Examine your own sensitivity to paralanguage variations by seeing if you get different meanings for each of the following questions based on where the emphasis is.

- Is *this the face that launched a thousand ships?*
- *Is* this *the face that launched a thousand ships?*
- *Is this the* face *that launched a thousand ships?*
- *Is this the face that* launched *a thousand ships?*
- *Is this the face that launched* a thousand ships?

In addition to stress and **pitch** (highness or lowness), paralanguage includes such **voice qualities** or vocal characteristics as **rate** (speed), **volume** (loudness), and rhythm as well as the vocalizations you make in crying, whispering, moaning, belching, yawning, and yelling (Trager, 1958, 1961; Argyle, 1988). A variation in any of these features communicates. When you speak quickly, for example, you communicate something different from when you speak slowly. Even though the words may be the same, if the speed (or volume, rhythm, or pitch) differs, the meanings people receive will also differ.

Judgments about People   We often use paralanguage cues as a basis for judgments about people; for example, evaluations of their emotional state or even their personality. A listener can accurately judge the emotional state of a speaker from vocal expression alone, if both speaker and listener speak the same language. Paralanguage cues are not so accurate when used to communicate emotions to those who speak a different language (Albas, McCluskey, & Albas, 1976). In studies in this field, speakers recite the alphabet or numbers while expressing emotions. Some emotions are easier to identify than others; it's easy to distinguish between hate and sympathy but more difficult to distinguish between fear and anxiety. And, of course, listeners vary in their ability to decode, and speakers in their ability to encode emotions (Scherer, 1986).

Less reliable are judgments made about personality. Some people, for example, may conclude that those who speak softly feel inferior, believing that no one wants to listen and nothing they say is significant, or that people who speak loudly have overinflated egos and think everyone in the world wants to hear them. Such conclusions may be mistaken, however. There are lots of reasons why people might speak softly or loudly.

Judgments about Communication Effectiveness   The rate or speed at which people speak is the aspect of paralanguage that has received the most attention (MacLachlan, 1979). Rates of speech are of interest to the advertiser, the politician, and, in fact, anyone who tries to convey information or influence others. They are especially important when time is limited or expensive.

In one-way communication (when one person is doing all or most of the speaking and the other person is doing all or most of the listening), those who talk fast (about 50 percent faster than normal) are more persuasive. People agree more with a fast speaker than with a slow speaker and find the fast speaker more intelligent and objective.

When we look at comprehension, rapid speech shows an interesting effect. When the speaking rate is increased by 50 percent, the comprehension level drops

Message Skills

Paralanguage: Vary paralinguistic features to communicate nuances of meaning and to add interest and color to your messages.

Praising and Criticizing

To consider how nonverbal messages can communicate praise and criticism, read aloud each of the following statements, first to communicate praise and second to express criticism. In the second and third columns, record the nonverbal signals you used to help you communicate praise and criticism. What cues are most often used to signal praise? To signal criticism?

Message	Nonverbal cues to communicate praise	Nonverbal cues to communicate criticism
1. You lost weight		
2. You look younger than that		
3. You're an expert		

Interpersonal messages are a combination of verbal and nonverbal signals; even subtle variations in, say, eye movements or intonation can drastically change the meaning communicated.

only by 5 percent. When the rate is doubled, the comprehension level drops only 10 percent. These 5 and 10 percent losses are more than offset by the increased speed; thus, the faster rates are much more efficient in communicating information. If speeds are more than twice the rate of normal speech, however, comprehension begins to fall dramatically.

Do exercise caution in applying this research to all forms of communication (MacLachlan, 1979). For example, if you increase your rate to increase efficiency, you may create an impression so unnatural that others will focus on your speed instead of your meaning.

Silence Messages

Like words and gestures, **silence,** too, communicates important meanings and serves important functions (Johannesen, 1974; Jaworski, 1993). Silence allows the speaker *time to think,* time to formulate and organize his or her verbal communications. Before messages of intense conflict, as well as before those confessing undying love, there is often silence. Again, silence seems to prepare the receiver for the importance of these messages.

Some people use silence as a *weapon* to hurt others. We often speak of giving someone "the silent treatment." After a conflict, for example, one or both individuals may remain silent as a kind of punishment. Silence used to hurt others may also take the form of refusal to acknowledge the presence of another person, as in disconfirmation (see Chapter 5); here silence is a dramatic demonstration of the total indifference one person feels toward the other.

Sometimes silence is used as a *response to personal anxiety,* shyness, or threats. You may feel anxious or shy among new people and prefer to remain silent. By remaining silent you preclude the chance of rejection. Only when you break your silence and make an attempt to communicate with another person do you risk rejection.

Silence may be used *to prevent communication* of certain messages. In conflict situations silence is sometimes used to prevent certain topics from surfacing and to prevent one or both parties from saying things they may later regret. In such situations silence often allows us time to cool off before expressing hatred, severe criticism, or personal attacks—which, as we know, are irreversible.

Like the eyes, face, or hands, silence can also be used *to communicate emotional responses* (Ehrenhaus, 1988). Sometimes silence communicates a determination to

> ❝ Speaking is silver, silence is gold. ❞
>
> —German proverb

Ethical messages

Interpersonal Silence

In the U.S. legal system, you have the right to remain silent and to refuse to reveal information about yourself that could be used against you or used to incriminate you. But in general you don't have the right to refuse to reveal information about, for example, the criminal activities of others that you may have witnessed. Rightly or wrongly (and this itself is an ethical issue), psychiatrists, clergy, and lawyers are often exempt from this general rule. Similarly, a wife can't be forced to testify against her husband or a husband against his wife.

In interpersonal situations, however, there are no such written rules; so it is not always clear if or when silence is ethical or unethical. For example, most people (though not all) would agree that you have the right to withhold information that has no bearing on the matter at hand. Thus, in most job-related situations your previous relationship history, affectional orientation, or religion is usually irrelevant to your ability to function and may be kept private. In situations in which these issues become relevant—say, when you're about to enter a new relationship—then there may be an obligation not to remain silent and to reveal certain information about yourself.

What Would You Do?

While at the supermarket, you witness a mother verbally abusing her three-year-old child. You worry that the mother might psychologically harm the child, and your first impulse is to speak up and tell this woman that verbal abuse can have lasting effects on the child and often leads to physical abuse. At the same time, you don't want to interfere with a mother's right to say what she wants to her child. What is your ethical obligation in this case? What would you do in this situation?

Message Skills

Silence: Examine silence for meanings just as you would eye movements or body gestures.

be uncooperative or defiant; by refusing to engage in verbal communication, you defy the authority or the legitimacy of the other person's position. Silence is often used to communicate annoyance, particularly when accompanied by a pouting expression, arms crossed in front of the chest, and nostrils flared. Silence may express affection or love, especially when coupled with long and longing gazes into each other's eyes.

Silence may also be used strategically, *to achieve specific effects.* You may, for example, strategically position a pause before what you feel is an important comment to make your idea stand out. A prolonged silence after someone voices disagreement may give the appearance of control and superiority. It's a way of saying, "I can respond in my own time." Generally research finds that people use silence strategically more with strangers than they do with close friends (Hesegawa & Gudykunst, 1998).

Of course, you may also use silence when you simply have *nothing* to say—when nothing occurs to you, or when you do not want to say anything. James Russell Lowell expressed this best: "Blessed are they who have nothing to say, and who cannot be persuaded to say it." Silence may also be used to avoid responsibility for wrongdoing (Beach, 1990–1991).

Time Messages

The study of **temporal communication,** known technically as **chronemics,** concerns the use of time—how you organize it, react to it, and communicate messages through it (Bruneau, 1985, 1990). Consider, for example, **psychological time:** the emphasis you place on the past, present, or future. In a past orientation, you have special reverence for the past. You relive old times and regard the old methods as the best. You see events as circular and recurring, so the wisdom of yesterday is applicable also to today and tomorrow. In a present orientation, however, you live in the present: for now, not tomorrow. In a future orientation, you look toward and live for the future. You save today, work hard in college, and deny yourself luxuries because you're preparing for the future. Before reading more about time, take the following self-test.

> **❝** Gather ye rose-buds while ye may. Old Time is still aflying, And this same flower that smiles today, Tomorrow will be dying. **❞**
>
> —Robert Herrick

What Time Do You Have?

INSTRUCTIONS: For each statement, indicate whether the statement is true (T) or untrue (F) of your general attitude and behavior.

_____ ❶ Meeting tomorrow's deadlines and doing other necessary work comes before tonight's partying.

_____ ❷ I meet my obligations to friends and authorities on time.

_____ ❸ I complete projects on time by making steady progress.

_____ ❹ I am able to resist temptations when I know there is work to be done.

_____ ❺ I keep working at a difficult, uninteresting task if it will help me get ahead.

_____ ❻ If things don't get done on time, I don't worry about it.

_____ ❼ I think that it's useless to plan too far ahead because things hardly ever come out the way you planned anyway.

_____ ❽ I try to live one day at a time.

_____ ❾ I live to make better what is rather than to be concerned about what will be.

_____ ❿ It seems to me that it doesn't make sense to worry about the future, since fate determines that whatever will be, will be.

_____ ⓫ I believe that getting together with friends to party is one of life's important pleasures.

_____ ⓬ I do things impulsively, making decisions on the spur of the moment.

_____ ⓭ I take risks to put excitement in my life.

_____ ⓮ I get drunk at parties.

_____ ⓯ It's fun to gamble.

_____ ⓰ Thinking about the future is pleasant to me.

_____ ⓱ When I want to achieve something, I set subgoals and consider specific means for reaching those goals.

_____ ⓲ It seems to me that my career path is pretty well laid out.

_____ ⓳ It upsets me to be late for appointments.

_____ ⓴ I meet my obligations to friends and authorities on time.

_____ ㉑ I get irritated at people who keep me waiting when we've agreed to meet at a given time.

_____ ㉒ It makes sense to invest a substantial part of my income in insurance premiums.

_____ ㉓ I believe that "A stitch in time saves nine."

_____ ㉔ I believe that "A bird in the hand is worth two in the bush."

_____ ㉕ I believe it is important to save for a rainy day.

_____ ㉖ I believe a person's day should be planned each morning.

_____ ㉗ I make lists of things I must do.

_____ ㉘ When I want to achieve something, I set subgoals and consider specific means for reaching those goals.

_____ ㉙ I believe that "A stitch in time saves nine."

HOW DID YOU DO? This time test measures seven different factors. If you selected true (T) for all or most of the questions within any given factor, you're high on that factor. If you selected untrue (F) for all or most of the questions within any given factor, you're low on that factor.

The first factor, measured by questions 1–5, is a future, work motivation, perseverance orientation. These people have a strong work ethic and are committed to completing a task despite difficulties. The second factor (questions 6–10) is a present, fatalistic, worry-free orientation. High scorers on this factor live one day at a time, not necessarily to enjoy the day but to avoid planning for the next day.

The third factor (questions 11–15) is a present, pleasure-seeking, partying orientation. These people enjoy the present, take risks, and engage in a variety of impulsive actions. The fourth factor (questions 16–18) is a future, goal-seeking, and planning orientation. These people derive pleasure from planning and achieving a variety of goals.

The fifth factor (questions 19–21) is a time-sensitivity orientation. People who score high are especially sensitive to time and its role in social obligations. The sixth factor (questions 22–25) is a future, practical action orientation. These people do what they have to do—take practical actions—to achieve the future they want.

The seventh factor (questions 26–29) is a future, somewhat obsessive daily planning orientation. High scorers make daily "to do" lists and devote great attention to detail.

WHAT WILL YOU DO? Now that you have some idea of how you treat time, consider how these attitudes and behaviors work for you. For example, will your time orientations help you achieve your social and professional goals? If not, what might you do about changing these attitudes and behaviors?

Source: From "Time in Perspective" by Alexander Gonzalez and Philip G. Zimbardo. Reprinted with permission from *Psychology Today* magazine. Copyright © 1985 Sussex Publishers, Inc.

> **"** Those who live to the future must always appear selfish to those who live to the present. **"**
>
> —Ralph Waldo Emerson

The time orientation you develop depends to a great extent on your socioeconomic class and your personal experiences. Gonzalez and Zimbardo (1985), who developed the scale in the time self-test and on whose research the scoring is based, observe: "A child with parents in unskilled and semiskilled occupations is usually socialized in a way that promotes a present-oriented fatalism and hedonism. A child of parents who are managers, teachers, or other professionals learns future-oriented values and strategies designed to promote achievement." In the United States, not surprisingly, future income is positively related to future orientation; the more future oriented you are, the greater your income is likely to be.

Different time perspectives also account for much intercultural misunderstanding, as different cultures often teach their members drastically different time orientations. For example, people from some Latin cultures would rather be late for an appointment than end a conversation abruptly or before it has come to a natural end. So the Latin may see lateness as a result of politeness. But others may see this as impolite to the person with whom he or she had the appointment (Hall & Hall, 1987).

Similarly, the future-oriented person who works for tomorrow's goals will frequently see the present-oriented person as lazy and poorly motivated for enjoying today and not planning for tomorrow. In turn, the present-oriented person may see those with strong future orientations as obsessed with amassing wealth or rising in status.

Message Skills

Time Cues: Be alert for time cues on the part of the person with whom you're interacting. Be especially sensitive to the person's leave-taking cues—remarks such as "It's getting late" or glances at his or her watch.

Smell Messages

Smell communication, or **olfactory communication,** is extremely important in a wide variety of situations and is now big business (Kleinfeld, 1992). There is some evidence (though clearly not very conclusive evidence) that the smell of lemon contributes to a perception of health; the smells of lavender and eucalyptus seem to increase alertness; and the smell of rose oil seems to reduce blood pressure. The smell of chocolate seems to reduce theta brain waves and thus produces a sense of relaxation and a reduced level of attention (Martin, 1998). Findings such as these have contributed to the growth of aromatherapy and to a new profession of aromatherapists (Furlow, 1996). Because humans possess "denser skin concentrations of scent glands than almost any other mammal," it has been argued that it only remains for us to discover how we use scent to communicate a wide variety of messages (Furlow, 1996, p. 41). Here are some of the most important messages scent seems to communicate.

> For the sense of smell, almost more than any other, has the power to recall memories and it is a pity that you use it so little.
> —Rachel Carson

- *Attraction messages.* Humans use perfumes, colognes, aftershave lotions, powders, and the like to enhance their attractiveness to others and to themselves. After all, you also smell yourself. When the smells are pleasant, you feel better about yourself. Women, research finds, prefer the scent of men who bear a close genetic similarity to themselves—a finding that may account, in part, for humans' attraction to people much like themselves (Ober, Weitkamp, Cox, Dytch, Kostyu, & Elias, 1997; Wade, 2002).

- *Taste messages.* Without smell, taste would be severely impaired. For example, without smell it would be extremely difficult to taste the difference between a raw potato and an apple. Street vendors selling hot dogs, sausages, and similar foods are aided greatly by the smells, which stimulate the appetites of passersby.

- *Memory messages.* Smell is a powerful memory aid; you often recall situations from months and even years ago when you happen upon a similar smell.

- *Identification messages.* Smell is often used to create an image or an identity for a product. Advertisers and manufacturers spend millions of dollars each year creating scents for cleaning products and tooth pastes, for example. These scents have nothing to do with the products' cleaning power; instead, they function solely to help create an image. There is also evidence that we can identify specific significant others by smell. In one study, for example, young children were able to identify the T-shirts of their brothers and sisters solely on the basis of smell (Porter & Moore, 1981). And one researcher goes so far as to advise: "If your man's odor reminds you of Dad or your brother, you may want genetic tests before trying to conceive a child" (Furlow, 1996, p. 41).

Skills toolbox

6 Ways to Communicate Power without Words

Your nonverbal communication greatly influences people's perceptions of your interpersonal power. Here are some suggestions for communicating your power nonverbally (Lewis, 1989; Burgoon, Buller, & Woodall, 1996; Guerrero, DeVito, & Hecht, 1999).

1. Other things being equal, dress relatively conservatively if you want to influence others; conservative clothing is associated with power and status.
2. Use facial expressions and gestures as appropriate to help you express your concern for and interest in the other person and the interaction.
3. When you break eye contact, direct your gaze downward; otherwise you'll signal a lack of interest in the other person.
4. Use consistent packaging; that is, be especially careful that your verbal and nonverbal messages reinforce rather than contradict each other.
5. To communicate dominance with your handshake, exert more pressure and hold the grip a bit longer than usual.
6. Walk slowly and deliberately. To appear hurried is to appear to be without power, as if you were rushing to meet the expectations of those who had power over you.

Applying Interpersonal Skills/Then and Now
Have you ever been in a situation in which you wanted to communicate power but for some reason failed to do so? Why do you think you failed? What might you do differently now?

You're mentoring a group of six interns from a variety of cultures who hope to be offered permanent jobs when their internship is over. One problem is that these interns are decorating their office spaces with items that seem wildly inappropriate and that communicate all the wrong messages. You need to help the interns tell the difference between artifacts that communicate the right impression and those that don't. What do you say?

> **Culture is communication, and communication is culture.**
>
> —Edward T. Hall

Culture and Nonverbal Messages

Not surprisingly, nonverbal communication is heavily influenced by culture. Consider a variety of differences.

Although Americans consider direct eye contact an expression of honesty and forthrightness, the Japanese often view this as a lack of respect. The Japanese will glance at the other person's face rarely and then only for very short periods (Axtell, 1990). Among some Latin Americans and American Indians, direct eye contact between, say, a teacher and a student is considered inappropriate, perhaps aggressive; appropriate student behavior is to avoid eye contact with the teacher. Table 6.3 presents a variety of other nonverbal signals, identified by Axtell (1993), that can get you into trouble if used in certain cultures.

TABLE 6.3	A Few Nonverbal Behaviors That Can Get You into Trouble

Can you identify other behaviors that can create cultural problems?

COMMUNICATION BEHAVIOR	MAY BE CONSIDERED
Blinking your eyes	impolite in Taiwan
Folding your arms over your chest	disrespectful in Fiji
Waving your hand	insulting in Nigeria and Greece
Gesturing with the thumb up	rude in Australia
Tapping your two index fingers together	an invitation to sleep together in Egypt
Pointing with the index finger	impolite in many Middle Eastern countries
Bowing to a lesser degree than your host	a statement of superiority in Japan
With a clenched fist, inserting your thumb between your index and middle finger	obscene in some southern European countries
Pointing at someone with your index and third fingers	a wish that evil fall on the person in some African countries
Resting your feet on a table or chair	insulting in some Middle Eastern countries

In the United States living next door to someone means that you're expected to be friendly and to interact with that person. This cultural expectation seems so natural that Americans and members of many other cultures probably don't even consider that it is not shared by all cultures. In Japan, the fact that your house is next to another's does not imply that you should become close or visit each other. Consider, therefore, the situation in which a Japanese person buys a house next to an American. The Japanese may see the American as overly familiar and as taking friendship for granted. The American may see the Japanese as distant, unfriendly, and unneighborly. Yet each person is merely fulfilling the expectations of his or her own culture (Hall & Hall, 1987).

Different cultures also assign different meanings to colors. Some of these cultural meanings are listed in Table 6.4—but before looking at the table, think about the meanings your own culture gives to such colors as red, green, black, white, blue, yellow, and purple.

Another aspect of artifactual communication that varies greatly from one culture to another is the meaning that gifts have. In some cultures a set of knives for the kitchen would be an appropriate house gift; in other cultures (for example, Chinese) it would be considered inappropriate and offensive.

Touching, too, varies greatly across cultures. For example, African Americans touch one another more than do whites. Among U.S. schoolchildren touching declines from kindergarten to the sixth grade for white but not for African American children (Burgoon, Buller, & Woodall, 1996). Similarly, Japanese touch one another much less than do Anglo-Saxons, who in turn touch one another much less than do southern Europeans (Morris, 1977; Burgoon, Buller, & Woodall, 1996).

Not surprisingly, the role of silence varies in different cultures (Basso, 1972). Among the Apache, for example, mutual friends do not feel the need to introduce strangers who may be working in the same area or on the same project. The strangers may remain silent

? SKILLS VIEWPOINT

What nonverbal cues should you look for in judging whether someone likes you? List the cues in the order of their importance, using 1 for the cue that is of most value in making your judgment, 2 for the cue that is next most valuable, and so on down to perhaps 10 or 12. Do you really need two lists? One for judging a woman's liking and one for a man's?

TABLE 6.4	Some Cultural Meanings of Color

This table, constructed from research reported by Henry Dreyfuss (1971), Nancy Hoft (1995), and Norine Dresser (1996), illustrates only some of the different meanings that colors may communicate in different cultures. As you read this table, consider the meanings you give to these colors and where your meanings came from.

COLOR	CULTURAL MEANINGS AND COMMENTS
Red	In China red signifies prosperity and rebirth and is used for festive and joyous occasions; in France and the United Kingdom, it signifies masculinity; in many African countries, blasphemy or death; and in Japan, anger and danger. Koreans, especially Korean Buddhists, use red ink only to write a person's name at the time of death or on the anniversary of the person's death.
Green	In the United States green signifies capitalism, "go ahead," and envy; in Ireland, patriotism; among some Native Americans, femininity; to the Egyptians, fertility and strength; and to the Japanese, youth and energy.
Black	In Thailand black signifies old age, in parts of Malaysia courage, and in much of Europe death.
White	In Thailand white signifies purity; in many Muslim and Hindu cultures, purity and peace; but in Japan and other Asian countries, death and mourning.
Blue	In Iran blue signifies something negative, in Egypt truth, and in Ghana joy; among the Cherokee it signifies defeat, and for Egyptians virtue and truth.
Yellow	In China yellow signifies wealth and authority, in the United States caution and cowardice, in Egypt happiness and prosperity; and in many countries throughout the world, femininity.
Purple	In Latin America purple signifies death, in Europe royalty, in Egypt virtue and faith, in Japan grace and nobility, and in China barbarism.

for several days. During this time the individuals look each other over, trying to determine if the other person is all right. Only after this period do the individuals talk. When courting, especially during the initial stages, the Apache remain silent for hours; if they do talk, they generally talk very little. Only after a couple has been dating for several months will they have lengthy conversations. These periods of silence are generally attributed to shyness or self-consciousness. But the use of silence is explicitly taught to Apache women, who are especially discouraged from engaging in long discussions with their dates. Silence during courtship is a sign of modesty to many Apache.

In Iranian culture there's an expression, *qahr*, which means not being on speaking terms with someone, giving someone the silent treatment. For example, when children disobey their parents, or are disrespectful, or fail to do their chores as they should, they are given this silent treatment. With adults *qahr* may be instituted when one person insults or injures another. After a cooling-off period, *ashti* (making up after *qahr*) may be initiated. *Qahr* last for a relatively short time when between parents and children but longer when between adults. *Qahr* is more frequently initiated between two women than between two men, but when men experience *qahr* it lasts much longer and often requires the intercession of a mediator to establish *ashti* (Behzadi, 1994).

Time is another communication channel with great cultural differences. Two types of **cultural time** are especially important in nonverbal communication: formal and informal. In U.S. culture, *formal time* is divided into seconds, minutes, hours, days, weeks, months, and years. Other cultures may use seasons or phases of the moon to delineate time periods. In some colleges courses are divided into 50- or 75-minute periods that meet two or three times a week for 14-week periods called semesters; eight semesters of 15 or 16 50-minute periods per week equal a college education. Other colleges use quarters or trimesters. As these examples illustrate, formal time units are arbitrary. The culture establishes them for convenience.

Informal time terms are more general—for example, expressions such as "forever," "immediately," "soon," "right away," "as soon as possible." Informal time creates the most communication problems, because the terms have different meanings for different people.

Another interesting distinction is that between **monochronic** and **polychronic time orientations** (Hall, 1959, 1976; Hall & Hall, 1987). Monochronic people or cultures (the United States, Germany, Scandinavia, and Switzerland are good examples) schedule one thing at a time. Time is compartmentalized; there is a time for everything, and everything has its own time. Polychronic people or cultures (Latin Americans, Mediterranean people, and Arabs are good examples), on the other hand, schedule multiple things at the same time. Eating, conducting business with several different people, and taking care of family matters may all be conducted at the same time. No culture is entirely monochronic or polychronic; rather, these are general tendencies that are found across a large part of the culture. Some cultures combine both time orientations; for example, in Japan and in parts of U.S. culture, both orientations are found. Table 6.5, based on Hall and Hall (1987), identifies some of the distinctions between these two time orientations.

General attitudes toward time vary from one culture to another. One study, for example, measured the accuracy of clocks in six cultures—Japan, Indonesia, Italy, England, Taiwan, and the United States. Japan had the most accurate clocks, Indonesia the least accurate. And a measure of the speed at which people in these six cultures walked found that the Japanese walked the fastest, the Indonesians the slowest (LeVine & Bartlett, 1984).

"Hello, I'm Nesbit. I'm three, and I'm right on track."

TABLE 6.5   Monochronic and Polychronic Time

Can you identify specific potentials for miscommunication that these differences might create when M-time and P-time people interact?

THE MONOCHRONIC PERSON	THE POLYCHRONIC PERSON
Does one thing at a time	Does several things at one time
Treats time schedules and plans very seriously; they may only be broken for the most serious of reasons	Treats time schedules and plans as useful, but not sacred; they may be broken for a variety of causes
Considers the job the most important part of life, ahead of even family	Considers the family and interpersonal relationships more important than the job
Considers privacy extremely important; seldom borrows or lends to others; works independently	Is actively involved with others; works in the presence of and with lots of people at the same time

Another interesting aspect of cultural time is your "social clock" (Neugarten, 1979). Your culture, as well as your more specific society, maintains a schedule for the right time to do a variety of important things; for example, the right time to start dating, to finish college, to buy your own home, to have a child. And you no doubt learned about this "clock" as you were growing up, as has Nesbit in the cartoon. You may well tend to evaluate your own social and professional development on the basis of this social clock. If you're on time relative to the rest of your peers—for example, if you all started dating at around the same age or you're all finishing college at around the same age—then you will feel well adjusted, competent, and a part of the group. If you're late, you will probably experience feelings of dissatisfaction. Recent research, however, shows that this social clock is becoming more flexible; people are becoming more willing to tolerate deviations from the established, socially acceptable timetable for accomplishing many of life's transitional events (Peterson, 1996).

Message Skills

Nonverbal Communication and Culture: Interpret the nonverbal cues of others with an awareness of the other person's cultural meanings (insofar as you can).

Summary of Concepts

This chapter explored nonverbal communication—communication without words—and considered such areas as body language, facial and eye messages, spatial and territorial communication, artifactual communication, touch communication, paralanguage, silence, and time communication.

1. Nonverbal messages often interact with verbal messages to accent, complement, contradict, regulate, repeat, or substitute.
2. Nonverbal researchers have focused their efforts on understanding how nonverbal messages function to form and manage impressions, form and define relationships, structure conversation and social interaction, influence or deceive, and allow for the expression of emotion.
3. The five categories of body movements are emblems (which rather directly translate words or phrases); illustrators (which accompany and literally "illustrate" verbal messages); affect displays (which communicate emotional meaning); regulators (which coordinate, monitor, maintain, or control the speaking of another individual); and adaptors (which usually are unconscious and serve some kind of need, as in scratching an itch).
4. Facial movements may communicate a variety of emotions. The most frequently studied are happiness, surprise, fear, anger, sadness, and disgust/contempt. Facial management techniques enable you to control your facial expression of emotions. The facial feedback hypothesis claims that facial display of an emotion can lead to physiological and psychological changes.
5. Eye movements may seek feedback, invite others to speak, signal the nature of a relationship, or compensate for physical distance.
6. The study of proxemics investigates the communicative functions of space and spatial relationships. Four ma-

jor proxemic distances are: (1) intimate distance, ranging from actual touching to 18 inches; (2) personal distance, ranging from 18 inches to 4 feet; (3) social distance, ranging from 4 to 12 feet; and (4) public distance, ranging from 12 to 25 or more feet.

7. Your treatment of space is influenced by such factors as status, culture, context, subject matter, sex, age, and positive or negative evaluation of the other person.

8. Territoriality involves people's possessive reactions to particular spaces or objects.

9. Artifactual communication consists of messages conveyed by objects or arrangements created by humans; for example, by the use of color, clothing, body adornment, or space decoration.

10. Touch communication, or haptics, may communicate a variety of meanings, the most important being positive affect, playfulness, control, ritual, and task-relatedness. Touch avoidance is the desire to avoid touching and being touched by others.

11. Paralanguage has to do with the vocal but nonverbal dimension of speech. It includes rate, pitch, volume, resonance, and vocal quality as well as pauses and hesitations. Based on paralanguage we make judgments about people, sense conversational turns, and assess believability.

12. Silence communicates a variety of meanings, from anger (as in the "silent treatment") to deep emotional responses.

13. Time communication, or chronemics, consists of messages communicated by our treatment of time.

14. Smell can communicate messages of attraction, taste, memory, and identification.

15. Cultural variations in nonverbal communication are great. Different cultures, for example, assign different meanings to facial expressions and colors, have different spatial rules, and treat time very differently.

Vocabulary Quiz: The Language of Nonverbal Communication

Match the terms of nonverbal communication with their definitions. Record the number of the definition next to the appropriate term.

_____ emblems

_____ affect displays

_____ proxemics

_____ territoriality

_____ haptics

_____ paralanguage

_____ chronemics

_____ artifactual communication

_____ social clock

_____ psychological time

1. Movements of the facial area that convey emotional meaning.
2. The study of how time communicates.
3. The time that a culture establishes for achieving certain milestones.
4. Nonverbal behaviors that directly translate words or phrases.
5. Communication by touch.
6. Your orientation to the past, present, or future.
7. The meanings communicated by clothing, jewelry, buttons, or the furniture in your house, for example.
8. The study of how space communicates.
9. A possessive or ownership reaction to an area of space or to particular objects.
10. The vocal but nonverbal aspects of speech; for example, rate and volume.

Four for Discussion

1. A popular defense tactic in sex crimes against women, gay men, and lesbians is to blame the victim by referring to the way the victim was dressed and to imply that the victim, by wearing certain clothing, provoked the attack. Currently, New York and Florida are the only states that prohibit defense attorneys from referring to the way a sex-crime victim was dressed at the time of the attack (*New York Times,* July 30, 1994, p. 22). What do you think of this? If you do not live in New York or Florida, have there been proposals in your state to similarly limit the use of this popular defense tactic?

2. A "Pygmalion gift" is a gift designed to change the person into what the donor wants that person to become. The parent who gives a child books or science equipment may be asking the child to be a scholar. What messages have you recently communicated in your gift-giving behavior? What messages do you think others have communicated to you by gifts they've given you?

3. On a 10-point scale, with 1 indicating "not at all important" and 10 indicating "extremely important," how important is body appearance to your own romantic interest in another person? Do the men and women you know conform to the stereotypes that say males are more concerned with the physical and females with personality?

4. As discussed in the text, research clearly shows that women are better encoders and decoders of nonverbal signals than are men. Among the reasons advanced for this are: (1) Women through the ages were subordinate and powerless and so needed to become more competent in nonverbal communication; (2) women are socialized to be more accommodating and need nonverbal information to accomplish this; and (3) biological differences cause women to be more expressive and men to hold back emotional expression (Burgoon & Hoobler, 2002). Why do you think research finds that women are better than men at nonverbal communication?

Web Explorations

 Explore our text website at **www.ablongman.com/devito** to find:

Exercises and Self-Tests

Exercises to help explain further the dynamics of nonverbal communication include (1) Facial Expressions, (2) Eye Contact, (3) Interpersonal Interactions and Space, (4) The Meanings of Color, (5) Artifacts and Culture: The Case of Gifts, and (6) Who? A self-test on touch avoidance will help you analyze your own touch tendencies: (7) Do You Avoid Touch?

Another aspect of psychological time is biorhythms. Biorhythms theory proposes that our bodies operate on physical, intellectual, and emotional cycles, each of which has its own distinctive time patterns. An interesting website that enables you to figure out your own biorhythms may be found at **www.kfu.com/~nsayer/compat.html**.

Writing Resources and Assignments

Suggestions are available for writing papers of personal experience (for example, your own territorial behavior), concept or principle explanation (for example, body adornment), review (for example, what we know about the effects of aromatherapy), or research on various aspects of nonverbal communication (for example, clothing and impression formation).

 Explore our research resources at **www.researchnavigator.com** and

Read an article.

Read a popular or scholarly article on one of the channels of nonverbal communication discussed in this chapter (for example, body, face, eyes, space, artifacts, touch, paralanguage, silence, or time). On the basis of this article, what can you add to the discussion presented here?

Investigate key terms.

Investigate one of the key terms discussed in this chapter (for example, body movements, facial management, facial feedback, eye contact, touch, paralanguage, silence, space, distance, territoriality, artifactual communication, time communication, social clock). What additional insights can you provide?

Find answers.

Try finding answers to one of the following questions, or design a research study to answer it.

1. How do men and women in different cultures express romantic interest?
2. Are concepts of body attractiveness universal across all cultures?
3. How are status and touching related?
4. In what ways do children born blind express themselves nonverbally?

Emotional Messages

7

Principles of Emotions and Emotional Communication

Obstacles to Communicating Emotions

Guidelines for Communicating Emotions

> A young wife leaves her house one morning to draw water from the local well; her husband watches from the porch. As she walks back from the well, a stranger stops her and asks for some water. She gives him a cupful, then invites him home to dinner. He accepts. The husband, wife, and guest have a pleasant meal together. The husband, in a gesture of hospitality, invites the guest to spend the night—with his wife. The guest accepts. In the morning the husband leaves early to bring home breakfast. When he returns, he finds his wife again in bed with the visitor.
>
> The question is: At what point in this story does the husband feel angry?
>
> The answer is: It depends on the culture to which you belong (Hupka, 1981). In the United States, a husband would feel rather angry at a wife who slept with a stranger; and a wife would feel rather angry at being offered to a guest as if she were a lamb chop. But these reactions are not universal.
>
> - A Pawnee Indian husband of the nineteenth century would have been enraged at any man who dared ask his wife for water.
> - An Ammassalik Eskimo husband finds it perfectly honorable to offer his wife to a stranger, but only once. He would be angry to find his wife and the guest having a second encounter.
> - A Toda husband at the turn of the century in India would not have been angry at all. The Todas allowed both husband and wife to take lovers, and women were even allowed to have several husbands. Both spouses might feel angry, though, if one of them had a *sneaky* affair without announcing it publicly.

This report by Carole Wade and Carol Tavris (1998) illustrates that the emotions you feel depend, in part at least, on your culture. In this chapter we'll look at the nature of emotions and the key principles of emotional expression. We'll consider the major obstacles to communicating emotions, and we'll examine ways to communicate emotions more effectively.

Principles of Emotions and Emotional Communication

Communicating emotions is both difficult and important. It's difficult because your thinking often gets confused when you're intensely emotional. It's also difficult because you probably weren't taught how to communicate emotions—and you probably have few effective models to imitate. Communicating emotions is also most important. Feelings constitute a great part of your meanings. If you leave your feelings out, or if you communicate them inadequately, you will fail to communicate a great part of your meaning. Consider what your communications would be like if you left out your feelings when talking about failing a recent test, winning the lottery, becoming a parent, getting engaged, driving a car for the first time, becoming a citizen, or being promoted to supervisor. Emotional expression is so much a part of communication that even in the cryptic e-mail message style, emoticons are becoming more popular. (Two excellent websites contain extensive examples of smileys, emoticons, acronyms, and shorthand abbreviations: www.netlingo.com/smiley.cfm and www.netlingo.com/emailsh.cfm.) Let's look at several general principles of emotions and emotional expression.

Emotions Are Influenced by Body, Mind, and Culture

Emotion involves at least three parts: bodily reactions (such as blushing when you're embarrassed); mental evaluations and interpretations (as in calculating the odds of

> " Emotion is not something shameful, subordinate, second-rate; it is a supremely valid phase of humanity at its noblest and most mature. "
>
> —Joshua Loth Liebman

drawing an inside straight at poker); and cultural rules and beliefs (such as the pride parents feel when their child graduates from college).

Bodily reactions are the most obvious aspect of our emotional experience, because we can observe them easily. Such reactions span a wide range. They include, for example, the blush of embarrassment, the sweating palms that accompany nervousness, and the self-touching that goes with discomfort. When you judge people's emotions, you probably look to these nonverbal behaviors. You conclude that Ramon is happy to see you because of his smile and his open body posture. You conclude that Lisa is nervous from her damp hands, vocal hesitations, and awkward movements.

The mental or cognitive part of emotional experience involves the evaluations and interpretations you make on the basis of your behaviors. For example, leading psychotherapist Albert Ellis (1988; Ellis & Harper, 1975), whose insights are used throughout this chapter, claims that your evaluations of what happens have a greater influence on your feelings than what actually happens. Let us say, for example, that your best friend, Sally, ignores you in the college cafeteria. The emotions you feel will depend on what you think this behavior means. You may feel pity if you figure that Sally is depressed because her father died. You may feel anger if you believe that Sally is simply rude and insensitive and snubbed you on purpose. Or you may feel sadness if you believe that Sally is no longer interested in being friends with you.

The culture you were raised in and live in gives you a framework for both expressing feelings and interpreting the emotions of others. A colleague of mine gave a lecture in Beijing, China, to a group of Chinese college students. The students listened politely but made no comments and asked no questions after her lecture. At first my colleague concluded that the students were bored and uninterested. Later, she learned that Chinese students show respect by being quiet and seemingly passive. They think that asking questions would imply that she was not clear in her lecture. In other words, the culture—whether American or Chinese—influenced the interpretation of the students' feelings.

Emotions May Be Primary or Blends

How would you feel in each of the following situations?

- *You won the lottery!*
- *You got the job you applied for.*
- *Your best friend just died.*
- *Your parents tell you they're getting divorced.*

You would obviously feel very differently in each of these situations. In fact, each feeling is unique and unrepeatable. Yet amid all these differences, there are some similarities. For example, most people would claim that the feelings in the first two examples are more similar to each other than they are to the last two. Similarly, the last two are more similar to each other than they are to the first two.

To capture the similarities among emotions, many researchers have tried to identify basic or primary emotions. Robert Plutchik (1980; Havlena, Holbrook, & Lehmann, 1989) developed a most helpful model. In this model there are eight basic emotions (Figure 7.1): joy, acceptance, fear, surprise, sadness, disgust, anger, and anticipation. Emotions that are close to each other on this wheel are also close to each other in meaning. For example, joy and anticipation are more closely related than are joy and sadness or acceptance and disgust. Emotions that are opposite each other on the wheel are also opposite each other in their meaning. For example, joy is the opposite of sadness; anger is the opposite of fear.

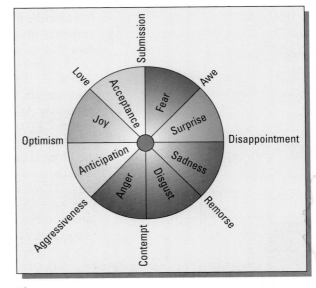

Figure 7.1

A Model of the Emotions

Do you agree with the basic assumptions of this model? For example, do you see love as a combination of joy and acceptance, and optimism as a combination of joy and anticipation?

From Robert Plutchik, *Emotion: A Psychoevolutionary Synthesis*, © 1980. Published by HarperCollins. Copyright © 2000 by Pearson Education. Reprinted by permission of Allyn & Bacon, Boston, MA.

Figure 7.2

Three Views of Emotion
How would you describe emotional
arousal?

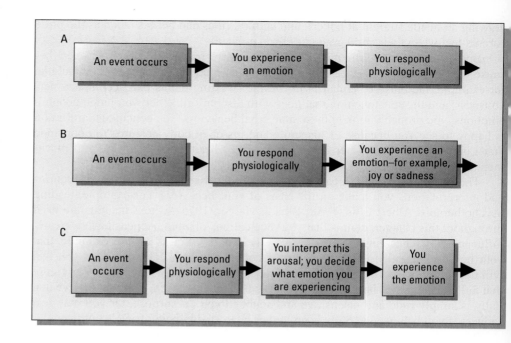

In this model there are also blends. These are emotions that are combinations of the primary emotions. These are noted outside the emotion wheel. For example, according to this model, love is a blend of joy and acceptance. Remorse is a blend of disgust and sadness.

Emotional Arousal Is a Multistep Process

If you were to describe the events leading up to emotional arousal, you would probably describe three stages: (1) An event occurs. (2) You experience an emotion such as surprise, joy, or anger. (3) You respond physiologically; your heart beats faster, your face flushes, and so on. Figure 7.2 (A) depicts this commonsense view of emotions.

Psychologist William James and physiologist Carl Lange offered a different explanation. Their theory places the physiological arousal before the experience of the emotion. The James–Lange sequence is: (1) An event occurs. (2) You respond physiologically. And (3) you experience an emotion; for example, you feel joy or sadness. Figure 7.2 (B) depicts the James–Lange view of emotions.

According to a third explanation, the **cognitive labeling theory,** you interpret the physiological arousal and, on the basis of this, experience the emotions of joy, sadness, or whatever (Schachter, 1971). The sequence goes like this: (1) An event occurs. (2) You respond physiologically. (3) You interpret this arousal—that is, you decide what emotion you're experiencing. And (4) you experience the emotion. Your interpretation of your arousal will depend on the situation you're in. For example, if you experience an increased pulse rate after someone you've been admiring smiles at you, you may interpret this as joy. If three suspicious-looking strangers approach you on a dark street, however, you may interpret that same increased heartbeat as fear. It's only after you make the interpretation that you experience the emotion; for example, the joy or the fear. Figure 7.2 (C) diagrams this sequence of events.

Emotions Are Communicated Verbally and Nonverbally

Although emotions are especially salient in conflict situations and in relationship development and dissolution, they are actually a part of all messages. Emotions are always present—sometimes to a very strong extent, though sometimes only mildly. Therefore, they must be recognized as a part of the communication experience. This

“ When dealing with people, remember you are not dealing with creatures of logic, but with creatures of emotion, creatures bristling with prejudice, and motivated by pride and vanity. ”

—Dale Carnegie

is not to say that emotions should always be talked about or that all emotions you feel should be expressed. Emotional feeling and **emotional communication** are two different things. In some instances you may want to say exactly what you feel, to reveal your emotions without any censorship. At other times, however, you may want to avoid revealing your emotions. For example, you might not want to reveal your frustration over a customer's indecision, or you might not want to share with your children your worries about finding a job.

Theorists do not agree over whether you can *choose* the emotions you feel. Some argue that you can; others argue that you cannot. You are, however, clearly in some control of the ways in which you *express* your emotions. Whether or not you choose to express your emotions will depend on your own attitudes about emotional expression. You may wish to explore these by taking the self-test below. Before taking the test, realize that people are more likely to receive expressions of positive affect positively and with approval, whereas negative affect is more likely to meet negative reactions (Sommers, 1984; Monahan, 1998; Metts & Planalp, 2002). But it's not always easy to determine how others will perceive an emotion; for example, jealousy, although a negative emotion, may be perceived positively, as a sign that you really care (Metts & Planalp, 2002, p. 359).

Test Yourself

How Do You Feel about Communicating Feelings?

INSTRUCTIONS: Respond to each of the following statements with T if you feel the statement is a generally true description of your attitudes about expressing emotions, or with F if you feel the statement is a generally false description of your attitudes.

_____ ❶ Expressing feelings is healthy; it reduces stress and prevents wasting energy on concealment.

_____ ❷ Expressing feelings can lead to interpersonal relationship problems.

_____ ❸ Expressing feelings can help others understand you.

_____ ❹ Emotional expression is often an effective means of persuading others to do as you wish.

_____ ❺ Expressing emotions may lead others to perceive you negatively.

_____ ❻ Emotional expression can lead to greater and not less stress; expressing anger, for example, may actually increase your feelings of anger.

HOW DID YOU DO? These statements are arguments that are often made for and against expressing emotions. Statements 1, 3, and 4 are arguments made in favor of expressing emotions; 2, 5, and 6 are arguments made against expressing emotions. You can look at your responses as revealing (in part) your attitude favoring or opposing the expression of feelings. "True" responses to statements 1, 3, and 4 and "False" responses to statements 2, 5, and 6 would indicate a favorable attitude to expressing feelings. "False" responses to statements 1, 3, and 4 and "True" responses to statements 2, 5, and 6 indicate a negative attitude.

WHAT WILL YOU DO? There is evidence suggesting that expressing emotions can lead to all six outcomes—the positives and the negatives—so general suggestions for increasing your willingness to express your emotions are not offered. These potential consequences underscore the importance of critically assessing your options for emotional expression. Be flexible, remembering that what will work in one situation will not work in another.

If you decide to communicate your feelings, you need to make several decisions. For example, you have to choose how to do so—face-to-face or by letter, phone, e-mail, or office memo. And you have to choose the specific emotions you will and will not reveal. Finally, you have to choose the language in which you'll express your emotions.

As with most meanings, emotions are encoded both verbally and nonverbally. Your words, the emphasis you give them, and the gestures and facial expressions that accompany them all help to communicate your feelings. Conversely, others decode emotional messages on the basis of both verbal and nonverbal cues. And of course emotions, like all messages, are most effectively communicated when verbal and nonverbal messages reinforce and complement each other.

Here is a list of terms for describing your emotions verbally. It's based on the eight primary emotions identified by Plutchik. Notice that the terms included for each basic emotion provide you with lots of choices for expressing the intensity level you're feeling. For example, if you're extremely happy, then *bliss, ecstasy,* or *enchantment* might be an appropriate description. If you're mildly happy, then perhaps *contentment, satisfaction,* or *well-being* would be more descriptive. Look over the list and try grouping the terms into three levels of intensity: high, middle, and low. Before doing that, however, look up the meanings of any words that are unfamiliar to you.

Happiness: bliss, cheer, contentment, delight, ecstasy, enchantment, enjoyment, felicity, joy, rapture, gratification, pleasure, satisfaction, well-being

Surprise: amazement, astonishment, awe, eye-opener, incredulity, jolt, revelation, shock, unexpectedness, wonder, startle, catch off-guard, unforeseen

Fear: anxiety, apprehension, awe, concern, consternation, dread, fright, misgiving, phobia, terror, trepidation, worry, qualm, terror

Anger: acrimony, annoyance, bitterness, displeasure, exasperation, fury, ire, irritation, outrage, rage, resentment, tantrum, umbrage, wrath, hostility

Sadness: dejected, depressed, dismal, distressed, grief, loneliness, melancholy, misery, sorrowful, unhappiness

Disgust: abhorrence, aversion, loathing, repugnance, repulsion, revulsion, sickness, nausea, offensiveness

Contempt: abhorrence, aversion, derision, disdain, disgust, distaste, indignity, insolence, ridicule, scorn, snobbery, revulsion, disrespect

Interest: attention, appeal, concern, curiosity, fascination, notice, spice, zest, absorb, engage, engross

Emotional Expression Is Governed by Display Rules

As explained in Chapter 6, different cultures' display rules govern what is and what is not permissible emotional communication. Even within the United States culture itself, there are differences. For example, in one study Americans classified themselves into four categories: Caucasian, African American, Asian, and Hispanic/Latino. Just to make the point that different cultures teach different rules for the display of emotions, here are a few of the study's findings (Matsumoto, 1994): (1) Caucasians found the expression of contempt more appropriate than did Asians; (2) African Americans and Hispanics felt disgust was less appropriate than did Caucasians; (3) Hispanics rated public displays of emotion as less appropriate than did Caucasians; and (4) Caucasians rated the expression of fear as more appropriate than Hispanics.

Responding to the Emotions of Others

Communicating emotions is one of the most important of all communication tasks. Equally important, and perhaps even more difficult, is responding appropriately to the emotions of others. Here are some situations to practice on. Visualize yourself in each of the following situations and for each indicate an appropriate response in which you *(a)* reflect the feelings of the other person to show you understand, *(b)* confirm the person's feelings, and *(c)* ask if there's anything you can do.

1. A neighbor who has lived next door to you for the last 10 years and who has had many difficult financial times has just won a lottery worth several million dollars. You meet in the hallway of your apartment house.
2. Your grandmother is dying and calls you to spend some time with her. She says that she knows she is dying, that she wants you to know how much she has always loved you, and that her only regret in dying is not being able to see you anymore.
3. A young child about six or seven years old is crying because the other children won't play with her.

Responding appropriately to the emotions of others requires you to know the other person and to have a firm grasp on the skills of effective interpersonal communication.

Researchers agree that men and women experience emotions similarly (Oatley & Duncan, 1994; Cherulnik, 1979; Wade & Tavris, 1998). The differences that are observed are differences in emotional expression. Men and women seem to have different **gender display rules**, much as different cultures have different cultural display rules.

Women talk more about feelings and emotions and use communication for emotional expression more than men (Barbato & Perse, 1992). Perhaps because of this, they also express themselves facially more than men. Even junior and senior high schoolers show this gender difference. Research findings suggest that this difference may be due to differences in the brains of men and women; women's brains have a significantly larger inferior parietal lobule, which seems to account for women's greater awareness of feelings (Barta, 1999).

Women are also more likely to express socially acceptable emotions than are men (Brody, 1985). For example, women smile significantly more than men. In fact, women smile even when smiling is not appropriate—for example, when reprimanding a subordinate. Men, on the other hand, are more likely than women to express anger and aggression (Fischer, 1993; DePaulo, 1992; Wade & Tavris, 1998). Similarly, women are more effective at communicating happiness and men are more effective at communicating anger (Coats & Feldman, 1996). Women also cry more than men (Metts & Planalp, 2002).

Women also seem to respond well to men who express emotions (Werrbach, Grotevant, & Cooper, 1990). In one study, while watching a movie, a confederate of the experimenter displayed a variety of emotions; the experimenter then asked participants what they thought of this person. Results showed that people liked men best when they cried and women best when they did not cry (Labott, Martin, Eason, & Berkey, 1991).

"I've been thinking—it might be good for Andrew if he could see you cry once in a while."

Emotional Messages Are Influential

Emotional messages influence other people. One way this influence occurs is through **emotional contagion.** If you've ever watched an infant and mother interacting, you

Message Skills

Emotional Display: Express emotions and interpret the emotions of others in light of the cultural and gender rules dictating what is and what isn't "appropriate."

can readily see how quickly the infant mimics the emotional expressions of the mother. If the mother smiles, the infant smiles; if the mother frowns, the infant frowns. As children get older, they begin to pick up more subtle expressions of emotions. For example, children quickly identify and often mimic a parent's anxiety or fear. In a study of college roommates, the depression of one roommate spread to the other over a period of just three weeks (Joiner, 1994). In short, emotions pass easily from one person to another. In conversation and in small groups, the strong emotions of one person can easily prove contagious to others present; this can be productive when the emotions are productive or unproductive when the emotions are unproductive.

You also can see the influence of emotions in most attempts at persuasion. Emotional appeals are all around us. One popular appeal, which organizations use frequently in fund-raising for children's orphanages, is to the emotion of pity. By showing you images of hungry and sad children, these fund-raisers hope to get you to experience so much pity that you'll help finance their efforts. Similarly, people who beg for money often emphasize their difficulties in an effort to evoke pity and donations.

Another popular appeal is to guilt. If someone does something for you, he or she may try to make you feel guilty unless you do something in return. Or someone may present himself or herself as in desperate need of money and make you feel guilty for having what you have and not sharing it.

Part of the art of interpersonal communication is to listen carefully to emotional messages, keeping in mind several important points:

- Facial management techniques can easily disguise emotions. Recall from Chapter 6 that people can intensify, deintensify, neutralize, or mask emotions to make you think they're feeling something different from what they're really feeling.

- Emotional appeals do not constitute proof; no matter how passionate the speaker is, remember that passion does not prove the case.

- Some speakers may use emotional appeals instead of evidence and logical arguments; some, in fact, may try to use emotional appeals to divert attention away from a lack of evidence.

Obstacles to Communicating Emotions

The expression of feelings is a part of most meaningful relationships. Yet it's often very difficult. Three major obstacles stand in the way of effective emotional commu-

Ethical messages

Motivational Appeals

Appeals to motives are commonplace. For example, if you want a friend to take a vacation with you, you're likely to appeal to such motives as the friend's desire for fun and excitement, and perhaps to the friend's hopes of meeting his or her true love. If you look at the advertisements for cruises and vacation packages, you'll see appeals to very similar motives. **Fear appeals** also are common: Persons who want to censor the Internet may appeal to your fear of children's accessing pornographic materials; those who want to restrict media portrayals of violence may appeal to your fear of increased violence in your community. Advertisers appeal to your vanity and your desire for increased sexual attractiveness in trying to sell you cosmetics and expensive clothing.

There can be no doubt that such motivational appeals are effective. But are they ethical?

What Would You Do?

Suppose you wanted to dissuade your teenage children from engaging in sexual relationships. Would it be ethical to use emotional appeals to fear—to scare them so that they'd avoid such relationships? Would it be ethical to use the same appeals if your goal were to get them to stop smoking?

nication: (1) society's rules and customs, (2) fear, and (3) inadequate interpersonal skills. Let's look more closely at each of these barriers.

Societal Rules and Customs

If you grew up in the United States, you probably learned that many people frown on emotional expression. This is especially true for men and has been aptly called "the cowboy syndrome," after a pattern of behavior seen in the old Westerns (Balswick & Peck, 1971). The cowboy syndrome describes the closed and unexpressive male. This man is strong but silent. He never feels any of the softer emotions (such as compassion, love, or contentment). He would never ever cry, experience fear, or feel sorry for himself. And he would never ask—as does our hero in the cartoon—for "a bigger emotional share." Unfortunately, many men grow up trying to live up to

"Rebecca, I'm looking for a bigger emotional share here."

this unrealistic image. It's a syndrome that prevents open and honest expression. Researcher Ronald Levant (*Time,* January 20, 1992, p. 44) has argued that men's inability to deal with emotions as effectively as women is a "trained incompetence." Such training begins early in life when boys are taught not to cry and to ignore pain. This is not necessarily to suggest, however, that men should communicate their emotions more openly. Unfortunately, there are many who will negatively evaluate men who express emotions openly and often; such men may be judged ineffective, insecure, or unmanly.

Nor are women exempt from the difficulties of emotional expression. At one time our society permitted and encouraged women to express emotions openly. The tide now is turning, especially for women in executive and managerial positions. Today the executive woman is being forced into the same cowboy syndrome. She is not allowed to cry or to show any of the once acceptable "soft" emotions. She is especially denied these feelings while she is on the job.

For both men and women, the best advice (as with self-disclosure or any of the characteristics of communication effectiveness discussed in this book) is to express your emotions selectively. Carefully weigh the arguments for and against expressing your emotions. Consider the situation, the people you're with, the emotions themselves, and all the elements that make up the communication act. And, most important, consider your options for communicating—not only what you'll say but also how you'll say it.

Fear

A variety of types of fear stand in the way of emotional expression. Emotional expression exposes a part of you that makes you vulnerable to attack. For example, if you express your love for another person, you risk being rejected. That is, by exposing a "weakness," you can now easily be hurt by the uncaring and the insensitive. Of course, you may also fear hurting someone else by, say, voicing your feelings about past loves. Or you may be angry and want to say something but fear that you might hurt the person and then feel guilty yourself.

In addition, you may not reveal your emotions for fear of causing a conflict. Expressing your dislike for Pat's friends, for example, may create difficulties for the two of you, and you may not be willing to risk the argument and its aftermath.

Because of fears such as these, you may deny to others and perhaps even to yourself that you have certain feelings. In fact, this kind of **denial** is the way many people were taught to deal with emotions.

? SKILLS VIEWPOINT

Your supervisor seems to constantly belittle your experience, which you thought was your strong point. Often your supervisor will say that your experiences were "in school" or "with only a few people" or some such negative phrase. You think your experience has more than prepared you for this job, and you want to make sure your supervisor knows this. What do you say?

Communicating Emotions Effectively

Before reading about the principles and guidelines for emotional expression, try your hand at analyzing and rewriting some ineffective emotional messages. In your rewrites, try to *(a)* describe your feelings and their intensity as accurately as possible; *(b)* identify the reasons for your feelings and what influenced or stimulated you to feel as you do; *(c)* anchor your feelings to the present; *(d)* use I-messages to own your own feelings, to claim responsibility for these feelings; and *(e)* describe what (if anything) you want the other person to do because of your feelings.

1. Your lack of consideration makes me so angry I can't stand it anymore.
2. You hurt me when you ignore me. If you ever do that again, I'm out of here.
3. Look. I really can't bear to hear about your problems of deciding whom to date tomorrow and the next day and the next. Give me a break. It's boring. Boring.
4. You did that just to upset me. You enjoy seeing me get upset, don't you?
5. Don't talk to me in that tone of voice. Don't you dare insult me with that attitude of yours.

Some ways of expressing emotions are better than others; it's possible to communicate difficult messages without generating ill feeling.

Inadequate Interpersonal Skills

Perhaps the most important obstacle to effective emotional communication is lack of interpersonal skills. Many people simply don't know how to express their feelings. Some people, for example, can express anger only through violence or avoidance. Others can deal with anger only by blaming and accusing others. And many people cannot express love. They literally cannot say, "I love you."

Expressing negative feelings is doubly difficult. Many of us suppress or fail to communicate negative feelings for fear of offending the other person or making matters worse. But failing to express negative feelings will probably not help the relationship, especially if these feelings are concealed frequently and over a long time.

Guidelines for Communicating Emotions

Both communicating your emotions and responding appropriately to the emotional expressions of others are as important as they are difficult (Burleson, 2003). And to complicate matters further, as noted in the self-test earlier in this chapter, emotional expression can be good but also can be bad. On the one hand, expressing emotions can be cathartic to yourself and can benefit a relationship. Expressing emotions can help you air dissatisfactions and perhaps reduce or even eliminate them. Through emotional expression you can come to understand each other better, which may lead to a closer and more meaningful relationship.

On the other hand, expressing emotions may cause relationship difficulties. For example, expressing your anger with a worker's customary way of answering the phone may generate hostility; expressing jealousy when your partner spends time with friends may cause your partner to fear being controlled and losing autonomy.

In many cases, despite these cautions, you'll want to express your emotions. When you do so, your first tasks are intrapersonal.

SKILLS VIEWPOINT

Your neighbors just had their apartment broken into, their jewelry stolen, and their furnishings trashed. They come to you in tears. What do you say?

- Understand your emotions. Think about your emotions as objectively as possible. Identify, in terms as specific as possible, the antecedent conditions that may be influencing your feelings. Try to answer the question "Why am I feeling this way?" or "What happened to lead me to feel as I do?"

Listening to the Emotions of Others

Expressing your feelings is only half of the process of emotional communication; the other half is listening to the feelings of others. Here are a few guidelines for making an often difficult process a little easier.

- Don't equate (as the stereotypical male supposedly does) "responding to another's feelings" with "solving the other person's problems." Instead, provide a supportive atmosphere that encourages the person to express his or her feelings.
- Empathize. See the situation from the point of view of the speaker. Don't evaluate the other person's feelings. For example, comments such as "Don't cry; it wasn't worth it" or "You'll get promoted next year" can easily be interpreted to mean "Your feelings are wrong or inappropriate."
- Focus on the other person. Interjecting your own similar past situations is often useful for showing your understanding, but it may create problems if it refocuses the conversation away from the other person.
- Show interest by encouraging the person to explore his or her feelings. Use simple encouragers like "I see" or "I understand." Or ask questions to let the speaker know that you're listening and that you're interested.

Applying Listening Skills

Your best friend tells you that he suspects his girlfriend is seeing someone else. He's extremely upset; he tells you that he wants to confront her with his suspicions but is afraid of what he'll hear. What listening skills would you suggest he use?

- Ask yourself whether you wish to express your emotions. Consider also whether your emotional expression will be a truthful expression of your feelings. When emotional expressions are faked—when, for example, you smile though feeling angry—you may actually be creating emotional and physical stress (Grandey, 2000). Remember, too, the irreversibility of communication; once you communicate something, you cannot take it back.
- Evaluate your communication options in terms of both effectiveness (what will work best and help you achieve your goal) and ethics (what is right or morally justified).

> *Message Skills*
>
> **Listening to the Feelings of Others:** Empathize, focus on the other person, and encourage the person to explore his or her feelings.

Now that you understand your emotions, have decided that you want to express them, and have carefully assessed your available options, consider the following suggestions for effective emotional expression.

Describe Your Feelings

Be as specific as possible. Consider, for example, the frequently heard "I feel bad." Does it mean "I feel guilty" (because I lied to my best friend)? "I feel lonely" (because I haven't had a date in the last two months)? "I feel depressed" (because I failed that last exam)? Specificity helps. Describe also the intensity with which you feel the emotion: "I feel so angry I'm thinking of quitting the job." "I feel so hurt I want to cry." Learn the vocabulary to describe your emotions and feelings in specific and concrete terms.

Identify the Reasons for Your Feelings

Describe the reasons you're feeling as you are. "I'm feeling guilty because I lied to my best friend." "I feel lonely; I haven't had a date for the last two months." "I'm really depressed from failing that last exam." If your feelings were influenced by something the person you're talking to did or said, describe this also. For example, "I felt so angry when you said you wouldn't help me. I felt hurt when you didn't invite me to the party."

5 Ways to Communicate with the Grief-Stricken

Dealing with people who are experiencing grief is a common but difficult communication interaction and requires special care (Zunin & Zunin, 1991). A person may experience grief because of illness or death, the loss of a job or highly valued relationship (such as a friendship or romantic breakup), the loss of certain physical or mental abilities, or the loss of material possessions (a house fire or stock losses). Here are a few suggestions for easing this difficult form of communication.

1. Confirm the other person and the person's emotions. A simple "You must be worried about finding another position" confirms the person's feelings. This type of expressive support lessens feelings of grief (Reed, 1993).
2. Give the person permission to grieve. Let the person know that it's acceptable and okay with you if he or she grieves in the ways that feel most comfortable—for example, crying or talking about old times.
3. Avoid trying to focus on the bright side. Avoid expressions such as "You're lucky you have some vision left" or "It was better this way; Pat was suffering so much."
4. Encourage the person to express feelings and talk about the loss. Most people will welcome this opportunity. On the other hand, don't try to force the person to talk about experiences or feelings she or he may not be willing to share. Be especially sensitive to leave-taking cues. Don't overstay your welcome.
5. Communicate empathy. Let the grief-stricken person know that you can feel (to some extent) what he or she is going through. But don't assume that your feelings, however empathic you are, are the same in depth or in kind.

Applying Interpersonal Skills/Then and Now

Can you recall a situation in which you interacted with someone who was experiencing grief but for some reason didn't communicate very effectively? Did you violate any of the suggestions identified here? What would you do differently if this situation occurred today?

Anchor Your Feelings to the Present

In expressing feelings—inwardly or outwardly—try to link your emotions to the present. Coupled with specific description and the identification of the reasons for your feelings, such statements might look like this: "I feel like a failure right now; I've erased this computer file three times today." "I felt foolish when I couldn't think of that formula." "I feel stupid when you point out my grammatical errors."

Own Your Own Feelings

Message Skills

I-Messages: Use I-messages when communicating your feelings; take responsibility for your own feelings rather than attributing them to others.

Perhaps the most important guideline for effective emotional communication is: Own your feelings, take personal responsibility for your feelings. Consider the following statements: "You make me angry." "You make me feel like a loser." "You make me feel stupid." "You make me feel like I don't belong here." In each of these statements, the speaker blames the other person for the way he or she is feeling. Of course, you know, on more sober reflection, that no one can make you feel anything. Others may do things or say things to you, but it is you who interpret them. That is, you develop feelings as a result of the interaction between what these people say, for example, and your own interpretations. **Owning feelings** means taking responsibility for them—acknowledging that your feelings are *your* feelings. The best way to own your statements is to use **I-messages** rather than the kinds of **you-messages** given above. With this acknowledgment of responsibility, the above statements would look like these: "I get angry when you come home late without calling." "I begin to think of myself as a loser when you criticize me in front of my friends." "I feel so stupid when you use medical terms that I don't understand." "When you ignore me in public, I feel like I don't belong here."

These rephrased statements identify and describe your feelings about those behaviors; they don't attack the other person or demand that he or she change certain behaviors and consequently don't encourage defensiveness. With I-message statements, it's easier for the other person to acknowledge behaviors and to offer to change them.

Also use I-messages to describe what, if anything, you want the listener to do: "I'm feeling sorry for myself right now; just give me some space. I'll give you a call in a few days." Or, more directly: "I'd prefer to be alone right now."

Handle Your Anger: A Special Case

As a kind of summary of emotional communication, this section looks at anger. Anger is one of the eight basic emotions identified in Plutchik's model (Figure 7.1, page 145). It's also an emotion that can create considerable problems if not managed properly. Anger varies from mild annoyance to intense rage; increases in pulse rate and blood pressure usually accompany these feelings.

Anger is not always necessarily bad. In fact, anger may help you protect yourself, energizing you to fight or flee. Often, however, anger does prove destructive—as when, for example, you allow it to obscure reality or to become an obsession.

Anger doesn't just happen; you make it happen by your interpretation of events. Yet life events can contribute mightily. There are the road repairs that force you to detour so you wind up late for an important appointment. There are the moths that attack your favorite sweater. There's the water leak that ruins your carpet. People, too, can contribute to your anger: the driver who tailgates, the clerk who overcharges you, the supervisor who ignores your contributions to the company. But it is you who interpret these events and people in ways that stimulate you to generate anger.

Writing more than a hundred years ago, Charles Darwin observed in his *The Expression of the Emotions in Man and Animals* (1872): "The free expression by outside signs of an emotion intensifies it . . . the repression, as far as this is possible, of all outside signs softens our emotions. He who gives way to violent gestures will increase his rage." Popular psychology ignored Darwin's implied admonition in the 1960s and '70s, when the suggested prescription for dealing with anger was to "let it all hang out" and "tell it like it is." Express your anger, many people advised, or risk its being bottled up and eventually exploding. Later thinking has returned to Darwin, however, and suggests that venting anger may not be the best strategy (Tavris, 1989). Expressing anger doesn't get rid of it but makes it grow: Angry expression increases anger, which promotes more angry expression, which increases anger, and on and on.

A better strategy seems to be to reduce the anger. With this principle in mind, here are some suggestions for analyzing and communicating anger.

SKILLS VIEWPOINT

A colleague at work has revealed to other workers personal information about you that you confided in him and him alone. You're steaming as you pass a group of colleagues commenting on your current relationship problems. You decide to try the SCREAM technique. What effects will this procedure have?

Anger Management: SCREAM before You Scream

Perhaps the most popular recommendation for dealing with anger is to count to 10. The purpose is to give you a cooling-off period, and the advice is not bad. A somewhat more difficult but probably far more effective strategy would be to use that cooling-off period not merely for counting but for mindfully analyzing and ultimately managing your anger. The procedure offered here is similar to those available in popular books on anger management but is couched in a communication framework. It's called SCREAM, an acronym for the major issues (that is, the major components of the communication process) that you need to consider:

> " People *can* change their feelings. No matter what happens to them, they *can* creatively decide to feel one way or another about it. And they have quite a range of possible feelings to choose from! "
>
> —Albert Ellis

- *Self.* How important is this to you? Is it worth the high blood pressure and the general aggravation? For example, are you interpreting the "insult" as the other person intended, or could you be misperceiving the situation or the intent? Is "insult" _{to you} the same as "insult" _{to your mother-in-law}? Are you confusing factual with inferential knowledge? Are you sure that what you think happened really happened? Or might you be filling in the gaps with what could have or might have happened or with what you expected to happen?

- *Context.* Is this the appropriate time and place to express your anger? Do you have to express your anger right now? Do you have to express it right here? Might a better time and place be arranged?

- *Receiver.* Is this person the one to whom you wish to express your anger? For example, do you want to express your anger to your life partner if you're really angry with your supervisor for not recommending your promotion?

- *Effect* (immediate). What effect do you want to achieve? Do you want to express your anger to help you get the promotion? To hurt the other person? To release pent-up emotions? To stand up for your rights? Each purpose would obviously require a different communication strategy. Consider, too, what may be the likely immediate effect of your anger display. For example, will the other person also become angry? And if so, is it possible that the entire situation will snowball and get out of hand?

- *Aftermath* (long-range). What are the likely long-term repercussions of this expression of anger? What will be the effects on your relationship? Your continued employment?

- *Messages.* Suppose that after this rather thorough analysis, you do decide to express your anger. What messages would be appropriate? How can you best communicate your feelings to achieve your desired results? This question brings us to the subject of anger communication.

Anger Communication   Anger communication is not angry communication. In fact, it might be argued that the communication of anger ought to be especially calm and dispassionate. Here, then, are a few suggestions for communicating your anger in a nonangry way.

1. Get ready to communicate calmly and logically. First, relax. Try to breathe deeply; think pleasant thoughts; perhaps tell yourself to "take it easy," "think rationally," and "calm down." Try to get rid of any unrealistic ideas you may have that might contribute to anger; for example, is what this person did so reprehensible, or was it perhaps just a selfish act of a frightened individual?

2. Examine your communication options. In most situations there are lots of different ways to express yourself, so don't jump to the first possibility that comes to mind. Assess your options for the form of the communication—should you communicate face-to-face? By e-mail? By telephone? Similarly, assess your options for the timing of your communication, for the specific words and gestures you might use, for the physical setting, and so on.

3. Consider the advantages of delaying the expression of anger. For example, consider writing the e-mail but sending it to yourself, at least until the next morning. Then the options of revising it or not sending it at all will still be open to you.

4. Remember that different cultures have different display rules—norms for what is and what is not appropriate to display. Assess the culture you're in as well as the cultures of the other people involved, especially these cultures' display rules for communicating anger.

5. Apply the relevant skills of interpersonal communication. For example, be specific, use I-messages, avoid allness, avoid polarized terms, and in general communicate with all the competence you can muster.

> **❝** One of the greatest gifts you can give the people you love is to hear their anger and frustration without judging or contradicting them. **❞**
>
> —Harold H. Bloomfield

6. Recall the irreversibility of communication. Once you say something, you'll not be able to erase or delete it from the mind of the other person.

These suggestions are not going to solve the problems of road rage, gang warfare, or domestic violence. Yet they may help—a bit—in reducing some of the negative consequences of anger and perhaps even some of the anger itself.

Summary of Concepts

This chapter explored the nature and principles of emotions in interpersonal communication, the obstacles to meaningful emotional communication, and some guidelines that will help you communicate your feelings and respond to the feelings of others more effectively.

1. Emotions consist of a physical part (our physiological reactions), a cognitive part (our interpretations of our feelings), and a cultural part (our cultural traditions' influence on our emotional evaluations and expressions).

2. Emotions may be primary or blends. The primary emotions, according to Robert Plutchik, are joy, acceptance, fear, surprise, sadness, disgust, anger, and anticipation. Other emotions, such as love, awe, contempt, and aggressiveness, are blends of primary emotions.

3. There are different views as to how emotions are aroused. One proposed sequence is this: An event occurs, you respond physiologically, you interpret this arousal, and you experience emotion based on your interpretation.

4. Emotions are communicated verbally and nonverbally, and the way in which you express emotions is largely a matter of choice.

5. Cultural and gender display rules identify what emotions may be expressed, where, how, and by whom.

6. Emotions are influential, as in emotional contagion and emotional persuasion.

7. Among the obstacles to effective communication of feelings are societal rules and customs, fear of making oneself vulnerable, and inadequate communication skills.

8. The following guidelines should help make your emotional expression more meaningful: Understand your feelings, decide if you wish to express your feelings (not all feelings need be or should be expressed), assess your communication options, describe your feelings as accurately as possible, identify the reasons for your feelings, anchor your feelings and their expression to the present time, own your own feelings, and handle your anger as appropriate.

9. In responding to the emotions of others, try to see the situation from the perspective of the other person. Avoid refocusing the conversation on yourself. Show interest and provide the speaker with the opportunity to talk and explore his or her feelings. Avoid evaluating the feelings of the other person.

Vocabulary Quiz: The Language of Emotions

Match the terms concerning the communication of emotions with their definitions. Record the number of the definition next to the appropriate term.

_____ emotion

_____ emotional contagion

_____ cognitive labeling theory

_____ emotional expression

_____ cowboy syndrome

_____ owning feelings

_____ I-messages

_____ emotional appeals

_____ gender display rules

_____ display rules

1. Many males' lack of ability to reveal emotions, influenced by a belief that men should be strong and silent.
2. The process by which we take responsibility for our own feelings.
3. Messages that explicitly acknowledge responsibility for your own feelings.
4. Rules for the appropriate expression of emotions.
5. The process by which emotional expression influences others also to experience the emotion.
6. The feelings you have; for example, your feelings of guilt, anger, or sorrow.
7. Rules for the gender-appropriate expression of emotions.
8. An often effective but nonlogical means of persuasion.
9. Theory that describes the sequence of events in feeling emotions as follows: An event occurs, you respond physiologically, you interpret this arousal (that is, you decide what emotion you're experiencing), and you experience the emotion.
10. The way you choose to communicate your feelings.

Four for Discussion

1. Some societies permit and even expect men to show strong emotions. They expect men to cry, to show fear, to express anger openly. Other societies—including many groups within general U.S. culture—criticize men for experiencing and expressing such emotions. What did your culture teach you about gender and the expression of emotions—in particular, the expression of strongly felt emotions and emotions that show weakness (such as fear, discomfort, or uncertainty)?

2. One implication of the cognitive labeling theory of emotions is that you and only you can make yourself feel angry or sad or anxious. This view is often phrased popularly as, "Other people can hurt you physically, but only you can hurt yourself emotionally." Do you agree with this? What evidence can you advance to support or refute this position?

3. What has your experience revealed about the ways men and women express emotions? In what ways are men and women similar? In what ways are they different?

4. For each of the following situations, identify (1) the nature of the problem and (2) the one solution you would recommend to the parties involved.

- Joe is extremely honest and open; he regularly says everything he feels without self-censorship. Not surprisingly, he often offends people. Joe is entering a new work environment and worries that his frankness may not be the best way to win friends and influence people.
- Alex and Deirdre have dated steadily for the last four years. Deirdre is extremely unexpressive but believes that Alex—because of their long and close relationship—should know how she feels without her having to spell it out. When Alex doesn't respond appropriately, Deirdre becomes angry, saying that Alex doesn't really love her; if he did, he would know what she's feeling. Alex says this is crazy, "I'm no mind reader; if Deirdre wants something, she has the obligation to say so."
- Tobin has recently been put in charge of a group of workers at a small printer repair firm. Tobin is extremely reserved and rarely reveals any emotion. He gives instructions, praises, and criticizes all with the same tone of voice and facial expressions. This had led the workers to feel he's insincere and isn't really feeling what he says.

Web Explorations

Explore our text website at
www.ablongman.com/devito
to find:

Explore our research resources at
www.researchnavigator.com
and

Exercises and Self-Tests

Exercises to help you understand the nature of emotional communication include (1) Communicating Emotions Nonverbally, (2) Communicating Your Emotions, (3) Expressing Negative Feelings, and (4) Emotional Advice.

Writing Resources and Assignments

Suggestions are available for writing papers of personal experience (for example, how your beliefs influence your emotional expression), concept or principle explanation (for example, cultural display rules), review (for example, gender differences in emotional expression), or research on emotional communication (for example, what we know about emotional contagion).

Read an article.

Read a popular or scholarly article on one of the topics covered in this chapter (for example, emotions, emotional communication, emotions on the job, anger management, or grief). On the basis of this article, what can you add to the discussion presented here?

Investigate key terms.

Investigate one of the key terms discussed in this chapter (for example, emotion, display rules, emotional appeals, emotional expression, grief, emotional contagion). What additional insights can you provide?

Find answers.

Try finding answers to one of the following questions, or design a research study to answer it.

1. How do children and adults differ in the way they deal with anger?
2. How do men and women differ in their emotional expression?
3. What motivational appeals are used to appeal to 18- to 35-year-olds? To 55- to 70-year-olds?

Conversation Messages

8

The Process of Conversation

Managing Conversation

Effective Conversation

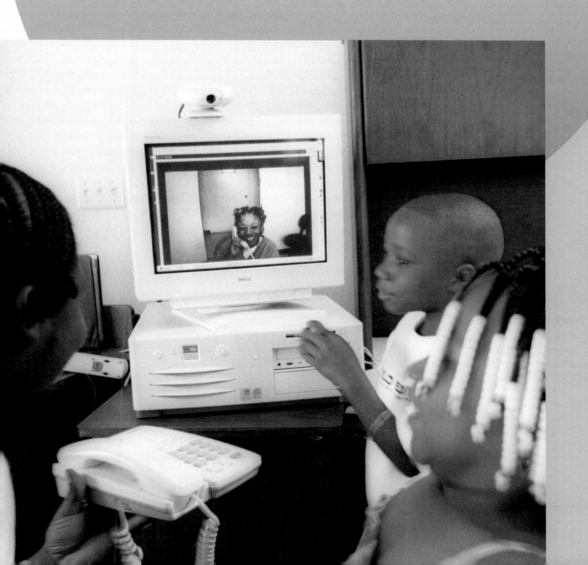

> "The time has come," the Walrus said,
> "To talk of many things:
> Of shoes—and ships—and sealing wax—
> Of cabbages—and kings—
> And why the sea is boiling hot—
> And whether pigs have wings."

Of course, you're not likely to spend much of your time talking (as Lewis Carroll suggested in *Through the Looking-Glass*) about sealing wax or pigs with wings. But you are likely to spend a great deal of time talking about other things, in the seemingly simple but actually quite complex process of conversation.

Interpersonal researcher Margaret McLaughlin (1984) defines **conversation** as "relatively informal social interaction in which the roles of speaker and hearer are exchanged in a nonautomatic fashion under the collaborative management of all parties." In this chapter we look at the conversation process—what the process is; the principles you follow in conversing; how you manage a conversation (for example, opening, maintaining, and closing); and how you try to prevent and repair conversational problems.

The Process of Conversation

Most often, of course, conversation takes place face-to-face; and this is the type of interaction that probably comes to mind when you think of conversation. But today much conversation also takes place online. Online communication is becoming a part of people's experience worldwide. Such communications are important personally, socially, and professionally. Recall from earlier discussions of online conversation (e-mail or listservs and chat groups, for example) the ways in which they differ from face-to-face interaction. Keep online communication in mind as you think about the conversation process.

When reading about the process of conversation, keep in mind that not everyone speaks with the fluency and ease that many textbooks often assume. Speech and language disorders, for example, can seriously disrupt the conversation process when some elementary guidelines aren't followed. Table 8.1 offers suggestions for making such conversations run more smoothly.

With the understanding that conversation can take place in a wide variety of channels, let's look at the way conversation works. Conversation takes place in five steps: opening, feedforward, business, feedback, and closing (Figure 8.1).

Figure 8.1

The Conversation Process
The process is viewed as occurring in five basic steps: opening, feedforward, business, feedback, and closing. Can you break down the conversation process into steps or stages that are significantly different from those identified here?

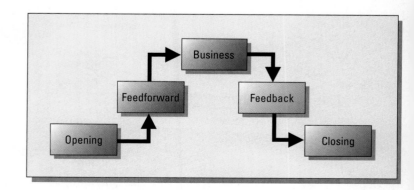

TABLE 8.1 *Interpersonal Communication Tips*

BETWEEN PEOPLE WITH AND WITHOUT SPEECH AND LANGUAGE DISORDERS

Speech and language disorders vary widely—from fluency problems in stuttering, to indistinct articulation, to difficulty in finding the right word in aphasia. Here are some guidelines that will help facilitate communication between people with and without speech and language disorders.

If you're the person without a speech or language disorder:

1. Avoid finishing sentences for someone who stutters or has difficulty in finding words (aphasia). Finishing sentences may communicate the idea that you're impatient and don't want to spend the extra time necessary to interact effectively.

2. Avoid giving directions to the person with a speech disorder. Saying things like "slow down" or "relax" will often prove insulting and will make further communication more difficult.

3. Maintain eye contact and avoid showing any signs of impatience or embarrassment.

4. If you don't understand what the person said, ask him or her to repeat it. Don't pretend that you understand when you don't.

5. Don't treat people who have language problems like children. A person with aphasia, say, may have difficulty with names or with nouns generally but is in no way childlike.

If you're the person with a speech or language disorder:

1. Let the other person know what your special needs are. For example, if you stutter, you might tell others that you have difficulty with certain sounds and that they need to be patient.

2. Demonstrate your comfort with and positive attitude toward the interpersonal situation. If you appear comfortable and positive, others will also.

Sources: These suggestions were drawn from the National Stuttering Association, **http://www.nsastutter.org**, the National Aphasia Association, **http://www.aphasia.org**, and Constance Dugan, M.A./CCC-SLP, **http://www.conniedugan.com**, all accessed April 5, 2002.

Step One: Opening

The first step is to open the conversation, usually with some verbal or nonverbal greeting: "Hi," "How are you?" "Hello, this is Joe," a smile, or a wave.

You can accomplish a great deal in your opening (Krivonos & Knapp, 1975). First, your greeting can tell others that you're accessible, that you're available to them for conversation. You can also reveal important information about the relationship between yourself and the other person. For example, a big smile and a warm "Hi, it's been a long time" may signal that your relationship is still a friendly one, that you aren't angry any longer, or any of numerous other messages. Your greeting also helps maintain the relationship. You see this function served between workers who pass each other frequently. This greeting-in-passing assures both people that even though they do not stop and talk for an extended period, they still have access to each other.

In normal conversation, your greeting is returned by the other person with a greeting that is similar in its formality and intensity. When it isn't—when the other person turns away or responds coldly to your friendly "Good morning"—you know that something is wrong. Similarly, openings are generally consistent in tone with the main part of the conversation; you would not normally follow a cheery "How ya doing today, big guy?" with news of a family death.

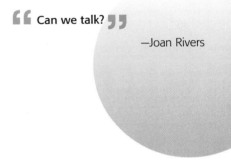

" Can we talk? "

—Joan Rivers

Step Two: Feedforward

At the second step there is usually some kind of feedforward (see Chapter 1). Here you give the other person a general idea of what the conversation will focus on: "I got to tell you about Jack," "Did you hear what happened in class yesterday?" or "We need to talk about our vacation plans." When feedforwards are misused—for example, when they are overly long or insensitive—they can create conversational problems.

As with the greeting, you can accomplish a great deal with feedforward. For example, you can (1) open the channels of communication, (2) preview the message, (3) altercast, and (4) disclaim. Let's look at each in more detail.

Open the Channels of Communication   **Phatic communication** (messages that open the channels of communication) is a perfect example of feedforward. Phatic communication tells us that the normal, expected, and accepted rules of interaction will be in effect. It's information that tells us another person is willing to communicate.

Preview Future Messages   Feedforward messages frequently preview other messages. Feedforward may, for example, preview the content ("I'm afraid I have bad news for you"), the importance ("Listen to this before you make a move"), the form or style ("I'll tell you all the gory details"), and the positive or negative quality ("You're not going to like this, but here's what I heard") of subsequent messages.

Altercast   Feedforward is often used to place someone in a specific role and to request that he or she respond to you in terms of this assumed role. This process, known as **altercasting,** asks the person to approach your message from a particular perspective or even as someone else (Weinstein & Deutschberger, 1963; McLaughlin, 1984). For example, you might ask a friend, "As an advertising executive, what would you think of corrective advertising?" This question casts your friend in the role of advertising executive (rather than that of, for example, parent, Democrat, or Baptist). It asks your friend to respond from a particular point of view.

Disclaim   A **disclaimer** is a statement that aims to ensure that your message will be understood and will not reflect negatively on you (Hewitt & Stokes, 1975; McLaughlin, 1984). Suppose, for example, you fear that your listeners will think

Message Skills

Disclaimers: Use disclaimers if you feel you might be misunderstood. But avoid them when they're not necessary; too many disclaimers can make you appear unprepared or unwilling to state an opinion.

Listen to this

Listening to Disclaimers

Listen to disclaimers (statements that ask the listener to receive what you're saying in a positive light) that others offer as well as those you make yourself (Hewitt & Stokes, 1975; McLaughlin, 1984). Listening to the functions disclaimers serve and the effects they have will sensitize you to the crucial role that these comments play in everyday conversation.

- In *hedging* you disclaim the importance of the message to your own identity; you make it clear that listeners may reject the message without rejecting you: "I didn't read the entire report, but. . . ."
- In *credentialing* you seek to establish special qualifications so as to avoid listeners' drawing undesirable inferences: "Don't get the wrong idea; I'm not sexist, but. . . ."
- With *sin licenses* you announce that you will violate some social or cultural rule but should be "forgiven" or given a "license to sin" in advance: "I realize that this may not be the time to talk about money, but. . . ."
- With *cognitive disclaimers* you seek to reaffirm your cognitive abilities in anticipation of any listener doubts: "I know you think I'm drunk, but I'm as sober as. . . ."
- With *appeals for the suspension of judgment,* you ask listeners to delay making judgments until you have had the chance to present a more complete account: "Don't say anything until I explain the real story. . . ."

Applying Listening Skills

A colleague regularly uses credentialing as a preface to culturally insensitive jokes and stories. You really don't want to listen to this insensitivity. What might you say if the colleague were your supervisor? What if the colleague were someone you were supervising? What if the colleague were a peer?

your comment is inappropriate, or that they may rush to judge you without hearing your full account, or that they may think you're not in full possession of your faculties. In such cases you may use some form of disclaimer and say, for example, "This may not be the place to say this, but . . ." or "Just hear me out before you hang up." Five popular disclaimers, along with their definitions and examples, are discussed in the Listen to This box on page 164.

Step Three: Business

The third step in the conversational process is the "business," the substance or focus of the conversation. The business is conducted through exchanges of speaker and listener roles. Usually, brief (rather than long) speaking turns characterize most satisfying conversations.

Business is a good word to use for this stage, because the term emphasizes that most conversations are goal-directed. You converse to fulfill one or several of the purposes of interpersonal communication: to learn, relate, influence, play, or help (Chapter 1). The term is also general enough to include all kinds of interactions. During the business stage you talk about Jack, what happened in class, or your vacation plans. This is obviously the longest part of the conversation and the reason for both the opening and the feedforward. Not surprisingly, each culture has its own conversational **taboos**—topics or language that should be avoided, especially by visitors from other cultures (see Table 8.2 on page 166).

Step Four: Feedback

The feedback step is the reverse of the feedforward step. Here you reflect back on the conversation to signal that the business is completed: "So, you may want to send Jack a get-well card," "Wasn't that the craziest class you ever heard of?" or "I'll call for reservations while you shop for what we need."

In another sense, as described in Chapter 1, feedback takes place throughout the interpersonal communication process. Speakers and listeners constantly exchange feedback—messages sent back to the speaker concerning reactions to what is said

SKILLS VIEWPOINT

The first 20 minutes of just about every meeting at work invariably revolves around personal talk about the last weekend or the next. You really don't enjoy this interaction; you want to participate in the work part of the meeting but not in the interpersonal part. What do you say?

TABLE 8.2 Conversational Taboos around the World

This table lists several examples of topics that Roger Axtell (in *Do's and Taboos Around the World,* 1993) recommends that visitors from the United States avoid when in other countries. These examples are not intended to be exhaustive, but rather should serve as a reminder that each culture defines what is and what is not an appropriate topic of conversation. Note that this list was published in 1993. How would you revise this list to better represent today's conversational taboos?

COUNTRY	CONVERSATIONAL TABOOS
Belgium	Politics, language differences between French and Flemish, religion
Norway	Salaries, social status
Spain	Family, religion, jobs, negative comments on bullfighting
Egypt	Middle Eastern politics
Nigeria	Religion
Libya	Politics, religion
Iraq	Religion, Middle Eastern politics
Japan	World War II
Pakistan	Politics
Philippines	Politics, religion, corruption, foreign aid
South Korea	Internal politics, socialism or communism, criticism of the government
Bolivia	Politics, religion
Colombia	Politics, criticism of bullfighting
Mexico	Mexican-American war, illegal aliens
Caribbean nations	Race, local politics, religion

(Clement & Frandsen, 1976). Feedback tells the speaker what effect he or she is having on listeners. On the basis of this feedback, the speaker may adjust, modify, strengthen, deemphasize, or change the content or form of the messages.

Feedback can take many forms. A frown or a smile, a yea or a nay, a pat on the back or a punch in the mouth—all are types of feedback. We can think about feedback in terms of five important dimensions: positive–negative, person focused–message focused, immediate–delayed, low monitoring–high monitoring, and supportive–critical. To use feedback effectively, you need to make educated choices along these dimensions.

Positive feedback (applause, smiles, head nods signifying approval) tells the speaker that his or her message is being well received and that essentially the speaker should continue speaking in the same general mode. **Negative feedback** (boos, frowns and puzzled looks, gestures signifying disapproval) tells the speaker that something is wrong and that some adjustment needs to be made. The art of feedback involves giving positive feedback without strings and giving negative feedback positively.

Feedback may be *person focused* ("You're sweet," "You have a great smile") or *message focused* ("Can you repeat that phone number?" "Your argument is a good one"). Especially when you are giving criticism, it's important to make clear that your feedback relates to, say, the organization of the budget report and not to the person himself or herself.

Feedback can be *immediate* or *delayed*. Generally, the most effective feedback is that which is most immediate. In interpersonal situations feedback is most often sent immediately after the message is received. Feedback, like reinforcement, loses its effectiveness with time. The longer you wait to praise or punish, for example, the less effect it will have. In other communication situations, however, the feedback may be

66 There is nothing you can say in answer to a compliment. I have been complimented myself a great many times, and they always embarrass me—I always feel that they have not said enough. 99

—Mark Twain

delayed. Instructor evaluation questionnaires completed at the end of the course provide feedback long after the class is over. In interview situations the feedback may come weeks afterwards.

Feedback varies from the spontaneous and totally honest reaction (*low-monitored* feedback) to the carefully constructed response designed to serve a specific purpose (*high-monitored* feedback). In most interpersonal situations you probably give feedback spontaneously; you allow your responses to show without any monitoring. At other times, however, you may be more guarded, as when your boss asks you how you like your job or when your grandfather asks what you think of his new motorcycle outfit.

Feedback is *supportive* when you console another or when you simply encourage the other to talk or affirm another's self-definition. *Critical* feedback, on the other hand, is evaluative. When you give critical feedback, you judge another's performance—as in, for example, evaluating a speech or coaching someone who is learning a new skill.

Step Five: Closing

The fifth and last step in conversation, the opposite of the first step, is the closing, the good-bye (Knapp, Hart, Friedrich, & Shulman, 1973; Knapp & Vangelisti, 2000). Most obviously, this step signals the end of accessibility. Just as the opening signaled access, the closing signals the end of access. The closing may also signal some degree of supportiveness; for example, you might express your pleasure in interacting through a comment such as "Well, it was good talking with you." In some conversations the closing summarizes the interaction. Like the opening, the closing may be verbal or nonverbal but is usually a combination of both. Examples of verbal closings include expressions of appreciation ("Well, I appreciate the time you've given me"), concern for the other's welfare ("Do take care of yourself"), or reinforcement ("It was great seeing you again") as well as leave-taking phrases ("Good-bye," "So long"). Nonverbal closings include breaking eye contact, positioning your legs or feet toward the door and away from the person you're talking with, leaning forward, and placing your hands on your knees or legs (often accompanied by forward leaning) to signal the intention to stand up. As with openings, usually the verbal and the nonverbal are combined; for example, you might say "It was good seeing you again" while leaning forward with hands on your knees.

Reflections on the Model of Conversation

Not all conversations will be neatly divided into these five steps. Often the opening and the feedforward are combined—as when you see someone on campus, for example, and say "Hey, listen to this"; or when, in a work situation, someone says, "Well, folks, let's get the meeting going." In a similar way, the feedback and the closing might be combined: "Look, I've got to think more about this commitment, okay?"

As already noted, the business is the longest part of the conversation. The opening and the closing are usually about the same length, and the feedforward and feedback are usually about equal in length. When these relative lengths are severely distorted, you may feel that something is wrong. For example, when someone uses a too-short opening or a long feedforward, you may suspect that what is to follow is extremely serious.

This conversational process model can help us to identify conversational skill deficits and to distinguish effective and satisfying from ineffective and unsatisfying conversations. Consider, for example, how people can damage entire conversations through the following violations:

- using openings that are insensitive; for example, "Wow, you've gained a few pounds"
- using openers that fail to acknowledge the listener; for example, never asking "How are you?"

> **"** Their remarks and responses were like a Ping-Pong game with each volley clearing the net and flying back to the opposition. **"**
> —Maya Angelou

> **"** The real art of conversation is not only to say the right thing at the right place but to leave unsaid the wrong thing at the tempting moment. **"**
> —Dorothy Nevill

- using overly long feedforwards that make you wonder if the speaker will ever get to the business
- omitting feedforward before a truly shocking message (for example, the death or illness of a friend or relative), which leads you to see the other person as insensitive or uncaring
- doing business without the normally expected greeting; as when, for example, your doctor begins the conversation with "Well, what's wrong?"
- omitting feedback, which leads you to wonder if the listener heard or cared about what you said
- omitting an appropriate closing, which makes you wonder if the other person is disturbed or angry with you
- not giving clear closure (say, on the phone) so it's not clear if the person wants to hang up or continue talking

Of course, each culture will alter the five basic steps in different ways. In some cultures the openings are especially short; in others the openings are elaborate, lengthy, and sometimes highly ritualized. It's easy in intercultural communication situations to violate another culture's conversational rules. Being overly friendly, too formal, or too forward may easily hinder the remainder of the conversation. The reason why such violations may have significant consequences is that people are not aware of these rules and therefore do not see violations as simply cultural differences. Rather, we see the rule violator as too aggressive, too stuffy, or too pushy—almost immediately we dislike the person and put a negative cast on the future conversation.

Managing Conversation

Speakers and listeners have to work together to make conversation an effective and satisfying experience. We can look at **conversational management** in terms of opening, maintaining, repairing, and closing conversations.

Opening Conversations

Opening a conversation is especially difficult. At times you may not be sure of what to say or how to say it. You may fear being rejected or having someone not understand your meaning. One way to develop opening approaches is to focus on the elements of the interpersonal communication process we discussed in Chapter 1. From these we can derive several avenues for opening a conversation:

"Would you mind talking to me for a while? I forgot my cell phone."

- *Self-references.* Say something about yourself. Such references may be of the name, rank, and serial number type; for example, "My name is Joe, I'm from Omaha." Or, on the first day of class, a student might say, "I'm worried about this class" or "I took this instructor last semester; she was excellent."
- *Other-references.* Say something about the other person, or ask a question: "I like that sweater" or "Didn't we meet at Charlie's?"
- *Relational references.* Say something about the two of you; for example, "May I buy you a drink?" "Would you like to dance?" or simply "May I join you?"
- *Context references.* Say something about the physical, cultural, social–psychological, or temporal context. The familiar "Do you have the time?" is of this type. But you can be more creative; for example, "This place seems real friendly" or "That painting is just great."

Keep in mind two general rules. First, be positive. Lead off with something positive rather than something negative. Say, for example, "I really enjoy coming here" instead of "Don't you just hate this place?" Second, do not be too revealing; don't self-disclose too much early in an interaction. If you do, people will think it strange.

The Opening Line   Another way of looking at the process of initiating conversations is to examine the infamous "opening line." For example, consider your own opening lines (and perhaps some opening lines that have been used on you). Let's say you're at a club and want to strike up a conversation—and perhaps spark a relationship. Which of the following are you most likely to use (Kleinke, 1986)?

- *a cute–flippant opener—"Is that really your hair?" "I bet the cherry jubilee isn't as sweet as you are."*
- *an innocuous (highly ambiguous) opener—"What do you think of the band?" "Could you show me how to work this machine?"*
- *a direct opener—"I feel a little embarrassed about this, but I'd like to meet you"; "Would you like to have a drink with me?" "May I join you?"*

Cute–flippant openers are humorous, indirect, and ambiguous as to whether the person opening the conversation actually wants an extended encounter. One advantage of these opening lines is that they're indirect enough to cushion any rejection. These are also, however, the lines both men and women like least.

Innocuous openers are highly ambiguous as to whether they're simple comments that might be made to just anyone or whether they're in fact openers designed to initiate an extended encounter. Men and women generally like these openers; they're indirect enough to allow for an easy out if the other person doesn't want to talk.

Direct openers clearly demonstrate the speaker's interest in meeting the other person. Men like direct openers that are very clear in meaning, possibly because men are not used to having another person initiate a meeting. Women prefer openers that aren't too strong and that are relatively modest.

In e-mail the situation is a bit different. Even before the receiver opens your message, he or she knows who you are, when you sent your message, and, from the title or subject line, something about the nature of the message. In addition to providing this general hint at the nature of the message, most e-mail users begin with a

? SKILLS VIEWPOINT

You're new at college and have been hanging out with a group of fellow students for the last several months. You'd like to ask one of them on a date but are worried that you'll be rejected and it will ruin the friendship. You want to find out what your chances are before making a move. What do you say?

Opening a Conversation

Here are a few situations in which you might want to open a conversation. For each situation, develop a possible opening message in which you seek to accomplish one or more of the following: *(a)* telling others that you're accessible and open to communication, *(b)* showing that you're friendly, and/or *(c)* showing that you like the other person.

1. On the first day of class, you and another student are the first to come into the classroom and are seated in the room alone.
2. You're a guest at a friend's party. You're one of the first guests to arrive and are now there with several other people to whom you've only just been introduced. Your friend, the host, is busy with other matters.
3. You're in the college cafeteria eating alone. You see another student who is also eating alone and who you recognize from your English literature class. But you're not sure if this person has noticed you in class.

Opening a conversation is difficult and exciting; how you do it is going to influence the person's early impression of you, an impression that's likely to be long lasting and highly resistant to change.

kind of preface; for example, "I'm writing to ask the name of your acupuncturist" or "I want to fill you in on what happened at the party." Generally, such openers are direct and relate closely to what is to follow.

Maintaining Conversations

In maintaining conversations you follow a variety of principles and rules. Let's consider first the principle of cooperation and its several maxims; then we'll look at the principles of dialogue and turn-taking.

The Principle of Cooperation   During conversation you probably follow the **principle of cooperation,** tacitly agreeing with the other person that you will both cooperate in trying to understand each other (Grice, 1975). If you didn't agree on **cooperation,** then communication would be extremely difficult, if not impossible. You cooperate largely by adhering to four **conversational maxims**—rules that speakers and listeners in the United States and in many other cultures follow in conversation. Although the names for these maxims may be new to you, you will easily recognize the rules themselves from your own experiences.

You follow the **quantity maxim** when you're only as informative as necessary to communicate the intended meaning. Thus, you include information that makes the meaning clear but omit what does not. The maxim of quantity requires that you give neither too little nor too much information. You see people violate this simple principle when they try to relate an incident and digress to give unnecessary information. You find yourself thinking, or even saying, "Get to the point; what happened?" This maxim is also violated when a person omits necessary information. In this situation, you find yourself constantly interrupting to ask questions: "Where were they?" "When did this happen?" "Who else was there?"

E-mail communication frequently violates the quantity maxim. Here are three examples and some suggestions on how to avoid these violations:

- Chain e-mails often violate the maxim of quantity by sending people information they don't need or want. Suggestion: Avoid chain e-mail, at least most of the time. When something comes along that you think some specific person would like to read, then send it to that person.
- Chain e-mails often contain the e-mail addresses of everyone on the chain. These extensive headers clog the system and also reveal e-mail addresses that

> **"** Conversation should be pleasant without scurrility, witty without affectation, free without indecency, learned without conceitedness, novel without falsehood. **"**
>
> —William Shakespeare

Gossiping about Secrets

Gossiping seems universal among all cultures (Laing, 1993), and among some it's a commonly accepted ritual (Hall, 1993). **Gossip** may be defined as evaluative messages about a person who is not a party to or present during the conversation (Eder & Enke, 1991; Rosnow, 1977; Leaper & Holliday, 1995). Often gossip involves telling secrets about the third party.

In *Secrets* (1983) ethicist Sissela Bok identifies three types of situations in which she argues it would be unethical to reveal the secrets of another person.

- It's unethical to reveal information that you have promised to keep secret. When you promise to keep information hidden, you take on an ethical responsibility.
- It's unethical to talk about another person when you know the information is false. When you try to deceive listeners by saying things about another person that you know to be false, your messages are unethical.
- It's unethical to invade the privacy to which everyone has a right, to reveal information that no one else has a right to know. This is especially unethical when such disclosures can hurt the individual involved.

What Would You Do?

As Bok suggests, consider an 18-year-old friend who confides that he intends to commit suicide. Using Bok's guidelines, how would you evaluate the ethics involved in revealing this secret? What ethical justification might be offered for revealing such a secret? What would you do in this situation?

some people may want to keep private. Suggestion: When you do send chain e-mails (and in some situations they serve useful purposes), conceal the recipients' e-mail addresses by using some general description such as "undisclosed recipients."

- Lengthy attachments take time to download and often create problems for people who do not have compatible technology. Not everyone wants to see all the photos of your last vacation. Suggestion: Use attachments in moderation; find out first who would like to receive photos and who would not.

The **quality maxim** states that speakers should say what they know or believe to be true and not say what they know to be false. When you're in conversation, you assume that the other person's information is true—at least as far as he or she knows. When you speak with a person who frequently violates the maxim of quality by lying, exaggerating, or minimizing, you come to distrust what the person is saying and wonder what is true and what is fabricated.

You follow the **relation maxim** when you talk about what is relevant to the conversation. Thus, if you're talking about Pat and Chris and say, for example, "Money causes all sorts of relationship problems," others will assume that your comment is somehow related to Pat and Chris. Speakers who digress widely and frequently interject irrelevant comments violate the maxim of relation.

You follow the **manner maxim** by being clear, by avoiding ambiguities, by being relatively brief, and by organizing your thoughts into a meaningful sequence. Thus, you use terms that the listener understands and omit or clarify terms that you suspect the listener will not understand. You see the maxim of manner in action when you adjust your speech on the basis of your listener. For example, when talking to a close friend, you can refer to mutual acquaintances and to experiences you've shared. When talking to a stranger, however, you either omit such references or explain them. Similarly, when talking with a child, you simplify your vocabulary so that the child will understand your meaning.

The four maxims just discussed aptly describe most conversations as they take place in much of the United States. Recognize, however, that these maxims may not apply in all cultures; also, other cultures may have other maxims. Some of these other maxims may

Message Skills

Conversational Maxims: Follow (generally) the basic maxims of conversation, such as quantity, quality, relations, manner, and politeness.

> The art of conversation consists as much in listening politely, as in talking agreeably.
>
> —Atwell

contradict the advice generally given to persons communicating in the United States or in other cultures (Keenan, 1976). Here are a few maxims appropriate in countries other than the United States, but also appropriate to some degree throughout the United States.

Researchers on Japanese conversations and group discussions have noted a maxim of *preserving peaceful relationships* with others (Midooka, 1990). The ways in which such peaceful relationships may be maintained will vary with the person with whom you're interacting. For example, in Japan your status or position in the hierarchy will influence the amount of self-expression you're expected to engage in. Similarly, there is a great distinction made between public and private conversations. The maxim of peaceful relationships is much more important in public than in private conversations, in which the maxim may be and often is violated.

The maxim of *self-denigration,* observed in the conversations of Chinese speakers, may require that you avoid taking credit for some accomplishment or make less of some ability or talent you have (Gu, 1990). To put yourself down in this way is a form of politeness that seeks to elevate the person to whom you're speaking.

The maxim of *politeness* is probably universal across all cultures (Brown & Levinson, 1987). Cultures differ, however, in how they define politeness and in how important politeness is in comparison with, say, openness or honesty. Cultures also differ in their rules for expressing politeness or impoliteness and in their punishments for violating the accepted rules of politeness (Mao, 1994; Strecker, 1993). You may wish to take the self-test below to help you think about your own level of politeness.

 Test Yourself

How Polite Is Your Conversation?

INSTRUCTIONS: This is an approach to a conversational politeness scale—a device for measuring politeness in conversation. Try estimating your own level of politeness. For each item below indicate how closely the statement describes your *typical* behavior in conversations with peers. Avoid giving responses that you feel might be considered "socially acceptable"; instead, give responses that accurately represent your typical conversational behaviors. Use a 10-point scale, with 10 being "very accurate description of my typical communications in conversations" and 1 being "very inaccurate description of my typical communications in conversations."

_____ ❶ I make jokes at the expense of another nationality, race, religion, or affectional orientation.

_____ ❷ I say "please" when asking someone to do something.

_____ ❸ When talking with guests in my home, I leave the television on.

_____ ❹ I make an effort to make sure that other people are not embarrassed.

_____ ❺ I use body adaptors when in conversation—for example, touching my hair or face, playing with a pen or Styrofoam cup, or touching the clothing of the other person.

_____ ❻ I ask people I call if it's a good time to talk.

_____ ❼ I will raise my voice to take charge of the conversation.

_____ ❽ I give the speaker cues to show that I'm listening and interested.

_____ ❾ I avoid using terms that might prove offensive to people with whom I'm talking, such as terms that might be considered sexist, racist, or heterosexist.

_____ ❿ I interrupt the speaker when I think I have something important to say.

HOW DID YOU DO? This scale was developed to encourage you to consider some of the ways in which politeness is signaled in conversations and to encourage you to examine your own politeness behaviors. Nevertheless, you may want to compile a general politeness score that you can compare with those of others. To compile your politeness score, follow these steps:

- Step 1. Add up your scores for items 2, 4, 6, 8, and 9.

- Step 2. Reverse your scores for items 1, 3, 5, 7, and 10. That is, if you ranked a statement 10, it becomes 1; if you ranked a statement 9, it becomes 2; 8 becomes 3; 7 becomes 4; 6 becomes 5; 5 becomes 6; 4 becomes 7; 3 becomes 8; 2 becomes 9; and 1 becomes 10.

- Step 3. Add the scores for Steps 1 and 2 (using the reversed scores for items 1, 3, 5, 7, and 10).

- Your score should fall somewhere between 10 (extremely impolite) and 100 (extremely polite).

WHAT WILL YOU DO? Realize that this "scale" is only a pedagogical tool; it's not a scientifically valid research instrument. So use it to stimulate thinking about your own interpersonal politeness behaviors rather than to give yourself a label. Notice that your score indicates your evaluation of your own conversational behaviors, so this score may be very different from the scores others would assign to you. Generally, do you think you see yourself as more (or less) polite than your peers see you? What might you do to increase your level of perceived politeness?

In New York City, to take one example, the low level of politeness between cab drivers and riders has elicited a great deal of criticism. In an attempt to combat this negative attitude, cab drivers have been given 50 polite phrases and are instructed to use these frequently: "May I open (close) the window for you?" "Madam (Sir), is the temperature OK for you?" "I'm sorry, I made a wrong turn. I'll take care of it, and we can deduct it from the fare" (*New York Times,* May 6, 1996, p. B1).

People in Asian cultures, especially the Chinese and Japanese, are often singled out because they emphasize politeness more and mete out harsher social punishments for violations of courtesy norms than would most people in, say, the United States or western Europe. This pattern has led some to propose that a maxim of politeness operates in Asian cultures (Fraser, 1990). When this maxim operates, it may actually conflict with other maxims. For example, the maxim of politeness may require that you not tell the truth—a situation that would violate the maxim of quality.

In Internet communication, politeness is covered very specifically by the rules of netiquette, which are very clearly stated in most computer books (see the Skills Toolbox in Chapter 5). For example: Find out what a group is talking about before breaking in with your own comment; be tolerant of newbies (those who are new to newsgroups or chat groups); don't send duplicate messages; don't attack other people.

There are also large gender differences (as well as some similarities) in the expression of politeness (Holmes, 1995). Generally, studies from several different cultures show that women use more polite forms than men (Brown, 1980; Wetzel, 1988; Holmes, 1995). For example, both in informal conversation and in conflict situations, women tend to seek areas of agreement more than do men. Young girls are more apt to try to modify expressions of disagreement, whereas young boys are more apt to express more "bald disagreements" (Holmes, 1995). There are also similarities. For example, both men and women in the United States and New Zealand seem to pay compliments in similar ways (Manes & Wolfson, 1981; Holmes,

? SKILLS VIEWPOINT

You're with a group of friends and you really have to leave. But Pat keeps talking, never pausing even for a moment to allow you to say you have to go. What do you do?

Figure 8.2

Wolfson's Bulge Model of Politeness
Do you find this model a generally accurate representation of your own level of politeness in different types of relationships? Can you build a case for an inverted U theory, in which politeness would be high with both strangers and intimates and low with friends?

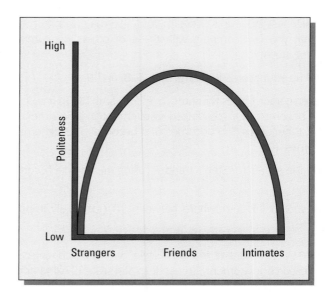

1986, 1995), and both men and women use politeness strategies when communicating bad news in an organization (Lee, 1993).

Politeness also varies with the type of relationship. One researcher, for example, has proposed that politeness is considerably greater with friends than with either strangers or intimates (Wolfson, 1988; Holmes, 1995). Wolfson (1998) depicts this relationship as in Figure 8.2.

The Principle of Dialogue   Think about your own conversational tendencies. Which of the following paired statements *generally* characterize your interpersonal interactions?

- *You frequently use negative criticism ("I didn't like that explanation") and negative personal judgments ("You're not a very good listener, are you?").*

- *You frequently use dysfunctional communication, such as expressing unwillingness to talk or using messages that are unrelated to the topic of discussion ("There's no sense discussing this; I can see you're not rational").*

- *You rarely demonstrate (by paraphrasing or summarizing) that you understand the other person's meaning.*

- *You rarely request clarification of the other person's perspectives or ideas.*

- *You frequently request personal positive statements or statements of approval ("How did you like the way I told that guy off? Clever, no?").*

- *You avoid negative criticism and negative personal judgments; you practice using positive criticism ("I liked those first two explanations best; they were really well reasoned").*

- *You keep the channels of communication open ("I really don't know what I did that offended you; please tell me, because I don't want to hurt you again").*

- *You frequently paraphrase or summarize what the other person has said to ensure accurate understanding.*

- *You request clarification as necessary, and you ask for the other person's point of view because of a genuine interest in the other person's perspective.*

- *You avoid requesting personal endorsement or approval statements.*

> ❝ Most conversations are monologues delivered in the presence of witnesses. ❞
>
> —Margaret Millar

> ❝ There is no such thing as conversation. It is an illusion. There are intersecting monologues, that is all. ❞
>
> —Rebecca West

> ❝ Two monologues do not make a dialogue. ❞
>
> —Jeff Daly

Figure 8.3

	To speak	**To listen**
Speaker	1 Turn-maintaining cues	2 Turn-yielding cues
Listener	3 Turn-requesting cues	4 Turn-denying cues

Turn-Taking and Conversational Wants
Quadrant 1 represents the speaker who wishes to continue to speak and uses turn-maintaining cues; quadrant 2, the speaker who wishes to listen and uses turn-yielding cues. Quadrant 3 represents the listener who wishes to speak and uses turn-requesting cues; quadrant 4, the listener who wishes to continue listening and uses turn-denying cues. Backchanneling cues would appear in quadrant 4, as they are cues that listeners use while they continue to listen. Interruptions would appear in quadrant 3, though they are not so much cues that request a turn as actual takeovers of the speaker's position.

The conversational behaviors described in the left column are examples of monologue; statements on the right are examples of dialogue. **Monologue** is communication in which one person speaks and the other listens—there's no real interaction between participants. The term *monologic communication* is an extension of this basic definition. The monologic communicator is focused only on his or her own goals and has no concern for the listener's feelings or attitudes; this speaker is interested in the other person only insofar as that person can serve the speaker's purposes.

Not surprisingly, effective communication is based not on monologue but on its opposite, **dialogue** (Buber, 1958; Yau-fair Ho, Chan, Peng, & Ng, 2001; McNamee & Gergen, 1999). In dialogue there is two-way interaction. Each person is both speaker and listener, sender and receiver. In *dialogic communication* there is deep concern for the other person and for the relationship between the two people. The objective of dialogue is mutual understanding and empathy. There is respect for the other person, not because of what this person can do or give but simply because this person is a human being and therefore deserves to be treated honestly and sincerely.

In a dialogic interaction you respect the other person enough to allow that person the right to make his or her own choices without coercion, without the threat of punishment, without fear or social pressure. A dialogic communicator believes that other people can make decisions that are right for them and implicitly or explicitly lets them know that whatever choices they make, they will still be respected as people.

The Principle of Turn-Taking   The defining feature of conversation is that the roles of speaker and listener are exchanged throughout the interaction. We use a wide variety of verbal and nonverbal cues to signal **conversational turns**—the changing (or maintaining) of the speaker or listener roles during the conversation. Figure 8.3 summarizes the various turn-taking cues and how they correspond to the conversational wants or desires of speaker and listener. Combining the insights of a variety of communication researchers (Duncan, 1972; Burgoon, Buller, & Woodall, 1996; Pearson & Spitzberg, 1990), let's examine conversational turns in terms of speaker cues and listener cues.

Speaker Cues.   As a speaker you regulate the conversation through two major types of cues. *Turn-maintaining cues* enable you to maintain the role of speaker. You communicate these cues by, for example, audibly inhaling breath to show that you have more to say; continuing a gesture to show that your thought is not yet complete; avoiding eye contact with the listener so as not to indicate that you're passing the speaking turn on to the listener; or vocalizing **pauses** ("er," "umm") rather than

> " It is all right to hold a conversation but you should let go of it now and then. "
>
> —Richard Armour

Message Skills

Conversational Turns: Maintain relatively short conversational turns; after taking your turn, pass the speaker's turn to another person nonverbally or verbally.

pausing silently, so as to prevent the listener from speaking and to show that you're still talking.

Turn-yielding cues tell the listener that you're finished and wish to exchange the role of speaker for the role of listener. You may communicate these cues by dropping your intonation, by a prolonged silence, by making direct eye contact with a listener, by asking a question, or by nodding in the direction of a particular listener.

Listener Cues.   As a listener you can regulate the conversation by using three types of cues. First, *turn-requesting cues* tell the speaker that you would like to take a turn as speaker; you might transmit these cues by using some vocalized "er" or "um" that tells the speaker that you would now like to speak, by opening your eyes and mouth as if to say something, by beginning to gesture with a hand, or by leaning forward.

Second, through *turn-denying cues* you indicate your reluctance to assume the role of speaker by, for example, intoning a slurred "I don't know"; giving the speaker some brief grunt that signals you have nothing to say; avoiding eye contact with the speaker who wishes you now to take on the speaker role; or engaging in some behavior that is incompatible with speaking—for example, coughing or blowing your nose.

Third, through **backchanneling cues** you communicate various meanings back to the speaker—but without assuming the role of the speaker. For example, you can indicate your *agreement* or *disagreement* with the speaker through smiles or frowns, nods of approval or disapproval; brief comments such as "right," "exactly," or "never"; or vocalizations such as "uh-huh" or "uh-uh." You convey your *involvement* or *boredom* with the speaker through attentive posture, forward leaning, and focused eye contact, which tell the speaker that you're involved in the conversation—or through an inattentive posture, backward leaning, and avoidance of eye contact, which communicate your lack of involvement. You can also request that the speaker *pace* the conversation differently, perhaps asking the speaker to slow down by raising your hand near your ear and leaning forward, or to speed up by continually nodding your head. Or you can signal the speaker to give you *clarification;* a puzzled facial expression, perhaps coupled with a forward lean, will probably tell most speakers that you need something clarified.

Some backchanneling cues are actually *interruptions*. Backchanneling interruptions, however, are generally confirming rather than disconfirming. They tell the speaker that you're listening and are involved (Kennedy & Camden, 1988). Other interruptions are not as confirming and simply take the speaking turn away from the speaker, either temporarily or permanently. Sometimes the interrupter may apologize for breaking in; at other times the interrupter may not even seem aware of interrupting.

Interruptions can, of course, serve a variety of specific functions. For example, interruptions may be used to change the topic ("I gotta tell you this story before I bust"); to correct the speaker ("You mean four months, not years, don't you?"); to seek information or clarification ("Are you talking about Jeff's cousin?"); or to introduce essential information ("Your car's on fire"). And, of course, you can interrupt to end the conversation ("I hate to interrupt, but I really have to get back to the office").

Not surprisingly, research finds that superiors (bosses, supervisors) and those in positions of authority (police officers, interviewers) interrupt those in inferior positions more than the other way around (Carroll, 1994; Ashcraft, 1998). In fact, it would probably strike you as strange to see a worker repeatedly interrupting a supervisor or a student repeatedly interrupting a professor.

Another and even more often studied aspect of interruption is that of gender difference. Do men or women interrupt more? Research here is conflicting. These few research findings will give you an idea of the differing results (Pearson, West, & Turner, 1995):

- The more malelike the person's gender identity—regardless of the person's biological sex—the more likely it is that the person will interrupt (Drass, 1986).
- There are no significant differences between boys and girls (aged two to five) in interrupting behavior (Greif, 1980).

❝ To listen closely and reply well is the highest perfection we are able to attain in the art of conversation. ❞

—Francois de La Rochefoucauld

- Fathers interrupt their children more than mothers do (Greif, 1980).
- Women judge "simultaneous talk" as being interruptions more than men do (Bresnahan & Cai, 1996).
- Men interrupt more than women do (Zimmerman & West, 1975; West & Zimmerman, 1977).
- Men and women do not differ in their interrupting behavior (Roger & Nesshoever, 1987).
- No single linguistic feature has been found that definitely identifies a message as an interruption (Coon & Schwanenflugel, 1996).

Repairing Conversations

At times it's necessary to repair a conversation that has hit a snag. Unfortunately, even if you realize you've said the wrong thing, you can't erase the message—communication really is irreversible. So you may try to account for it. Perhaps the most common way of doing this is with an excuse (Snyder, 1984; Snyder, Higgins, & Stucky, 1983).

You learn early in life that when you do something that others will view negatively, an **excuse** is in order to justify your performance. In conversation you're especially likely to offer an excuse when you say or are accused of saying something that runs counter to what is expected, sanctioned, or considered "right" by your listeners. Ideally, the excuse lessens the negative impact of the message.

Motives for Excuse Making   The major motive for excuse making seems to be to maintain self-esteem, to project a positive image to yourself and to others. You also may offer an excuse to reduce the stress that may result from a bad performance. In other words, you may feel that if you can offer an excuse—especially a good one that is accepted by those around you—it will reduce the negative reaction to your performance and the subsequent stress.

Excuses also enable you to maintain effective interpersonal relationships, even after some negative behavior. For example, after criticizing a friend's behavior and observing the friend's negative reaction to your criticism, you might offer an excuse such as "Please forgive me; I'm really exhausted. I'm just not thinking straight." Excuses place your messages—even your failures—in a more favorable light.

Types of Excuses   One categorization describes three basic classes of excuses (Snyder, 1984). Think of recent excuses you have used or heard. Did they fall into any of these classes?

- I didn't do it: *You deny that you did what you're accused of. "I never said that." "I wasn't even near the place when it happened." "She did it, not me."*
- It wasn't so bad: *You admit to doing it, but you claim the offense was not really so bad or perhaps that there was justification for it. "I only padded the expense account by a few dollars." "Sure, I hit him, but he was asking for it."*
- Yes, but: *You claim that extenuating circumstances account for the behavior. "It was the liquor talking." "I was too upset to think clearly."*

Good Excuses   The most important question to most people is what makes a good excuse (Snyder, 1984; Slade, 1995). Bad excuses only make matters worse—so how can you make good excuses and thus get out of problems?

The best excuses contain five elements (Slade, 1995; Coleman, 2002):

1. You demonstrate that you really see the problem and that your partner's feelings are legitimate and justified. Avoid minimizing the issue or your partner's feelings ("You're overreacting," "I was only two hours late").

> ❝ To make excuses before they are needed is to blame one's self. ❞
>
> —Spanish proverb

2. You acknowledge your responsibility for doing what you did. Avoid qualifying responsibility ("I'm sorry *if* I did anything wrong") or expressing a lack of sincerity ("OK, I'm sorry; it's obviously my fault—*again*").

2. You acknowledge your responsibility for doing what you did. Avoid qualifying responsibility ("I'm sorry *if* I did anything wrong") or expressing a lack of sincerity ("OK, I'm sorry; it's obviously my fault—*again*").

3. You say that you regret what you did; you make it clear that you're not happy with yourself for doing what you did.

4. You request forgiveness for what you did. It's important to be specific.

5. You make it clear that this will never happen again.

Table 8.3 provides examples of how you might deploy these five messages in excuses in romantic and business situations.

Closing Conversations

Closing a conversation is almost as difficult as opening a conversation. It's frequently an awkward and uncomfortable part of interpersonal interaction. Here are a few **leave-taking cues** you might consider for closing a conversation.

- Reflect back on the conversation and briefly summarize it to bring it to a close. For example, "I'm glad I ran into you and found out what happened at that union meeting. I'll probably be seeing you at the workshops."
- State the desire to end the conversation directly and to get on with other things. For example, "I'd like to continue talking but I really have to run. I'll see you around."
- Refer to future interaction. For example, "Why don't we get together next week sometime and continue this discussion."
- Ask for closure. For example, "Have I covered what you wanted to know?"
- Say that you enjoyed the interaction. For example, "I really enjoyed talking with you."

With any of these closings, it should be clear to the other person that you're attempting to end the conversation. Obviously, you will have to use more direct methods with those who don't take these sub-

? SKILLS VIEWPOINT

You took off from work to attend your brother's softball game, but you told your supervisor that you weren't feeling well. The next day, when your supervisor asks how you're feeling, you describe your illness and say that you're now feeling a little better. Almost immediately after you say your piece, a colleague joins you both, mentions the game, and says it was great that you were able to catch your brother's no-hitter. What do you say?

TABLE 8.3	Excuses in Romantic and Workplace Relationships

Here are the five key excuse messages along with some specific examples. As you read this table, visualize a specific situation in which you recently made an excuse. Can you reorganize what you said (or should have said) into this five-step sequence?

MESSAGE	IN ROMANTIC RELATIONSHIPS	AT WORK
1. I see	I should have asked you first; you have a right to be angry.	I understand that we lost the client because of this.
2. I did it	I was totally responsible.	I should have acted differently.
3. I'm sorry	I'm sorry that I didn't ask you first.	I'm sorry I didn't familiarize myself with the client's objections to our last offer.
4. Forgive me	Forgive me?	I'd really like another chance.
5. I'll do better	I'll never loan anyone money without first discussing it with you.	This will never happen again.

Formulating Excuses

Although excuses are not always appropriate, they are often helpful in lessening the possible negative effects of a mishap. Here are several situations in which you might want to offer an excuse. For any one situation, write an excuse that includes all five parts of the effective excuse as discussed in the text.

1. Your boss discovers that you've been making lots of long-distance personal phone calls from work, a practice that is explicitly forbidden.
2. In talking with your supervisor, you tell a joke that puts down lesbians and gay men. She tells you she finds the joke homophobic and offensive; she adds that she has a gay son and is proud of it. Because you just started the job, this supervisor's approval is important to you.
3. You're caught in a lie. You told your romantic partner that you were going to visit your parents, but you actually went to visit a former lover. Your partner has found out and confronts you.
4. Your life partner discovers that you had a history of alcoholism, which you kept hidden despite your mutual agreement to be totally honest.

Excuses will not reverse your errors or eliminate their negative impacts, but they may help repair—at least to some extent—conversational or relationship damage.

tle hints—who don't realize that *both* persons are responsible for managing the interpersonal interaction and for bringing it to a satisfying close.

Closing a conversation in e-mail follows the same principles as closing a face-to-face conversation. However, exactly when you end the e-mail exchange is often not clear, partly because the absence of nonverbal cues creates ambiguity. For example, if you ask someone a question and the other person answers, do you then e-mail again and say "thanks"? If so, should the other person e-mail you back and say "It was my pleasure"? And if so, should you then e-mail back again and say "I appreciate your willingness to answer my questions"? And should the other person then respond with something like "It was no problem"?

Clearly you don't want to prolong the interaction more than necessary. At the same time you don't want to appear impolite. So how do you signal (politely) that the e-mail exchange should stop? Here are a few suggestions (Cohen, 2002).

- Include in your e-mail the notation NRN (no reply necessary).
- If you're replying with information the other person requested, end your message with something like "I hope this helps."
- Title or head your message FYI (for your information), thus indicating that your message is just to keep someone in the loop.
- When you make a request for information, end your message with "thank you in advance."

Message Skills

Making Excuses: Repair conversational problems by offering excuses that demonstrate understanding, acknowledge your responsibility, acknowledge your regret, request forgiveness, and make clear that this will never happen again.

Effective Conversation

Because each conversation is unique, the specific skills of **interpersonal effectiveness** cannot be applied indiscriminately. Shortly we'll consider specific conversational skills, but you'll need to apply these skills selectively. For example, although openness is a generally positive quality in, say, romantic relationships, it may be quite inappropriate with your supervisor or postal worker. Fortunately, there are general skills to help you regulate your more specific skills.

Closing a Conversation

Here are a few situations in which you might want to bring a conversation to a close. For each situation, develop a possible closing message in which you seek to accomplish one or more of the following: *(a)* end the conversation without much more talk, *(b)* leave the other person with a favorable impression of you, and *(c)* keep the channels of communication open for future interaction.

1. You and a friend have been talking on the phone for the last hour, but not much new is being said. You have a great deal of work to do and want to wrap it up. Your friend just doesn't seem to hear your subtle cues.
2. You're at a party and are anxious to meet a person with whom you've exchanged eye contact for the last 10 minutes. The problem is that a friendly and talkative older relative of yours is demanding all your attention. You don't want to insult your relative, but at the same time you want to make contact with this other person.
3. You're at a welcoming meeting at your new job and are in conversation with a supervisor who has had too much to drink. You've listened to the supervisor's sad tales for the last 20 minutes; now you really want to get away and join others.

The way you close a conversation can leave an important impression; it will influence heavily what the other person remembers about you.

General Conversational Skills

Four general skills will prove especially valuable in helping you decide how to apply your specific skills; these are mindfulness, flexibility, cultural sensitivity, and metalinguistic abilities.

Mindfulness   **Mindfulness** is a state of awareness in which you're conscious of your reasons for thinking or behaving. In its opposite, **mindlessness,** you lack conscious awareness of what or how you're thinking (Langer, 1989). To apply interpersonal skills effectively in conversation, you need to be mindful of the unique communication situation you're in, of your available communication options, and of the reasons why one option is likely to be better than the others (Elmes & Gemmill, 1990; Burgoon, Berger, & Waldron, 2000).

Increasing Mindfulness.   To increase mindfulness, try the following suggestions (Langer, 1989).

- *Create and recreate categories.* Learn to see objects, events, and people as belonging to a wide variety of categories. Try to see, for example, your prospective romantic partner in a variety of roles—child, parent, employee, neighbor, friend, financial contributor, and so on. Avoid storing in memory an image of a person with only one specific label.

- *Be open to new information and points of view,* even when these contradict your most firmly held beliefs. New information forces you to reconsider what might be outmoded ways of thinking and can help you challenge long held but now inappropriate beliefs and attitudes. Be willing to see your own and others' behaviors from the viewpoints of people very different from yourself.

- *Beware of relying too heavily on first impressions* (Chanowitz & Langer, 1981; Langer, 1989). Treat first impressions as tentative, as hypotheses that need further investigation. Be prepared to revise, reject, or accept these initial impressions.

Message Skills

Mindfulness: Increase your mindfulness by creating and recreating categories and being open to new information and points of view; also, beware of relying too heavily on first impressions.

5 Ways to Avoid Being Conversationally Difficult

At work meetings or at the water cooler, some people make conversation extremely difficult. Here's a brief list of types of conversationally difficult people and some suggestions for how to avoid becoming one of them.

1. The Detour Taker begins to talk about a topic, but then a key word or idea suggests another topic and off this person goes pursuing the other topic. *Follow a logical pattern in conversation; avoid frequent and/or long detours.*
2. The Storyteller has difficulty talking about the here and now and so tells stories. Mention a topic and the storyteller has a ready tale that makes you sorry you ever mentioned the topic in the first place. *Talk about yourself in moderation; be other-oriented.*
3. The Interrogator is a mixture of police officer, lawyer, and teacher and seems to do nothing but ask questions. No sooner have you answered one question than you are hit with another. *Ask questions in moderation—to secure needed information, not to get every detail imaginable.*
4. The Egotist is interested only in himself or herself and shows this by connecting even the most wide-ranging topics to self-related concerns. *Be other-oriented; focus on the other person as an individual; listen as much as you speak, and speak about the listener at least as much as you speak about yourself.*
5. The Advisor, whenever you express a doubt, assumes that you want advice and proceeds to analyze the situation and offer a solution. The idea that you simply wanted to express a doubt never occurs to the advisor. *Avoid giving unsolicited advice. Don't assume that discussing a problem is the same as asking you to come up with a solution.*

Applying Interpersonal Skills/Then and Now
Have you ever been in a conversation in which you fell into the role of one or more of these conversationally difficult people? What specifically did you do to make the conversation difficult? If you were having the same conversation today, what would you do differently?

Flexibility **Flexibility** is a quality of thinking and behaving in which you vary your messages based on the unique situation. One test of flexibility asks you how true you believe certain statements are; for example, "People should be frank and spontaneous in conversation" or "When angry, a person should say nothing rather than say something he or she will be sorry for later." The "preferred" answer to all such questions is "sometimes true," underscoring the importance of flexibility in all interpersonal situations (Hart, Carlson, & Eadie, 1980).

Increasing Flexibility.   Here are a few ways to cultivate flexibility.

- Realize that no two situations or people are exactly alike. Ask yourself what is different about this situation or person, and take these differences into consideration as you construct your messages.
- Realize that communication always takes place in a context; ask yourself what is unique about this specific context and how this should influence your messages.
- Realize that everything is in a state of flux. Maybe the way you communicated last month was effective, but that doesn't necessarily mean it will be effective today or tomorrow. Realize too that sudden changes (a breakup with a lover or a fatal illness) will influence what are and what are not appropriate messages.
- Realize that every situation offers you different options for communicating. Think about these options, and try to predict the effects each option might have.

Cultural Sensitivity   Cultural sensitivity is an attitude and way of behaving in which you're aware of and acknowledge cultural differences. Cultural sensitivity is crucial on a global scale, as in efforts toward world peace and economic growth; it's

Message Skills

Flexibility: Because no two communication situations are identical, because everything is in a state of flux, and because everyone is different, cultivate flexibility and adjust your communication to the unique situation.

Message Skills

Cultural Sensitivity: Increase your cultural sensitivity by learning about different cultures, recognizing and facing your fears, recognizing relevant differences, and becoming conscious of the cultural rules of other cultures.

also essential for effective interpersonal communication and for general success in life (Franklin & Mizell, 1995). Without cultural sensitivity there can be no effective interpersonal communication between people who are different in gender or race or nationality or affectional orientation. So be mindful of the cultural differences between yourself and the other person. The close physical distance that is normal in Arab cultures may prove too familiar or too intrusive in much of the United States and northern Europe. The empathy that most Americans welcome may be uncomfortable for most Koreans (Yun, 1976).

Increasing Cultural Sensitivity. Here are a few guidelines to follow for achieving greater cultural sensitivity.

- Prepare yourself. Read about and listen carefully for culturally influenced behaviors.
- Recognize and face your own and others' fears of acting inappropriately with members of different cultures.
- Recognize differences between yourself and culturally different groups.
- At the same time, recognize that there are often enormous differences within any given cultural group.
- Recognize differences in meaning; words rarely mean the same thing to members of different cultures.
- Become conscious of the cultural rules and customs of others.

Metacommunication   **Metacommunication** is communication that refers to other communications; it's communication about communication. Both verbal and nonverbal messages can be metacommunicational. Verbally, you can convey **metamessages** such as "Do you understand what I'm trying to say?" Nonverbally, you can lean forward in an exaggerated conspiratorial fashion when confiding some dubious tidbit of gossip. Interpersonal effectiveness often hinges on the ability to metacommunicate. For example, in conflict situations it's often helpful to talk about the way you fight. In romantic relationships, it's often helpful to talk about what each of you means by "steady" or "really care." On the job, it's often necessary to talk about the ways people delegate orders or express criticism.

Metacommunicating.   Here are a few suggestions for increasing your metacommunicational effectiveness:

- Explain the feelings that go with the thoughts. Often people communicate only the thinking part of their message, with the result that listeners aren't able to appreciate the other parts of the meaning.
- Give clear feedforward to help the other person get a general picture of the messages that will follow.
- Paraphrase your own complex messages to make your meaning extra clear. Similarly, check on your understanding of another's message by paraphrasing what you think the other person meant and asking for confirmation.
- If you have doubts about another's meaning, ask for clarification.
- Use metacommunication when you want to clarify the communication patterns between yourself and another person. Say, for example, "I'd like to talk about the way you talk about me to our friends" or "I think we should talk about the way we talk about sex."

Message Skills

Metacommunication: Metacommunicate when you want to clarify the way you're talking or what you're talking about by, for example, giving clear feedforward and paraphrasing your complex messages.

Specific Conversational Skills

A wide spectrum of ongoing research has identified seven specific qualities or skills of **interpersonal effectiveness:** (1) openness, (2) empathy, (3) positiveness, (4) immediacy, (5) interaction management, (6) expressiveness, and (7) other-orientation (Bochner & Kelly, 1974; Wiemann, 1977; Spitzberg & Hecht, 1984; Spitzberg & Cupach, 1984, 1989; Rubin, 1985, 1986; Rubin & Graham, 1988). As you read about these specific conversational skills, keep in mind the general skills we've just surveyed.

Openness   **Openness** involves your willingness to self-disclose—to reveal information about yourself that might normally be kept hidden. Openness also includes your willingness to listen openly and to react honestly to the messages of others.

Communicating Openness.   Consider these few ideas.

- Self-disclose when appropriate. Be mindful about your self-disclosures, remembering that this form of intimate communication has both benefits and dangers.

- Respond to those with whom you're interacting with spontaneity and with appropriate honesty—but also with an awareness of what you're saying and what the possible outcomes of your messages might be.

- Own your own feelings and thoughts. Take responsibility for what you say. Use I-messages instead of you-messages. For example, instead of saying, "You make me feel stupid when you don't ask my opinion," say, "I feel stupid when you ask everyone else what they think but don't ask me." When you use I-messages, you say, in effect, "This is how *I* feel," "This is how *I* see the situation," and "This is what *I* think."

Empathy   **Empathy** is an ability to feel what another person feels from that person's point of view, to feel as the person feels, to walk in the same shoes, to feel the feelings in a somewhat similar way. To empathize is to understand emotionally, without losing your own identity, what another person is experiencing. (To sympathize, in contrast, is to feel *for* the person—to feel sorry or happy for the person, for example.)

Communicating Empathy.   Here are a few suggestions to help you communicate empathy effectively (Authier & Gustafson, 1982).

- Avoid evaluating, judging, or criticizing the other person's behaviors. Make it clear that your're not evaluating or judging but trying to understand.

- Focus your concentration. Maintain eye contact, an attentive posture, and physical closeness. Express your involvement through appropriate facial expressions and gestures.

"Just take a seat, Mr. Bern. You're acting as if you were the only one here who's been shot."

- Reflect back to the speaker the feelings that you think are being expressed so as to check the accuracy of your perceptions and to show your commitment to understanding the speaker. Try offering tentative statements about what you think the person is feeling, as in "You seem really angry with your father" or "I hear some doubt in your voice."

- When appropriate, use your own self-disclosures to communicate your understanding. Be careful, however, not to get so caught up in your own disclosures that you refocus the discussion on yourself.

- To foster more open and honest communication, address **mixed messages.** When your friend verbally expresses contentment but shows nonverbal signs of depression it may be prudent to question the possible discrepancy.

Positiveness   **Positiveness** in interpersonal communication involves the use of positive rather than negative messages. For example, instead of the negative "I wish you wouldn't ignore my opinions," consider the positive alternative: "I feel good when you ask my opinions." Instead of the negative "You look horrible in stripes," consider the positive " I think you look great in solid colors."

Communicating Positiveness. Here are a few suggestions for communicating positiveness. Following these tips may be a bit easier for women than for men, because women generally are more apt to express positiveness in their evaluations in both face-to-face and computer-mediated communication (Adrianson, 2001).

- Look for the positive in the person or in the person's work and compliment it. Compliment specifics; overly general compliments ("Your project was interesting") are rarely as effective as those that are specific and concrete ("Your proposal will produce a great financial saving").
- Express satisfaction when communicating with others by, for example, using positive facial expressions, maintaining a reasonably close but appropriate distance, focusing eye contact, and avoiding glancing away from the other person for long periods of time.
- Recognize cultural differences in expressing positive messages (Dresser, 1996; Chen, 1992). For example, in the United States it's considered appropriate for a supervisor to compliment a worker for doing an exceptional job. But in other cultures (collectivist cultures, for example) this would be considered inappropriate, because it singles out one individual and separates that person from the group.

Immediacy   **Immediacy** has to do with the joining of speaker and listener; it's the creation of a sense of togetherness, of oneness. When you communicate immediacy you convey a sense of interest and attention, a linking for the other person. People respond to communication that is immediate more favorable than to communication that is not. In various studies, for example, students of instructors who communicated immediacy felt that the instruction was better and the course more valuable than students of instructors who did not communicate immediacy (Moore, Masterson, Christophel, & Shea, 1996; Witt & Wheeless, 2001). Students and teachers liked each other largely on the basis of immediacy (Wilson & Taylor, 2001; Baringer & McCroskey, 2000).

Communicating Immediacy.   Here are a few suggestions for communicating immediacy.

- Express psychological closeness and openness by, for example, maintaining physical closeness and arranging your body to exclude third parties. Maintain appropriate eye contact and limit looking around at others.
- Smile and express your interest in the other person.
- Use the other person's name; for example, say, "Joe, what do you think?" instead of "What do you think?"
- Focus on the other person's remarks. Make the speaker know that you heard and understood what he or she said, and give the speaker appropriate verbal and nonverbal feedback.
- Express immediacy with cultural sensitivity. In the United States immediacy is generally seen as friendly and appropriate. In other cultures, however, the same behaviors may be viewed as overly familiar, as presuming that relationship is close when it's only one of acquaintanceship (Axtell, 1993).

Interaction Management   **Interaction management** consists of the techniques and strategies by which you regulate and carry on an interpersonal interaction. Effective interaction management results in an interaction that's satisfying to both parties. Neither person feels ignored or on stage; each contributes to and benefits from the interpersonal exchange.

Managing Communication Interactions. Of course, this entire text is devoted to the effective management of interpersonal interactions—but here are a few specific suggestions.

- Maintain your role as speaker or listener—and pass the opportunity to speak back and forth—through appropriate eye movements, vocal expressions, and body and facial gestures.
- Keep the conversation fluent, avoiding long and awkward pauses. For example, researchers have found that patients are less satisfied with their interaction with their doctor when the silences between their comments and the doctor's responses are overly long (Rowland-Morin & Carroll, 1990).
- Communicate by means of verbal and nonverbal messages that are consistent and reinforce one another. Avoid sending contradictory signals—for example, a nonverbal message that contradicts the verbal message.

Expressiveness   Expressiveness is the skill of communicating genuine involvement and includes, for example, taking responsibility for your thoughts and feelings, encouraging expressiveness or openness in others, and providing appropriate feedback.

Communicating Expressiveness.   Here are a few suggestions for communicating expressiveness.

- Use appropriate variations in vocal rate, pitch, volume, and rhythm to convey involvement and interest. Use appropriate variations in verbal language, avoiding clichés and trite expressions—which can signal a lack of originality and personal involvement.

Skill building exercise

Managing Difficult Conversations

Putting all your insights into interpersonal communication and conversation to work, identify what each of these individuals might say in these relatively difficult communication situations. In framing these messages, indicate (1) how the person might open the conversation; (2) how the person would follow the principles of cooperation, dialogue, and turn-taking; and (3) the ways in which the message would include the skills of effective conversation.

1. Tanya just discovered that she has AIDS and wants to tell members of her immediate family (her mother, father, brother, and sister) as well as her relationship partner of two years and some of her close friends. But she's so upset that she can't think how to convey the news. What might Tanya say?
2. C.J. lied on his résumé and fears it may come to light now that his company is reviewing the accuracy of all résumés. On his résumé he claimed that he earned an MBA from Columbia University. The truth is that he took one course in the program and dropped out. What might C.J. say?
3. Sofia's partner of four years had an affair with a coworker about six months ago. The strange thing is that the affair has never been mentioned. And although it's over and things at home are somewhat back to normal, Sofia now feels the need to discuss the matter with her partner in order to put it behind them. What might Sofia say?
4. Pat and Chris have been dating exclusively for the last three years, but recently Pat has decided that this relationship is not working and wants out. Chris is an especially emotional individual and will take this breakup very hard. What might Pat say?

Effective conversation is a lot more difficult than it might at first seem. But with the application of some basic principles, difficult conversational problems can be managed.

Message Skills

Expressiveness: Communicate active involvement by using active listening, addressing mixed messages, using I-messages, and using appropriate variations in paralanguage and gestures.

- Use appropriate gestures, especially those that focus on the other person rather than on yourself. For example, maintain eye contact and lean toward the person; at the same time, avoid making self-touching gestures or directing your eyes to others in the room.

- Be conscious of different cultures' approaches to expressiveness. Some cultures (Italian, for example) encourage expressiveness and teach children to be expressive. Other cultures (Japanese and Thai, for example) encourage a more reserved response style (Matsumoto, 1996). Some cultures (Arab and many Asian cultures, for example) consider expressiveness by women in business settings to be generally inappropriate (Lustig & Koester, 1999; Axtell, 1993; Hall & Hall, 1987).

- Give verbal and nonverbal feedback to show that you're listening. Such feedback—called "conversational pitchback" by one researcher—promotes relationship satisfaction (Ross, 1995).

Other-Orientation   **Other-orientation** is the ability to adapt interpersonal messages to the other person; it involves communicating attentiveness and interest in the other person and in what the person says.

Communicating Other-Orientation.   You'll recognize the following behaviors in those with whom you enjoy talking.

- Show consideration and respect. For example, ask if it's all right to dump your troubles on someone before doing so; ask if your phone call comes at a good time before launching into your conversation.

- Acknowledge the other person's feelings as legitimate: "You're right" or "I can understand why you're so angry; I would be, too." Such responses help focus the interaction on the other person and assure the person that you're listening.

- Acknowledge the importance of the other person. Ask the other person for suggestions and opinions. Similarly, ask for clarification as appropriate to make sure that you understand what the other person means.

- Focus your messages on the other person. Verbally, use open-ended questions (as opposed to questions that merely ask for a yes or no answer) to involve the other person in the interaction, and make statements that directly address the person. Nonverbally, use focused eye contact and appropriate facial expressions; smile, nod, and lean toward the other person.

- Grant the other person permission to express (or to not express) feelings. A simple statement such as "I know how difficult it is to talk about feelings" opens up the topic of feelings and gives the person permission to pursue such a discussion or to say nothing.

Message Skills

Other-Orientation: Acknowledge the importance of the other person: Use focused eye contact and appropriate facial expressions; smile, nod, and lean toward the other person.

Summary of Concepts

This chapter examined conversation and looked first at five conversational stages that are especially important; second at the process of initiating, maintaining, repairing, and closing conversations; and finally at the skills of conversational effectiveness.

1. Conversation consists of five general stages: opening, feedforward, business, feedback, and closing.
2. Initiating conversations can be accomplished in various ways; for example, with self, other, relational, and context references.
3. People maintain conversations are maintained by taking turns at speaking and listening. Turn-maintaining and turn-yielding cues are used by the speaker; turn-requesting, turn-denying, and backchanneling cues are used by the listener.
4. You can close a conversation through a variety of methods. For example: Reflect back on the conversation, as in summarizing; directly state your desire to end the conversation; refer to future interaction; ask for closure; and/or state your pleasure with the interaction.
5. Conversational repair is frequently undertaken through excuses (statements of explanation designed to lessen the negative impact of a speaker's messages). "I didn't do it," "It wasn't so bad," and "Yes, but" are the major general categories of excuses.
6. The skills of conversational effectiveness need to be applied with mindfulness, flexibility, cultural sensitivity, and metacommunication (as appropriate). Among the skills of conversational effectiveness are openness, empathy, positiveness, immediacy, interaction management, expressiveness, and other-orientation.

Vocabulary Quiz: The Language of Conversation

Match the following conversation-related terms with their definitions. Record the number of the definition next to the appropriate term.

_____ excuse

_____ disclaimer

_____ business

_____ turn-yielding cues

_____ feedforward

_____ backchanneling cues

_____ altercasting

_____ conversation

_____ immediacy

_____ phatic communication

1. An interaction in which speaker and listener exchange their roles nonautomatically.
2. A form of conversation repair.
3. Messages about messages to follow.
4. A statement aiming to ensure that your message will not reflect on you negatively.
5. A conversation stage during which the major purpose of the interaction is accomplished.
6. Cues that announce that the speaker is finished and wishes to assume the listener's role.
7. A process by which the speaker or listener assumes a specific role.
8. Conversational messages through which the listener communicates information back to the speaker but does not ask to assume the speaker's role.
9. Messages that open the channels of communication.
10. A way of communicating that joins speaker and listener.

Four for Discussion

1. In dialogic interaction between, say, a fluent speaker and a speaker who has a severe physical or psychological communication problem, the more fluent speaker tries to help the speaker with the problem communicate more effectively. In fact, some researchers have argued that the more competent communicator has an ethical responsibility to equalize the interaction by helping the other person to better convey his or her meaning (von Tetzchner & Jensen, 1999). Do you consider this an ethical responsibility?

2. Not surprisingly, each culture has its own conversational taboos—topics that should be avoided, especially by visitors from other cultures. Table 8.2 (p. 166) listed a few examples. Are there certain taboo topics that you do not want members of other cultures to talk about? Why?

3. If you were compiling a book on *The World's Worst Excuses,* which ones would you include? Which would you include in *The World's Best Excuses?* What standards did you use to classify excuses as bad or good?

4. Consider the influence of gender on your own topics of conversation. Can you identify two or three topics of conversation that you would feel comfortable talking to men about? Uncomfortable talking to men about? Can you identify two or three topics that you would feel comfortable talking to women about? Uncomfortable talking to women about? How does gender impact on your conversational life?

Web Explorations

 Explore our text website at **www.ablongman.com/devito** to find:

Exercises and Self-Tests

Exercises on the varied aspects of conversation include (1) Conversational Analysis: A Chance Meeting, (2) Giving and Taking Directions, (3) Gender and the Topics of Conversation, (4) Responding Effectively in Conversation, and (5) The Qualities of Effectiveness. Several self-tests on qualities of conversation also are available: (6) How Satisfying Is Your Conversation? (also see the related test, [7] How Satisfying Is Your Public Speaking?) (8) How Flexible Are You in Conversation? (9) How Polite Is Your Conversation? (a longer form than appears in this chapter), and (10) How Much Do You Self-Monitor?

Writing Resources and Assignments

Suggestions are available for writing papers of personal experience (for example, your experience with excuses), concept or principle explanation (for example, chat groups), review (for example, gender differences in opening lines), or research on different aspects of conversation (for example, what communication qualities make for satisfying first dates).

 Explore our research resources at **www.researchnavigator.com** and

Read an article.

Read a popular or scholarly article on the conversation process, conversational management, or conversational effectiveness. On the basis of this article, what can you add to the discussion presented here?

Investigate key terms.

Investigate one of the key terms discussed in this chapter (for example, conversation, disclaimer, excuse, conversational turns, opening lines, conversational maxims, dialogue, monologue, empathy, flexibility, mindfulness). What additional insights can you provide?

Find answers.

Try finding answers to one of the following questions or design a research study to answer it.

1. How are people who monologue perceived? How are people who dialogue perceived?
2. Do men and women engage in conversation for the same purposes?
3. Do happy and unhappy couples use the same kinds of excuses?

Culture and Interpersonal Communication

9

Nacirema culture is characterized by a highly developed market economy which has evolved in a rich natural habitat. While much of the people's time is devoted to economic pursuits, a large part of the fruits of these labors and a considerable portion of the day are spent in ritual activity. The focus of this activity is the human body, the appearance and health of which loom as a dominant concern in the ethos of the people. While such a concern is certainly not unusual, its ceremonial aspects and associated philosophy are unique.

The fundamental belief underlying the whole system appears to be that the human body is ugly and that its natural tendency is to debility and disease. Incarcerated in such a body, man's only hope is to avert these characteristics through the use of the powerful influences of ritual and ceremony. Every household has one or more shrines devoted to this purpose. The more powerful individuals in the society have several shrines in their houses and, in fact, the opulence of a house is often referred to in terms of the number of such ritual centers it possesses. Most houses are of wattle and daub construction, but the shrine rooms of the more wealthy are walled with stone. Poorer families imitate the rich by applying pottery plaques to their shrine walls.

While each family has at least one such shrine, the rituals associated with it are not family ceremonies but are private and secret. The rites are normally only discussed with children, and then only during the period when they are being initiated into these mysteries. I was able, however, to establish sufficient rapport with the natives to examine these shrines and to have the rituals described to me.

The focal point of the shrine is a box or chest which is built into the wall. In this chest are kept the many charms and magical potions without which no native believes he could live. These preparations are secured from a variety of specialized practitioners. The most powerful of these are the medicine men, whose assistance must be rewarded with substantial gifts. However, the medicine men do not provide the curative potions for their clients, but decide what the ingredients should be and then write them down in an ancient and secret language. This writing is understood only by the medicine men and by the herbalists who, for another gift, provide the required charm. . . .

There remains one other kind of practitioner, known as a "listener." This witch-doctor has the power to exorcise the devils that lodge in the heads of people who have been bewitched. The Nacirema believe that parents bewitch their own children. Mothers are particularly suspected of putting a curse on children while teaching them the secret body rituals. The counter-magic of the witch-doctor is unusual in its lack of ritual. The patient simply tells the "listener" all his troubles and fears, beginning with the earliest difficulties he can remember. The memory displayed by the Nacirema in these exorcism sessions is truly remarkable. It is not uncommon for the patient to bemoan the rejection he felt upon being weaned as a babe, and a few individuals even see their troubles going back to the traumatic effects of their own birth.

From these observations of anthropologist Horace Miner (1956, pp. 503–504) you might conclude that the Nacirema are a truly strange people. Look more carefully, however, and you will see that we are the Nacirema and the rituals are our own: *Nacirema* is *American* spelled backwards. In the passage quoted, Miner describes the bathroom, the doctor writing prescriptions for the druggist, and the psychiatrist.

This excerpt brings into focus the fact that cultural customs (our own and those of others) are not necessarily logical or natural. Rather, they are better viewed as useful or not useful to the members of that particular culture. This passage is an appropriate reminder against ethnocentrism—the tendency to think that your culture's customs are right and the customs of others are wrong. It also awakens our consciousness, our mindful state, to our own customs and values.

> " From the moment of his birth the customs into which [a person] is born shape his experience and behavior. By the time he can talk, he is the little creature of his culture. "
>
> —Ruth Benedict

Culture and Intercultural Communication

A good way to start the exploration of culture and intercultural communication is to define exactly what is meant by *culture* and to look at significant cultural processes and the nature of intercultural communication.

Culture and Cultural Processes

The word *culture,* you'll recall from Chapter 1, refers to the lifestyle of a group of people: their values, beliefs, artifacts, ways of behaving, and ways of communicating. Culture includes everything that members of a social group have produced and developed—their language, ways of thinking, art, laws, and religion—and that is transmitted from one generation to another through communication rather than genes. You learn the values and **cultural rules** of your culture through the teachings of your parents, peer groups, schools, religious institutions, government agencies, and media; this process is known as **enculturation.** Through enculturation you develop an ethnic identity, a commitment to the beliefs and philosophy of your culture (Chung & Ting-Toomey, 1999). The degree to which you identify with your cultural group can be measured by your responses to such questions as these (from Ting-Toomey, 1981). Using a five-point scale from 1 (strongly disagree) to 5 (strongly agree), indicate how true of you the following statements are:

- *I am increasing my involvement in activities with my ethnic group.*
- *I involve myself in causes that will help members of my ethnic group.*
- *It feels natural being part of my ethnic group.*
- *I have spent time trying to find out more about my own ethnic group.*
- *I am happy to be a member of my ethnic group.*
- *I have a strong sense of belonging to my ethnic group.*
- *I often talk to other members of my group to learn more about my ethnic culture.*

High scores (say, 5s and 4s) indicate a strong commitment to your culture's values and beliefs; low numbers (1s and 2s) indicate a relatively weak commitment.

Acculturation refers to the processes by which a person's culture is modified through direct contact with or exposure to (say, through the mass media) another culture (Kim, 1988). For example, when immigrants settle in the United States (the host culture), their own culture becomes influenced by the host culture. Gradually the values, ways of behaving, and beliefs of the host culture become more and more a part of the immigrants' culture. At the same time, of course, the host culture changes too. Generally, however, the culture of the immigrants changes more. As Young Yun Kim (1988) puts it, "a reason for the essentially unidirectional change in the immigrant is the difference between the number of individuals in the new environment sharing the immigrant's original culture and the size of the host society."

The acceptance of the new culture depends on several factors (Kim, 1988). Immigrants who come from cultures similar to the host culture will become accultur-

> " If you see in any given situation only what everybody else can see, you can be said to be so much a representative of your culture that you are a victim of it. "
>
> —S. I. Hayakawa

Figure 9.1

A Model of Intercultural Communication

This model of intercultural communication illustrates that culture is a part of every communication act. More specifically, it illustrates that the messages you send and the messages you receive will be influenced by your cultural beliefs, values, and attitudes.

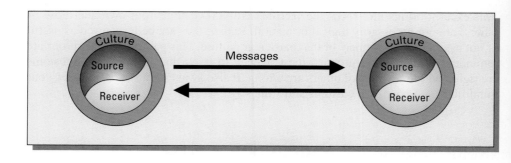

ated more easily. Similarly, those who are younger and better educated become acculturated more quickly than do older and less educated persons. Personality factors are also relevant. Persons who are risk takers and open-minded, for example, have a greater acculturation potential. Also, persons who are familiar with the host culture before immigration—whether through interpersonal contact or through mass media—will be acculturated more readily.

Intercultural Communication

Intercultural communication is communication between persons who have different cultural beliefs, values, or ways of behaving. The model in Figure 9.1 illustrates this concept. The larger circles represent the cultures of the individual communicators. The inner circles identify the communicators (the sources–receivers). In this model each communicator is a member of a different culture. In some instances the cultural differences are relatively slight—say, between persons from Toronto and New York. In other instances the cultural differences are great—say, between persons from Borneo and Germany, or between persons from rural Nigeria and industrialized England.

All messages originate from a specific and unique cultural context, and that context influences their content and form. You communicate as you do largely as a result of your culture. Culture (along with the processes of enculturation and acculturation) influences every aspect of your communication experience. And, of course, you receive messages through the filters imposed by a unique culture. Cultural filters, like filters on a camera, color the messages you receive. They influence what you receive and how you receive it. For example, some cultures rely heavily on television or newspapers for their news and trust them implicitly. Others rely on face-to-face interpersonal interactions, distrusting any of the mass communication systems. Some look to religious leaders as guides to behavior; others generally ignore them.

The term *intercultural* is used broadly to refer to all forms of communication among persons from different groups as well as to the more narrowly defined area of communication between different cultures. The model of intercultural communication presented in Figure 9.1 applies equally to communication between a smaller culture and the dominant or majority culture, communication between different smaller cultures, and communication between a variety of other groups. The following types of communication may all be considered "intercultural" and, more important, subject to the same barriers and gateways to effective communication identified in this chapter:

? SKILLS VIEWPOINT

How many intercultural differences can you identify in this photo? How many might be hidden to visual inspection? What one interpersonal communication skill would you think would be most important to the woman speaking in this particular situation?

- Communication between cultures—for example, between Chinese and Portuguese, or between French and Norwegian.

- Communication between races (sometimes called *interracial communication*)—for example, between African Americans and Asian Americans.

- Communication between ethnic groups (sometimes called *interethnic communication*)—for example, between Italian Americans and German Americans.

- Communication between people of different religions—for example, between Roman Catholics and Episcopalians, or between Muslims and Jews.

- Communication between nations (sometimes called *international communication*)—for example, between the United States and Argentina, or between China and Italy.

- Communication between smaller cultures existing within the larger culture—for example, between doctors and patients, or between research scientists and the general public.

- Communication between a smaller culture and the dominant culture—for example, between homosexuals and heterosexuals, or between older people and the younger majority.

- Communication between genders—between men and women. Some researchers would consider intergender communication as a separate area—as a form of intercultural communication only when the two people are also from different races or nationalities. But gender roles are largely learned through culture, so it seems useful to consider male–female communication as intercultural (Tannen, 1994a, b). That is, even though gender itself is transmitted genetically and not by communication, it is cultures that teach boys and girls different attitudes, beliefs, values, and ways of communicating and relating to one another (Payne, 2001). You act like a man or a woman partly because of what your culture has taught you about how men and women should act. Further, you can view male–female communication as cross-cultural because of the numerous differences in the way

Message Skills

Cultural Influences: Communicate with an understanding that culture influences communication in all its forms.

Culture and Ethics

Throughout history there have been numerous cultural practices that would be judged unethical and even illegal in much of today's world. Sacrificing virgins to the gods, burning people who held different religious beliefs, and sending children to fight religious wars are obvious examples. But even today there are practices woven deep into the fabric of different cultures that many people would find unethical. Consider just a few of these:

- Some cultures support bronco-riding events at which the bull's testicles are tied so that it will experience pain and will buck and try to throw off the rider.

- Some cultures support clitoridectomy, the practice of cutting a young girl's genitals so that she can never experience sexual intercourse without pain; the goal is to keep the girl a virgin until marriage.

- Some cultures support and enforce the belief that a woman must be subservient to her husband's will.

- Some cultures support the practice of wearing fur. In some cases this means catching wild animals in extremely painful traps; in others, raising captive animals so they can be killed when their pelts are worth the most money.

What Would You Do?

Imagine that you're on a television talk show dealing with the topic of cultural differences and diversity. During the discussion different members of the panel speak in support of each of the practices mentioned above, arguing that each culture is entitled to its own practices and beliefs and that no outsider has the right to object. Given your own beliefs about these issues and about cultural diversity in general, what ethical obligiations do you have as a member of this panel?

"Because my genetic programming *prevents* me from stopping to ask directions—*that's* why!"

men and women speak and listen (Eckstein & Goldman, 2001). This does not deny that biological differences also play a role. In fact, research continues to uncover biological roots of behavior once thought to be entirely learned, such as happiness and shyness (McCroskey, 1997).

Regardless of your own cultural background, you will surely come into close contact with people from a variety of other cultures—people who speak different languages, eat different foods, practice different religions, and approach work and relationships in very different ways. It doesn't matter whether you're a longtime resident or a newly arrived immigrant: You are or soon will be living, going to school, working, and forming relationships with people who are from very different cultures. Your day-to-day experiences are sure to become increasingly intercultural.

Cultural Differences

Cultures differ in terms of their (1) orientation (whether individualistic or collectivist), (2) context (whether high or low), and (3) masculinity–femininity; and each of these dimensions of difference has a significant impact on interpersonal communication (Hofstede, 1997; Hall & Hall, 1987; Gudykunst, 1991). Cultures also differ in their characteristic attitudes toward uncertainty, a topic discussed in Chapter 3.

Individualist and Collectivist Cultures

The distinction between **individualist** and **collectivist cultures** revolves around the extent to which the individual's goals or the group's goals are given greater importance. Individualist and collectivist tendencies are not mutually exclusive; this is not an all-or-none orientation but rather one of emphasis. Thus, you may, for example, compete with other members of your basketball team for most baskets or most valuable player award. In a game, however, you will act in a way that will benefit the group. In actual practice both individualist and collectivist tendencies will help you and your team each achieve your goals. Even so, at times these tendencies may conflict; for example, do you shoot for the basket and try to raise your own individual score, or do you pass the ball to another player who is better positioned to score the basket and thus benefit your team?

In an individualist culture you're responsible for yourself and perhaps your immediate family; in a collectivist culture you're responsible for the entire group. In an individualist culture success is measured by the extent to which you surpass other members of your group; you will take pride in standing out from the crowd. And your heroes—in the media, for example—are likely to be those who are unique and who stand apart. In a collectivist culture success is measured by your contribution to the achievements of the group as a whole; you will take pride in your similarity to other members of your group. Your heroes are more likely to be team players who do not stand out from the rest of the group's members.

In an individualist culture you're responsible to your own conscience, and responsibility is largely an individual matter. In a collectivist culture you're responsible to the rules of the social group, and responsibility for an accomplishment or a failure is shared by all members. In individualist cultures competition is promoted; in collectivist cultures cooperation is promoted.

Distinctions between in-group members and out-group members are extremely important in collectivist cultures. In individualistic cultures, which prize a person's individuality, these distinctions are likely to be less important.

Message Skills

Individualist and Collectivist Cultures: Adjust your messages and your listening with an awareness of differences between individualist and collectivist cultures.

High- and Low-Context Cultures

In a **high-context culture** much of the information in communication is in the context or in the person—for example, information shared through previous communications, through assumptions about each other, and through shared experiences. The information is not explicitly stated in the verbal message. In a **low-context culture** most information is explicitly stated in verbal messages or, in formal transactions, in written (contract) form.

To appreciate the distinction between high and low context, consider giving directions ("Where's the voter registration center?") to someone who knows the neighborhood and to a newcomer to your city. With someone who knows the neighborhood (a high-context situation), you can assume the person knows the local landmarks. So you can give directions such as "next to the laundromat on Main Street" or "the corner of Albany and Elm." With the newcomer (a low-context situation), you cannot assume the person shares any information with you. So you have to use directions that a stranger will understand; for example, "Make a left at the next stop sign" or "Go two blocks and then turn right."

High-context cultures are also collectivist cultures. These cultures (Japanese, Arabic, Latin American, Thai, Korean, Apache, and Mexican are examples) place great emphasis on personal relationships and oral agreements (Victor, 1992). Low-context cultures, on the other hand, are individualistic cultures. These cultures (German, Swedish, Norwegian, and American are examples) place less emphasis on personal relationships; they tend to emphasize explicit explanations and, for example, written contracts in business transactions.

Members of high-context cultures spend lots of time getting to know each other before engaging in any important transactions. Because of this prior personal knowledge, a great deal of information is shared and therefore does not have to be explicitly stated. High-context societies, for example, rely more on nonverbal cues in reducing uncertainty (Sanders, Wiseman, & Matz, 1991). Members of low-context cultures spend less time getting to know each other and therefore do not have that shared knowledge. As a result everything has to be stated explicitly.

When this simple difference is not taken into account, misunderstandings can easily result. For example, the directness and explicitness characteristic of the low-context culture may prove insulting, insensitive, or unnecessary to members of a high-context culture. Conversely, to members of a low-context culture, someone from a high-context culture may appear vague, underhanded, even dishonest in his or her reluctance to be explicit or to engage in communication that a low-context culture would consider open and direct.

Another frequent difference and source of misunderstanding between high- and low-context cultures is face-saving (Hall & Hall, 1987). People in high-context cultures place a great deal more emphasis on face-saving. For example, they are more likely to avoid argument for fear of causing others to lose face, whereas people in low-context cultures (with their individualistic orientation) will use argument to win a point. Similarly, in high-context cultures criticism should take place only in private so the person can save face. Low-context cultures may not make this public–private distinction.

Members of high-context cultures are reluctant to say no for fear of offending and causing a person to lose face. So, for example, it's necessary to understand when a Japanese executive's yes means yes and when it means no. The difference is not in the words but in the way they are used. It's easy to see how a low-context individual may interpret this reluctance to be direct—to say no when you mean no—as a weakness or as an unwillingness to confront reality.

Members of high-context cultures also are reluctant to question the judgments of their superiors. So, for example, if a product were being manufactured with a defect, workers might be reluctant to communicate this back to management (Gross, Turner, & Cederholm, 1987). Similarly, workers might detect problems in proce-

Message Skills

High- and Low-Context Cultures: Adjust your messages and your listening in light of the differences between high- and low-context cultures.

dures proposed by management but never communicate their concerns back to management. In an intercultural organization knowledge of this tendency would alert a low-context management to look more deeply into the absence of communication.

Masculine and Feminine Cultures

Cultures differ in the extent to which gender roles are distinct or overlap (Hofstede, 1997). A **masculine culture** typically views men as assertive, oriented to material success, and strong; people in such a culture tend to see women as modest, focused on the quality of life, and tender. In a **feminine culture** both men and women are supposed to be modest, oriented to maintaining the quality of life, and tender. On the basis of Hofstede's research on 53 countries, the 10 countries with the highest masculinity scores (starting from the top) are Japan, Austria, Venezuela, Italy, Switzerland, Mexico, Ireland, Jamaica, Great Britain, and Germany. The 10 countries with the highest femininity scores (starting from the top) are Sweden, Norway, the Netherlands, Denmark, Costa Rica, Yugoslavia, Finland, Chile, Portugal, and Thailand. Of the 53 countries ranked, the United States ranks 15th most masculine.

A study of babies raised in Japan and the United States illustrates the ways in which masculine and feminine cultures teach boys and girls differently (Otaki et al., 1986). Boys raised in Japan are significantly noisier than girls; girls raised in the United States are significantly noisier than boys. This difference is most likely due to the ways in which mothers and (to a somewhat lesser extent) fathers react to the babies. Both of these cultures are relatively high on masculinity and so, not surprisingly, teach girls and boys differently. In the dominant cultures of the United States, Japan, and Germany, for example, the emphasis on material success is seen in the importance that students place on grades. Students in such cultures are conditioned to strive to be the best, and school failure is shameful and extremely significant. Students from more feminine cultures place greater emphasis on the quality of life and give much less importance to such issues as grades. Students in these cultures are content to be average, and failing in school is unpleasant but nothing serious (Hofstede, 1997).

The masculine culture socializes its children to be assertive, ambitious, and competitive. A masculine organization emphasizes the bottom line and rewards its workers on the basis of their contribution to the organization. The feminine culture socializes its children to be modest and to emphasize close interpersonal relationships. A feminine organization is more likely to emphasize worker satisfaction and

Skill building exercise

Facilitating Intercultural Communication

Here are three scenarios involving people from different cultural orientations. For each situation *(a)* identify at least one difference between the two extremes that might cause communication difficulties, and *(b)* identify at least one thing the individuals can do so as not to let this difference obstruct effective communication.

1. An associate at work (high masculine) tells a colleague (high feminine) of a history of chronic fatigue syndrome and is now awaiting results of new blood tests.
2. A group of new advertising executives (three are from high-context cultures and three from low-context cultures) prepare to interact for the first time.
3. A couple (one from an individualist and one from a collectivist culture) see two children fighting in the street; no other adults are around, and the passersby worry that the children may get hurt.

Cultural teachings and orientations exert powerful (but often unconscious) influences on the way people communicate. A knowledge of such influences will often help suggest remedies for misperceptions and misunderstandings.

to reward its workers on the basis of need; an employee with a large family, for example, may get raises that a single person would not get even if the single person contributed more to the organization.

Masculine cultures are more likely to confront conflicts directly and to competitively fight out any differences; they are more likely to emphasize win–lose conflict strategies. Feminine cultures are more likely to emphasize compromise and negotiation; they are more likely to emphasize win–win solutions to conflicts.

Message Skills
Masculine and Feminine Cultures: Adjust your messages and your listening to allow for differences in cultural masculinity and femininity.

Improving Intercultural Communication

Murphy's law ("If anything can go wrong, it will") is especially applicable to intercultural communication. Intercultural communication is, of course, subject to all the same barriers and problems as are the other forms of communication discussed throughout this text. Here, however, are some suggestions designed to counteract the barriers that are unique to intercultural communication (Barna, 1997; Ruben, 1985; Spitzberg, 1991).

Prepare Yourself

There's no better preparation for intercultural communication than learning about the other culture. Fortunately, there are numerous sources to draw on. View a video or film that presents a realistic view of the culture. Read what members of the culture as well as "outsiders" write about the culture. Scan magazines and websites from the culture. Talk with members of the culture. Chat on international IRC channels. Read materials addressed to people who need to communicate with those from other cultures. The easiest way to do this is to search the online bookstores (for example, Barnes and Noble at **www.bn.com**, Borders at **www.borders.com**, and

7 Ways to Effective Intercultural Communication

The skills and qualities of conversational effectiveness (Chapter 8) are especially useful in intercultural interactions. Of course, exercise caution, as there may be important differences in the ways various cultures regard these qualities. Generally, however:

1. Be open to differences among people; specifically, be open to different values, beliefs, and attitudes as well as to ways of behaving.
2. Empathize; put yourself in the position of the person from another culture. Try to see the world from this different perspective. Let the person know that you feel as he or she is feeling.
3. Communicate positiveness; it helps put the other person at ease. However, the appropriateness of positive statements about yourself varies greatly with the culture.
4. Use immediacy to unite yourself with others and to surmount differences; be aware, however, that members of some cultures prefer to maintain greater interpersonal distance.
5. Engage in effective interaction management; be sensitive to differences in turn-taking. Be especially wary of interrupting; some cultures consider this extremely rude.
6. Communicate expressiveness and a genuine involvement in the interaction. Smile. Allow your facial muscles to express your interest and concern. At the same time, recognize that some cultures may frown on too much expressiveness.
7. Be other-oriented; focus your attention and the conversation on the other person. Listen actively, ask questions, and maintain eye contact. But go carefully—some cultures may find these messages too intrusive, so be guided by feedback from the listener.

Applying Interpersonal Skills/Then and Now
Recall a recent intercultural interaction that did not go as well as it might have. If you were having the same conversation today, what could you do to make it more effective?

Amazon at www.Amazon.com) for such keywords as *culture, international,* and *foreign travel.*

Another part of this preparation is to recognize and face fears that may stand in the way of effective intercultural communication (Gudykunst, 1991; Stephan & Stephan, 1985). For example, you may fear for your self-esteem. You may be anxious about your ability to control the intercultural situation, or you may worry about your own level of discomfort. You may fear saying something that will be considered politically incorrect or culturally insensitive and thereby losing face.

You may fear that you'll be taken advantage of by a member of the other culture. Depending on your own stereotypes, you may fear being lied to, financially duped, or made fun of.

You may fear that members of this other group will react to you negatively. You may fear, for example, that they will not like you or will disapprove of your attitudes or beliefs or perhaps even reject you as a person. Conversely, you may fear negative reactions from members of your own group. They might, for example, disapprove of your socializing with culturally different people.

Some fears, of course, are reasonable. In many cases, however, fears are groundless. Either way, you need to assess your concerns logically and weigh their consequences carefully. Then you'll be able to make informed choices about your communications.

Reduce Your Ethnocentrism

Before reading about reducing ethnocentrism, examine your own cultural thinking by taking the self-test below.

 Test Yourself

How Ethnocentric Are You?

Here are 18 statements representing your beliefs about your culture. For each statement indicate how much you agree or disagree, using the following scale: strongly agree = 5, agree = 4, neither agree nor disagree = 3, disagree = 2, and strongly disagree = 1.

_____ ❶ Most cultures are backward compared to my culture.

_____ ❷ My culture should be the role model for other cultures.

_____ ❸ Lifestyles in other cultures are just as valid as those in my culture.

_____ ❹ Other cultures should try to be like my culture.

_____ ❺ I'm not interested in the values and customs of other cultures.

_____ ❻ People in my culture could learn a lot from people in other cultures.

_____ ❼ Most people from other cultures just don't know what's good for them.

_____ ❽ I have little respect for the values and customs of other cultures.

_____ ❾ Most people would be happier if they lived like people in my culture.

_____ ❿ People in my culture have just about the best lifestyles of anywhere.

_____ ⓫ Lifestyles in other cultures are not as valid as those in my culture.

_____ ⓬ I'm very interested in the values and customs of other cultures.

_____ ⓭ I respect the values and customs of other cultures.

_____ ⓮ I do not cooperate with people who are different.

_____ ⑮ I do not trust people who are different.

_____ ⑯ I dislike interacting with people from different cultures.

_____ ⑰ Other cultures are smart to look up to my culture.

_____ ⑱ People from other cultures act strange and unusual when they come into my culture.

HOW DID YOU DO? This test was presented to give you the opportunity to examine some of your own cultural beliefs, particularly those cultural beliefs that contribute to ethnocentrism. The person low in ethnocentrism would have high scores (4s and 5s) for items 3, 6, 12, and 13 and low scores (1s and 2s) for all the others. The person high in ethnocentrism would have low scores for items 3, 6, 12, and 13 and high scores for all the others.

WHAT WILL YOU DO? Use this test to bring your own cultural beliefs to consciousness so you can examine them logically and objectively. Ask yourself if your beliefs are productive and will help you achieve your professional and social goals, or if they're counterproductive and will actually hinder your achieving your goals.

Source: Adapted from James W. Neuliep & James C. McCroskey (1997). The development of a U.S. and generalized ethnocentrism scale, _Communication Research Reports, 14,_ 393.

As you've probably gathered from taking this test, **ethnocentrism** is the tendency to see others and their behaviors through your own cultural filters, often as distortions of your own behaviors. It's the tendency to evaluate the values, beliefs, and behaviors of your own culture as superior; as more positive, logical, and natural than those of other cultures. To achieve effective interpersonal communication, you need to see yourself and others as different but as neither inferior nor superior—not a very easily accomplished task.

Ethnocentrism exists on a continuum. People are not either ethnocentric or non-ethnocentric; rather, most people are somewhere along the continuum (Table 9.1 on page 200), and we're all ethnocentric to at least some degree. Most important for our purposes is that your degree of ethnocentrism will influence your interpersonal (intercultural) communications.

Message Skills

Ethnocentric Thinking: Recognize your own ethnocentric thinking and be aware of how it influences your verbal and nonverbal messages.

? SKILLS VIEWPOINT

What do you say to someone who tries to appear totally without prejudice and yet talks in the most offensive stereotypes and uses all the offensive cultural labels?

TABLE 9.1 The Ethnocentrism Continuum

Drawing from several researchers (Lukens, 1978; Gudykunst & Kim, 1992; Gudykunst, 1991), this table summarizes some interconnections between ethnocentrism and communication. The table identifies five levels of ethnocentrism; the general terms under "Communication Distances" characterize the major communication attitudes that dominate the various levels. Under "Communications" are some ways people might behave given their particular degree of ethnocentrism. How would you rate yourself on this scale?

DEGREES OF ETHNOCENTRISM	COMMUNICATION DISTANCE	COMMUNICATIONS
Low	Equality	Treats others as equals; evaluates other ways of doing things as equal to own ways
	Sensitivity	Wants to decrease distance between self and others
	Indifference	Lacks concern for others but is not hostile
	Avoidance	Avoids and limits interpersonal interactions with others; prefers to be with own kind
High	Disparagement	Engages in hostile behavior; belittles others; views own culture as superior to other cultures

Be Mindful

Being mindful rather than mindless (a distinction considered in Chapter 8), is especially helpful in intercultural communication (Hajek & Giles, 2003). When you're in a mindless state, you behave in accordance with assumptions that would not normally pass intellectual scrutiny. For example, you know that cancer is not contagious, and yet many people will avoid touching cancer patients. You know that people who cannot see do not have hearing problems, and yet many people use a louder voice when talking to persons without sight. When the discrepancies between available evidence and behaviors are pointed out and your mindful state is awakened, you quickly realize that these behaviors are not logical or realistic.

When you deal with people from other cultures, you're often in a mindless state and therefore may function nonrationally in many ways. When your mindful state is awakened, you may then shift to a more critical thinking mode—and recognize, for example, that other people and other cultural systems are different but not inferior or superior. Thus, these suggestions for increasing intercultural communication effectiveness may appear logical (even obvious) to your mindful state, even though they are probably frequently ignored in your mindless state.

Avoid Overattribution

You'll recall from Chapter 3 that overattribution is the tendency to attribute too much of a person's behavior or attitudes to one of that person's characteristics ("She thinks that way because she's a woman," "He believes that because he was raised a Catholic"). In intercultural communication situations, overattribution takes two forms. First, it's the tendency to see too much of what a person believes or does as caused by the person's cultural identification. Second, it's the tendency to see a person as a spokesperson for his or her particular culture—for example, to assume because a man is African American (as in the accompanying cartoon) that he is therefore knowledgeable about the entire African American experience or that his thoughts are always focused on African American issues. As demonstrated in the discussion of perception in Chapter 3, people's ways of thinking and ways of behaving are influenced by a wide variety of factors; culture is only one factor of many.

Listening without Bias

Just as racist, sexist, heterosexist, and ageist attitudes influence your language, they also influence your listening. In biased listening you hear what the speaker says through your preconceptions. You assume that what the speaker is saying merely reflects, for example, the speaker's gender, race, affectional orientation, or age.

Such biased listening occurs in a wide variety of situations. For example, when you dismiss a valid argument or give credence to an invalid argument, when you refuse to give someone a fair hearing, or when you attribute less credibility (or more credibility) to a speaker *because* the speaker is of a particular gender, race, affectional orientation, or age—and when these characteristics have nothing to do with the position or argument advanced—you're listening with bias.

To be sure, there are many instances in which speakers' characteristics are relevant and pertinent to your evaluation of the message. For example, the gender of a speaker who is discussing pregnancy, fathering a child, birth control, or surrogate motherhood is, most would agree, probably relevant to the message. On such topics it is not biased listening to hear the discussion in light of the gender of the speaker. But it is sexist listening to assume that only one gender has anything to say that's worth hearing—or that what one gender says can be discounted without a fair hearing. The same is true in regard to a person's race, age, or affectional orientation.

Applying Listening Skills

Chloe, a good friend of yours, has been assigned to train under the supervision of someone of a different race. Chloe confides in you that she just can't get herself to work with this person; she admits she is just too prejudiced to appreciate anything her supervisor says or does. What listening advice would you give Chloe?

Reduce Uncertainty

All communication interactions involve uncertainty and ambiguity. Not surprisingly, this uncertainty and ambiguity is greater when there are wide cultural differences (Berger & Bradac, 1982; Gudykunst, 1989, 1993). Because of this, in intercultural communication it takes more time and effort to reduce uncertainty and thus to communicate meaningfully. Reducing your uncertainty about another person is worth the effort, however; it not only will make your communication more effective but also will increase your liking for the person (Douglas, 1994).

Techniques such as active listening (Chapter 4) and perception checking (Chapter 3) help you check on the accuracy of your perceptions and allow you to revise

Confronting Intercultural Differences

Here are a few cases of obvious intercultural differences. Select any one of them and indicate how you might communicate. For example: (1) What attitude would you approach the situation with? (2) What specific purpose would you hope to achieve? (3) What subordinate purposes might you hope to achieve? And (4) what would you say, and how would you say it?

1. You're in an interracial, interreligious relationship. Your partner's family ignores your "couplehood." For example, you and your partner are never invited to dinner as a couple or included in any family affairs. You decide to confront your partner's family.
2. Your parents persist in holding and verbalizing stereotypes about other religious, racial, and ethnic groups. You feel you must tell your parents how incorrect you think these stereotypes are.
3. Lenny, a colleague at work, recently underwent a religious conversion. He now persists in trying to get you and everyone else to undergo this same conversion. You decide to tell him that you find this behavior offensive.

Confronting intercultural insensitivity is extremely difficult, especially because most people will deny it. So approach these situations carefully, relying heavily on the skills of interpersonal communication identified throughout this text.

and amend any incorrect perceptions. Also, being specific reduces ambiguity and the chances of misunderstandings; misunderstanding is a lot more likely if you talk about "neglect" (a highly abstract concept) than if you refer to "forgetting my last birthday" (a specific event).

Finally, seeking feedback helps you correct any possible misconceptions almost immediately. Seek feedback on whether you're making yourself clear ("Does that make sense?" "Do you see where to put the widget?"). Similarly, seek feedback to make sure you understand what the other person is saying ("Do you mean that you'll never speak with them again? Do you mean that literally?").

Recognize Differences

To communicate interculturally you need to recognize the differences between yourself and people who are culturally different, the differences within the culturally different group, and the numerous differences in meaning that arise from cultural differences.

Differences between Yourself and Culturally Different People   A common barrier to intercultural communication is the assumption that similarities exist but that differences do not. For example, although you may easily accept different hairstyles, clothing, and foods, you may assume that in basic values and beliefs, everyone is really alike. But that's not necessarily true. When you assume similarities and ignore differences, you'll fail to notice important distinctions. As a result, you'll risk communicating to others that your ways are the right ways and that their ways are not important to you. Consider: An American invites a Filipino coworker to dinner. The Filipino politely refuses. The American is hurt, feels that the Filipino does not want to be friendly, and does not repeat the invitation. The Filipino is hurt and concludes that the invitation was not extended sincerely. Here, it seems, both the American and the Filipino assume that their customs for inviting people to dinner are the same—when, in fact, they aren't. A Filipino expects to be invited several times before accepting a dinner invitation. In the Philippines, an invitation given only once is viewed as insincere.

Or consider age. If you were raised in the United States, you probably grew up with a youth bias (young is good, old is not so good—an attitude the U.S. media reinforce daily) and may well have assumed that this reverence for youth was universal

> **"** I was raised to believe that excellence is the best deterrent to racism or sexism. And that's how I operate my life. **"**
>
> —Oprah Winfrey

across all cultures. But it isn't; and if you assume it is, you may be in line for intercultural difficulties. A good example is the case of the American journalist in China who remarked to a government official that the official was probably too young to remember a particular event. The comment would have been taken as a compliment by most youth-oriented Americans. But the official perceived it as an insult—as a suggestion that he was too young to deserve respect (Smith, 2002).

Differences within the Culturally Different Group   Within every cultural group there are wide and important differences. Just as all Americans are not alike, neither are all Indonesians, Greeks, Mexicans, and so on. When you ignore these differences—when you assume that all persons covered by the same label (in this case a national or racial label) are the same—you're guilty of stereotyping. A good example of this is the use of the term "African American." The term stresses the unity of Africa and those who are of African descent and is analogous to "Asian American" or "European American." At the same time, if the term is used in the same sense as "German American" or "Japanese American," it ignores the great diversity within the African continent. More analogous terms would be "Nigerian American" or "Ethiopian American." Within each culture there are smaller cultures that differ greatly from one another and from the larger culture as well as from other large cultures.

Differences in Meaning   Meanings exist not in words but in people (Chapter 5). Consider, for example, the different meanings of the word *woman* to an American and a Muslim, of *religion* to a born-again Christian and an atheist, or of *lunch* to a Chinese rice farmer and a Madison Avenue advertising executive. Even though different groups may use the same word, its meanings will vary greatly depending on the listeners' cultural definitions.

   Similarly, nonverbal messages have different meanings in different cultures. For example, a left-handed American who eats with the left hand may be seen by a Muslim as obscene. Muslims do not use the left hand for eating or for shaking hands but to solely clean themselves after excretory functions. So using the left hand to eat or to shake hands is considered insulting and obscene.

Message Skills

Intercultural Communication: Become mindful of (1) differences between yourself and people who are culturally different, (2) differences within the other cultural groups, and (3) cultural differences in meanings.

Adjust Your Communication

Intercultural communication (in fact, all interpersonal communication) takes place only to the extent that you and the person you're trying to communicate with share the same system of symbols. Your interaction will be hindered to the extent that your language and nonverbal systems differ. Therefore, it's important to adjust your communication to compensate for cultural differences.

   This principle takes on particular relevance when you realize that even within a given culture, no two persons share identical symbol systems. Parents and children, for example, not only have different vocabularies but also, even more important, associate different meanings with some of the terms they both use. People in close relationships—either as intimate friends or as romantic partners—realize that learning the other person's signals takes a long time and, often, great patience. If you want to understand what another person means—by smiling, by saying "I love you," by arguing about trivial matters, by self-deprecating comments—you have to learn the person's system of signals.

   In the same way, part of the art of intercultural communication is learning the other culture's signals, how they're used, and what they mean. Furthermore, you have to share your own system of signals with others so that they can better understand you. Although some people may know what you mean by your silence or by your

❓ SKILLS VIEWPOINT

   Of all the interpersonal communication skills considered so far, which would you identify as the most significant in effective intercultural communication?

avoidance of eye contact, others may not. You cannot expect others to decode your behaviors accurately without help.

Adjusting your communication is especially important in intercultural situations, largely because people from different cultures use different signals—or sometimes use the same signals to signify quite different things. For example, focused eye contact means honesty and openness in much of the United States. But in Japan and in many Hispanic cultures, that same behavior may signify arrogance or disrespect, particularly engaged in by a youngster with someone significantly older.

Communication accommodation theory, as explained in Chapter 1, holds that speakers will adjust or accommodate to the communication style of their listeners in order to interact more pleasantly and efficiently (Giles, Mulac, Bradac, & Johnson, 1987). As you adjust your messages, recognize that each culture has its own rules and customs for communication (Barna, 1997; Ruben, 1985; Spitzberg, 1991). These rules identify what is appropriate and what is inappropriate. Thus, for example, in U.S. culture you would call a person you wished to date three or four days in advance. In certain Asian cultures you might call the person's parents weeks or even months in advance. In U.S. culture you say, as a general friendly gesture and not as a specific invitation, "come over and pay us a visit sometime." To members of other cultures, this comment is sufficient to prompt the listeners actually to visit at their convenience. Table 9.2 presents a good example of a set of cultural rules—guidelines for communicating with an extremely large and important culture that many people don't know.

Recognize Culture Shock

Culture shock is the psychological reaction you experience when you encounter a culture very different from your own (Furnham & Bochner, 1986). Culture shock is normal; most people experience it when entering a new and different culture. Going away to college, moving in together, or joining the military, for example, can also result in culture shock. Nevertheless, it can be unpleasant and frustrating. Entering a new culture often engenders feelings of alienation, conspicuousness, and difference from everyone else. When you lack knowledge of the rules and customs of the new society, you cannot communicate effectively. You're apt to blunder frequently and seriously. In your culture shock you may not know basic things:

- how to ask someone for a favor or pay someone a compliment
- how to extend or accept an invitation
- how early or how late to arrive for an appointment, or how long to stay
- how to distinguish seriousness from playfulness and politeness from indifference

? SKILLS VIEWPOINT

You're assigned to help a group of students at your school prepare for the inevitable culture shock that they'll experience when they take their senior year at a foreign university. What do you say?

TABLE 9.2 *Interpersonal Communication Tips*

BETWEEN PEOPLE WITH AND WITHOUT DISABILITIES

Consider communication between people with general disabilities—such as people in wheelchairs or people with cerebral palsy—and those who have no such disability. Note that the suggestions offered here are considered appropriate in the United States but not necessarily in other cultures. For example, although most people in the United States accept the phrase "person with mental retardation," it's considered offensive to many in the United Kingdom (Fernald, 1995).

If you're the one without a general disability:

1. Avoid negative terms and terms that define the person in terms of the disability, such as "the disabled" or "the handicapped." Instead, say "person with a disability," putting the person, not the disability, first. Similarly, say "seizure" instead of "fit," "person with cerebral palsy," instead of "cerebral palsy victim," and "wheelchair user" instead of "wheelchair bound."

2. Treat assistive devices such as wheelchairs, canes, walkers, or crutches as the personal property of the user; be careful not to move these out of your way, as they're needed by the person with a disability.

3. If you shake hands with others in a group, also shake hands with the person with a disability. Don't avoid shaking hands, say, because the individual's hand is crippled.

4. Avoid talking about the person with a disability in the third person. For example, don't make remarks like "Doesn't he get around beautifully with the new crutches." Always direct your comments directly to the individual.

5. Don't assume that people who have a disability (such as slurred speech, as may occur with people who have cerebral palsy or cleft palate) are intellectually impaired. This definitely may not be the case, so be especially careful not to talk down to such people as, research shows, many people do (Unger, 2001).

6. If you're not sure how to act—for example, whether or not to offer walking assistance—ask: "Would you like me to help you into the dining room?"

7. If the person is in a wheelchair, it may be helpful for you to sit down or kneel down to get on the same eye level.

If you're the one with a disability:

1. Let the other person know if he or she can do anything to assist you in communicating. For example, if you want someone to speak louder, ask. If you want to relax and have someone push your wheelchair, say so.

2. Be patient and understanding with those who may not know how to act or what to say. Put them at ease as best you can.

3. If you detect discomfort in the other person, you might talk a bit about your disability to show that you're not uncomfortable and that you understand that others may not know how you feel. But, of course, you are under no obligation to educate the public—so don't feel this is something you ought to or have to do. If it makes you more comfortable, then do it; otherwise, don't.

Sources: These suggestions are based on a wide variety of sources; for example, **http://www.empowermentzone.com/etiquet.txt** (the website for the National Center for Access Unlimited), U.S. Department of Labor, **http://www.dol.gov**, **http://www.dissvcs.uga.edu/com-peodis.html**, and United Cerebral Palsy National, **http://www.ucpa.org**, all accessed April 5, 2002.

- how to dress for an informal, formal, or business function
- how to order a meal in a restaurant or how to summon a waiter

Culture shock occurs in four general stages, which apply to a wide variety of encounters with the new and the different (Oberg, 1960).

Stage One: The Honeymoon　At first you experience fascination, even enchantment, with the new culture and its people. You finally have your own apartment. You're your own boss. Finally, on your own! Among people who are culturally different, the early (and superficial) relationships of this stage are characterized by cordiality and friendship. Many tourists remain at this stage, because their stays in foreign countries are so brief.

Stage Two: The Crisis　In the crisis stage the differences between your own culture and the new one create problems. For example, students no longer find dinner ready or their clothes washed or ironed unless they do them themselves. Feelings of

> ❝ Prejudice is a raft onto which the shipwrecked mind clambers and paddles to safety. ❞
>
> —Ben Hecht

frustration and inadequacy come to the fore. This is the stage at which you experience the actual shock of the new culture. For example, in a study of students from more than 100 countries who were studying in 11 foreign countries, 25 percent of the students experienced depression (Klineberg & Hull, 1979).

Stage Three: The Recovery   During the recovery period you gain the skills necessary to function effectively in the new culture. You learn how to shop, cook, and plan a meal. You find a local laundry and figure you'll learn how to iron later. You learn the language and ways of the society. Your feelings of inadequacy subside.

Stage Four: The Adjustment   At the final stage you adjust to and come to enjoy the new culture and the new experiences. You may still experience periodic difficulties and strains, but on a whole, the experience is pleasant. Actually, you're now a pretty decent cook. You're even coming to enjoy it. And you're making a good salary, so why learn to iron?

People also may experience a kind of reverse culture shock when they return to their original culture after living in a foreign culture (Jandt, 2000). Consider, for example, Peace Corps volunteers who work in economically deprived rural areas around the world. On returning to Las Vegas or Beverly Hills, they too may experience culture shock. Sailors who serve long periods aboard ship and then return to, for example, isolated farming communities may also experience culture shock. In these cases, however, the recovery period is shorter and the sense of inadequacy and frustration is less.

Message Skills

Appreciating Cultural Differences:
Look at cultural differences not as deviations or deficiencies but as the differences they are. Recognizing different ways of doing things, however, does not necessarily mean accepting them.

Summary of Concepts

This chapter explored culture and intercultural communication, the ways in which cultures differ, and ways to improve intercultural communication.

1. A culture is the specialized lifestyle of a group of people—their values, beliefs, artifacts, ways of behaving, and ways of communicating. Each generation transmits its culture to the next generation through the process of enculturation. In acculturation, one culture is modified through direct contact with or exposure to another culture.

2. Intercultural communication encompasses a broad range of interactions. Among them are communication between cultures, between races, between genders, between socioeconomic and ethnic groups, between age groups, between religions, and between nations.

3. Cultures differ in the degree to which they teach an individualist orientation (the individual is the most im-

portant consideration) or a collectivist orientation (the group is the most important consideration).

4. In high-context cultures much information is in the context or in the person's nonverbals; in low-context cultures most of the information is explicitly stated in the message.

5. Cultures differ in the degree to which gender roles are distinct or overlap. Highly "masculine" cultures view men as assertive, oriented to material success, and strong and view women as modest, focused on the quality of life, and tender.

6. Many tactics can help make intercultural communication more effective. For example, prepare yourself by learning about the culture, reduce ethnocentrism, communicate mindfully, avoid overattribution, reduce uncertainty, recognize differences, adjust your communication on the basis of cultural differences, and recognize culture shock.

Vocabulary Quiz: The Language of Intercultural Communication

Match the terms of intercultural communication with their definitions. Record the number of the definition next to the appropriate term.

____ high-context culture

____ acculturation

____ intercultural communication

____ low-context culture

____ ethnocentrism

____ culture

____ mindfulness

____ enculturation

____ individualist cultures

____ collectivist cultures

1. A culture in which most information is explicitly encoded in the verbal message.
2. The values, beliefs, artifacts, and ways of communicating of a group of people.
3. The process by which culture is transmitted from one generation to another.
4. Communication that takes place between persons of different cultures or persons who have different cultural beliefs, values, or ways of behaving.
5. The process through which a person's culture is modified through contact with another culture.
6. The tendency to evaluate other cultures negatively and our own culture positively.
7. A mental state in which we are aware of the logic that governs your behaviors.
8. Cultures that emphasize competition and individual success, and in which your responsibility is largely to yourself.
9. A culture in which much information is in the context or the person and is not made explicit in the verbal message.
10. Cultures that emphasize the member's responsibility to the group.

Four for Discussion

1. In this age of multiculturalism, how do you feel about Article II, Section 1 of the U.S. Constitution? The relevant section reads: "No person except a natural born citizen, or citizen of the United States at the time of the adoption of this Constitution, shall be eligible to the office of President."
2. Social Darwinism holds that much as the human species evolved from lower life forms to homo sapiens, cultures also evolve. Consequently, some cultures may be considered "advanced" and others "primitive." Cultural relativism, on the other hand, holds that although all cultures are different, that no culture is either superior or inferior to any other (Berry, Poortinga, Segall, & Dasen, 1992). What arguments can you advance in support of or against each position?
3. Men and women from different cultures were asked the following question: "If a man (woman) had all the other qualities you desired, would you marry this person if you were not in love with him (her)?" (LeVine, Sato, Hashimoto, & Verma, 1994). Fifty percent of the respondents from Pakistan, 49 percent from India, and 19 percent from Thailand said yes. At the other extreme were respondents from Japan (only 2 percent said yes), the United States (3.5 percent), and Brazil (4 percent). How would you answer this question? How is your answer influenced by your culture?
4. Some cultures frown on sexual relationships outside of marriage; others consider sex a normal part of intimacy. Intercultural researchers (Hatfield & Rapson, 1996) recall a discussion between colleagues from Sweden and the United States on ways of preventing AIDS. When researchers from the United States suggested promoting abstinence, their Swedish counterparts asked, "How will teenagers ever learn to become loving, considerate sexual partners if they don't practice?" "The silence that greeted the question," note Hatfield and Rapson (1996, p. 36), "was the sound of two cultures clashing." How have your cultural beliefs and values influenced what you consider appropriate relationship behavior?

Web Explorations

Explore our text website at **www.ablongman.com/devito** to find:

Explore our research resources at **www.researchnavigator.com** and

Exercises and Self-Tests

Exercises on culture and intercultural communication include (1) Random Pairs, (2) Cultural Beliefs, (3) From Culture to Gender, (4) Cultural Identities, and (5) The Sources of Your Cultural Beliefs. Two relevant self-tests are (6) How Open Are You Interculturally? and (7) Can You Distinguish Universal from Culture-Specific Icons?

Writing Resources and Assignments

Suggestions are available for writing papers of personal experience (for example, your experiences with intercultural communication), concept or principle explanation (for example, culture shock or ethnocentrism), review (the role of intercultural relationships in TV situation comedies), or research on culture and intercultural communication (for example, ethnocentrism of college students).

Read an article.

Read a popular or scholarly article on the nature of culture, cultural differences, or intercultural communication. On the basis of this article, what can you add to the discussion presented here?

Investigate key terms.

Investigate one of the key terms discussed in this chapter (for example, culture, masculine and feminine cultures, individualist and collectivist orientations, high- and low-context cultures, uncertainty reduction, culture shock, intercultural communication). What additional insights can you provide?

Find answers.

Try finding answers to one of the following questions, or design a research study to answer it.

1. How do cultures differ in their ways of communicating?
2. What are some of the culturally influenced communication differences between men and women?
3. What is the current status of interracial romantic relationships in the United States?

Relationships and Interpersonal Communication

10

Interpersonal Relationships

Relationship Stages

Relationship Types

> The story is told that in ancient Greece a young man named Pythias was condemned to death by the tyrant Dionysius for speaking out against the government. Pythias begged Dionysius to delay his execution until he was able to put his family affairs in order. Dionysius agreed but insisted that someone remain in Pythias's place just in case he didn't come back. Damon, Pythias's friend, volunteered and agreed to be executed if Pythias did not return. Damon was then placed in prison while Pythias traveled home. On the day of the scheduled execution, Pythias was nowhere to be found. Without any anger or animosity toward his friend, Damon prepared to die. But just before the execution could be carried out, Pythias arrived and begged the court's forgiveness for his unavoidable delay; he was ready to be executed and asked that his friend be set free. Dionysius was so impressed that he not only freed Damon but pardoned Pythias and asked if he could join the two of them in this extraordinary friendship.

The legend of Damon and Pythias is the story of an exceptional relationship. In a way, however, all relationships are exceptional and all tell exceptional stories.

Interpersonal Relationships

Although we think of relationships as largely face-to-face interactions, the Internet is playing an ever greater role in the world of interpersonal relationships. As the number of Internet users increases, commercial services are adding, expanding, and improving their services for computer relationships. Even television talk shows have been focusing on computer relationships, often getting people together who have established a relationship online but who have never met. Clearly, many people turn to the Internet to find friends and romantic partners. Some people use the Internet as their only means of interaction; others use it to begin relationships and later supplement computer talk with photographs, phone calls, and face-to-face meetings.

One of the great advantages of online relationships is that rapport and mutual self-disclosure become more important than physical attractiveness in promoting intimacy (Cooper & Sportolari, 1997). And, contrary to some popular opinion, online relationships rely as heavily on the ideals of trust, honesty, and commitment as do face-to-face relationships (Whitty & Gavin, 2001). Still, it's easy to misrepresent yourself online—a fact that probably accounts for the higher incidence of fakery in computer relationships (Cornwell & Lundgren, 2001).

Characteristics of Interpersonal Relationships

You can view relationships as existing on a continuum, from the impersonal at one end to the highly personal (that is, interpersonal) at the other end. Interpersonal relationships are those that exist between people who are interdependent; that is, one person's behavior has a significant impact on the other person. You can distinguish interpersonal relationships from impersonal relationships on the basis of three main factors (Miller, 1978, 1990): psychological data, explanatory knowledge, and personally established rules.

Psychological Data   In impersonal relationships people respond to each other chiefly as members of the classes or groups to which they belong. For example, initially you respond to a particular college professor as you respond to college professors in general. Similarly, the college professor responds to you as he or she responds to students generally. As your relationship becomes more personal, however, both of you begin to respond to each other not as members of groups but as unique individuals. Put differently, in impersonal relationships, the social or cultural role of the person governs your interaction; in interpersonal relationships, it is the psychological uniqueness of the person that tells you how to interact.

This general move from emphasis on social data (group membership) to emphasis on psychological data prevails in the United States and in most European cultures. In many Asian and African cultures, however, your group membership is always important; it never recedes into the background. Thus, in these cultures your group membership—even in the closest intimate relationships—is always important, often more important than your individual or psychological characteristics (Moghaddam, Taylor, & Wright, 1993).

Explanatory Knowledge   In impersonal relationships you can do little more than *describe* a person or a person's way of communicating. As you get to know someone a bit better, you can *predict* his or her behavior. If you get to know the person even better, you'll become able to *explain* the behavior. The college professor, in an impersonal relationship, may be able to describe, say, your lateness and perhaps also can predict that you'll be five minutes late to class each Friday. In an interpersonal situation, however, the professor can go beyond these levels to explain the behavior—in this case, give reasons why you're late.

Personally Established Rules   In impersonal relationships general social norms set the rules of interaction. For example, in impersonal contexts students and professors behave toward one another according to the social norms established by their culture and society. However, as the relationship between student and professor becomes interpersonal, the social rules no longer totally regulate the interaction. Student and professor begin to establish rules of their own—largely because they begin to see each other as unique individuals rather than merely as members of the social groups "student" and "professor."

Advantages and Disadvantages of Interpersonal Relationships

A good way to begin the study of interpersonal relationships is to examine your own relationships (past, present, or those you look forward to) by taking the accompanying self-test. The test highlights the advantages and the disadvantages of relationships.

 Test Yourself

What Do Your Relationships Do for You?

For this test you may focus on your own relationships in general (friendship, romantic, family, and work) or on one particular relationship (say, with your life partner or your child or your best friend) or on one type of relationship (say, friendships). Respond to the statements below by indicating the extent to which your relationship(s) serve each function. Use a 10-point scale, with 1 indicating "never," 10 indicating "always," and the numbers in between indicating levels between these extremes.

_____ ❶ My relationships help to lessen my loneliness.

_____ ❷ My relationships put uncomfortable pressure on me to expose my vulnerabilities.

_____ ❸ My relationships help me to secure stimulation (intellectual, physical, and emotional).

> People are more frightened of being lonely than of being hungry, or being deprived of sleep, or of having their sexual needs unfulfilled.
>
> —Frieda Fromm Reichman

_____ ④ My relationships increase my obligations.

_____ ⑤ My relationships help me gain in self-knowledge and in self-esteem.

_____ ⑥ My relationships prevent me from developing other relationships.

_____ ⑦ My relationships help enhance my physical and emotional health.

_____ ⑧ My relationships scare me because they may be difficult to dissolve.

_____ ⑨ My relationships maximize my pleasures and minimize my pains.

_____ ⑩ My relationships hurt me.

HOW DID YOU DO? Your responses to these statements should give you some idea of how strongly your relationships serve positive or negative functions.

The odd-numbered statements (1, 3, 5, 7, and 9) reflect what most people would consider advantages of interpersonal relationships: (1) Relationships help to lessen loneliness (Rokach, 1998; Rokach & Brock, 1995). They make you feel that someone cares, that someone likes you, that someone will protect you, that someone ultimately will love you. (3) As plants are heliotropic and orient themselves to light, humans are stimulotropic and orient themselves to sources of stimulation (M. Davis, 1973). Human contact is one of the best ways to secure intellectual, physical, and emotional stimulation. (5) Through contact with others you learn about yourself and see yourself from different perspectives and in different roles: as a child or parent, as a coworker, as a friend. Healthy interpersonal relationships help enhance self-esteem and self-worth. (7) Research consistently shows that interpersonal relationships contribute significantly to physical and emotional health (Rosen, 1998; Goleman, 1995a; Rosengren, et al, 1993; Pennebacker, 1991) and to personal happiness (Berscheid & Reis, 1998). Without close interpersonal relationships you're more likely to become depressed, and depression contributes significantly to physical illness. Isolation, in fact, correlates as closely with mortality as does high blood pressure, high cholesterol, obesity, smoking, or lack of physical exercise (Goleman, 1995). (9) Above all, interpersonal relationships tend to maximize pleasure and minimize pain. Good friends, for example, will make you feel even better at times of good fortune and less hurt in the face of hardships.

The even-numbered statements (2, 4, 6, 8, and 10) suggest what most people consider disadvantages of interpersonal relationships. (2) Close relationships put pressure on you to reveal yourself and to expose your vulnerabilities. This is generally worthwhile in the context of a supporting and caring relationship, but if the relationship deteriorates these weaknesses can be used against you. (4) Close relationships increase your obligations, sometimes to a great extent. Although you enter relationships in order to spend more time with special people, you also incur time (and perhaps financial) obligations with which you may not be happy. (6) Close relationships can limit other relationships. Sometimes this issue involves someone you like but your partner can't stand. More often, however, it's simply a matter of time and energy: You have less to give to other and less intimate relationships. (8) The closer your relationship, the more emotionally difficult it is to dissolve. A deteriorating relationship can cause distress or depression. In some cultures religious pressures may prevent unhappily married couples from separating. And if lots of money is at stake, the end of a relationship can involve a huge financial blow. (10) Your partner may break your heart. If you care a great deal, you're likely to experience great hurt. Ironically, if you care less, the hurt will be less.

WHAT WILL YOU DO? One way to use this self-test is to consider how you might lessen the disadvantages of your interpersonal relationships, at least those disadvantages that you indicate are always or almost always present in your relationships. Consider, for example, if your own behaviors are contributing to the disadvantages. For example, do you bury yourself in one or two relationships and discourage the development of others? At the same time, consider how you can maximize the advantages that your relationships currently offer.

Message Skills

Advantages and Disadvantages of Relationships: In evaluating, entering, or dissolving relationships, consider both the advantages and the disadvantages.

Cultural Influences on Interpersonal Relationships

Cultural factors play important roles in the formation of relationships. In most of the United States, interpersonal friendships are drawn from a relatively large pool. Out of all the people you come into regular contact with, you choose relatively few as friends. And with computer chat groups the number of friends you can have has increased enormously, as has the range of people from which you can choose these friends. In rural areas and in small villages throughout the world, however, people have very few choices. The two or three other children your age become your friends; there's no real choice, because these are the only possible friends you could make.

Most cultures assume that relationships should be permanent or at least long lasting. Consequently, it's assumed that people want to keep relationships together and will exert considerable energy to maintain relationships. Because of this bias, there is little research that has studied how to move effortlessly from one intimate relationship to another or that advises you how to do this more effectively and efficiently.

Culture influences heterosexual relationships by assigning different roles to men and women. In the United States men and women are supposed to be equal; at least that is the stated ideal. As a result, both men and women can initiate relationships and both can dissolve them. Both men and women are expected to derive satisfaction from their interpersonal relationships; and when that satisfaction isn't present, either partner may seek to exit the relationship. In Iran, on the other hand, only the man has the right to dissolve a marriage without giving reasons. And in Jordan it was only recently (May 2002) that the first wife was granted a divorce; before this only men could obtain divorces (*New York Times*, May 15, 2002, p. A6).

In some cultures gay and lesbian relationships are accepted, and in others they are condemned. In some areas of the United States, formally registered "domestic partnerships" grant gay men, lesbians, and (in some cases) unmarried heterosexuals rights that were formerly reserved only for married couples—such as health insurance benefits and one partner's right to make decisions when the other is incapacitated. In Norway, Sweden, and Denmark, same-sex relationship partners have the same rights as married partners. Belgium and the Netherlands, too, now give gay and lesbian couples essentially the same rights and freedoms as heterosexual couples.

? SKILLS VIEWPOINT

Your friend asks you for a loan of $150 to pay off some bills. But you've never been paid back when you've lent money to friends in the past, and you simply don't want to risk the same disappointment again. Yet you don't want to lose this friend. Aside from a slight inability to manage money, your friend is a really wonderful person. What do you say?

Message Skills

Cultural Influences on Interpersonal Relationships: Culture exerts influences on all types of relationships, encouraging some and discouraging others.

Relationship Stages

The six-stage model shown in Figure 10.1 on page 214 describes the significant stages you may go through as you try to achieve your relationship goals. As a general description of **relationship development** (and sometimes dissolution), the stages seem standard: They apply to all relationships, whether friendship or love. The six stages are *contact, involvement, intimacy, deterioration, repair,* and *dissolution*. Each stage can be divided into an initial and a final phase.

Contact

At the **contact** stage there is first *perceptual contact*—you see what the person looks like, you hear what the person sounds like, you may even smell the person. From this

Figure 10.1

The Six Stages of Relationships
Can you provide a specific example or examples, from literature or from your own experience, that would illustrate some or all of these six stages?

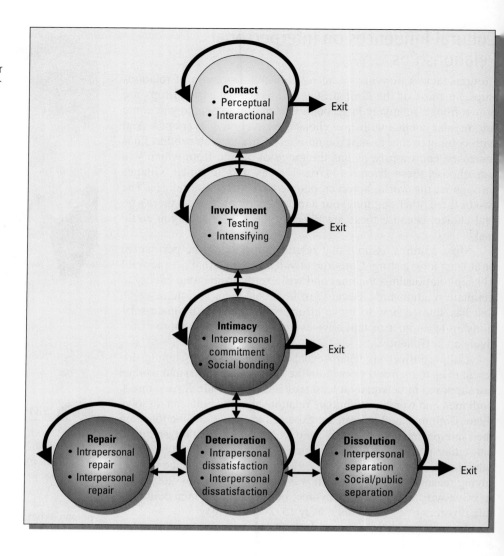

you get a physical picture: gender, approximate age, height, and so on. After this perception there is usually *interactional contact*. Here the interaction is superficial and impersonal. This is the stage of "Hello, my name is Joe"—the stage at which you exchange basic information that needs to come before any more intense involvement. This interactional contact may also be nonverbal, as in, for example, exchanging smiles, concentrating your focus on one person, or decreasing the physical distance between the two of you.

This is the stage at which you initiate interaction ("May I join you?") and engage in invitational communication ("May I buy you a drink?"). According to some researchers, it's at this contact stage—within the first four minutes of initial interaction—that you decide if you want to pursue the relationship or not (Zunin & Zunin, 1972).

Physical appearance is especially important in the initial development of **attraction,** because it's the most readily available to sensory inspection. Yet through both verbal and nonverbal behaviors, qualities such as friendliness, warmth, openness, and dynamism are also revealed at the contact stage.

Involvement

At the **involvement** stage a sense of mutuality, of being connected, develops. During this stage you experiment and try to learn more about the other person. At the initial phase of involvement a kind of preliminary *testing* goes on. You want to see if your initial judgment—made perhaps at the contact stage—proves reasonable. So you may ask questions—"Where do you work?" "What are you majoring in?"

If you're committed to getting to know the person even better, you continue your involvement by *intensifying* your interaction. Here you not only try to get to know the other person better but also begin to reveal yourself. It's at this stage that you begin to share your feelings and your emotions. If this is to be a romantic relationship, you might date. If it's to be a friendship, you might share in activities related to mutual interests—go to the movies or to some sports event together.

And throughout the relationship process, but especially during the involvement and early stages of intimacy, partners continue testing each other. Each person tests the other; each tries to find out how the other feels about the relationship. For example, you might ask your partner directly how he or she feels; or you might disclose your own feelings on the assumption that your partner will also self-disclose; or you might joke about a shared future together, touch more intimately, or hint that you're serious about the relationship; or you might question mutual friends as to your partner's feelings (Bell & Buerkel-Rothfuss, 1990; Baxter & Wilmot, 1984).

Intimacy

One way to define *intimacy* is the feeling that you can be honest and open when talking about yourself; you can express thoughts and feelings that you don't reveal in other relationships (Mackey, Diemer, & O'Brien, 2000). At the **intimacy** stage you commit yourself still further to the other person and, in fact, establish a kind of relationship in which this individual becomes your best or closest friend, lover, or companion. Your communication becomes more personalized, more synchronized, and easier (Gudykunst, Nishida, & Chua, 1987). Usually the intimacy stage divides itself quite neatly into two phases: an *interpersonal commitment* phase in which you commit yourselves to each other in a kind of private way, and a *social bonding* phase in which the commitment is made public—perhaps to family and friends, perhaps to the public at large through formal marriage. Here the two of you become a unit, a pair.

Commitment may take many forms; it may be an engagement or a marriage, a commitment to help the person or to be with the person, or a commitment to reveal your deepest secrets. It may consist of living together or agreeing to become lovers. The type of commitment varies with the relationship and with the individuals. The important characteristic is that the commitment made is a special one; it's a commitment that you do not make lightly or to everyone. Each of us reserves this level of intimacy for very few people at any given time—sometimes just one person; sometimes two, three, or perhaps four. Rarely do people have more than four intimates, except in a family situation.

Intimacy and Risk   To some people relational intimacy seems extremely risky. To others it involves only low risk. Consider your own view of relationship risk by responding to the following questions.

- *Is it dangerous to get really close to people?*
- *Are you afraid to get really close to someone because you might get hurt?*
- *Do you find it difficult to trust other people?*
- *Do you believe that the most important thing to consider in a relationship is whether you might get hurt?*

People who answer yes to these and similar questions see intimacy as involving considerable risk (Pilkington & Richardson, 1988). Such people have fewer close friends, are less likely to have romantic relationships, have less trust in others, have

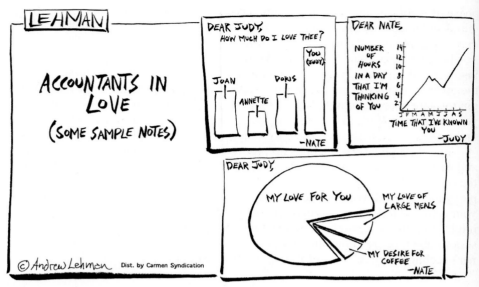

OFF THE DEEP END © Andrew Lehman. Reprinted by permission.

lower levels of dating assertiveness, have lower self-esteem, are more possessive and jealous, and are generally less sociable and extraverted than those who see intimacy as involving little risk (Pilkington & Woods, 1999).

Deterioration

Although many relationships remain at the intimacy stage, some enter the stage of **deterioration**—the stage that focuses on the weakening of bonds between the parties and that represents the downside of the relationship progression. Relationships deteriorate for many reasons. When the reasons for coming together are no longer present or change drastically, relationships may deteriorate. Thus, for example, when your relationship no longer lessens your loneliness or provides stimulation or self-knowledge, or when it fails to increase your self-esteem or maximize pleasures and minimize pains, it may be in the process of deteriorating. Among the other reasons for deterioration are third-party relationships, sexual dissatisfaction, dissatisfaction with work, or financial difficulties (Blumstein & Schwartz, 1983).

The first phase of deterioration is usually *intrapersonal dissatisfaction.* You begin to feel that this relationship may not be as important as you had previously thought. You may experience personal dissatisfaction with everyday interactions and begin to view the future together negatively. If this dissatisfaction continues or grows, you may pass to the second phase, *interpersonal deterioration,* in which you discuss these dissatisfactions with your partner.

During the process of deterioration, communication patterns change drastically. These patterns are in part a response to the deterioration; you communicate as you do because of the way you feel your relationship is deteriorating. However, the way you communicate (or fail to communicate) also influences the fate of your relationship. During the deterioration stage you may, for example, increase withdrawal, talk and listen less, and self-disclose less.

Repair

The first phase of **repair** is *intrapersonal repair,* in which you analyze what went wrong and consider ways of solving your relational difficulties. At this stage you may consider changing your behaviors or perhaps changing your expectations of

> ❝ After all, my erstwhile dear,
> My no longer cherished,
> Need we say it was not love,
> Just because it perished? ❞
>
> —Edna St. Vincent Millay

your partner. You may also weigh the rewards of your relationship as it is now against the rewards you could anticipate if your relationship ended.

If you decide that you want to repair your relationship, you may discuss this with your partner at the *interpersonal repair* level. Here you may talk about the problems in the relationship, the corrections you would want to see, and perhaps what you would be willing to do and what you would want the other person to do. This is the stage of negotiating new agreements, new behaviors. You and your partner may try to solve your problems yourselves, seek the advice of friends or family, or perhaps enter professional counseling.

You can look at the strategies for repairing a relationship in terms of the following six suggestions (see Figure 10.2)—which conveniently spell out the word REPAIR, a useful reminder that repair is not a one-step but a multistep process: Recognize the problem, Engage in productive conflict resolution, Pose possible solutions, Affirm each other, Integrate solutions into normal behavior, and Risk.

? SKILLS VIEWPOINT

You lied to a friend about being out of town so you wouldn't have to attend his retirement party—but you got caught, and this soured your friendship. What was once a best friend is now "barely an acquaintance." Several months have gone by, and you want to repair the relationship. What do you say?

- *Recognize* the problem. What, in concrete terms, is wrong with your present relationship? What changes would be needed to make it better—again, in specific terms? Create a picture of your relationship as you would want it to be and compare that picture to the way the relationship looks now.

- *Engage* in productive conflict resolution. Interpersonal conflict is an inevitable part of relationship life. It's not so much the conflict that causes relationship difficulties as the way in which the conflict is approached (Chapter 11). If it's confronted through productive strategies, the conflict may be resolved, and the relationship may actually emerge stronger and healthier. If, however, unproductive and destructive strategies are used, the relationship may well deteriorate further.

- *Pose* possible solutions. Ideally, each person will ask, "What can we do to resolve the difficulty that will allow both of us to get what we want?"

- *Affirm* each other. For example, happily married couples engage in greater positive behavior exchange; that is, they communicate more agreement, approval, and positive affect than do unhappily married couples (Dindia & Fitzpatrick, 1985).

- *Integrate* solutions into your life—make the solutions a part of your normal behavior.

- *Risk.* Risk giving favors without any certainty of reciprocity. Risk rejection by making the first move to make up or say you're sorry. Be willing to change, to adapt, to take on new tasks and responsibilities.

Message Skills

Relationship Repair: Recognize the problem, engage in productive conflict resolution, pose possible solutions, affirm each other, integrate solutions into normal behavior, and take risks as appropriate.

Dissolution

The **dissolution** stage, in both friendship and romance, is the cutting of the bonds tying you together. At first it usually takes the form of *interpersonal separation,* in which you may not see each other anymore. If you live together, you move into separate apartments and begin to lead lives apart from each other. If this relationship is a marriage, you may seek a legal separation. If this separation period proves workable and if the original relationship is not repaired, you may enter the phase of *social or public separation.* In marriage this phase corresponds to divorce. Avoidance of each other and a return to being "single" are among the primary identifiable features of dissolution. In some cases, however, the former partners change the definition of

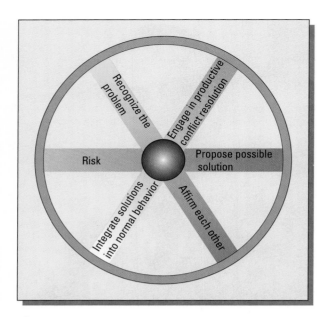

Figure 10.2

The Relationship Repair Wheel
The wheel seems an apt metaphor for the repair process: The specific repair strategies—the spokes—all work together in a constant process. The wheel is difficult getting started, but once in motion it becomes easier. And, of course, it's easier to start when two people are pushing. How would you describe the repair process?

their relationship; for example, ex-lovers become friends, or ex-friends become "just" business partners.

This final, "good-bye," phase of dissolution is the point at which you become an ex-lover or ex-friend. In some cases this is a stage of relief and relaxation; finally it's over. In other cases this is a stage of anxiety and frustration, of guilt and regret, of resentment over time ill spent and now lost. In more materialistic terms, the good-bye phase is the stage when property is divided and when legal battles may ensue over who should get what.

No matter how friendly the breakup, there is likely to be some emotional difficulty. Here are some suggestions for dealing with this.

Break the Loneliness–Depression Cycle   Realize, first, that your feelings of loneliness and depression are not insignificant (Rubenstein & Shaver, 1982). And keep in mind that research shows that both men and women get depressed when their relationships deteriorate (Spangler & Burns, 2000) and that men are more likely than women to commit suicide as a result of relationship breakups (Kposow, 2000). Avoid *sad passivity,* a state in which you feel sorry for yourself, sit alone, and perhaps cry. This may actually make you feel worse. Instead, try to engage in *active solitude* (exercise, write, study, play computer games) and seek *distraction* (do things to put loneliness out of your mind; for example, take a long drive or shop). The most effective way to deal with loneliness is through *social action,* especially through helping people in need.

Take Time Out   Take some time for yourself. Renew your relationship with yourself. If you were in a long-term relationship, you probably saw yourself as part of a team, as one of a pair. Get to know yourself as a unique individual, standing alone now but fully capable of entering a meaningful relationship in the future.

Bolster Self-Esteem   If your relationship failed, you may experience a lowering of self-esteem. Positive and successful experiences are most helpful in building self-esteem. As in dealing with loneliness, helping others is one of the best ways to raise your own self-esteem. And engage in other activities that you enjoy, that you do well, and that are likely to result in success.

Seek the Support of Others   Avail yourself of your friends and family for support; it's an effective antidote to the discomfort and unhappiness that occurs when a relationship ends. Seek out people who are positive and nurturing, and avoid negative individuals who will paint the world in even darker tones. Also, make the distinction between seeking support and seeking advice. If you feel you need advice, seek out a professional.

Avoid Repeating Negative Patterns   Many people repeat unsuccessful patterns, entering second and third relationships with the same blinders and unrealistic expectations with which they entered earlier relationships. Ask, at the start of a new relationship, if you're entering a relationship modeled on the previous one. If the answer is yes, be especially careful that you do not repeat the problems. At the same time, avoid becoming a prophet of doom. Do not see in every new relationship vestiges of the old. Do not jump at the first conflict and say, "Here it goes again." Treat the new relationship as the unique relationship it is. Use past relationships and experiences as guides, not filters.

Listen to this

Listening to Stage Talk

Listening for stage-talk messages—messages expressing a desire to move the relationship in a particular way or to maintain it at a particular stage—will help you understand and manage your interpersonal relationships, whether business or personal. It will help you see when, for example, your partner's messages are inconsistent with the stage you think the relationship is at, or when your partner wants to intensify or deintensify the relationship. Stage-talk messages can be classified in the following categories.

1. *Contact messages* express a desire for contact: "Hi, my name is Joe."
2. *Closeness messages* express a desire for increased closeness, involvement, or intimacy: "I'd like to see you more often."
3. *Maintenance messages* express a desire to stabilize the relationship at one stage: "Let's stay friends for now; I'm afraid to get more involved at this point."
4. *Distancing messages* express a desire for more "space": "I think we need a few weeks apart."
5. *Repair messages* express a desire to repair the relationship: "Let's discuss this issue again. I didn't mean to hurt your feelings."
6. *Dissolution messages* express a desire to break up or dissolve the existing relationship: "It's just not working out; let's each go our own way."

Applying Listening Skills

Grace has been dating Thomas for the past few months and admits that she really can't tell if Tom wants the relationship to become more intimate or more distant. And Tom admits that he has difficulty reading Grace's stage talk. What specific advice would you give both Grace and Tom to help them listen more effectively to each other's stage talk?

Reflections on the Model of Relationships

Before we move on to examine relationship types, consider some of the implications of the six-stage model of relationships.

1. Because relationships differ so widely, it's best to think of any relationship model as a tool for talking about relationships rather than as a specific map that indicates how you move from one relationship position to another. The six-stage model is certainly not the only way you can look at relationships. Table 10.1 on page 220, for example, presents a somewhat different model of relationship stages.

2. Within each relationship and within each relationship stage, there are dynamic tensions. According to **relational dialectics theory,** is that all relationships can be defined by a series of competing opposite desires or motivations. For example: (1) The tension between autonomy and connection reflects your desire to remain an individual but also to be intimately connected to another person and to a relationship. (2) The tension between novelty and predictability focuses on your desires for newness and adventure on the one hand and for sameness and comfortableness on the other. (3) The tension between closedness and openness relates to your desires to be in an exclusive relationship yet at the same time to be in a relationship that is open to different people (Baxter, 1988, 1990; Baxter & Simon, 1993).

3. More accurate than a linear progression from stage to stage is the movement depicted in Figure 10.1 by the different types of arrows. The exit arrows show that each stage offers the opportunity to exit the relationship: After saying hello you can say good-bye and exit. The vertical or movement arrows going to the next stage and back again represent the fact that you can move either to a more intense stage (say, from involvement to intimacy) or to a less intense stage (say, from intimacy to deterioration). The self-reflexive arrows—the arrows that re-

> " Falling out of love is very enlightening; for a short while you see the world with new eyes. "
>
> —Iris Murdoch

TABLE 10.1 Knapp's Model of Relationship Stages

The first five stages of Knapp's model describe the processes of coming together and moving toward greater connection and intimacy.

- *Initiation* is the stage at which you first perceive and interact with the other person. Here you try to present yourself in a positive light and to open the channels of communication.
- *Experimenting* involves trying to learn about the other person.
- *Intensifying* involves interacting on a more personal and intimate level; your speech becomes more informal, and you use lots of terms that have meaning only for the two of you.
- *Integrating* consists of a fusion of the two individuals, a stage when mutual opinions and attitudes are cultivated.
- *Bonding* has to do with the social naming of the relationship; for example, as marriage or domestic partnership or exclusive partnership.

The next five stages describe the stages of coming apart and moving away from intimacy.

- *Differentiating* is the process by which the individuals begin to think of themselves as different and distinct from each other.
- *Circumscribing* involves restricting communication, perhaps to topics that are safe and will not cause conflict.
- *Stagnating* is the stage of inactive communication; when you do communicate it's with difficulty and awkwardness.
- *Avoiding* involves active physical separation and the absence of face-to-face interaction.
- *Terminating* involves the breaking of the bonds that once held the relationship together.

Source: Adapted from Mark L. Knapp & Anita L. Vangelisti, *Interpersonal Communication and Human Relationships,* 4/e. Published by Allyn & Bacon, Boston, MA. Copyright © 2000 by Pearson Education. Reprinted by permission of the publisher.

turn to the beginning of the same level or stage—signify that any relationship may become stabilized at any point. In **relationship maintenance** you may, for example, continue to maintain a relationship at the intimate level without its deteriorating or going back to a less intense stage of involvement. Or you may remain at the "Hello, how are you?" stage—the contact stage—without getting any further involved.

4. Movement from one stage to another depends largely on your **relationship communication** skills—the skills you deploy to initiate and open a relationship, to present yourself as likable, to express affection, and to self-disclose appropriately—and in fact all the interpersonal skills you've been acquiring throughout this course (cf. Dindia & Timmerman, 2003).

Relationship Types

In this section we look at friendship, love, family, and work relationships and their various types.

Friendship

> Laughter is not at all a bad beginning for a friendship.
>
> —Oscar Wilde

Friendship is an interpersonal relationship between two persons that is mutually productive and characterized by mutual positive regard.

Friendship is an interpersonal relationship; communication interactions must have taken place between the people. Further, the interpersonal relationship involves a "personalistic focus" (Wright, 1978, 1984). That is, friends react to each other as complete persons; as unique, genuine, and irreplaceable individuals.

Friendships must be mutually productive; by definition, they cannot be destructive to either person. Once destructiveness enters into a relationship, it can no longer be charac-

Q & A

One of the most difficult issues in interpersonal relationships occurs when you're asked a question and there is a tension between your desire to be truthful and your wish to be effective in achieving your communication goal.

What Would You Do?

Here are a few questions that others might ask you. For each question, however, certain circumstances may make it difficult for you to respond fully or even truthfully; these are noted as the "Thoughts" you have as you consider your possible answers. What would you do in each of these three situations?

Question *[A romantic partner asks:] Do you love me?*

Thought *I don't want to commit myself, but I don't want to end the relationship, either. I want to allow the relationship to progress further before making any commitment.*

Question *[An interviewer says:] You seem a bit old for this type of job. How old are you?*

Thought *I am old for this job, but I need it anyway. Further, it's really illegal for the interviewer to ask my age. I don't want to turn the interviewer off, because I really need this job. Yet I don't want to reveal my age either.*

Question *[A 15-year-old asks:] Was I adopted? Who are my real parents?*

Thought *Yes, you were adopted, but I fear that you will look for your biological parents and will be hurt when you find that they're drug dealers and murderers.*

terized as friendship. Love relationships, marriage relationships, parent–child relationships, and just about any other possible relationship can be either destructive or productive. But friendship must enhance the potential of each person and can only be productive.

Friendships are characterized by mutual positive regard. Liking people is essential if we are to call them friends. Three major characteristics of friendship—trust, emotional support, and sharing of interests (Blieszner & Adams, 1992)—testify to this positive regard.

The closer friends are, the more *interdependent* they become; that is, when friends are especially close, the actions of one will impact more significantly on the other than they would if the friends were just casual acquaintances. At the same time, however, the closer friends are, the more *independent* they are of, for example, the attitudes and behaviors of others. Also, they're less influenced by the societal rules that govern more casual relationships. In other words, close friends are likely to make up their own rules for interacting with each other; they decide what they will talk about and when, what they can say to each other without offending and what they can't, when and for what reasons one friend can call the other, and so on.

Friends serve a variety of needs; as your needs change, the qualities you look for in friendships also change. In many instances, old friends are dropped from your close circle to be replaced by new friends who better meet new needs. For example, as your own experience is likely to confirm, friendships serve such needs as *utility* (friends may have special talents, skills, or resources that prove useful to you), *affirmation* (friends may affirm your personal value), *ego support* (friends help you to view yourself as a worthy and competent individual), *stimulation* (friends introduce you to new ideas and new ways of seeing the world), and *security* (friends do nothing to hurt you or to emphasize your inadequacies or weaknesses) (Wright, 1978, 1984). And you'll be better able to serve such friendship needs when you apply the interpersonal communication skills discussed throughout this text (cf. Samter, 2003).

> " Friendship makes prosperity more shining and lessens adversity by dividing and sharing it. "
>
> —Cicero

Types of Friendships Not all friendships are the same. But how do they differ? One way of answering this question is by distinguishing among the three major types of friendship: reciprocity, receptivity, and association (Reisman, 1979, 1981).

The friendship of *reciprocity* is the ideal type, characterized by loyalty, self-sacrifice, mutual affection, and generosity. A friendship of reciprocity is based on equality: Each individual shares equally in giving and receiving the benefits and rewards of the relationship. In the friendship of *receptivity,* in contrast, there is an imbalance in giving and receiving; one person is the primary giver and one the primary receiver. This imbalance, however, is a positive one, because each person gains something from the relationship. The different needs of both the person who receives and the person who gives are satisfied. This is the friendship that may develop between a teacher and a student or between a doctor and a patient. In fact, a difference in status is essential for the friendship of receptivity to develop.

The friendship of *association* is a transitory one. It might be described as a friendly relationship rather than a true friendship. Associative friendships are the kind we often have with classmates, neighbors, or coworkers. There is no great loyalty, no great trust, no great giving or receiving. The association is cordial but not intense.

Cultural and Gender Differences in Friendship

Your friendships and the way you look at friendships will be influenced by your culture and your gender. In the United States you can be friends with someone yet never really be expected to go much out of your way for this person. Many Middle Easterners, Asians, and Latin Americans would consider going significantly out of their way an absolute essential ingredient in friendship; if you're not willing to sacrifice for your friend, then this person is really not your friend (Dresser, 1996).

Generally, friendships are closer in collectivist cultures than in individualist cultures (see Chapter 9). In their emphasis on the group and on cooperating, collectivist cultures foster the development of close friendship bonds. Members of collectivist cultures are expected to help others in the group. When you help or do things for someone else, you increase your own attraction to—and attractiveness to—the person, and this is certainly a good start for a friendship. And of course the culture continues to reward these close associations. Members of individualist cultures, on the other hand, are expected to look out for number one. Consequently, they're more likely to compete and to try to do better than one another—conditions that don't support, generally at least, the development of friendships. Do realize that these characteristics are extremes: Most people have both collectivist and individualist values but have them to different degrees, and that is what we are talking about here—differences in degree of collectivist and individualist orientations.

Perhaps the best-documented finding, already noted in our discussion of self-disclosure in Chapter 2, is that women self-disclose more than men do (e.g., Dolgin, Meyer, & Schwartz, 1991). This difference holds throughout male and female friendships: Male friends self-disclose less often and with less intimate details than female friends do. Men generally don't view intimacy as a necessary quality of their friendships (Hart, 1990).

Women engage in significantly more affectional behaviors with their friends than do males (Hays, 1989). This difference, Hays notes, may account for the greater difficulty men experience in beginning and maintaining close friendships. Women engage in more casual communication; they also share greater intimacy and more confidences with their friends than do men. Communication, in all its forms and functions, seems a much more important dimension of women's friendships.

Men's friendships are often built around shared activities—attending a ball game, playing cards, working on a project at the office. Women's friendships, on the other hand, are built more around a sharing of feelings, support, and "personalism." One study found that similarity in status, in willingness to protect one's friend in uncomfortable situations, in academic major, and even in proficiency in playing Password were significantly related to the relationship closeness of male–male friends but not of female–female or female–male friends (Griffin & Sparks, 1990). Perhaps similarity is a criterion for male friendships but not for female or mixed-sex friendships.

Message Skills

Friendships: Establish friendships to help serve such needs as utility, ego support, stimulation, and security. At the same time, seek to serve your friends' similar needs.

8 Ways to Create Sticky Relationships

A "sticky" website is one that holds visitors, keeping them at the website and deterring them from visiting others. In a similar way relationships vary in stickiness; in fact, you can view interpersonal communication as the glue that makes some relationships sticky and others glueless. Here then are eight ways you can build a sticky relationship—a relationship that your partner will want to stay with and not stray from. Conveniently, the word POSITIVE is both the central concept and a useful acronym; it stands for positiveness, openness, supportiveness, interest, truthfulness, involvement, value, and equality.

1. In relationship communication, *positiveness* means a favorable attitude toward the relationship and toward the prospect of continued couplehood. It also includes expressing positive statements and compliments when the two of you are alone as well as in the presence of others.
2. Foster *openness* and honesty, such that your intrapersonal and interpersonal messages, especially those about yourself and your partner, are similar. The less discrepancy between how you talk about yourself and your partner with yourself and how you talk with others, the stickier your relationship is likely to be.
3. Communicate *supportiveness*. Empower your partner—help him or her to be the best he or she can be—by raising his or her self-esteem and by sharing the skills you have that your partner may need.
4. Demonstrate *interest*. The more interested you are in your partner, the greater your partner's interest in you is likely to be.
5. *Truthfulness* does not necessarily mean total disclosure; rather, it means that what you do reveal will be an honest reflection of what you feel rather than, say, attempts to manipulate your partner's feelings.
6. *Involvement* means participating actively in the relationship and in the other person's life, though not to the point of being intrusive. It includes taking responsibility for the relationship's maintenance, level of satisfaction, and growth.
7. Be mindful of the *value* of the person and of the relationship. And express in words this value that you see and want to maintain.
8. *Equality* entails a sharing of power and decision making in significant relationship undertakings: Each person has something to contribute, and each person recognizes and acknowledges this.

Applying Interpersonal Skills/Then and Now

Have you ever been in a relationship in which communication lapses led to a lack of stickiness? How would you communicate differently today?

The ways in which men and women develop and maintain their friendships will undoubtedly change considerably—as will all gender-related variables—in coming years. Perhaps there will be a further differentiation, or perhaps an increase in similarities. In the meantime, given the present state of research in gender differences, we need to be careful not to exaggerate or to treat small differences as if they were highly significant. We need to avoid stereotyping and stressing opposites to the neglect of the huge number of similarities between men and women (Wright, 1988; Deaux & LaFrance, 1998).

Love

Although there are many theories about **love,** a model that has long interested interpersonal researchers is Lee's (1976) proposal that not one but six types of love exist. View the following descriptions of the six types as broad characterizations that are generally but not always true. As a preface to this discussion of the types of love, you may wish to respond to the self-test on page 224.

Skill building exercise

Talking Cherishing

Cherishing behaviors are an especially effective way to affirm another person and to increase "favor exchange," a concept that comes from the work of William Lederer (1984). **Cherishing behaviors** are those small gestures you enjoy receiving from your partner (a smile, a wink, a phone call, a kiss).

Prepare a list of 10 cherishing behaviors that you would like to receive from your real or imagined relationship partner. Identify cherishing behaviors that are

1. specific and positive—nothing overly general or negative;
2. focused on the present and future rather than related to issues about which the partners have argued in the past;
3. capable of being performed daily; and
4. easily executed—nothing you really have to go out of your way to accomplish.

After each partner prepares a list, they exchange lists and, ideally, perform the desired cherishing behaviors. At first these behaviors may seem self-conscious and awkward. In time, however, they'll become a normal part of your interaction, which is exactly what you hope to achieve. If you have a relationship partner, you may want to try out this idea.

Lists of cherishing behaviors—yours or your partner's—will also give you insight into your relationship needs and the kind of communicating partner you want.

 Test Yourself

What Kind of Lover Are You?

INSTRUCTIONS: Respond to each of the following statements with T if you believe the statement to be a generally accurate representation of your attitudes about love, or with F if you believe the statement does not adequately represent your attitudes about love.

_____ ❶ My lover and I have the right physical "chemistry" between us.

_____ ❷ I feel that my lover and I were meant for each other.

_____ ❸ My lover and I really understand each other.

_____ ❹ I believe that what my lover doesn't know about me won't hurt him/her.

_____ ❺ My lover would get upset if he/she knew of some of the things I've done with other people.

_____ ❻ When my lover gets too dependent on me, I want to back off a little.

_____ ❼ I expect to always be friends with my lover.

_____ ❽ Our love is really a deep friendship, not a mysterious, mystical emotion.

_____ ❾ Our love relationship is the most satisfying because it developed from a good friendship.

_____ ❿ In choosing my lover, I believed it was best to love someone with a similar background.

_____ ⑪ An important factor in choosing a partner is whether or not he/she would be a good parent.

_____ ⑫ One consideration in choosing my lover was how he/she would reflect on my career.

_____ ⑬ Sometimes I get so excited about being in love with my lover that I can't sleep.

_____ ⑭ When my lover doesn't pay attention to me, I feel sick all over.

_____ ⑮ I cannot relax if I suspect that my lover is with someone else.

_____ ⑯ I would rather suffer myself than let my lover suffer.

_____ ⑰ When my lover gets angry with me, I still love him/her fully and unconditionally.

_____ ⑱ I would endure all things for the sake of my lover.

HOW DID YOU DO? This scale is from Hendrick and Hendrick (1990) and is based on the work of Lee (1976), as is the text's discussion of the six types of love. The statements refer to the six types of love described in the text: eros, ludus, storge, pragma, mania, and agape. Statements 1–3 are characteristic of the eros lover. If you answered "true" to these statements, you have a strong eros component to your love style; if you answered "false," you have a weak eros component. Statements 4–6 refer to ludus love, 7–9 to storge love, 10–12 to pragma love, 13–15 to manic love, and 16–18 to agapic love.

WHAT WILL YOU DO? Are there things you can do to become more aware of the different love styles and to become a more well-rounded lover? Incorporating the qualities of effective interpersonal communication—for example, being more flexible, more polite, and more other-oriented—will go a long way toward making you a more responsive love partner.

Source: Scale from "A Relationship-Specific Version of the Love Attitudes Scale" by Clyde Hendrick and Susan Hendrick, *Journal of Social Behavior and Personality, 5,* 1990. Reprinted by permission of Select Press.

> **❝** If you have ever loved, been loved, or wanted to be in love, you have had to face a frustrating fact: different people can mean different things by that simple phrase 'I love you.' **❞**
>
> —John Alan Lee

Types of Love

The self-test above identified six types of love: *eros, ludus, storge, pragma, mania,* and *agape.*

Eros: Beauty and Sexuality. Like Narcissus, who fell in love with the beauty of his own image, the *erotic* lover focuses on beauty and physical attractiveness, sometimes to the exclusion of qualities you might consider more important and more lasting. Also like Narcissus, the erotic lover has an idealized image of beauty that is unattainable in reality. Consequently, the erotic lover often feels unfulfilled. Not surprisingly, erotic lovers are particularly sensitive to physical imperfections in the ones they love.

Ludus: Entertainment and Excitement. *Ludus* love is experienced as a game, as fun. The better the lover can play the game, the greater the enjoyment. Love is not to be taken too seriously; emotions are to be held in check lest they get out of hand and make trouble; passions never rise to the point where they get out of control. A ludic lover is self-controlled, always aware of the need to manage love rather than allowing it to be in control. Perhaps because of this need to control love, some researchers have proposed that ludic love tendencies may reveal tendencies to sexual aggression (Sarwer, Kalichman, Johnson, Early, et al., 1993). Not surprisingly, the ludic lover retains a partner only as long as he or she is interesting and amusing. When interest fades, it's time to change partners. Perhaps because love is a game, sexual fidelity is of little importance to ludic lovers. In fact, research shows that people who score high on ludic love are more likely to engage in extradyadic (outside-the-couple) dating and sex than those who score low on ludus (Wiederman & Hurd, 1999).

Storge: Peace and Slowness. *Storge* love lacks passion and intensity. Storgic lovers set out not to find a lover but to establish a companionable relationship with someone they know and with whom they can share interests and activities. Storgic love is a gradual process of unfolding thoughts and feelings; the changes seem to

> **❝** True love comes quietly, without banners or flashing lights. If you hear bells, get your ears checked. **❞**
>
> —Erich Segal

come so slowly and so gradually that it's often difficult to define exactly where the relationship is at any point in time. Sex in storgic relationships comes late, and when it comes it assumes no great importance.

Pragma: Practicality and Tradition. The *pragma* lover is practical and seeks a relationship that will work. Pragma lovers want compatibility and a relationship in which their important needs and desires will be satisfied. They're concerned with the social qualifications of a potential mate even more than with personal qualities; family and background are extremely important to the pragma lover, who relies not so much on feelings as on logic. The pragma lover views love as a useful relationship, a relationship that makes the rest of life easier. So the pragma lover asks such questions of a potential mate as "Will this person earn a good living?" "Can this person cook?" "Will my family get along with this person?" Pragma lovers' relationships rarely deteriorate. This is partly because pragma lovers choose their mates carefully and emphasize similarities. Another reason is that they have realistic romantic expectations.

Mania: Elation and Depression. *Mania* is characterized by extreme highs and extreme lows. The manic lover loves intensely and at the same time worries intensely about the loss of the love. This fear often prevents the manic lover from deriving as much pleasure as possible from the relationship. With little provocation, the manic lover may experience extreme jealousy. Manic love is obsessive; the manic lover has to possess the beloved completely. In return, the manic lover wishes to be possessed, to be loved intensely. The manic lover's poor self-image seems capable of being improved only by being loved; self-worth comes from being loved rather than from any sense of inner satisfaction. Because love is so important, danger signs in a relationship are often ignored; the manic lover believes that if there is love, then nothing else matters.

Agape: Compassion and Selflessness. *Agape* (ah-guh-pay) is a compassionate, egoless, self-giving love. The agapic lover loves even people with whom he or she has no close ties. This lover loves the stranger on the road even though they will probably never meet again. Agape is a spiritual love, offered without concern for personal reward or gain. This lover loves without expecting that the love will be reciprocated. Jesus, Buddha, and Gandhi practiced and preached this unqualified love (Lee, 1976). In one sense, agape is more a philosophical kind of love than a love that most people have the strength to achieve.

Cultural and Gender Differences in Love Although most of the research on the six love styles has been done in the United States, some research has been conducted in other cultures. Here is a brief sampling of the research findings—just enough to illustrate that culture is an important factor in love. The test and the love styles have been found to have validity among Germans (Bierhoff & Klein, 1991). Asians have been found to be more friendship oriented in their love style than are Europeans (Dion & Dion, 1993b). Members of individualistic cultures (for example, Europeans) are likely to place greater emphasis on romantic love and on individual fulfillment. Members of collectivist cultures are likely to spread their love over a large network of relatives (Dion & Dion, 1993a).

In the United States the differences between men and women in love are considered great. Poetry, novels, and the mass media depict women and men as acting very differently when falling in love, being in love, and ending a love relationship. As Lord Byron put it in *Don Juan*, "Man's love is of man's life a thing apart, / 'Tis

"I wonder if there is ever a perfect time to tell someone his hands are sticky."

woman's whole existence." Women are portrayed as emotional, men as logical. Women are supposed to love intensely; men are supposed to love with detachment.

Women and men seem to experience love to a similar degree (Rubin, 1973). However, women indicate greater love for their same-sex friends than men do. This may reflect a real difference between the sexes, or it may be a function of the greater social restrictions on men: A man is not supposed to admit his love for another man. Women are permitted greater freedom to communicate their love for other women.

Men and women also differ in the types of love they prefer (Hendrick, Hendrick, Foote, & Slapion-Foote, 1984). For example, on one version of the love self-test on page 224, men have been found to score higher on erotic and ludic love, whereas women score higher on manic, pragmatic, and storgic love. No difference has been found for agapic love.

? SKILLS VIEWPOINT

Your dating partner communicates as if you're at the intimacy stage, whereas you see the relationship in much less intimate (even casual) terms. You want to correct this misinterpretation. What do you say?

Family Relationships

If you had to define the word *family,* your first instinct might be to say that a family consists of a husband, a wife, and one or more children. When pressed, you might add that some families also consist of other relatives: brothers and sisters, grandparents, aunts and uncles, in-laws, and so on. But there are other types of relationships that are, to their own members, "families." Table 10.2 provides a few statistics on the American family as constituted in 1970 and in 2000.

What other trends do you see occurring in the family? One obvious example is the family with one parent. There are now almost 12 million single-family households in the United States. In 1998 about 28 percent of children under 18 lived with just one parent (about 23 percent with their mother and about 4 percent with their father), according to the *World Almance and Book of Facts, 2002.*

Another obvious example is the family that consists of people living together in an exclusive relationship who are not married. For the most part these cohabitants live as if they were married: There is an exclusive sexual commitment; there may be children; there are shared financial responsibilities, shared time, and shared space. These relationships mirror traditional marriages, except that in marriage the union is recognized by a religious body, the state, or both, whereas in a relationship of cohab-

TABLE 10.2	The Changing Face of the Family			

Here are a few statistics on the nature of the American family in 1970 and in 2000, as reported by the 2002 *New York Times Almanac,* and some possible trends theses figures indicate.

FAMILY CHARACTERISTICS	1970	2000	TRENDS
Number of members in average family	3.58	3.17	Tendency toward smaller families
Families without children	44.1%	52.9%	Growing number of families that opt not to have children
Families headed by married couples	86.9%	76.8%	Growing trends for heterosexual couples to live as a family without marriage, for singles to have children, and for gay men and lesbians to form families
Female heads of households	10.7%	17.6%	Growing trend of women's having children without marriage and high rate of divorce and separation
Unmarried couples living together	523,000	4,700,000	Growing trend for couples to form families without being married
Unmarried couples living together with children under 15	196,000	1,675,000	Growing trend for couples to form families and have children without marriage

itants it generally is not. In the most comprehensive study to date, *American Couples* (Blumstein & Schwartz, 1983), the authors reported that although cohabiting couples represented only about 2 percent to 3.8 percent of all couples in the early 1980s, their number was increasing. One bit of supporting evidence at that time was that among couples in which the male was under age 25, the percentage of cohabiting couples was 7.4 percent. In Sweden, a country that often leads in sexual trends, 12 percent of all couples were cohabitants.

The gay male or lesbian couple who live together as "domestic partners"—a relatively new term for people living in a committed relationship—often have all the typical characteristics of a family. Many of these couples have children, whether from previous heterosexual unions, through artificial insemination, or by adoption. Although accurate statistics are difficult to secure, primary relationships (couplehoods) among gays and lesbians seem more common than the popular media lead us to believe. Researchers estimate that gay and lesbian couples constitute 70 percent to more than 80 percent of the gay population (itself estimated variously at between 4 percent and 16 percent of the total population, depending on the definitions used and the studies cited). In summarizing previous studies and their own research, Blumstein and Schwartz (1983) concluded, "'Couplehood,' either as a reality or as an aspiration, is as strong among gay people as it is among heterosexuals."

Let's look at several key characteristics of both traditional nuclear families (mother–father–child families) and the many new kinds of family groups. In the following discussion, the term **primary relationship** denotes the relationship that the two principal parties—the husband and wife, the lover, or the domestic partners, for example—consider most important. The term **family** denotes the broader constellation that includes children, relatives, and assorted significant others.

All primary relationships and families have characteristics that further define these relationship types: defined roles, recognition of responsibilities, shared history and future, shared living space, and established rules for communicating.

For example, primary relationship partners have relatively *defined roles* that each person is expected to play in relation to the other and to the relationship as a whole. Each has acquired the rules of the culture and social group; each knows approximately what his or her obligations, duties, privileges, and responsibilities are. The partners' roles might include those of wage earner, cook, housecleaner, child caregiver, social secretary, home decorator, plumber, carpenter, food shopper, money manager, nurturer, philosopher, comedian, organizer, and so on. At times the roles may be shared, but even then it's generally assumed that one person has primary responsibility for certain tasks and the other person for others.

Family members have a *recognition of responsibilities* to one another; for example, responsibilities to help others financially; to offer comfort when family members are distressed; to take pleasure in family members' pleasures, to feel their pain, to raise their spirits.

Primary relationships have *a shared history and the prospect of a shared future.* For a relationship to become a primary relationship, there must be some history, some significant past interaction. This interaction enables the members to get to know each other, to understand each other a little better, and ideally to like and even love each other. Similarly, the individuals view the relationship as having a potential future.

All families teach *rules for communicating;* for example, never contradict the family in front of outsiders, or never talk finances with outsiders.

Workplace Relationships

Workplace relationships are becoming more and more important as we spend growing amounts of time in work relationship situations, whether face-to-face in the traditional office or online. Online work groups are also on the increase—and have been found to be more task oriented and more efficient than face-to-face groups

Skill building exercise

Changing the Distance between You

Here are two sets of strategies: (1) **Affinity-seeking strategies** are strategies that people use to make others like them, to draw people closer to them (Bell & Daly, 1984). (2) **Disengagement strategies** are strategies people use in trying to distance themselves from a close relationship partner (Cody, 1982). As you read and think about each group of qualities and behaviors, try composing at least one message that would help you communicate the desired qualities. Be sure to coordinate both verbal and nonverbal messages.

Affinity-Seeking Strategies

Altruism: Be of help to the other person.

Assumption of equality: Present yourself as socially equal to the other.

Comfortable self: Present yourself as comfortable and relaxed with the other.

Conversational rule-keeping: Follow the cultural rules for polite, cooperative conversation.

Dynamism: Appear active, enthusiastic, and dynamic.

Self-concept confirmation: Show respect for the other person and help the person feel positive about himself or herself.

Disengagement Strategies

Positive tone: Try to maintain a positive relationship and to express positive feelings: "I really care for you a lot, but I'm not ready for such a relationship."

Justification: Give reasons for the breakup: "I'm going away to college; there's no point in not dating others." Avoid negativity and blaming the other person, as in "I can't stand your jealousy, your checking up on me. I need my freedom."

Behavioral deescalation: Reduce the intensity of the relationship by avoiding the other person, cutting down on phone calls, reducing time spent together.

Explicit deescalation: Explain that you'd like to reduce the exclusivity and hence the intensity of the relationship: "I'm not ready for so exclusive a relationship. We should see other people."

All communication abounds with such strategies; practicing with these strategies will help increase your arsenal of ways to best achieve some of your most important interpersonal purposes.

(Lantz, 2001). Online groups can provide a sense of belongingness that may once have been thought possible only in face-to-face interactions (Silverman, 2001). Here we look at three kinds of workplace relationships: romantic, mentoring, and networking relationships.

Romantic Relationships   In television depictions coworkers always seem to be best friends who would do anything for one another, and characters move in and out of interoffice romances with no difficulties—at least with no difficulties that can't be resolved in 24 minutes. Real life is quite different.

Opinions concerning workplace romances vary widely. Some organizations, on the assumption that romantic relationships are basically detrimental to the success of the workplace, have explicit rules prohibiting such relationships. In some organizations workers can even be fired for getting involved in workplace romances.

On the positive side, the work environment seems a perfect place to meet a potential romantic partner. After all, by virtue of the fact that you're working in the same office, you both are probably interested in the same field, have similar training and ambitions, and will spend considerable time together—all factors that foster the development of a successful interpersonal relationship.

Similarly, office romances can lead to greater work satisfaction. If you're romantically attracted to another worker, it can make going to work, working together,

> 66 Whenever I date a guy, I think, is this the man I want my children to spend their weekends with? 99
>
> —Rita Rudner

and even working added hours more enjoyable and more satisfying. If the relationship is good and mutually satisfying, the individuals are likely to develop empathy for each other and act in ways that are supportive, cooperative, and friendly; in short, the workers are more likely to act with all the characteristics of effective communication noted throughout this book.

However, even when the relationship is good for the two individuals, it may not necessarily be positive for other workers. Seeing the loving couple every day in every way may generate destructive office gossip. Or fellow workers may see the lovers as a team that has to be confronted as a pair, feeling that they can't criticize one lover without incurring the wrath of the other.

Similarly, such relationships may cause problems for management when, for example, promotion or relocation decisions are necessary. Can you legitimately ask one lover to move to Boston and the other to move to San Francisco? Will it prove difficult for management to put one lover in the position of supervising the other?

The workplace also puts pressure on the individuals. Most organizations in the United States are highly competitive, and one person's success often means another's failure. In this environment a romantic couple may find, for example, that the self-disclosures that normally accompany increased intimacy (and which often reveal weaknesses, self-doubts, and misgivings), may actually prove a competitive liability.

There's a popular belief that women see office romances as a route to some kind of personal gain. For example, researchers who surveyed 218 male and female business school graduates found that despite a lack of any evidence, people perceived women as entering office romances in order to achieve advancement (Anderson & Fisher, 1991). So the woman who does participate in an office romance may have to deal with both male and female colleagues' assumptions that she is in this relationship to advance her career.

When an office romance goes bad or when it's one-sided, there are even more disadvantages. One obvious problem is that it can be stressful for the former partners to see each other regularly and perhaps to work together. And other workers may feel they have to take sides, being supportive of one partner and critical of the other. This can easily cause friction throughout the organization. Another and perhaps more serious issue is the potential for charges of workplace sexual harassment, especially if the romance is between a supervisor and a worker. Whether the charges are legitimate or merely the result of an unhappy love affair that has nothing to do with the organization, management will find itself in the middle, facing the expenditure of time and money to investigate and ultimately act on the charges—or, still worse, to defend against lawsuits.

On balance, the generally negative attitude of management toward office love affairs and the problems of dealing with the normal stress of both work and romance seem to outweigh the positive benefits that could be derived from such relationships, so workers are generally advised not to romance their colleagues. Friendships seem the much safer course.

Mentoring Relationships In a **mentoring relationship** an experienced individual helps to train a person who is less experienced. An accomplished teacher, for example, might mentor a young teacher who is newly arrived or who has never taught before. The mentor guides the new person through the ropes, teaches the strategies and techniques for success, and otherwise communicates his or her accumulated knowledge and experience to the "mentee."

? SKILLS VIEWPOINT

One way to improve communication during difficult times is to ask your partner for positive behaviors rather than asking him or her to stop negative behaviors. You decide to turn negative statements such as these into positive suggestions: (1) "I hate it when you ignore me at business functions." (2) "I can't stand going to these cheap restaurants; when are you going to start spending a few bucks?" (3) "Stop being so negative; you criticize everything and everyone." What do you say?

Message Skills

Romantic Workplace Relationships: Establish romantic relationships at work with a clear understanding of the potential problems.

The mentoring relationship provides an ideal learning environment. It's usually a supportive and trusting one-on-one relationship between expert and novice. There's a mutual and open sharing of information and thoughts about the job. The relationship enables the novice to try out new skills under the guidance of an expert, to ask questions, and to obtain the feedback so necessary to the acquisition of complex skills. Mentoring is perhaps best characterized as a relationship in which the experienced and powerful mentor empowers the novice, giving the novice the tools and techniques for gaining the same power the mentor now holds.

One study found the mentoring relationship to be one of the three primary paths to career achievement among African American men and women (Bridges, 1996). And another study (of middle-level managers) found that people who had mentors and participated in mentoring relationships got more promotions and higher salaries than those who did not have mentors (Scandura, 1992).

At the same time, the mentor benefits from clarifying his or her thoughts, from seeing the job from the perspective of a newcomer, and from considering and formulating answers to a variety of questions. Much as a teacher learns from teaching, a mentor learns from mentoring.

Networking Relationships   We often think of networking simply as a technique for securing a job. But it's actually a much broader process. **Networking** can be viewed as using other people to help you solve your problems, or at least to offer insights that bear on your problems—for example, how to publish your manuscript, where to look for low-cost auto insurance, how to find an affordable apartment, or how to defrag your hard drive.

Networking comes in at least two forms: informal and formal. Informal networking is what we do every day when we find ourselves in a new situation or unable to answer questions. Thus, for example, if you're new at a school, you might ask someone in your class what's the best place to eat or shop for clothes or who's the best teacher for interpersonal communication. In the same way, when you enter a new work environment, you might ask more experienced workers how to perform certain tasks or whom to avoid or approach when you have questions.

Formal networking is the same thing, except that it's a lot more systematic and strategic. It's establishing connections with people who can help you—who can answer questions, help you get a job, help you get promoted, help you relocate or accomplish any task you want to accomplish.

Here are a few suggestions for making networking more effective. Begin by reviewing the list of your friends, relatives, and acquaintances; you'll probably find that you know lots of people with specialized knowledge who can help you in a variety of ways. In some cultures—Brazil is one example—friendships are often established partly for the sake of potential networking connections (Rector & Neiva, 1996). Starting with people you know, you can then branch out to network with people who know people you know. Thus, you may contact a friend's friend to find out if the firm he or she works for is hiring. Or you may contact people you have no connection with. Perhaps you've read something a person wrote or you've heard the person's name raised in connection with an area in which you're interested. With e-mail addresses readily available, it's now quite common to e-mail individuals who have particular expertise and ask them questions.

Try to establish relationships that are mutually beneficial. After all, much as others are useful sources of information for you, you're likely to be a useful source of information for others. And if you can help others, it's more likely that they will be helpful to you.

Consider developing files of people you can contact. For example, if you're a freelance artist, come up with a list of persons who might be in positions to offer you work. Authors, editors, art directors, administrative assistants, people in advertising, and a host of others might eventually provide useful leads and can often simplify your search for freelance work.

> It is wise to apply the oil of refined politeness to the mechanisms of friendship.
>
> —Colette

Message Skills

Networking: Establish a network of relationships to provide insights into issues relevant to your personal and professional life, and be willing to lend your expertise to others.

Take an active part in locating and establishing networking connections. Be proactive; initiate contacts rather than waiting for them to come to you. Don't overdo it; you don't want to rely on other people to do work you can easily do yourself. Yet if you're also willing to help others, there's nothing wrong in asking these same people to help you. If you're respectful of their time and expertise, most people will respond positively to your networking attempts. Following up your requests with thank-you notes, for example, will help you establish networks that can be ongoing productive relationships rather than one-shot affairs.

Summary of Concepts

This chapter explored the nature of interpersonal relationships, the stages relationships go through, and the major types of relationships.

1. Interpersonal relationships may be characterized as those that are based on psychological data, involve explanatory knowledge, and rely on personally established rules.
2. Interpersonal relationships have both advantages and disadvantages. Among the advantages are that they stimulate you, help you learn about yourself, and generally enhance your self-esteem. Among the disadvantages are that they force you to expose your vulnerabilities, make great demands on your time, and often cause you to abandon other relationships.
3. Most relationships involve various stages. Recognize at least these: contact, involvement, intimacy, deterioration, repair, and dissolution.
4. In contact there is first perceptual contact and then interaction.
5. Involvement includes a testing phase (will this be a suitable relationship?) and an intensifying of the interaction; often a sense of mutuality, of connectedness, begins.
6. In intimacy there is an interpersonal commitment and perhaps a social bonding, in which the commitment is made public.
7. Some relationships deteriorate, proceeding through a period of intrapersonal dissatisfaction to interpersonal deterioration.

8. Along the process, repair may be initiated. Intrapersonal repair generally comes first (should I change my behavior?); it may be followed by interpersonal repair, in which you and your partner discuss your problems and seek remedies.
9. If repair fails, the relationship may dissolve, moving first to interpersonal separation and later, perhaps, to public or social separation.
10. Among the major interpersonal relationships are friendship, love, family, and work relationships.
11. Friendship is an interpersonal relationship between two persons that is mutually productive and characterized by mutual positive regard.
12. Love refers to the romantic relationship existing between two people and comes in a variety of forms. Eros, ludus, storge, pragma, mania, and agape are some of the commonly distinguished types of love.
13. Family relationships are those existing between two or more people who have defined roles, recognize their responsibilities to each other, have a shared history and a prospect of a shared future, and interact according to a shared system of communication rules.
14. Among the workplace relationships that need to be considered are romantic relationships (their positives and their negatives), mentoring relationships (in which one experienced worker helps a less experienced one), and networking relationships (in which helping relationships are established either informally or formally).

Vocabulary Quiz: The Language of Interpersonal Relationships

Match the terms dealing with interpersonal relationships with their definitions. Record the number of the definition next to the appropriate term.

_____ friendship

_____ agape

_____ interpersonal repair

_____ mentoring

_____ networking

_____ family

_____ dissolution

_____ reciprocity

_____ personally established rules

_____ relational dialectics theory

1. A type of friendship based on loyalty, self-sacrifice, and equality.
2. A selfless, compassionate love.
3. A relationship characterized by a shared history and a prospect of a shared future, recognition of mutual responsibilities, defined roles, and rules for communicating.
4. An interpersonal relationship that is mutually productive and characterized by mutual positive regard.
5. One of the qualities defining interpersonal relationships.
6. A theory that all relationships can be defined by a series of competing opposite motivations or desires.
7. A stage in some relationships that involves recognizing problems and engaging in productive conflict resolution.
8. A relationship in which an experienced worker helps train a less experienced worker.
9. Establishment of connections with people who can help you.
10. A stage in some relationships that involves interpersonal separation followed by social or public separation.

Four for Discussion

1. The "matching hypothesis" claims that people date and mate people who are comparable to themselves in physical attractiveness (Walster & Walster, 1978). When this does not happen—for example, when a very attractive person dates someone of average attractiveness—you may begin to look for "compensating factors," or attributes of the less attractive person that compensate or make up for his or her appearance. What evidence can you find to support or contract this theory? Why do you think people date and mate people who are roughly equal in attractiveness?

2. Do you "comparison shop" (compare your own relationship against potential alternative relationships) regardless of the type of relationship you're in, or do you stop "shopping" when the relationship reaches a certain level of commitment?

3. It's been argued that you don't actually develop an attraction to people who are similar to you but rather develop a repulsion toward those who are dissimilar (Rosenbaum, 1986). For example, you may exclude people who disagree with you from those with whom you might develop a relationship. You're therefore left with a pool of possible partners whose ideas are similar to yours. What do you think of this "repulsion hypothesis"?

4. Not surprisingly, a great deal of relationship maintenance takes place through e-mail (Stafford, Kline, & Dimmick, 1999; Howard, Rainie, & Jones, 2001). Because an increasing number of relationships develop online, and because online contact is so easy even when partners are widely separated geographically, this use of e-mail is likely to increase in frequency and importance. Incidentally, the use of e-mail to maintain relationships, is more common among women than men; women also find such e-mail contact more gratifying than do men (Boneva, Kraut, & Frohlich, 2001). What role does Internet communication play in your relationship life?

Web Explorations

Explore our text website at
www.ablongman.com/devito
to find:

Explore our research resources at
www.researchnavigator.com
and

Exercises and Self-Tests

Exercises that will enable you to work actively with the concepts discussed in this chapter are (1) Analyzing Stage Talk, (2) Giving Repair Advice, (3) Til' This Do Us Part, (4) Interpersonal Relationships in Songs and Greeting Cards, (5) Applying Theories to Problems, (6) Male and Female, (7) Relational Repair from Advice Columnists, (8) How Can You Get Someone to Like You? (9) How Might You Repair Relationships? (10) Friendship Behaviors, (11) Mate Preferences: I Prefer Someone Who . . . , and (12) The Television Relationship. Relevant self-tests are (13) What Do You Believe about Relationships? (14) How Committed Are You? (15) How Romantic Are You? and (16) What Type of Relationship Do You Prefer?

You may at this point wish to explore the genealogy of your own family. For this there are many useful websites. You might begin with **www.ancestralfindings.com**; or you can go to any search engine and ask it to search genealogy (your last name) or genealogy (cultural identifiers such as nationality or religion).

Writing Resources and Assignments

Suggestions are available for writing papers of personal experience (for example, your strategies of relationship repair), concept or principle explanation (for example, online relationships), review (for example, the reasons for relationship breakup), or research (for example, the role of money in contemporary relationships) on interpersonal relationships.

Read an article.

Read a popular or scholarly article on interpersonal relationships; the stages that relationships go through; or the influence of culture, gender, or technology on relationships. On the basis of this article, what can you add to the discussion presented here?

Investigate key terms.

Investigate one of the key terms discussed in this chapter (for example, interpersonal relationship, online relationship, relationship development, relationship deterioration, relationship repair, intimacy, friendship, love, family). What additional insights can you provide?

Find answers.

Try finding answers to one of the following questions, or design a research study to answer it.

1. Do the advantages and disadvantages of relationships change with age?
2. Do men and women see relationship fidelity in the same way?
3. What types of lovers (eros, ludus, storge, pragma, mania, agape) were the great lovers of history and literature?
4. In what ways are primary relationships among heterosexuals and homosexuals different? In what ways are they the same?

Conflict and Interpersonal Communication

11

> In ancient times the beautiful woman Mi Tzu-hsia was the favorite of the king of Wei. According to the law of Wei, anyone who rode in the king's carriage without permission would be punished by amputation of the foot. When Mi Tzu-hsia's mother fell ill, she took the king's carriage and went out, and the king only praised her for it. "Such filial devotion!" he said. "For her mother's sake she risked the punishment of amputation!"
>
> Another day she was dallying with the king in the fruit garden. She took a peach, which she found so sweet that instead of finishing it she handed it to the king to taste. "How she loves me," said the king, "forgetting the pleasure of her own taste to share with me!"
>
> But when Mi Tzu-hsia's beauty began to fade, the king's affection cooled. And when she offended the king, he said, "Didn't she once take my carriage without permission? And didn't she once give me a peach that she had already chewed on?"

This folktale—taken from *Chinese Fairy Tales and Fantasies* (Roberts, 1979)—captures our common tendency to evaluate the same behavior in very different ways, depending on how we feel about the person. This tendency is especially clear in interpersonal conflict, the subject of this chapter. More specifically, this chapter considers the principles of interpersonal conflict, the stages you can go through in a conflict, and the strategies that you can use to resolve conflicts without damaging your relationships.

Principles of Interpersonal Conflict

Interpersonal conflict is disagreement between or among connected individuals—coworkers, close friends, lovers, or family members. The word *connected* emphasizes the transactional nature of interpersonal conflict—the fact that each person's position affects the other person. The positions in conflicts are to some degree interrelated and incompatible. Let's look at the fundamental principles of interpersonal conflict.

Interpersonal Conflict Is Inevitable

Conflict, or dissension, is a part of every interpersonal relationship, whether between parents and children, brothers and sisters, friends, lovers, or coworkers. If conflict doesn't exist, then the relationship is probably dull, irrelevant, or insignificant.

One of the difficulties in dealing with interpersonal conflict is that many people think that if they experience conflict in their friendships or romantic relationships, it means that something is wrong or that the relationship is in jeopardy or that the relationship will be damaged if these differences are brought up for discussion. These myths often get in the way of meaningful communication about differences and disagreements. As we'll see, conflict itself doesn't necessarily damage the relationship; more often, the crucial difference is in how the participants manage and resolve the conflict. If conflict is managed fairly and with mutual respect, the relationship is likely to prosper. If it's managed unfairly, the relationship is likely to suffer.

To appreciate the inevitability of conflict, consider the broad range of topics on which relationship partners disagree to the point of conflict (Canary, 2003). For example, one study on the issues argued about by gay, lesbian, and heterosexual couples, identified six major sources of conflict that were virtually identical for all couples (Kurdek, 1994). The issues are arranged here in order, with the first being the most often mentioned. How many of these do you argue about?

" It is seldom the fault of one when two argue. "

—Swedish proverb

- *intimacy issues* such as affection and sex
- *power issues* such as excessive demands or possessiveness, lack of equality in the relationship, friends, or leisure time
- *personal flaws issues* such as drinking or smoking, personal grooming, or driving style
- *personal distance issues* such as frequent absences or school or job commitments
- *social issues* such as politics and social issues, parents, or personal values
- *distrust issues* such as previous lovers or lying

Another study found that four conditions typically led up to couples' "first big fight": uncertainty over commitment, jealousy, violation of expectations, and personality differences (Siegert & Stamp, 1994). Among top managers, conflict most often revolved around issues of executive responsibility and coordination. Other conflicts focused on differences in organizational objectives, on allocation of resources, and on appropriate management style (Morrill, 1992). In a study of same-sex and opposite-sex friends, the four issues most often argued about involved problems with sharing living space or possessions, violations of friendship rules, difficulties in sharing activities, and incompatible ideas or opinions (Samter & Cupach, 1998).

Just as you experience conflict in face-to-face communication, you can experience conflicts online. Spamming and flaming, although having parallels in face-to-face communication, are especially troublesome in Internet communication.

Spamming is sending someone unsolicited mail, repeatedly sending the same mail, or posting the same message on lots of bulletin boards even when the message is irrelevant to the focus of the group. Spam wastes people's time and energy, obliging them to deal with something they didn't want in the first place. Spam also clogs the system, slowing it down for everyone.

Flaming, especially common in newsgroups, is sending messages that personally attack another user. Flaming frequently leads to flame wars in which everyone in the group gets into the act. Generally, flaming and flame wars are counterproductive.

Conflict Can Be Negative or Positive

Although interpersonal conflict is always stressful, it's important to recognize that it has both negative and positive aspects.

Negative Aspects Conflict often leads to increased negative regard for the opponent. One reason for this is that many conflicts involve unfair fighting methods and are focused largely on hurting the other person. When one person hurts the other, increased negative feelings are inevitable; even the strongest relationship has limits.

At times conflict may lead you to close yourself off from the other person. When you hide your true self from an intimate, you prevent meaningful communication from taking place. Because the need for intimacy is so strong, one or both parties may then seek intimacy elsewhere. This often leads to further conflict, mutual hurt, and resentment—qualities that add heavily to the costs carried by the relationship. Meanwhile, rewards may become difficult to exchange. In this situation, the costs increase and the rewards decrease, which often results in relationship deterioration and eventual dissolution.

> **❝❝** Where there is no difference, there is only indifference. **❞❞**
>
> —Louis Nizer

Positive Aspects The major value of interpersonal conflict is that it forces you to examine a problem and work toward a potential solution. If the participants use productive conflict strategies, the relationship may well emerge from the encounter stronger, healthier, and more satisfying than before. And you may emerge stronger, more confident, and better able to stand up for yourself (Bedford, 1996).

Through conflict and its resolution we also can stop resentment from increasing and let our needs be known. For example, suppose I need lots of attention when I come home from work, but you need to review and get closure on the day's work. If we both can appreciate the legitimacy of these needs, then we can find solutions. Perhaps you can make your important phone call after my attention needs are met, or perhaps I can delay my need for attention until you get closure about work. Or perhaps I can learn to provide for your closure needs and in doing so get my attention needs met. We have a win–win solution; each of us gets our needs met.

Consider, too, that when you try to resolve conflict within an interpersonal relationship, you're saying in effect that the relationship is worth the effort; otherwise you would walk away from such a conflict. Usually, confronting a conflict indicates commitment and a desire to preserve the relationship.

Conflict Is Influenced by Culture and Gender

As in other areas of interpersonal communication, it helps to view conflict in light of culture and gender. Both exert powerful influences on how people view and resolve conflicts.

Conflict and Culture   Culture influences not only the issues that people fight about but also what is considered appropriate and inappropriate in terms of dealing with conflict. Researchers have found, for example, that cohabitating 18-year-olds are more likely to experience conflict with their parents about their living style if they live in the United States than if they live in Sweden, where cohabitation is much more accepted. Similarly, male infidelity is more likely to cause conflict between American spouses than in southern European couples. Students from the United States are more likely to engage in conflict with another U.S. student than with someone from another culture. Chinese students, on the other hand, are more likely to engage in a conflict with a non-Chinese student than with another Chinese (Leung, 1988).

The types of conflicts that arise depend on the cultural orientation of the individuals involved. For example, in collectivist cultures, such as those of Ecuador, Indonesia, and Korea, conflicts are more likely to center on violations of collective or group norms and values. Conversely, in individualist cultures, such as those of the United States, Canada, and western Europe, conflicts are more likely to occur when people violate individual norms (Ting-Toomey, 1985).

Americans and Japanese differ in their view of the aim or purpose of conflict. The Japanese (a collectivist culture) see conflicts and conflict resolution in terms of compromise; Americans (an individualist culture), on the other hand, see conflict in terms of winning (Gelfand, Nishii, Holcombe, Dyer, Ohbuchi, & Fukuno, 2001). Also, different cultures seem to teach their members different views of conflict strategies (Tardiff, 2001). For example, in Japan it's especially important that you not embarrass the person with whom you are in conflict, especially if the disagreement occurs in public. This face-saving principle prohibits the use of such strategies as personal rejection or verbal aggressiveness. In another example, many Middle Eastern and Pacific Rim cultures discourage women from direct and forceful expressions; rather, these societies expect more agreeable and submissive postures. Also, in general, members of collectivist cultures tend to avoid conflict more than members of individualist cultures (Dsilva & Whyte, 1998; Haar & Krabe, 1999; Cai & Fink, 2002).

Even within a given general culture, more specific cultures differ from one another in their methods of conflict management. African American men and women and European American men and women, for example, engage in conflict in very different ways (Kochman, 1981). The issues that cause conflict and aggravate conflict, the conflict strategies that are expected and accepted, and the entire attitude toward conflict vary from one group to the other. For example, African American men preferred clear arguments and a focus on problem solving. African American women, however, preferred assertiveness and respect (Collier, 1991).

Among Mexican Americans, studies found that men preferred to achieve mutual understanding by discussing the reasons for the conflict, whereas women focused on being supportive of the relationship. Among Anglo Americans, men preferred direct and rational argument; women preferred flexibility (Collier, 1991). These, of course, are merely examples—but the underlying principle is that techniques for dealing with interpersonal conflict will be viewed differently by different cultures.

The cultural norms of organizations also influence the types of conflicts that occur and the ways people may deal with them. Some work environments, for example, would not tolerate the expression of disagreement with high-level management; others might welcome it. In individualist cultures there is greater tolerance for conflict, even when it involves different levels of an organizational hierarchy. In collectivist cultures there's less tolerance. And, not surprisingly, the culture influences how the conflict will be resolved. For example, managers in the United States (an individualist culture) deal with workplace conflict by seeking to integrate the demands of the different sides; managers in China (a collectivist culture) are more likely to call on higher management to make decisions—or not to resolve the conflict at all (Tinsley & Brett, 2001).

Conflict and Gender Do men and women engage in interpersonal conflict differently? One of the few stereotypes that is supported by research is that of the withdrawing and sometimes aggressive male. Men are more apt to withdraw from a conflict situation than are women. It has been argued that this may happen because men become more psychologically and physiologically aroused during conflict (and retain this heightened level of arousal much longer than do women) and so may try to distance themselves and withdraw from the conflict to prevent further arousal (Gottman & Carrere, 1994; Canary, Cupach, & Messman, 1995; Goleman, 1995a). Women, on the other hand, want to get closer to the conflict; they want to talk about it and resolve it. Even adolescents reveal these differences; in a study of boys and girls aged 11 to 17, boys withdrew more than girls but were more aggressive when they didn't withdraw (Lindeman, Harakka, & Keltikangas-Jarvinen, 1997). Similarly, a study of offensive language found that girls were more easily offended by language than boys; but boys were more apt to fight when they were offended by the words used (Heasley, Babbitt, & Burbach, 1995). Another study showed that young girls used more prosocial strategies than boys (Rose & Asher, 1999).

Other research has found that women tend to be more emotional and men more logical when they argue (Schaap, Buunk, & Kerkstra, 1988; Canary, Cupach, & Messman, 1995). Women have been defined as conflict "feelers" and men as conflict "thinkers" (Sorenson, Hawkins, & Sorenson, 1995). Another difference is that women are more apt to reveal their negative feelings than are men (Schaap, Buunk, & Kerkstra, 1988; Canary, Cupach, & Messman, 1995).

Nevertheless, from a close examination of the research it would have to be concluded that the differences between men and women in interpersonal conflict are a lot less clear in reality than they are in popular stereotypes. Much research fails to find the differences that cartoons, situation comedies, novels, and films portray so readily. For example, several studies dealing with both college students and men and women in business found no significant differences in the way men and women engage in conflict (Wilkins & Andersen, 1991; Canary & Hause, 1993; Canary, Cupach, & Messman, 1995).

? SKILLS VIEWPOINT

After you do some things you're not very proud of, you and your partner have a fight. You're really sorry about what you did and want to show your understanding for your partner's distress and anger. What do you say if you're male? If you're female?

Message Skills

Conflict, Culture, and Gender: Approach conflict with an understanding of the cultural and gender differences in attitudes toward what constitutes conflict and toward how it should be pursued.

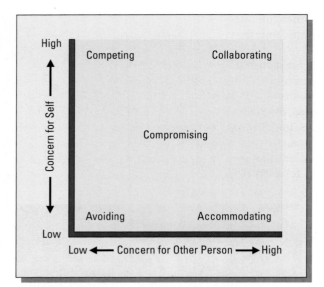

Figure 11.1

Five Conflict Styles
This figure is adapted from Blake and Mouton's (1985) approach to managerial leadership and conflict.

Source: R. R. Blake & J. S. Mouton, *The Managerial Grid III.* Gulf Publishing Company, 1985. Reprinted by permission of Grid International, Inc.

Conflict Styles Have Consequences

The way in which you engage in conflict has consequences for the resolution conflict and for the relationship between the conflicting parties. Figure 11.1 identifies five basic styles or ways of engaging in conflict and is especially relevant to understanding interpersonal conflicts (Blake & Mouton, 1985). Descriptions of the five styles, plotted among the dimensions of concern for self and concern for the other person, provide insight into the ways people engage in conflict and highlight some of the advantages and disadvantages of each style. As you read through these styles, try to identify your own conflict style as well as the styles of those with whom you have close relationships.

Competing: I Win, You Lose   The competitive style involves great concern for your own needs and desires and little for those of others. As long as your needs are met, the conflict has been dealt with successfully (for you). In conflict motivated by competitiveness, you'd be likely to be verbally aggressive and to blame the other person.

This style represents an *I win, you lose* philosophy. As you can tell, this style might be appropriate in a courtroom or at a used-car lot, two settings where one person benefits from the other person's losses. But in interpersonal situations this philosophy can easily lead to resentment on the part of the person who loses, which can easily morph into additional conflicts. Further, the fact that you win and the other person loses probably means that the conflict hasn't really been resolved but only concluded (for now).

Avoiding: I Lose, You Lose   Conflict avoiders are relatively unconcerned with their own or with their opponents' needs or desires. They avoid any real communication about the problem, change topics when the problem is brought up, and generally withdraw from the scene both psychologically and physically.

As you can appreciate, the avoiding style does little to resolve any conflicts and may be viewed as an *I lose, you lose* philosophy. Interpersonal problems rarely go away of their own accord; rather, if they exist, they need to be faced and dealt with effectively. Avoidance merely allows the conflict to fester and probably grow, only to resurface in another guise.

Accommodating: I Lose, You Win   In accommodating you sacrifice your own needs for the needs of the other person(s). Your major purpose is to maintain harmony and peace in the relationship or group. This style may help maintain peace and may satisfy the opposition; but it does little to meet your own needs, which are unlikely to go away.

Accommodation represents an *I lose, you win* philosophy. And although this style may make your partner happy (at least on this occasion), it's not likely to prove a lasting resolution to an interpersonal conflict. You'll eventually sense unfairness and inequality and may easily come to resent your partner and perhaps even yourself.

Collaborating: I Win, You Win   In collaborating you address both your own and the other person's needs. This style, often considered the ideal, takes time and a willingness to communicate—and especially to listen to the perspectives and needs of the other person.

Ideally, collaboration enables each person's needs to be met, an *I win, you win* situation. This is obviously the style that, in an ideal world, most people would choose for interpersonal conflict.

Message Skills

Conflict Styles: Chose your conflict style carefully; each style has consequences. In relationship conflict, look for win–win solutions rather than solutions in which one person wins and the other loses.

Compromising: I Win and Lose, You Win and Lose   The compromising style is in the middle: There's some concern for your own needs and some concern for the other's needs. Compromise is the kind of strategy you might refer to as "meeting each other halfway," "horse trading," or "give and take." This strategy is likely to result in maintaining peace, but there will be a residue of dissatisfaction over the inevitable loses that each side has to endure.

Compromise represents an *I win and lose, you win and lose* philosophy. There are lots of times when you can't both get exactly what you want. You can't both get a new car if the available funds allow for only one. And yet you might each get a better used car than the one you now have. So each of you might win something, though not everything.

Conflict Can Focus on Content or Relationship Issues

Using concepts developed in Chapter 1, we can distinguish between content conflict and relationship conflict. *Content conflict* centers on objects, events, and persons in the world that are usually, though not always, external to the parties involved in the conflict. Content conflicts have to do with the millions of issues that we argue and fight about every day—the merit of a particular movie, what to watch on television, the fairness of the last examination or job promotion, the way to spend our savings.

Relationship conflicts are equally numerous and include such examples as a younger brother who refuses to obey his older brother, two partners who each want an equal say in making vacation plans, and a mother and daughter who each want to have the final word concerning the daughter's lifestyle. Here the conflicts are concerned not so much with some external object as with the relationships between the individuals—with issues like who is in charge, how equal are the members in a primary relationship, or who has the right to set down rules of behavior.

Of course, content and relationship dimensions are always easier to separate in a textbook than they are in real life, in which many conflicts contain elements of both. For example, you can probably imagine both content and relationship dimensions in each of the "content" issues mentioned earlier. And yet certain issues seem more one way than the other. For example, intimacy and power issues are largely relational, whereas differences on political and social issues are largely content focused.

> " The ultimate test of a relationship is to disagree but to hold hands. "
>
> —Alexandria Penney

Message Skills

Content and Relationship Conflicts: Analyze conflict messages in terms of content and relationship dimensions, and respond to each accordingly.

Conflict Resolution Stages

The model in Figure 11.2 on page 242 helps explain conflict more fully and at the same time provides guidance for dealing with conflicts effectively. This five-stage model is based on the problem-solving technique first introduced by John Dewey (1910) and still used by many contemporary theorists (e.g., Beebe & Masterson, 2000; Patton, Giffin, & Patton, 1989). The assumption made here is that interpersonal conflict is essentially a problem that needs to be solved. This model should not be taken as suggesting that there is only one path to conflict resolution, however. It is a general way of envisioning the process that should help you better understand how conflict works and how you can work toward resolving the conflict.

Before getting to the five stages of conflict, consider a few "before the conflict" suggestions.

- Try to fight in private. When you air your conflicts in front of others you create other problems. You may not be willing to be totally honest when third parties are present; you may feel you have to save face and therefore must win the fight at all costs.

"Is this a good time to have a big fight?"

Figure 11.2

The Stages of Conflict Resolution

This model derives from John Dewey's stages of reflective thinking and is a general pattern for understanding and resolving any type of problem.

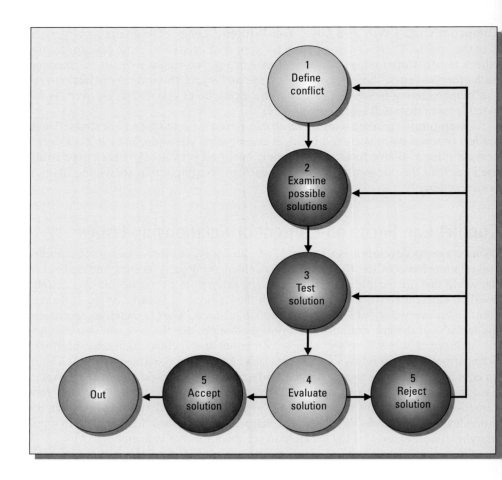

You also run the risk of embarrassing your partner in front of others, which will cause resentment and hostility.

- Make sure you're both relatively free of other problems and ready to deal with the conflict at hand. The moment when your partner comes home after a hard day of work may not be the right time to tackle a conflict.

- Fight about problems that can be solved. Fighting about past behaviors or about family members or situations over which you have no control solves nothing; in fact, it's more likely to create additional difficulties. Often such conflicts are really relationship conflicts—concealed attempts at expressing frustration or dissatisfaction.

Define the Conflict

Your first and most essential step is to define the conflict. Here are several techniques to keep in mind.

- *Define both content and relationship issues.* Define the obvious content issues (who should do the dishes, who should take the kids to school) as well as the underlying relationship issues (who has been avoiding household responsibilities, whose time is more valuable).

- *Define the problem in specific terms.* Conflict defined in the abstract is difficult to deal with and resolve. It's one thing for a husband to say that his wife is "cold and unfeeling" and quite another for him to say that she does not call him at the office, kiss him when he comes home, or hold his hand when they're at a party. Specific behaviors can be agreed upon and dealt with, but the abstract "cold and unfeeling" remains elusive.

> " The aim of an argument or discussion should not be victory, but progress. "
>
> —Joseph Joubert

Dealing with Conflict Starters

This exercise helps you look at your own pattern for dealing with conflict "starters"—remarks that signal an impending interpersonal conflict. For each situation below: (1) Write an unproductive response; that is, a response that will probably cause the conflict to escalate. (2) Write a productive response; that is, a response that will likely lessen the potential conflict. And (3) in one sentence, explain the major difference that you see between the productive and the unproductive responses.

1. You're late again. You're always late. Your lateness is so inconsiderate!
2. I just can't bear another weekend of sitting home watching cartoon shows with the kids.
3. Well, there goes another anniversary that you forgot.
4. You think I'm fat, don't you?
5. You never want to do what I want. We always have to do what you want.

Impending conflicts are often signaled at a stage when it's still possible to confront and resolve them. Once conflicts escalate, they generally become more difficult to resolve.

- *Empathize.* Try to understand the nature of the conflict from the other person's point of view. Why is your partner disturbed that you're not doing the dishes? Why is your neighbor complaining about taking your kids to school? Once you have empathically understood the other person's feelings, validate those feelings when appropriate. If your partner is hurt or angry and you believe such feelings are legitimate and justified, say so: "You have a right to be angry; I shouldn't have said what I did about your mother. I'm sorry. But I still don't want to go on vacation with her." In expressing validation, you're not necessarily expressing agreement; you're merely stating that your partner has feelings that you recognize as legitimate.

- *Avoid mind reading.* Don't try to read the other person's mind. Ask questions to make sure you understand the problem as the other person is experiencing it. Ask directly and simply: "Why are you insisting that I take the dog out now when I have to call three clients before nine o'clock?"

Let's now select an example and work with it through the remaining conflict stages. This conflict revolves around Raul's not wanting to socialize with Julia's friends. Julia is devoted to her friends, but Raul actively dislikes them. Julia thinks they're wonderful and exciting; Raul thinks they're unpleasant and boring.

Examine Possible Solutions

The second step in conflict is to look for possible ways of resolving the issue. Most conflicts can probably be resolved in a variety of ways. At this stage, try to identify as many solutions as possible.

As noted in the discussion of conflict styles earlier, win–win solutions are the ideal; so look for these whenever possible. Most solutions, of course, will involve costs to one or both parties (after all, someone has to take the dog out), so it's unlikely that solutions to real interpersonal problems are going to involve only rewards for both persons. But you can try to seek solutions in which the costs and the rewards will be evenly shared.

In our example, let's say Raul and Julia identify these possible solutions:

1. Julia should not interact with her friends anymore.
2. Raul should interact with Julia's friends.
3. Julia should see her friends without Raul.

? SKILLS VIEWPOINT

What one skill do you find especially useful for conflict resolution with friends? Romantic partners? Work colleagues? Family?

Generating Win–Win Solutions

To get into the habit of looking for win–win solutions, consider the following conflict situations. For each situation *(a)* generate as many win–lose solutions as you can—solutions in which one person wins and the other loses; *(b)* generate as many possible win–win solutions as you feel the individuals could reasonably accept; and *(c)* explain in one sentence the major difference between win–lose and win–win solutions

1. For their vacation, Pat wants to go to the shore and relax by the water; Chris wants to go hiking and camping in the mountains.
2. Pat, who recently got a $3,000 bonus, wants to buy a new computer and printer; Chris wants to take a vacation.
3. Pat hangs around the house in underwear. Chris really hates this, and they argue about it almost daily.

Win–win solutions exist for most conflict situations (though not necessarily all); with a little effort win–win solutions can be identified for most interpersonal conflicts.

Clearly solutions 1 and 2 are win–lose solutions. In 1, Raul wins and Julia loses; in 2, Julia wins and Raul loses. Solution 3, however, might be a possibility. Both might win and neither must necessarily lose. The next step would be to test this possible solution.

Test a Solution

Once you have examined all possible solutions, select one and test it out. First test the solution mentally. How does it feel now? How will it feel tomorrow? Are you comfortable with the solution? Will Raul be comfortable about Julia's socializing with her friends without him? Some of Julia's friends are attractive unmarried men; is this going to make a difference? Will Julia be comfortable socializing with her friends without Raul? Will she give people too much to gossip about? Will she feel guilty? Will she enjoy herself without Raul?

Then test the solution in actual practice. How does it work? Give each solution a fair chance. Perhaps Julia might go out once without Raul to try it out. How was it? Did her friends think there was something wrong with her relationship with Raul? Did she feel guilty? Did she enjoy herself? How did Raul feel? Did he feel jealous? Did he feel lonely or abandoned?

Evaluate the Solution

In the evaluation stage, ask whether the test solution helped resolve the conflict. Is the situation better now than it was before the solution was tentatively put into operation? Share your feelings and evaluations of the solution. Use the skills for expressing emotions covered in Chapter 7.

Raul and Julia now need to share their perceptions of this possible solution. Would they be comfortable with this solution on a monthly basis? Is the solution worth the costs that each will pay? Are the costs and the rewards about evenly distributed? Might other solutions be more effective?

Critical thinking pioneer Edward deBono (1987) suggests that in evaluating problems or proposed solutions, you use six "thinking hats." With each hat you look at the problem or the solution from a different perspective. Here's how looking at Julia and Raul's problem with the six hats might work:

- *The fact hat* focuses attention on the facts and figures that bear on the problem. For example, How can Raul learn more about the rewards that Julia gets from her friends? How can Julia find out why Raul doesn't like her friends?

- *The feeling hat* focuses attention on the emotional responses to the problem. How does Raul feel when Julia goes out with her friends? How does Julia feel when Raul refuses to meet them?

- *The negative argument hat* asks you to become the devil's advocate. How might this relationship deteriorate if Julia continues seeing her friends without Raul or if Raul resists interacting with Julia's friends?

- *The positive benefits hat* asks you to look at the upside. What are the opportunities that Julia's seeing friends without Raul might yield? What benefits might Raul and Julia get from this new arrangement?

- *The creative new idea hat* focuses on new ways of looking at the problem. In what other ways can Raul and Julia look at this problem? What other possible solutions might they consider?

- *The control of thinking hat* helps you analyze what you're doing. It asks you to reflect on your own thinking. Have Raul and Julia adequately defined the problem? Are they focusing too much on insignificant issues? Have they given enough attention to possible negative effects?

Accept or Reject the Solution

If you accept a solution, you're ready to put this solution into more permanent operation. But if you decide, on the basis of your evaluation, that this is not the right solution for the conflict, then there are two major alternatives. First, you might test another solution. Perhaps you might now reexamine a runner-up idea or approach. Second, you might go back to the definition of the conflict. As the diagram in Figure 11.2 illustrates, you can reenter the conflict-resolution process at any of the first three stages.

Let us say that Raul is actually quite happy with the solution. He takes the opportunity of his evening alone to visit his brother. Next time Julia goes out with her friends, Raul intends to go to wrestling. And Julia feels pretty good about seeing her friends without Raul. She simply explains that occasionally she and Raul socialize separately and that both are comfortable with this.

Message Skills

Problem-Solving Conflicts: Deal with interpersonal conflicts systematically, as problems to be solved: Define the problem, examine possible solutions, test a solution, evaluate the solution, and accept or reject the solution.

Listen to this

Listening to Messages in Conflict

Perhaps the most difficult type of listening occurs in conflict situations; tempers may be running high, and you may be finding yourself under attack. Here are some suggestions for listening more effectively in this difficult situation.

- Act and think as a listener. Turn off the television, stereo, or computer; face the other person. Devote your total attention to the other person.
- Make sure you understand what the person is saying and feeling. Use perception checking (Chapter 3) and active listening techniques (Chapter 4).
- Express your support or empathy: "I can understand how you feel. I can appreciate that my handling the checkbook could create a feeling of inequality."
- If appropriate, indicate your agreement: "You're right to be disturbed."
- State your thoughts and feelings as objectively as you can; avoid criticism or blame.
- Get ready to listen to the other person's responses to your statement.

Applying Listening Skills

You're a new teacher at an elementary school. The parents of a student who has been doing very poorly and has created all sorts of discipline problems (in your opinion, she's a brat) complain that their daughter hates school and isn't learning anything. They want her transferred to another class with another teacher. What listening skills would you try to practice in your conversation with these parents?

After a conflict is resolved, it is not necessarily over. Consider a few "after the conflict" suggestions.

- Learn from the conflict and from the process you went through in trying to resolve it. For example, can you identify the fight strategies that aggravated the situation? Do you, or does your partner, need a cooling-off period? Can you tell when minor issues are going to escalate into major arguments?
- Attack your negative feelings. Often such feelings arise because unfair fight strategies were used (as we'll see in the next section)—for example, blame or verbal aggressiveness. Resolve to avoid such unfair tactics in the future, but at the same time let go of guilt and blame. Don't view yourself, your partner, or your relationship as a failure simply because you have conflicts.
- Increase the exchange of rewards and cherishing behaviors. These will show your positive feelings and demonstrate that you're over the conflict and want the relationship to survive.

Conflict Management Strategies

Throughout the process of resolving conflict, try to avoid the common but damaging **unproductive conflict strategies** that can destroy a relationship. At the same time, seek to apply strategies that will help to resolve the conflict and even improve the relationship.

Avoidance and Fighting Actively

Message Skills

Active Interpersonal Conflict: Engage in interpersonal conflict actively; be appropriately revealing, and listen to your partner.

Avoidance may involve actual physical flight. You may leave the scene of the conflict (walk out of the apartment or go to another part of the office or shop), fall asleep, or blast the stereo to drown out all conversation. It may also take the form of emotional or intellectual avoidance, in which you may leave the conflict psychologically by not dealing with any of the arguments or problems raised.

Nonnegotiation is a special type of avoidance. Here you refuse to discuss the conflict or to listen to the other person's argument. At times nonnegotiation takes the form of hammering away at your own point of view until the other person gives in—a technique called "steamrolling."

Skills toolbox

5 Ways to Deal with Complaints

Because complaints are often preludes to conflict, they need to be listened to and responded to appropriately. Here are some suggestions for dealing with complaints.

1. Let the person know you're open to complaints, that you view them as helpful, and that you're listening.
2. Understand both the thoughts and the feelings that go with the complaint. Respond both to the substance of the complaint and to the emotional frustration that the person feels.
3. Respect confidentiality if needed. Let the person know that the complaint will be treated in strict confidence or that it will be revealed only if he or she wishes.
4. Ask what the person would like you to do about the complaint. Sometimes all a person wants is to be heard.
5. Thank the person for voicing the complaint and stress your intention to follow up on the complaint.

Applying Interpersonal Skills/Then and Now

Has someone ever voiced a complaint to you that you did not take in the positive spirit advocated here? What happened? If you received the same complaint today, would you handle it any differently?

Instead of avoiding the issues, take an active role in your interpersonal conflicts. Involve yourself on both sides of the communication exchange. Be an active participant as a speaker and as a listener; voice your own feelings and listen carefully to the voicing of your opponent's feelings. This is not to say that periodic moratoriums are not helpful; sometimes they are. But in general, be willing to communicate.

Another part of active fighting involves owning your thoughts and feelings. For example, when you disagree with your partner or find fault with her or his behavior, take responsibility for these feelings. Say, for example, "I disagree with . . ." or "I don't like it when you. . . ." Avoid statements that deny your responsibility; for example, "Everybody thinks you're wrong about . . ." or "Chris thinks you shouldn't. . . ."

"What ever happened to 'Never go to bed angry'?"

Force and Talk

When confronted with conflict, many people prefer not to deal with the issues but rather to force their position on the other person. The **force** may be emotional or physical. In either case, however, the issues are avoided and the "winner" is the combatant who exerts the most force. This is the technique of warring nations, quarreling children, and even some normally sensible and mature adults.

In one study more than 50 percent of both single people and married couples reported that they had experienced physical violence in their relationships. If symbolic violence was included (for example, threatening to hit the other person or throwing something), the percentages were above 60 percent for singles and above 70 percent for marrieds (Marshall & Rose, 1987). In another study, 47 percent of a sample of 410 college students reported some experience with violence in a dating relationship. In most cases the violence was reciprocal—each person in the relationship used violence. In cases in which only one person was violent, the research results are conflicting. For example, some surveys (e.g., Deal & Wampler, 1986; Cate et al., 1982) have found that in cases in which only one partner was violent, the aggressor was significantly more often the female partner. Other research, however, has tended to confirm the widespread view that men are more likely to use force than women (DeTurck, 1987): Men are more apt than women to use violent methods to achieve compliance.

The only real alternative to force is talk. Instead of resorting to force, talk and listen. The qualities of openness, empathy, and positiveness, for example, are suitable starting points (see Chapter 8).

Message Skills

Talk, Not Force: Talk about problems rather than using physical or emotional force.

Skill building exercise

Responding to Complaints

Write a response to one of the following complaints in which you *(a)* let the person know that you're open to complaints and view them as useful information, *(b)* show that you understand both the substance of the complaint and the feelings that go with it; and *(c)* ask the person what he or she would like you to do about the complaint.

1. You're calling these meetings much too often and much too early to suit us. We'd like fewer meetings scheduled for later in the day.
2. There's a good reason why I don't say anything. I don't say anything because you never listen to me anyway.
3. I'm tired of having to take care of everything to do with the kids—attending PTA meetings, driving them to soccer practice, checking their homework, making their lunch.

Complaints can give you valuable information, feedback that will help you improve. If responded to appropriately, complaints can actually improve your interpersonal relationship.

Defensiveness and Supportiveness

Although talk is preferred to force, not all talk is equally productive in conflict resolution. One of the best ways to look at destructive versus productive talk is to look at how the style of your communications can create unproductive **defensiveness** or a productive sense of **supportiveness** (Gibb, 1961). The type of talk that generally proves destructive and sets up defensive reactions in the listener is talk that is evaluative, controlling, strategic, indifferent or neutral, superior, and certain.

Evaluation.   When you evaluate or judge another person or what that person has done, that person is likely to become resentful and defensive and is likely to respond with attempts to defend himself or herself and perhaps at the same time to become equally evaluative and judgmental. In contrast, when you describe what happened or what you want, it creates no such defensiveness and is generally seen as supportive. The distinction between evaluation and description can be seen in the differences between you-messages and I-messages.

Evaluative You-Messages	Descriptive I-Messages
You never reveal your feelings.	I sure would like hearing how you feel about this.
You just don't plan ahead.	I need to know what our schedule for the next few days will be.
You never call me.	I'd enjoy hearing from you more often.

If you put yourself in the role of the listener hearing these statements, you probably can feel the resentment or defensiveness that the evaluative messages (you-messages) would create and the supportiveness from the descriptive messages (I-messages).

Control.   When you try to control the behavior of the other person, when you order the other person to do this or that, or when you make decisions without mutual discussion and agreement, defensiveness is a likely response. Control messages deny the legitimacy of the person's contributions and in fact deny his or her importance. They say, in effect, "You don't count; your contributions are meaningless." When, on the other hand, you focus on the problem at hand—not on controlling the situation or getting your own way—defensiveness is much less likely. This problem orientation invites mutual participation and recognizes the significance of each person's contributions.

Strategy.   When you use **strategy** and try to get around other people or situations through **manipulation**—especially when you conceal your true purposes—others are likely to resent it and to respond defensively. But when you act openly and with **spontaneity,** you're more likely to create an atmosphere that is equal and honest.

Neutrality.   When you demonstrate **neutrality**—in the sense of indifference or a lack of caring for the other person—it's likely to create defensiveness. Neutrality seems to show a lack of empathy or interest in the thoughts and feelings of the other person; it is especially damaging when intimates are in conflict. This kind of talk says, in effect, "You're not important or deserving of attention and caring." When, on the other hand, you demonstrate empathy, defensiveness is unlikely to occur. Although it can be especially difficult in conflict situations, try to show that you can understand what the other person is going through and that you accept these feelings.

Superiority.   When you present yourself as superior to the other person, you're in effect putting the other person in an inferior

? SKILLS VIEWPOINT

What types of messages would most members of your class see as causing them to lose face? What types of messages would they find supportive of their public image?

position, and this is likely to be resented. Such **superiority** messages say in effect that the other person is inadequate or somehow second-class. It's a violation of the implicit **equality** contract that people in a close relationship have—namely, the assumption that each person is equal. The other person may then begin to attack your superiority; the conflict can easily degenerate into a conflict over who's the boss, with personal attack being the mode of interaction.

Certainty. The person who appears to know it all is likely to be resented, so **certainty** often sets up a defensive climate. After all, there is little room for negotiation or mutual problem solving when one person already has the answer. An attitude of **provisionalism**—"Let's explore this issue together and try to find a solution"—is likely to be much more productive than **closed-mindedness.**

Face-Detracting and Face-Enhancing Strategies

Another dimension of conflict strategies is that of face orientation. Face-detracting or face-attacking strategies involve treating the other person as incompetent or untrustworthy, as unable or bad (Donohue & Kolt, 1992). Such attacks can vary from mildly embarrassing the other person to severely damaging his or her ego or reputation. When such attacks become extreme, they may be similar to verbal aggressiveness—a tactic explained below. So be especially careful to avoid "fighting words"—words that are sure to escalate the conflict rather than help to revolve it. Words like *stupid, liar,* and *bitch* as well as words like *always* and *never* (as in "you always . . ." or "you never . . .") invariably create additional problems.

One popular but destructive face-detracting strategy is **beltlining** (Bach & Wyden, 1968). Much like fighters in a ring, each of us has a "beltline" in interpersonal conflict. When you hit above the "belt," the person is able to absorb the emotional blow. When you hit below it, however, you can inflict serious injury. With most interpersonal relationships, especially those of long standing, you know where the beltline is. You know, for example, that to talk about Pat's infertility or Chris's failure to get a permanent job is to hit below the belt. This type of face-detracting strategy causes added problems for all persons involved in a conflict. Keep blows to areas your opponent can absorb and handle.

Face-enhancing techniques involve helping the other person maintain a positive image—the image of a person who is competent and trustworthy, able and good. There is some evidence to show that even when you get what you want, say in a bargaining situation, it's wise to help the other person retain positive face. This makes it less likely that future conflicts will arise (Donohue & Kolt, 1992). Not surprisingly, people are more likely to make an effort to support someone's "face" if they like the person than if they don't (Meyer, 1994).

Generally, collectivist cultures like those of Korea and Japan place greater emphasis on face, especially on maintaining a positive image in public. Face is generally less crucial in individualistic cultures such as that of the United States. And yet there are, of course, many shadings to any such broad generalization. For example, in parts of China, whose highly collectivist culture puts great stress on face-saving, criminals are paraded publicly at rallies and humiliated before being put to death (Tyler, 1996). Perhaps the importance of face-saving in China gives this particular punishment a meaning that it could not have in more individualistic cultures. But be careful not to think of all individualist or collectivist cultures as similar. For example, one study indicated that Germans had more face concerns than Americans, although both are individualist cultures; and Chinese had more face concerns than Japanese, although both are collectivist cultures (Oetzel, Ting-Toomey, Masumoto, Yokochi, Pan, Takai, & Wilcox, 2001).

Confirming the other person's definition of self (Chapter 5), avoiding attack and blame, and using excuses and apologies as appropriate are some generally useful face-enhancing strategies.

Message Skills

Supportive Conflict: Engage in conflict using a supportive approach, so as not to create defensiveness; avoid messages that evaluate or control, that are strategic or inappropriately neutral, or that express superiority or certainty.

Message Skills

Face-Saving Strategies: Use strategies that allow your opponents to save face; avoid beltlining, or hitting opponents with attacks that they will have difficulty absorbing and will resent.

Message Skills

Empathic Conflict: Engage in conflict with empathy rather than blame. Also, express this empathy ("I can understand how you must have felt").

Blame and Empathy

Sometimes conflict is caused by the actions of one of the individuals. Sometimes it's caused by clearly identifiable outside forces. Most of the time, however, it's caused by a wide variety of factors. Any attempt to single out one or two factors for **blame** is sure to fail. Yet a frequently used fight strategy is to blame someone for the situation. Consider, for example, a couple who are fighting over their child's getting into trouble with the police. Instead of dealing with the problem itself, the parents may blame each other for the child's troubles. Such blaming, of course, does nothing to resolve the problem or to help the child.

Perhaps the best alternative to blame is empathy. Do your best to pathically understand your opponent's feelings, and validate those feelings as appropriate. Once again, in expressing affirmation and validation you are not necessarily expressing agreement on the issue in conflict; you're merely respecting your partner's feelings. This simple strategy has also been found to reduce verbal aggressiveness (Infante, Rancer, & Jordan, 1996).

Message Skills

Open Expression in Conflict: Try to express your feelings openly rather than resorting to silence or avoidance.

Silencers and Facilitating Open Expression

Silencers are a wide variety of unproductive fighting techniques that literally silence the other individual. One frequently used silencer is crying. When a person is unable to deal with a conflict or when winning seems unlikely, he or she may cry and thus silence the other person.

Another silencer is to feign extreme emotionalism—to yell and scream and pretend to be losing control. Still another is to develop some "physical" reaction—headaches and shortness of breath are probably the most popular. One of the major problems with such silencers is that we as opponents can never be certain that they are mere tactics; they *may* be real physical reactions that we should pay attention to. Regardless of what we do, the conflict remains unexamined and unresolved.

In addition to avoiding silencers, avoid power tactics (raising your voice or threatening physical force) that suppress or inhibit freedom of expression. Such tactics are designed to put the other person down and to subvert real interpersonal equality. Grant other people permission to express themselves freely and openly, to be themselves.

Message Skills

Present-Focus Conflict: Focus your conflict resolution messages on the present; avoid gunnysacking, or dredging up and unloading old grievances.

Gunnysacking and Present Focus

As a conflict strategy, gunnysacking is generally highly unproductive. The immediate occasion for unloading stored-up grievances may be relatively simple (or so it may seem at first); for example, you come home late one night without calling. Instead of arguing about this, the gunnysacker pours out a mass of unrelated past grievances. As you probably know from experience, however, gunnysacking often begets gunnysacking. Frequently the trigger problem never gets addressed. Instead, resentment and hostility escalate. Therefore, focus on the present, on the here and now, rather than on issues that occurred two months ago. Similarly, focus your conflict on the person with whom you're fighting, not on the person's mother, child, or friends.

Verbal Aggressiveness and Argumentativeness

An especially interesting perspective on conflict emerges from work on verbal aggressiveness and argumentativeness (Infante & Rancer, 1982; Infante & Wigley, 1986; Infante, 1988). Understanding these two concepts will help you understand some of the reasons why things go wrong and some of the ways in which you can use conflict to actually improve your relationships.

In **verbal aggressiveness** one person attempts to win an argument by inflicting psychological pain, by attacking the other person's self-concept. Verbal aggressiveness is a type of disconfirmation (and the opposite of confirmation), in that it seeks to discredit the opponent's view of himself or herself (see Chapter 5). To explore this tendency further, take the self-test on verbal aggressiveness below.

Test Yourself

How Verbally Aggressive Are You?

INSTRUCTIONS: This scale is designed to measure how people try to win arguments through verbal aggression. For each statement, indicate the extent to which you feel it is true for you. Use the following scale: 1 = almost never true, 2 = rarely true, 3 = occasionally true, 4 = often true, and 5 = almost always true.

_____ ① I am extremely careful to avoid attacking individuals' intelligence when I attack their ideas.

_____ ② When individuals are very stubborn, I use insults to soften the stubbornness.

_____ ③ I try very hard to avoid having other people feel bad about themselves when I try to influence them.

_____ ④ When people refuse to do a task I know is important, without good reason, I tell them they are unreasonable.

_____ ⑤ When others do things I regard as stupid, I try to be extremely gentle with them.

_____ ⑥ If individuals I am trying to influence really deserve it, I attack their character.

_____ ⑦ When people behave in ways that are really in very poor taste, I insult them in order to shock them into proper behavior.

_____ ⑧ I try to make people feel good about themselves even when their ideas are stupid.

_____ ⑨ When people simply will not budge on a matter of importance, I lose my temper and say rather strong things to them.

_____ ⑩ When people criticize my shortcomings, I take it in good humor and do not try to get back at them.

_____ ⑪ When individuals insult me, I get a lot of pleasure out of really telling them off.

_____ ⑫ When I dislike individuals greatly, I try not to show it in what I say or how I say it.

_____ ⑬ I like poking fun at people who do things which are very stupid in order to stimulate their intelligence.

_____ ⑭ When I attack a person's ideas, I try not to damage their self-concepts.

_____ ⑮ When I try to influence people, I make a great effort not to offend them.

_____ ⑯ When people do things which are mean or cruel, I attack their character in order to help correct their behavior.

_____ ⑰ I refuse to participate in arguments when they involve personal attacks.

_____ ⑱ When nothing seems to work in trying to influence others, I yell and scream in order to get some movement from them.

_____ ⑲ When I am not able to refute others' positions, I try to make them feel defensive in order to weaken their positions.

_____ ⑳ When an argument shifts to personal attacks, I try very hard to change the subject.

HOW DID YOU DO? To compute your verbal aggressiveness score, follow these steps:

1. Add your scores on items 2, 4, 6, 7, 9, 11, 13, 16, 18, and 19.

2. Add your scores on items 1, 3, 5, 8, 10, 12, 14, 15, 17, and 20.

3. Subtract the sum obtained in step 2 from 60.

4. To compute your verbal aggressiveness score, add the total obtained in step 1 to the result obtained in step 3.

If you scored between 59 and 100, you're high in verbal aggressiveness; if you scored between 39 and 58, you're moderate in verbal aggressiveness; and if you scored between 20 and 38, you're low in verbal aggressiveness. In looking over your responses, make special note of the characteristics identified in the 20 statements that indicate a tendency to act verbally aggressive. Note those inappropriate behaviors that you're especially prone to commit. High agreement (4s or 5s) with statements 2, 4, 6, 7, 9, 11, 13, 16, 18, and 19 and low agreement (1s or 2s) with statements 1, 3, 5, 8, 10, 12, 14, 15, 17, and 20 will help you highlight any significant verbal aggressiveness you might have.

SKILLS VIEWPOINT

Your partner persists in being verbally aggressive when you have an argument: Regardless of what the conflict is about, your partner attacks your self-concept. You're determined to stop this behavior or, if necessary and as a last resort, to end the relationship. What do you say?

> **People generally quarrel because they cannot argue.**
>
> —Gilbert Keith Chesterton

WHAT WILL YOU DO? Because verbal aggressiveness is likely to seriously reduce interpersonal effectiveness, you probably want to reduce your tendencies to respond aggressively. Review the times when you acted verbally aggressive. What effect did such actions have on your subsequent interaction? What effect did they have on your relationship with the other person? What alternative ways of getting your point across might you have used? Might these have proved more effective? Interestingly, perhaps the most general suggestion for reducing verbal aggressiveness is to increase your argumentativeness.

Source: From Dominic Infante, "Verbal Aggressiveness," *Communication Monographs* (1986), Vol. 53, pp. 61–69. Reprinted by permission of Taylor & Francis Ltd, **http://www .tandf.co.uk/journals**.

Contrary to popular usage, **argumentativeness** is a quality to be cultivated rather than avoided. Your argumentativeness is your willingness to argue for a point of view, your tendency to speak your mind on significant issues. It's the mode of dealing with disagreements that is the preferred alternative to verbal aggressiveness. Before reading about ways to increase your argumentativeness, take the self-test on argumentativeness below.

 Test Yourself

How Argumentative Are You?

INSTRUCTIONS: This questionnaire contains statements about ways of dealing with controversial issues. Indicate how often each statement is true for you personally according to the following scale: 1 = almost never true, 2 = rarely true, 3 = occasionally true, 4 = often true, and 5 = almost always true.

_____ ❶ While in an argument, I worry that the person I am arguing with will form a negative impression of me.

_____ ❷ Arguing over controversial issues improves my intelligence.

_____ ❸ I enjoy avoiding arguments.

_____ ❹ I am energetic and enthusiastic when I argue.

_____ ⑤ Once I finish an argument, I promise myself that I will not get into another.

_____ ⑥ Arguing with a person creates more problems for me than it solves.

_____ ⑦ I have a pleasant, good feeling when I win a point in an argument.

_____ ⑧ When I finish arguing with someone, I feel nervous and upset.

_____ ⑨ I enjoy a good argument over a controversial issue.

_____ ⑩ I get an unpleasant feeling when I realize I am about to get into an argument.

_____ ⑪ I enjoy defending my point of view on an issue.

_____ ⑫ I am happy when I keep an argument from happening.

_____ ⑬ I do not like to miss the opportunity to argue a controversial issue.

_____ ⑭ I prefer being with people who rarely disagree with me.

_____ ⑮ I consider an argument an exciting intellectual challenge.

_____ ⑯ I find myself unable to think of effective points during an argument.

_____ ⑰ I feel refreshed and satisfied after an argument on a controversial issue.

_____ ⑱ I have the ability to do well in an argument.

_____ ⑲ I try to avoid getting into arguments.

_____ ⑳ I feel excitement when I expect that a conversation I am in is leading to an argument.

HOW DID YOU DO? To compute your argumentativeness score follow these steps:

1. Add your scores on items 2, 4, 7, 9, 11, 13, 15, 17, 18, and 20.

2. Add 60 to the sum obtained in Step 1.

3. Add your scores on items 1, 3, 5, 6, 8, 10, 12, 14, 16, and 19.

4. To compute your argumentativeness score, subtract the total obtained in step 3 from the total obtained in step 2.

    The following guidelines will help you interpret your score:

    Scores between 73 and 100 indicate high argumentativeness.
    Scores between 56 and 72 indicate moderate argumentativeness.
    Scores between 20 and 55 indicate low argumentativeness.

WHAT WILL YOU DO? Infante and Rancer (1982) note that both high and low argumentatives may experience communication difficulties. The high argumentative, for example, may argue needlessly, too often, and too forcefully. The low argumentative, on the other hand, may avoid taking a stand even when it seems necessary. Persons scoring somewhere in the middle are probably the more interpersonally skilled and adaptable, arguing when it is necessary but avoiding arguments that are needless and repetitive. Does your experience support these observations? What specific actions might you take to improve your argumentativeness?

Source: From Dominic Infante & Andrew Rancer, "A conceptualization and measure of argumentativeness," _Journal of Personality Assessment, 46_ (1982): 72–80. Reprinted by permission of Lawrence Erlbaum Associates, Inc.

> 66 Difficulties are meant to rouse, not discourage. The human spirit is to grow strong by conflict. 99
>
> —William Ellery Channing

The researchers who developed the argumentativeness test note that those who score high in argumentativeness have a strong tendency to state their position on controversial issues and to argue against the positions of others (Infante & Rancer, 1982). A high scorer sees arguing as exciting, intellectually challenging, and as an opportunity to win a kind of contest. The low scorer sees arguing as unpleasant and

Ethical Fighting

The text of this chapter emphasizes the distinction between effective and ineffective conflict strategies. But communication strategies also have an ethical dimension, and it's important to keep strategies' ethical implications in mind. For example:

- Does conflict avoidance have an ethical dimension? For example, is it unethical for one person to refuse to discuss issues of disagreement?
- Is it ever ethical to force someone physically to accept your position? Can you identify a situation in which it would be appropriate for someone to overpower another person to enforce his or her point of view?
- Are face-detracting strategies inherently unethical, or might it be appropriate to use them in certain situations? Can you identify such situations?
- What are the ethical implications of verbal aggressiveness?

What Would You Do?

At your job, which is stressful, you and your colleagues use coke several times a month. You yourself don't use drugs at any other times. At home one night, your partner—who you know hates drugs and people who use them—asks you if you take drugs. Because your use is so limited, but mostly because you know that admitting it will cause a huge conflict in a relationship that's already having difficulties, you wonder what to say. Can you ethically lie?

unsatisfying. Not surprisingly, this person has little confidence in his or her ability to argue effectively. The person who scores low in argumentativeness tries to prevent arguments. This person derives satisfaction not from arguing but from avoiding arguments. The moderately argumentative individual possesses some of the qualities of the high argumentative and some of the qualities of the low argumentative.

At this point you may wish to examine your own behavior and ask yourself how argumentative you are. Here are hints for cultivating constructive argumentativeness; hopefully, most of these approaches are already part of your communication behavior (Infante, 1988). If any are not, consider how you can adopt them. Do you

- *treat disagreements objectively? Avoid assuming that because someone takes issue with your position, they're attacking you as a person.*
- *avoid attacking the other person (rather than the person's arguments), even if this would give you a tactical advantage? Center your arguments on issues, not personalities.*
- *reaffirm the other person's sense of competence? Compliment the other person as appropriate.*
- *avoid interrupting? Allow the other person to state her or his position fully before you respond.*
- *stress equality and emphasize the similarities between you and the other person? Stress your areas of agreement before attacking the disagreements.*
- *express interest in the other person's point of view?*
- *avoid presenting your arguments too emotionally? Avoid using an overly loud voice or interjecting vulgar expressions.*
- *allow the other person to save face? Never humiliate the other person.*

Message Skills

Argumentativeness: Avoid aggressiveness (attacking the other person's self-concept); instead focus logically on the issues, emphasize finding solutions, and work to ensure that what is said will result in positive self-feelings for both individuals.

Summary of Concepts

This chapter examined interpersonal conflict and some of the myths that surround it, the distinction between content and relationship conflict, and conflict's positive and negative effects; it explained a model of conflict resolution and a described variety of unproductive conflict strategies and their more productive counterparts.

1. Interpersonal conflict involves disagreement between or among connected individuals. The positions in interpersonal conflicts are to some degree interrelated and incompatible.
2. There are five major principles of interpersonal conflict: Conflict is inevitable, conflict can be negative or positive, conflict is influenced by culture and gender, conflict styles have consequences, and conflict can focus on content or relationship issues.
3. Before the conflict: Try to fight in private, be sure you're each ready to fight, know what you're fighting about, and avoid fighting about problems that cannot be solved.
4. A five-stage model is often helpful in resolving conflict: Define the conflict, examine possible solutions, test a solution, evaluate the solution, and accept or reject the solution.
5. After the conflict: Learn from the conflict, challenge your negative feelings, and increase the exchange of rewards.
6. Unproductive and productive conflict strategies include avoidance and fighting actively, force and talk, face-detracting and face-enhancing strategies, blame and empathy, silencers and facilitating open expression, gunnysacking and present focus, fighting below and above the belt, and verbal aggressiveness and argumentativeness.
7. To cultivate argumentativeness, treat disagreements objectively and avoid attacking the other person; reaffirm the other's sense of competence; avoid interrupting; stress equality and similarities; express interest in the other's position; avoid presenting your arguments too emotionally; and allow the other to save face.

Vocabulary Quiz: The Language of Conflict

Match the terms dealing with interpersonal conflict with their definitions. Record the number of the definition next to the appropriate term.

_____ six hats technique

_____ accommodating

_____ argumentativeness

_____ gunnysacking

_____ beltline

_____ verbal aggressiveness

_____ compromising

_____ complaint

_____ interpersonal conflict

_____ conflict resolution model

1. A disagreement between connected individuals.
2. An unproductive conflict strategy of storing up grievances and holding these in readiness to dump on the person with whom one is in conflict.
3. A person's level of tolerance for absorbing personal attack.
4. A tendency or willingness to argue for a point of view.
5. A conflict strategy designed mainly to maintain peace and harmony in the relationship.
6. An expressed dissatisfaction that's a valuable source of feedback.
7. A tendency to try to win arguments at the expense of others' feelings.
8. A set of procedures for dealing with conflict consisting of five stages: define the conflict, examine possible solutions, test a solution, evaluate the solution, and accept or reject the solution.
9. Varied ways of looking at a particular issue to give you different perspectives.
10. A style of conflict management concerned with both the self and the other.

Four for Discussion

1. One theory accounting for the male tendency to withdraw from interpersonal conflict is that men experience flooding (a sense of being out of control, of extreme anger or rage) more easily and with less provocation than women (Gottman, 1993, 1994; Goleman, 1995a; Canary, Cupach, & Messman, 1995). Physiologically, flooding raises the heart rate to 10 beats per minute more than normal, and this response lasts for some time, even after the conflict is "settled." The male tendency to withdraw from argument may, therefore, be due to a desire to reduce the effects of flooding. What do you think of this idea?

2. How would you describe the issues that men and women argue about? Are there certain types of issues that men are more likely to argue about than women, and vice versa? In one sentence, how would you describe the differences in the issues argued about by men and women?

3. How would you describe the conflicts in your family in terms of the productive and unproductive conflict strategies discussed in this chapter? How might your family conflicts be resolved more effectively?

4. One of the most puzzling findings on violence is that many victims interpret it as a sign of love. For some reason, they see beatings or verbal abuse as a sign that their partner is fully in love with them. Also, many victims blame themselves for the violence instead of blaming their partners (Gelles & Cornell, 1985). Why do you think this is so? What part does force or violence play in your own interpersonal relationship conflicts?

Web Explorations

 Explore our text website at **www.ablongman.com/devito** to find:

Exercises and Self-Tests

Two useful exercises on interpersonal conflict are available: (1) Analyzing a Conflict Episode and (2) How Do You Fight? Like a Man? Like a Woman?

Writing Resources and Assignments

Suggestions are available for writing papers of personal experience (for example, your personal conflict resolution strategies), concept or principle explanation (for example, verbal aggressiveness), review (for example, online conflicts), or research (for example, gender differences in conflict strategies) on interpersonal conflict.

 Explore our research resources at **www.researchnavigator.com** and

Read an article.

Read a popular or scholarly article on conflict, its nature, the stages of conflict resolution, or conflict strategies. On the basis of this article, what can you add to the discussion presented here?

Investigate key terms.

Investigate one of the key terms discussed in this chapter (for example, conflict, interpersonal conflict, aggressiveness, argumentativeness, conflict styles, competition and collaboration, and conflict avoidance). What additional insights can you provide?

Find answers.

Try finding answers to one of the following questions, or design a research study to answer it.

1. Are men or women more likely to use avoidance (or blame, force, manipulation, ridicule, silencers, beltlining, gunnysacking, or personal rejection) as a romantic conflict strategy?
2. What are some of the advantages research has found (in addition to those discussed here) for argumentativeness as opposed to verbal aggressiveness?
3. How can mediation help in domestic conflicts?

Power and Interpersonal Communication

12

Principles of Power

....

Intrapersonal Power: Self-Esteem

....

Interpersonal Power: Assertiveness

....

> Pedro is a counselor at a local boys' club where his major problem is discipline. None of the younger boys respect him, and consequently none of them will listen to his admonitions. The administration is considering letting him go. He just doesn't seem able to exert the necessary control over the boys.

> Jackie has been having difficulties in all sorts of interpersonal situations. For example, although a competent worker, she has little confidence in her ability to do the work. She especially shies away from new tasks that may prove challenging, and as a result she has been overlooked repeatedly when promotions come around. Interpersonally, she has few friends and is seldom asked out. Although attractive and bright, she acts as if she is grossly unattractive and has little to offer another person.

> Clara is employed at the local automobile showroom, where she sells new Fords. Although a competent salesperson, Clara often finds herself used by her coworkers. For example, when the salespeople want coffee, they often ask Clara to get it. Clara doesn't really want to be the showroom gofer, but she doesn't know how to say no. Clara runs into similar problems at home, where her brothers and sisters and even her parents take advantage of her good nature.

All of these interpersonal difficulties revolve around interpersonal **power.** Pedro's problem centers on his lack of ability to communicate his authority, his power. He needs to learn the principles for communicating power to others. Jackie lacks self-esteem and communicates this both at work and in her personal life. Jackie has to raise her self-esteem and develop a kind of self-power. Clara is a classic example of the nonassertive person. She wants to stand up for her rights but doesn't know how. Clara needs training in assertiveness.

This chapter examines the principles of power and focuses especially on how you can increase your own intrapersonal and interpersonal power. More effective management of power will enable you to better control and influence both yourself and others.

Principles of Power

Power permeates all interpersonal relationships. It influences what you do, when, and with whom. It influences the employment you seek and the employment you get. It influences the friends you choose and do not choose and those who choose or do not choose you. It influences your romantic and family relationships—their success or failure, the level of satisfaction or dissatisfaction they provide. Interpersonal power is what enables the individual with power to control the behaviors of others.

Power in interpersonal relationships is governed by a few important principles. These principles spell out the basic characteristics of power. They help explain how power works interpersonally and how you may more effectively deal with power.

Power Varies from Person to Person

Many of the world's societies are moving in the direction of greater equality, endeavoring to offer people equality under the law and in their entitlement to education, legal protection, and freedom of speech. But even in the most egalitarian societies, people are not equal when it comes to just about everything else. Some are born into wealth, others into poverty. Some are born physically strong, good-looking, and healthy. Others are born weak, unattractive, and with a variety of inherited illnesses.

> " Communication is power. Those who have mastered its effective use can change their own experience of the world, and the world's experience of them. "
>
> —Anthony Robbins

As for power: Some people are born with assets that empower them—but some of those who are not still manage to achieve power. And everyone can increase his or her interpersonal power. You can, for example, learn the principles of effective communication and increase your power to persuade. Power can also be decreased, however. Perhaps the most frequent way in which power is decreased is through ineffective attempts to control others' behavior. For example, if you threaten someone with punishment and then fail to carry out the threat, you lose power.

Confidence communicates power. One of the clearest ways you can communicate power is by demonstrating confidence through your verbal and nonverbal behaviors. The confident communicator is relaxed (rather than rigid), flexible in voice and body (rather than locked into one or two ranges of voice or body movement), and controlled (rather than shaky or awkward). A relaxed posture, researchers find, communicates a sense of control, status, and power. Tenseness, rigidity, and apparent discomfort, on the other hand, signal a lack of self-control (Spitzberg & Hecht, 1984). This, in turn, signals a general inability to control other people or the environment.

Here are a few additional suggestions for communicating confidence:

- Take the initiative in introducing yourself to others and in introducing topics of conversation; try not to wait for others. When you react, rather than act, you're more likely to communicate a lack of confidence and control over the situation.

- Use open-ended questions to involve the other person in the interaction (as opposed to questions that merely ask for a yes or no answer). Follow up these questions with appropriate comments or additional questions.

- Use you-statements. These are statements that directly address the other person—not the accusatory kind, but messages that signal a direct and personalized focus on the other person, such as "Do you agree?" or "How do you feel about that?" This one behavior, incidentally, has been shown to increase men's attractiveness to women.

- Avoid various forms of powerless language, such as statements that express a lack of conviction or that are self-critical.

Power Is a Part of All Interpersonal Messages

Chapter 1 introduced the key principle that you cannot *not* communicate. By the same token, you cannot communicate without making some implicit comment on your power or lack of it. When in an interactional situation, therefore, recognize that on the basis of your verbal and nonverbal messages, people will assess your power—along with your competence, trustworthiness, honesty, openness, and so on.

No interpersonal relationship exists without a power dimension. Look at your own relationships and those of your friends and relatives. In each relationship, who has the greater power? In interpersonal relationships among most Americans, the more powerful person is often the one who is more attractive or the one who has more money. In other cultures the factors that contribute to power may be different and might include a person's family background, age, knowledge, or wisdom.

The ways in which people communicate powerfulness and powerlessness through speech have received lots of research attention (Molloy, 1981; Kleinke, 1986; Johnson, 1987; Dillard & Marshall, 2003). Generally, research finds that men use more powerful language forms than do women (Lakoff, 1975; Timmerman, 2002). Listed below are the major characteristics of powerless speech. As you consider this list, think of your own speech. Do you avoid the following speech behaviors?

- Hesitations *make the speaker sound unprepared and uncertain. Example: "I* er *want to say that* ah *this one is* er *the best,* you know?"

- Too many intensifiers *make your speech monotonous and don't allow you to stress what you do want to emphasize. Example: "Really, this was the greatest; it was truly phenomenal."*

6 Ways to Exert Power

Work, friendship, and romantic relationships differ in the types of power that the people use and to which they respond. Differences in amounts and types of power influence who makes important decisions, who will prevail in an argument, and who will control finances. It's useful to distinguish among six types of power: legitimate, referent, reward, coercive, expert, and information or persuasion power (French & Raven, 1968; Raven, Centers, & Rodrigues, 1975).

1. You hold *legitimate power* when others believe that by virtue of your position, you have a right to influence or control their behaviors. Your legitimate power derives from the role you occupy; for example, employers, judges, managers, and police officers have legitimate power by virtue of their roles. *Relate your persuasive arguments and appeals to your own role and credibility.*
2. You have *referent power* when others wish to be like you. Referent power holders are often attractive, have considerable prestige, and are well liked and well respected. For example, you might have referent power over a younger brother who wanted to be like you. *Demonstrate qualities that are admired by those you wish to influence.*
3. You have *reward power* when you control the rewards that others want. Rewards may be material (for example, money, promotion, jewelry) or social (for example, love, friendship, respect). *Make rewards contingent on compliance, and follow through and reward those who comply with your requests.*
4. You have *coercive power* when you have the ability to administer punishments to or remove rewards from others if they do not do as you wish. Usually, people who have reward power also have coercive power. *Make clear the negative consequences that are likely to follow noncompliance. But be careful; coercive power may reduce your other power bases and have a negative impact, as when wielded by supervisors in business settings* (Richmond et al., 1984; Kearney et al., 1984, 1985).
5. You have *expert power* when others see you as possessing important expertise or knowledge. For example, judges have expert power in legal matters and doctors have expert power in medical matters. *Cultivate your own expertise, and connect your persuasive appeals to this expertise.*
6. You have *information or persuasion power* when others see you as having the ability to communicate logically and persuasively. *Increase your communication competence; this book's major function, of course, is to explain ways for you to accomplish this.*

Applying Interpersonal Skills/Then and Now

Can you recall a situation in which you tried to exert power over another person but failed? To what do you attribute the failure? If this same situation occurred today, what might you do differently, to increase your chances for wielding power more effectively?

Message Skills

Communicating Power: Avoid powerless message forms such as hesitations, excessive intensifiers, disqualifiers, tag questions, one-word answers, self-critical statements, overly polite statements, and vulgar and slang expressions.

- Disqualifiers *signal a lack of competence and a feeling of uncertainty. Examples: "I didn't read the entire article, but. . . ." "I didn't actually see the accident, but. . . ."*
- Tag questions *ask for another's agreement and therefore may signal your need for agreement—and your own uncertainty. Examples: "That was a great movie, wasn't it?" "She's brilliant, don't you think?"*
- Self-critical statements *signal a lack of confidence and may make public your own inadequacies. Examples: "I'm not very good at this." "This is my first public speech."*
- Slang and vulgar language *signal low social class and hence little power. Examples: "@*+#?$!!" "No problem!"*

It's interesting to note that power also bears a close relationship to interpersonal violence. For example, in one study husbands who had less power in their relationship were more likely to be physically abusive toward their wives than husbands who had greater power (Babcock, Waltz, Jacobson, & Gottman, 1993). Further, in violent

SKILLS VIEWPOINT

Research finds that men are generally perceived to have higher levels of expert and legitimate power than women and that women are generally perceived to have higher levels of referent power than men. When it comes to exerting influence, these findings suggest, women will have greater difficulty influencing others by communicating competence and authority than will men; men, on the other hand, will have greater difficulty influencing others using their referent power (Carli, 1999). What would you suggest that men do to increase their referent power and that women do to increase their expert and legitimate power?

marriages the spouses often play out their interpersonal power struggles in unproductive and dysfunctional ways. For example, violent couples engage in greater blame and greater criticism of each other than do nonviolent couples (Rushe, 1996).

Just as you communicate your power (or lack of power) verbally, you also communicate it nonverbally—for example, through the things you wear and own. Trendy is powerless; cheap is powerless. Conservative is powerful; expensive is powerful. It's actually all very logical. Truly powerful people have no time for new trends that come and go every six months. Further, they don't wear or have anything cheap, because they have money to buy the real thing.

Using Compliance-Gaining Strategies

Compliance-gaining strategies are tactics that influence others to do what you want them to do (Marwell & Schmitt, 1967; Miller & Parks, 1982). One such strategy is *pregiving,* in which you reward the person you want to influence and then request compliance: "I'm glad you enjoyed that dinner. This really is the best restaurant in the city. How about going back to my place for a nightcap and whatever?" Another strategy is *promises:* offering to reward the other person if he or she does as you request. Still another is arguing on the basis of *positive or negative self-feelings:* saying that the person will feel better if he or she complies with your request or will feel horrible if he or she refuses to comply. And another strategy is *positive or negative altercasting,* in which you cast the other person in the role of the "good" or "bad" person and argue that a person with good qualities would comply with your request and a person with negative qualities would fail to comply: "Any intelligent person would grant their partner a divorce when the relationship has died."

What Would You Do?

Because you've fallen behind schedule on an important project, you need your colleague's help to complete the project on time. Would it be ethical to give your colleague an expensive watch she's been wanting, a few days before you ask for her help? You figure that if she accepts the watch, she'll find it difficult to refuse to help you. What would you do in this situation?

Similarly, nonverbal behavior often betrays a lack of power, as when someone fidgets and engages in lots of self-touching movements (adaptors) at a meeting, indicating discomfort. A powerful person may be bored but will not appear uncomfortable or ill at ease.

Territory also reflects a person's power. It's difficult for the junior executive who operates out of a cubbyhole in the basement of some huge office complex to appear powerful with an old metal desk and beat-up filing cabinet. Often, however, you're more in control of your **home territory** than you may realize. Clutter, metal ashtrays, and "cute" statues with signs like "Place your butt here" signify a lack of power and can easily be eliminated to communicate a more powerful image.

But perhaps the most important part of communicating power is to evidence your knowledge, your preparation, your organization in relation to whatever you're dealing with. If you can exhibit control over your own responsibilities, people generally conclude that you can and do also exhibit control over other aspects of life.

Power Follows the Principle of Less Interest

In any interpersonal relationship, the person who holds the power is the one less interested in and less dependent on the rewards and punishments controlled by the other person. If, for example, you can walk away from whatever rewards your partner has to offer or can handle whatever punishments your partner can mete out, then you control the relationship. If, on the other hand, you need the rewards or are unable or unwilling to suffer the punishments, then your partner has the power in the relationship.

In sum, the more you need a relationship, the less power you have in it. The less you need a relationship, the greater your power. In a love relationship, for example, the person who maintains greater power is the one who would find it easier to break up the relationship. The person who would be unwilling (or unable) to break up has

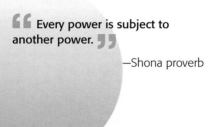

" Every power is subject to another power. "
—Shona proverb

Skill building exercise

Empowering Others

Here are three situations in which you might wish to empower the individuals involved. For each situation, write a response that would empower the other person, using such strategies as *(a)* raising the other person's self-esteem; *(b)* listening actively and supportively; *(c)* being open, positive, and empathic; and *(d)* avoiding verbal aggressiveness or any unfair conflict strategies.

1. Your partner is having lots of difficulties—recently he lost his job, received poor grades in a night class, and has been gaining a lot more weight than he wants to. At the same time, you're doing extremely well—you just got promoted, got admitted to a great MBA program, and are looking your best. You want to give your partner back his confidence. What do you say?
2. You're supervising four college interns, three men and one woman, who are redesigning your company's website. The men are extremely supportive of one another and regularly contribute ideas. Although equally competent, the woman doesn't contribute; she seems to lack confidence. But the objective of this redesign is to increase the number of female visitors, so you really need her input and want to empower her. What do you say?
3. You're a third-grade teacher. Most of your students are from the same ethnic–religious group; three, however, are from a very different group. The problem is that these students don't participate successfully; for example, they stumble when they have to read in front of the class (although they read well in private), and they make lots of arithmetic mistakes at the chalkboard. You want to empower these students to help them realize their potential. What do you say?

Empowering others enables you to help others but also to benefit yourself. Empowered partners and colleagues, for example, are likely to be happier, a lot less prone to violence or verbal abuse, and more satisfied with the relationship than those lacking in power.

little power, precisely because he or she is dependent on the relationship and on the rewards provided by the other person.

Power Has a Cultural Dimension

In some cultures power is concentrated in the hands of a few, and there is a great difference between the power held by these people and the power of the ordinary citizen. These are called high-power-distance cultures; examples are Mexico, Brazil, India, and the Philippines (Hofstede, 1997). In low-power-distance cultures power is more evenly distributed throughout the citizenry; examples include Denmark, New Zealand, Sweden, and to a lesser extent the United States.

In India (a high-power-distance culture), friendships and romantic relationships are expected to take place within your cultural class; in Sweden (a low-power-distance culture), a person is expected to select friends and romantic partners on the basis of individual factors such as personality, appearance, and the like—not on the basis of class.

In low-power-distance cultures you're expected to confront a friend, partner, or supervisor assertively; there is in these cultures a general feeling of equality that is consistent with an up-front approach (Borden, 1991). In high-power-distance cultures this kind of direct confrontation and assertiveness may be viewed negatively, especially when you are communicating with a superior.

? SKILLS VIEWPOINT

A manager from a high-power-distance culture has been put in charge of a group of workers who are all from low-power-distance cultures. What advice would you give this manager? What advice would you give if the manager came from a low-power-distance culture and the workers from high-power-distance cultures?

In high-power-distance cultures you're taught to have great respect for authority, and generally people in these cultures see authority as desirable and beneficial; challenges to authority are generally not welcomed (Westwood, Tang, & Kirkbride, 1992; also see Bochner & Hesketh, 1994). Low-power-distance cultures often share a certain distrust for authority, regarding it as a kind of necessary evil that should be limited as much as possible. This difference in attitudes toward authority can be seen right in the classroom. In high-power-distance cultures there is a great power distance between students and teachers; students are expected to be modest, polite, and totally respectful. In low-power-distance cultures students are expected to demonstrate their knowledge and command of the subject matter, participate in discussions with the teacher, and even challenge the teacher—something many high-power-distance culture members wouldn't even think of doing. The same differences can be seen in patient–doctor communication. Patients from high-power-distance cultures are less likely to challenge their doctor or to admit that they don't understand the medical terminology than are patients in low-power-distance cultures.

High-power-distance cultures rely more on symbols of power. For example, titles (Doctor, Professor, Chef, Inspector) are important in high-power-distance cultures. Failure to include these in forms of address is a serious breach of etiquette. Low-power-distance cultures rely less on symbols of power, and less of a problem is created if you fail to use a respectful title (Victor, 1992). But even in low-power-distance cultures you may create problems if, for example, you call a medical doctor, police captain, military officer, or professor Ms. or Mr.

Also, in the United States, two people quickly move from title plus last name (Mr. Smith) to first name (Joe). In low-power-distance cultures in general, it is not a serious problem if you're too informal or if you presume to exchange first names before sufficient interaction has taken place. Again, however, in even the lowest-power-distance culture, you may still create problems if you call your English professor Pat. And in high-power-distance cultures too great an informality—especially between those differing in power—would violate important cultural rules.

In many Asian, African, and Arab cultures (as well as in many European cultures such as Italian and Greek), there is a great power distance between men and women. Men have the greater power, and women are expected to recognize this and abide by its implications. Men, for example, make the important decisions and have the final word in any difference of opinion (Hatfield & Rapson, 1996).

In the United States the male–female power structure is undergoing considerable changes. In many families men still have the greater power. Partly because they earn more money, they also make the more important decisions. As economic equality becomes more a reality than an ideal, this power difference also may change. In Arab cultures, in contrast, the man makes the more important decisions not because he earns more money but because he is the man, and men are simply given greater power.

Power Is Frequently Used Unfairly

Although it would be nice if power were always wielded for the good of all, it's often used selfishly and unfairly. You see unethical uses of power in interpersonal relationships all the time. Here are two rather extensive examples: sexual harassment and the use of power plays.

Sexual Harassment   One type of unfair use of power is **sexual harassment,** a form of behavior that violates Title VII of the Civil Rights Act of 1964 as amended by the Civil Rights Act of 1991 (http://www.eeoc.gov/policy/cra91.html, last modified January 15, 1997; accessed May 4, 2002). There are two general categories of sexual harassment: quid pro quo (a term borrowed from the Latin that literally means "something for something") and the creation of a hostile environment.

In quid pro quo harassment, employment opportunities (as in hiring and promotion) are made dependent on the granting of sexual favors. Conversely, quid pro quo harassment also includes situations in which reprisals and various negative consequences would result from the failure to grant such sexual favors. Put more generally, quid pro quo harassment occurs when employment consequences (positive or negative) hinge on a person's response to sexual advancements.

Hostile environment harassment is broader and includes all sexual behaviors (verbal and nonverbal) that make a worker uncomfortable. Putting sexually explicit pictures on the bulletin board, using sexually explicit screen savers, telling sexual jokes and stories, and using sexual and demeaning language or gestures all constitute hostile environment harassment.

The Equal Employment Opportunity Commission (EEOC) definition of sexual harassment sums up these two basic types. In the definition below items 1 and 2 refer to quid pro quo harassment and item 3 to hostile environment harassment:

> Unwelcome sexual advances, requests for sexual favors and other verbal or physical conduct of a sexual nature constitute sexual harassment when (1) submission to such conduct is made either explicitly or implicitly a term or condition of an individual's employment, (2) submission to or rejection of such conduct by an individual is used as the basis for employment decisions affecting such individual, or (3) such conduct has the purpose or effect of unreasonably interfering with an individual's work performance or creating an intimidating, hostile, or offensive working environment. (Friedman, Boumil, & Taylor, 1992)

If you are trying to determine whether behavior constitutes sexual harassment, the following questions will help you assess your own situation objectively rather than emotionally (VanHyning, 1993):

1. Is it real? Does this behavior have the meaning it seems to have?
2. Is it job related? Does this behavior have something to do with or will it influence the way you do your job?

3. Did you reject this behavior? Did you make your rejection of unwanted messages clear to the other person?

4. Have these unwanted messages persisted? Is there a pattern, a consistency to these messages?

If you answer yes to all four questions, then the behavior is likely to constitute sexual harassment (VanHyning, 1993).

Keep in mind three additional facts that are often misunderstood. First, people of either gender may sexually harass either gender. Although most cases brought to public attention are committed by men against women, women may also harass men. Further, harassment may be committed by men against men and by women against women. Second, anyone in an organization can be guilty of sexual harassment. Although most cases of harassment involve persons in authority who harass subordinates, this is not a necessary condition. Coworkers, vendors, and even customers may be charged with sexual harassment. Third, sexual harassment is not limited to business organizations but can and does occur in schools, in hospitals, and in social, religious, and political organizations.

What can you do about sexual harassment? If you encounter sexual harassment and wish to do something about it, consider these suggestions recommended by workers in the field (Petrocelli & Repa, 1992; Bravo & Cassedy, 1992; Rubenstein, 1993):

1. Talk to the harasser. Tell this person, assertively, that you do not welcome the behavior and that you find it offensive. Simply informing Fred that his sexual jokes aren't appreciated and are seen as offensive may be sufficient to make him stop.

2. Collect evidence—perhaps corroboration from others who have experienced similar harassment at the hands of the same individual, and/or perhaps a log of the offensive behaviors.

3. Utilize appropriate channels within the organization. Most organizations have established channels to deal with such grievances. In most cases this step will eliminate any further harassment.

4. If necessary, file a complaint with an organization or governmental agency or perhaps take legal action.

Message Skills

Sexual Harassment Messages: Avoid behaviors that are sexual in nature, that might be considered unreasonable, that are severe or pervasive, and that are unwelcome and offensive.

Message Skills

Sexual Harassment Management: Talk to the harasser; if this doesn't stop the behavior, then consider collecting evidence, using appropriate channels within the organization, and filing a complaint.

? SKILLS VIEWPOINT

You've just been assigned to give a lecture to new employees on sexual harassment. During the brief time allotted (about 30 minutes), you want to teach the employees how to avoid even the appearance of sexual harassment. What do you tell them?

"The board of directors has given me new powers."

Power Plays   **Power plays** are patterns of communication (not isolated instances) that take unfair advantage of another person (Steiner, 1981). Put in terms of the concept of choice (see the Ethical Messages box in Chapter 4), power plays aim to rob us of our right to make our own choices, free of harassment or intimidation.

For example, in the power play *nobody upstairs,* the individual refuses to acknowledge your request, regardless of how or how many times you make it. One common form is the refusal to take no for an answer. Sometimes the *nobody upstairs* play takes the form of fake ignorance of common socially accepted (but unspoken) rules, such as the rules that require us to knock before entering someone's room or to refrain from opening another person's mail or wallet: "I didn't know you didn't want me to look in your wallet!" "Do you want me to knock the next time I come into your room?"

Another power play is *you owe me.* Here others do something for you and then demand something in return. They remind you of what they did for you and use your "debt" to get you to do what they want.

In *yougottobekidding* one person attacks the other by saying "You've got to be kidding" or some similar phrase: "You can't be serious." "You can't mean that." "You didn't say what I thought you said, did you?" The intention here is to express utter disbelief in the other's statement so as to make the statement—and the person—seem inadequate or stupid.

These power plays are just examples. There are, of course, many others that you have no doubt experienced on occasion. What do you do when you recognize such a power play? One common response is to ignore the power play and allow the other person to take control. Another response is to treat the power play as an isolated instance (rather than as a pattern of behavior) and object to it. For example, you might say quite simply, "Please don't come into my room without knocking first" or "Please don't look in my wallet without permission."

Listening to Empower

Much as you can empower others by complimenting or constructively criticizing them, you can also empower through your style of listening. When you wish to empower through listening, consider these suggestions:

1. Demonstrate your willingness and eagerness to listen. Acknowledge your understanding by appropriately nodding or using such minimal responses as "I see" or "I understand," ask questions if something isn't clear, maintain eye contact, and lean forward as appropriate.
2. Avoid interrupting to change the topic or to shift the focus to something else. When you interrupt, you say, in effect, that what the other person is saying is of less importance than what you're saying—a clear way to disempower and to imply that "you don't really count."
3. React supportively. Let the person know that you're listening and that you appreciate what he or she is saying. Couple any disagreements with positive comments such as "I really appreciate your bringing this to my attention, but we've tried what you're suggesting, and it didn't work. Is there another approach we could think about?"

Applying Listening Skills

John has been feeling depressed; he lost his job and his grades have been bad. John tells his friend Sam about what's been bothering him and why things have gotten so out of hand. What suggestions might you offer Sam to help him listen to empower John?

Managing Power Plays

Here are some examples of power plays. For each of the following situations, write an appropriate three-part management strategy as identified in the text: (1) State your feelings (remember to use I-messages); (2) describe the other person's behavior that you object to; and (3) state a cooperative response.

1. Fred continually ignores your objections to what you consider culturally insensitive humor. It's like he doesn't hear you.
2. One of your sisters often responds to your ideas with comments like "You've got to be kidding," "You can't mean that," and "You can't possibly be serious." When you say that you're going to date Harry, she says, "You can't be serious!" When you say that you're going to apply for a promotion, she says, "Promotion! You've got to be kidding!"
3. Your friend has helped you get a job in his company. Now, whenever he wants you to do something, he reminds you that he got you the job. Whenever you object that you have your own work to do, he reminds you that you wouldn't have any work to do if it wasn't for him.

Power plays are unfair but not necessarily motivated by malicious purposes. Cooperative responses can help stop the unfair power play without damaging your relationship.

A third response is a cooperative one (Steiner, 1981). In this response, you do the following:

- *Express your feelings.* Tell the person that you're angry, annoyed, or disturbed by his or her behavior.
- *Describe the behavior to which you object.* Tell the person—in language that describes rather than evaluates—the specific behavior you object to; for example, reading your mail, coming into your room without knocking, persisting in trying to hug you.
- *State a cooperative response you both can live with comfortably.* Tell the person—in a cooperative tone—what you want; for example, "I want you to knock before coming into my room." "I want you to stop reading my mail." "I want you to stop trying to hug me when I tell you to stop."

A cooperative response to *nobody upstairs* might go something like this: "I'm angry *[statement of feelings]* that you persist in opening my mail. You have opened my mail four times this past week alone *[description of the behavior to which you object]*. I want you to allow me to open my own mail. If there is anything in it that concerns you, I will let you know immediately *[statement of cooperative response]*."

Message Skills

Power Plays: Respond to power plays with cooperative strategies: Express your feelings, describe the behavior to which you object, and state a cooperative response.

Intrapersonal Power: Self-Esteem

How much do you like yourself? How valuable a person do you think you are? How competent do you think you are? The answers to these questions will reflect your **self-esteem,** the value that you place on yourself.

Success breeds success. When you feel good about yourself—about who you are and what you're capable of doing—you will perform better. When you think like a success, you're more likely to act like a success. When you think you're a failure, you're more likely to act like a failure. Increasing self-esteem will, therefore, help you to function more effectively in school, in interpersonal relationships, and in careers. Here are a few suggestions for increasing self-esteem.

> " Low self-esteem is like driving through life with your hand-brake on. "
>
> —Maxwell Maltz

Rewriting Unrealistic Beliefs

Here are five unrealistic beliefs that can get you into trouble and can lower your self-esteem (Butler, 1981). For each belief, create a rewritten version that is more realistic and productive.

1. The belief that you must *be perfect* impels you to try to perform at unrealistically high levels in everything. This belief suggests that anything short of perfection is unacceptable and that you're to blame for anything less than perfection.
2. The belief that you must *hurry up* compels you to do things quickly, to do more than can be reasonably expected in any given amount of time.
3. The belief that you must *be strong* tells you that weakness and vulnerable emotions like sadness, compassion, or loneliness are wrong.
4. The belief that you must *please others* leads you to seek approval from others. Pleasing yourself is secondary; in fact self-pleasure comes from pleasing others.
5. The belief that you must always *try harder* leads you to take on tasks that would be impossible for any normal person to handle; yet you take them on.

These beliefs are unrealistic and unproductive because they set goals and expectations that you cannot fulfill—a situation not very helpful to building self-esteem.

Attack Self-Destructive Beliefs

Actively challenge those beliefs you have about yourself that you find are unproductive or that make it more difficult for you to achieve your goals. Representative of such unproductive beliefs are the belief that you have to succeed in everything you do and the belief that you have to be loved by everyone. Replace these self-destructive beliefs with more productive ones, such as "I succeed in many things; I don't have to succeed in everything" and "It would be nice to be loved by everyone, but it isn't necessary to my well-being or my happines—and anyway, some pretty important people do love me."

Seek Out Nourishing People

Psychologist Carl Rogers (1970) drew a distinction between noxious and nourshing people. Noxious people criticize and find fault with just about everything. Nourishing people, on the other hand, are positive and optimistic. Most important, they reward us, they stroke us, they make us feel good about ourselves. To enhance your self-esteem, seek out these people. At the same time, avoid noxious others, those who make you feel negatively about yourself.

Secure Affirmation

It's frequently recommended that you remind yourself of your successes—that you focus on your good deeds; on your positive qualities, strengths, and virtues; and on your productive and meaningful relationships with friends, loved ones, and relatives (Aronson, Cohen, & Nail, 1998; Aronson, Wilson, & Akert, 1999).

The idea behind this advice is that the way you talk to yourself will influence what you think of yourself. If you affirm yourself—if you tell yourself that you're a success, that others like you, that you will succeed on the next test, and that you will be welcomed when asking for a date—you will soon come to feel more positive about yourself. Self-affirmations, such as the following, are often recommended:

- I'm a worthy person.
- I'm responsible and can be depended upon.
- I'm capable of loving and being loved.

> Most powerful is he who has himself in his own power.
>
> —Seneca

- I deserve to have good things happen to me.
- I can forgive myself for mistakes and misjudgments.

However, not all researchers agree with this advice. Some argue that such affirmations—although extremely popular in self-help books—may not be very helpful. These critics contend that if you have low self-esteem, you're not going to believe your self-affirmations, because you don't have a high opinion of yourself to begin with (Paul, 2001). They propose that the alternative to self-affirmation is to secure affirmation from others. You'd do this by, for example, becoming more interpersonally competent and inter-acting with more positive people. In this way you'd get more posi-tive feedback from others—which, these researchers argue, is more helpful than self-talk in raising self-esteem.

Work on Projects That Will Result in Success

Some people want to fail, or so it seems. Often, they select projects that will result in failure simply because they are impossible to complete. Avoid this trap and try consciously to select projects that will result in success. Each success will help build self-esteem. Each success will make the next success a little easier.

When a project does fail, recognize that this does not mean that you're a failure. Everyone fails somewhere along the line. Failure is something that happens. It's not necessarily something you have created, and it's not something inside you. Further, your failing once does not mean that you will fail the next time. So put failure in per-spective. Do not make it an excuse for not trying again.

Interpersonal Power: Assertiveness

If you disagree with other people in a group, do you speak your mind? Do you allow others to take advantage of you because you're reluctant to say what you want? Do you feel uncomfortable when you have to state your opinion in a group? Questions such a these revolve around your degree of **assertiveness.** Before reading further about this type of communication, take the self-test below.

"So, when he says, 'What a good boy am I,' Jack is really reinforcing his self-esteem."

Message Skills

Self-Esteem: Raise your self-esteem: Challenge self-destructive beliefs, seek out nourishing people, work on projects that will result in success, and secure affirmation.

Test Yourself

How Assertive Are Your Messages?

Indicate how true each of the following statements is about your own communication. Re-spond instinctively rather than in the way you feel you should respond. Use the following scale: 5 = always or almost always true; 4 = usually true; 3 = sometimes true, sometimes false; 2 = usually false; and 1 = always or almost always false.

_____ ❶ I would express my opinion in a group even if it contradicted the opinions of others.

_____ ❷ When asked to do something that I really don't want to do, I can say no without feeling guilty.

_____ ❸ I can express my opinion to my superiors on the job.

_____ ❹ I can start up a conversation with a stranger on a bus or at a business gathering without fear.

_____ ❺ I voice objection to people's behavior if I feel it infringes on my rights.

HOW DID YOU DO? All five items in this test identify characteristics of assertive communication. So high scores (say about 20 and above) would indicate a high level of assertiveness. Low scores (say about 10 and below) would indicate a low level of assertiveness.

WHAT WILL YOU DO? The remaining discussion in this chapter clarifies the nature of assertive communication and offers guidelines for increasing your own assertiveness. These suggestions can help you not only to increase your assertiveness but also, when appropriate, to reduce your aggressive tendencies.

Nonassertive, Aggressive, and Assertive Messages

In addition to identifying some specific assertive behaviors (as in the self-test above), we can further understand the nature of assertive communication by distinguishing it from nonassertiveness and aggressiveness (Alberti, 1977).

Nonassertive Messages   The term *nonassertiveness* refers to a lack of assertiveness in certain types of (or even in all) communication situations. People who are nonassertive fail to assert their rights. In many instances these people do what others tell them to do—parents, employers, and the like—without questioning and without concern for what is best for them. They operate with a "you win, I lose" philosophy; they give others what they want without concern for themselves (Lloyd, 2001). Nonassertive people often ask permission from others to do what is their perfect right. Social situations create anxiety for these individuals, and their self-esteem is generally low.

Aggressive Messages   Aggressiveness is the other extreme. Aggressive people operate with an "I win, you lose" philosophy; they care little for what the other person wants and focus only on their own needs. Some people communicate aggressively only under certain conditions or in certain situations (for example, after being taken advantage of over a long period of time); others communicate aggressively in all or at least most situations. Aggressive communicators think little of the opinions, values, or beliefs of others and yet are extremely sensitive to others' criticisms of their own behavior. Consequently, they frequently get into arguments with others.

Assertive Messages   Assertive behavior—behavior that enables you to act in your own best interests *without* denying or infringing on the rights of others—is the generally desired alternative to nonassertiveness or aggressiveness. Assertive people operate with an "I win, you win" philosophy; they assume that both people can gain something from an interpersonal interaction, even from a confrontation. Assertive people are willing to assert their own rights. Unlike their aggressive counterparts, however, they do not hurt others in the process. Assertive people speak their minds and welcome others' doing likewise.

People who are assertive in interpersonal communication display four major characteristics (Norton & Warnick, 1976). To what extent do these characteristics apply to you? Do you

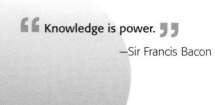

- *express your feelings frankly and openly to people in general as well as to those in whom you may have a romantic interest?*
- *volunteer opinions and beliefs and deal directly with interpersonal communication situations that may be stressful, and question others without fear?*
- *stand up and argue for your rights, even if this may entail a certain degree of disagreement or conflict with relatives or close friends?*
- *make up your own mind on the basis of evidence and argument instead of just accepting what others say?*

Research shows that people who are assertive generally answer yes to these questions. Assertive people are more open, less anxious, more contentious, and less likely to be intimidated or easily persuaded than nonassertive people. Assertive people also are more positive and more hopeful than nonassertive people (Velting, 1999). People who are unassertive generally answer no to the questions above. Unassertive people are less open, more anxious, less contentious, and more likely to be intimidated and easily persuaded.

Principles for Increasing Assertiveness

Most people are nonassertive in certain situations. If you're one of these people and if you wish to modify your behavior in some situations, there are steps you can take to increase your assertiveness. (If you're always and everywhere nonassertive and are unhappy about this, then you may need to work with a therapist to change your behavior.)

Analyze Assertive Messages   The first step in increasing your assertiveness skills is to understand the nature of these communications. Observe and analyze the messages of others. Learn to distinguish the differences among assertive, aggressive, and nonassertive messages. Focus on what makes one behavior assertive and another behavior nonassertive or aggressive.

After you've gained some skills in observing the behaviors of others, turn your analysis to yourself. Analyze situations in which you're normally assertive and situations in which you're more likely to act nonassertively or aggressively. What circumstances characterize these situations? What do the situations in which you're normally assertive have in common? How do you speak? How do you communicate nonverbally?

Rehearse Assertive Messages   To rehearse assertiveness, select a situation in which you're normally nonassertive. Build a hierarchy of visualizations that begins with a relatively nonthreatening message and ends with the desired communication. For example, let us say that you have difficulty voicing your opinion to your supervisor at work. The desired behavior, then, is to tell your supervisor your opinions. Con-

Practicing Assertiveness

For one of the following situations, write *(a)* an aggressive, *(b)* a nonassertive, and *(c)* an assertive response. Then, in one sentence of 15 words or less, explain why your assertiveness message will prove more effective than the aggressive or nonassertive message.

Decorating your apartment: You've just redecorated your apartment, expending considerable time and money in making it exactly as you want it. A good friend of yours brings you a house gift—the ugliest poster you've ever seen—and insists that you hang it over your fireplace, the focal point of your living room.

Lending money: A friend borrows $30 and promises to pay you back tomorrow. But tomorrow passes, as do 20 other tomorrows, and there is still no sign of the money. You know that your friend has not forgotten about the debt, and you also know that the person has more than enough money to pay you back.

Neighbor favors: A next-door neighbor repeatedly asks you to take care of her four-year-old while she runs some errand or another. You don't mind helping out in an emergency, but this occurs almost every day. You feel you're being taken advantage of and simply do not want to do this anymore.

Assertiveness is the most direct and honest response in situations such as these. Usually it's also the most effective.

In your weekly meetings at work, the supervisor who serves as group leader consistently ignores your cues that you want to say something—and even when you do manage to say something, no one seems to react or take special note of your comments. You're determined to change this situation. What do you say?

Message Skills

Increasing Assertiveness: Increase assertiveness by analyzing the assertive messages of others, rehearsing assertive messages, and communicating assertively.

struct a hierarchy of situations leading up to this desired behavior. Such a hierarchy might begin with visualizing yourself talking with your boss. Visualize this scenario until you can do it without any anxiety or discomfort. Once you have mastered this visualization, visualize a step closer to your goal; say, walking into your boss's office. Again, do this until your visualization creates no discomfort. Continue with these successive visualizations until you can visualize yourself telling your boss your opinion. As with the other visualizations, practice this until you can do it while totally relaxed. This is the mental rehearsal.

You might add a vocal dimension to this by actually acting out (with voice and gesture) your telling your boss your opinion. Again, do this until you experience no difficulty or discomfort. Next, try doing this in front of a trusted and supportive friend or group of friends. Ideally this interaction will provide you with useful feedback. After this rehearsal, you're probably ready for the next step: putting assertiveness into action.

Communicate Assertively Communicating assertively is naturally the most difficult step but obviously the most important. Here's a generally effective pattern to follow:

- Describe the problem; don't evaluate or judge it. "We're all working on this advertising project together. You're missing half our meetings, and you still haven't produced your first report."

- State how this problem affects you. But sure to use I-messages and to avoid messages that accuse or blame the other person. "My job depends on the success of this project, and I don't think it's fair that I have to do extra work to make up for what you're not doing."

- Propose solutions that are workable and that allow the person to save face. "If you can get your report to the group by Tuesday, we'll still be able to meet our deadline. And I could give you a call an hour before the meetings to remind you."

- Confirm understanding. "Is it clear that we just can't produce this project if you're not going to pull your own weight? Will you have the report to us by Tuesday?"

- Reflect on your own assertiveness. Think about what you did. How did you express yourself verbally and nonverbally? What would you do differently next time?

A note of caution should be added. It's easy to visualize a situation in which, for example, people are talking behind you in a movie and, with your newfound enthusiasm for assertiveness, you tell them to be quiet. It's also easy to see yourself getting smashed in the teeth as a result. In applying the principles of assertive communication, be careful that you do not go beyond what you can handle effectively.

Summary of Concepts

This chapter explored interpersonal power from three different points of view: the principles of power, self-esteem, and assertiveness.

1. Interpersonal power is the ability of one person to control the behaviors of another person. A has power over B if A can control B's behaviors.
2. The six types of power are referent, legitimate, reward, coercive, expert, and information or persuasion power.
3. Six principles governing power in interpersonal relationships are that power varies from person to person, power is a part of all interpersonal messages, power follows the principle of less interest, power has cultural dimension, and power is often used unfairly.
4. Sexual harassment consists of sexual behaviors that are unwelcome. In quid pro quo harassment sexual favors are required for employment or advancement, and in hostile environment harassment the sexual behaviors make people uncomfortable.
5. Among common types of interpersonal power plays are the kinds known as *nobody upstairs, you owe me,* and *yougottobekidding.*
6. An effective strategy for dealing with power plays cooperatively consist of three parts: stating your feelings, describing the behavior you object to, and outlining a cooperative solution.
7. Self-esteem is the way you see yourself, the value you place on yourself. Research differs on the value of self-affirmations.
8. Assertive people stand up for their rights without denying or infringing on the rights of others. They are open, not anxious, contentious (argumentative), and not easily intimidated.
9. To increase assertiveness, analyze assertive messages to understand what is unique about them, rehearse assertive messages so you'll feel comfortable with them, and try out these new assertive messages (with caution).

Vocabulary Quiz: The Language of Power

Match the terms of power with their definitions. Record the number of the definition next to the appropriate term.

____ self-esteem

____ power

____ assertive communication

____ tag questions, disqualifiers, and hesitations

____ nonassertive communication

____ low-power distance

____ compliance-gaining strategies

____ legitimate power

____ negative altercasting

____ cooperative management strategy for power plays

1. A willingness to speak out for your rights but with respect for others.
2. Power held by virtue of your position or role.
3. Stating your feelings, describing the behavior you object to, and stating a response both will find acceptable.
4. Often perceived as signs of powerlessness.
5. The value you place on yourself.
6. Tactics that influence people to do what you want them to do.
7. A compliance-gaining strategy in which you put another person into the role of the "bad" person.
8. An unwillingness to speak out for your rights.
9. A relatively even distribution of power among members.
10. The ability to control the behavior of another person.

Four for Discussion

1. Arguments for the benefits of self-esteem have come under a good deal of attack (e.g., Bushman & Baumeister, 1998; Baumeister, Bushman, & Campbell, 2000; Bower, 2001; Coover & Murphy, 2000; Hewitt, 1998). Much current thinking holds that high self-esteem is not desirable: It does nothing to improve academic performance; it does not predict success; and, in fact, it may lead to antisocial (especially aggressive) behavior. On the other hand, it's difficult to imagine a person functioning successfully without positive self-feelings. How do you feel about the benefits or liabilities of self-esteem?

2. Even the language of a culture may influence the extent of the "knowledge gap" (the difference in knowledge, and hence power, between the educated and powerful and the uneducated and powerless). For example, English dominates the Internet, so the Internet is more easily accessible to people in the United States and other English-speaking countries—and to educated people in non-English-speaking countries. Consider the fact that more than half the world's people do not use the Latin alphabet; Chinese, Japanese, Korean, and Arab people, for example, use alphabets that make software development and Internet access more difficult. Do you see this issue changing over the next 10 or 15 years? If so, in what ways?

3. How is interpersonal power illustrated on prime-time television? For example: (1) Do male and female characters wield the same types of power? (2) Do the story lines in sitcoms and dramas reward the exercise of some types of power and punish the exercise of other types? (3) How do these programs deal with the process of empowering others? Is it rewarded? Are men and women portrayed as empowering in the same way?

4. In each of the following dyads (pairs), there is a power difference. One person is significantly richer, of higher status, more educated, or more attractive than the other. How might the power differences create communication difficulties when the individuals are engaged (a) in informal conversation and (b) in romantic encounters?

   - a young nurse and the chief of surgery at a prestigious hospital
   - an uneducated parent and the high school principal
   - two coworkers, one extremely attractive and one extremely unattractive

Web Explorations

Explore our text website at
www.ablongman.com/devito
to find:

Exercises and Self-Tests

Two self-tests will enable you to examine your own inter-personal power: (1) How Machiavellian Are You? and (2) When Is Persuasion Unethical?

Writing Resources and Assignments

Suggestions are available for writing papers of personal experience (for example, your own experience with inter-personal power), concept or principle explanation (for example, self-esteem, empowerment), review (for example, types of sexual harassment), or research (for example, the assertive personality) on interpersonal power.

Explore our research resources at
www.researchnavigator.com
and

Read an article.

Read a popular or scholarly article on a principle or type of power, the ways of communicating power, or empowering others. On the basis of this article, what can you add to the discussion presented here?

Investigate key terms.

Investigate one of the key terms discussed in this chapter (for example, power, power play, reward power, coercive power, empowerment, power distance, sexual harassment). What additional insights can you provide?

Find answers.

Try finding answers to one of the following questions, or design a research study to answer it.

1. What types of power work best in the elementary or high school classroom? Which work best in the college class-room?
2. Which compliance-gaining strategies work best in same-sex and opposite-sex interactions? Which are least ef-fective?
3. Do women and men differ in assertiveness?

Glossary of Interpersonal Communication Concepts

acculturation. The process by which your culture is modified or changed through contact with or exposure to another culture.

active listening. The process by which a listener expresses his or her understanding of the speaker's total message, including the verbal and nonverbal, the thoughts and feelings.

adaptors. Nonverbal behaviors that, when engaged in either in private or in public, serve some kind of need and occur in their entirety—for example, scratching one's head until the itch is relieved.

adjustment (principle of). The principle of verbal interaction that claims that effective communication depends on the extent to which communicators share the same system of signals.

affect displays. Movements of the facial area that convey emotional meaning such as anger, fear, and surprise.

affinity-seeking strategies. Behaviors designed to increase interpersonal attractiveness.

affirmation. The communication of support and approval.

ageism. Discrimination based on age, usually against older people.

allness. The illogical assumption that all can be known or said about a given person, issue, object, or event.

alter-adaptors. Body movements you make in response to your current interactions; for example, crossing your arms over your chest when someone unpleasant approaches or moving closer to someone you like.

altercasting. Placing a person in a specific role for a specific purpose and asking that he or she assume the perspective of this specific role; for example, "As a professor of communication, please comment on. . . ."

ambiguity. The condition in which a message may be interpreted as having more than one meaning.

argumentativeness. A willingness to argue for a point of view, to speak one's mind. *Distinguished from* **verbal aggressiveness.**

assertiveness. A willingness to stand up for your rights but with respect for the rights of others.

attention. The process of responding to a stimulus or stimuli; usually some consciousness of responding is implied.

attitude. A predisposition to respond for or against an object, person, or position.

attraction. The process by which one individual is emotionally drawn to another and finds that person satisfying to be with.

attractiveness. A person's visual appeal and/or pleasantness in personality.

attribution. The processes by which we assign causation or motivation to a person's behavior.

avoidance. An **unproductive conflict strategy** in which you take mental or physical flight from the actual conflict.

backchanneling cues. Responses a listener makes to a speaker (while the speaker is speaking) but which do not ask for the speaking role; for example, interjections such as "I understand" or "You said what?"

barriers to intercultural communication. Physical or psychological factors that prevent or hinder effective communication.

behavioral synchrony. The similarity in the behavior, usually nonverbal (for example, postural stance or facial expressions) of two persons; generally taken as an indicator of liking.

belief. Confidence in the existence or truth of something; conviction.

beltlining. An **unproductive conflict strategy** in which one person hits the other at a vulnerable level—at the level at which the other person cannot withstand the blow.

blame. An **unproductive conflict strategy** in which we attribute the cause of the conflict to the other person or devote our energies to discovering who is the cause, avoiding talking about the issues at hand.

boundary marker. A **marker** that sets boundaries around or divides one person's territory from another's—for example, a fence.

breadth. The number of topics about which individuals in a relationship communicate.

censorship. Restrictions imposed on a person's right to produce, distribute, or receive various communications.

central marker. A **marker** or item that is placed in a territory to reserve it for a specific person—for example, the sweater thrown over a library chair to signal that the chair is taken.

certainty. An attitude of **closed-mindedness** that creates defensiveness among communicators. *Opposed to* **provisionalism.**

channel. The vehicle or medium through which signals are sent; for example, the vocal–auditory channel.

cherishing behaviors. Small behaviors you enjoy receiving from others, especially from your relational partner—for example, a kiss before you leave for work.

chronemics. The study of the communicative nature of time; of how a person's or a culture's treatment of time reveals something about the person or culture. Often divided into psychological and cultural time.

civil inattention. Polite ignoring of others (after a brief sign of awareness) so as not to invade their privacy.

closed-mindedness. An unwillingness to receive certain communication messages.

code. A set of symbols used to translate a message from one form to another.

cognitive labeling theory. A theory of emotions that holds that emotional feelings begin with the occurrence of an event; you respond physiologically to the event, then you interpret the arousal (you in effect decide what it is you're feeling), and then you experience (give a name to) the emotion.

collectivist culture. A culture in which the group's goals are given greater importance than the individual's and in which, for example, benevolence, tradition, and conformity are given special emphasis. *Opposed to* **individualist culture.**

color communication. The use of color to communicate different meanings; each culture seems to define the meanings colors communicate somewhat differently.

communication. (1) The process or act of communicating; (2) the actual message or messages sent and received; (3) the study of the processes involved in the sending and receiving of messages.

communication apprehension. Fear or anxiety of communicating.

communicology. The study of communication, particularly the subsection concerned with human communication.

competence. "Language competence" is a speaker's ability to use the language; it is a knowledge of the elements and rules of the language. "Communication competence" generally refers both to the knowledge of communication and also to the ability to engage in communication effectively.

complementarity. A principle of **attraction** holding that you are attracted by qualities that you do not possess or wish to possess, and to people who are opposite or different from yourself. *Opposed to* **similarity.**

complementary relationship. A relationship in which the behavior of one person serves as the stimulus for the complementary behavior of the other; in complementary relationships, behavioral differences are maximized.

compliance-gaining strategies. Behaviors designed to gain the agreement of others, to persuade others to do as you wish.

compliance-resisting strategies. Behaviors directed at resisting the persuasive attempts of others.

confidence. A quality of interpersonal effectiveness (and a factor in interpersonal **power**); a comfortable, at-ease feeling in interpersonal communication situations.

confirmation. A communication pattern that acknowledges another person's presence and indicates an acceptance of this person, this person's self-definition, and the relationship as defined or viewed by this other person. *Opposed to* **rejection** *and* **disconfirmation.**

conflict. A disagreement or difference of opinion; a form of competition in which one person tries to bring a rival to surrender; a situation in which one person's behaviors are directed at preventing something or at interfering with or harming another individual. *See also* **interpersonal conflict.**

congruence. A condition in which both verbal and nonverbal behaviors reinforce each other.

connotation. The feeling or emotional aspect of a word's meaning; generally viewed as consisting of evaluation (for example, good–bad), potency (strong–weak), and activity (fast–slow) dimensions. *Opposed to* **denotation.**

consistency. A tendency to maintain balance in your **perception** of messages or people; because of this process, you tend to see what you expect to see and to be uncomfortable when your perceptions run contrary to expectations.

contact. The first stage in **relationship development,** consisting of perceptual contact (you see or hear the person) and interactional contact (you talk with the person).

content and relationship dimensions. Two aspects to which messages may refer: the world external to both speaker and listener (content) and the connections existing between the individuals who are interacting (relationship).

context of communication. The physical, psychological, social, and temporal environment in which communication takes place.

conversation. Two-person communication, usually following five stages: opening, feedforward, business, feedback, and closing.

conversational management. The management of the way in which messages are exchanged in **conversation;** consists of procedures for opening, maintaining, repairing, and closing conversations.

conversational maxims. Principles that participants in **conversation** follow to ensure that the goal of the conversation is achieved.

conversational turns. The process of passing the speaker and listener roles back and forth during **conversation.**

cooperation. An interpersonal process by which individuals work together for a common end; the pooling of efforts to produce a mutually desired outcome.

cooperation (principle of). In **conversation,** an implicit agreement between speaker and listener to cooperate in trying to understand each other.

credibility. The degree to which people see a person as believable; competence, character, and charisma (dynamism) are major factors in credibility.

critical thinking. The process of logically evaluating reasons and evidence and reaching a judgment on the basis of this analysis.

cultural assimilation. The process by which people leave behind their culture of origin and take on the values and beliefs of another culture; as when, for example, immigrants give up their native culture to become members of their new adopted culture.

cultural display. Signs that communicate a person's cultural identification, such as clothing or religious jewelry.

cultural display rules. Rules that identify what are and what are not appropriate forms of expression for members of the culture.

cultural rules. Rules that are specific to a given culture.

cultural time. The meanings given to the ways time is treated in a particular culture.

date. An **extensional device** used to emphasize the notion of constant change and symbolized by a subscript: For example, John Smith$_{2000}$ is not John Smith$_{2005}$.

decoder. Something that takes a message in one form (for example, sound waves) and translates it into another form (for example, nerve impulses) from which meaning can be formulated. In human communication the decoder is the auditory mechanism; in electronic communication the decoder is, for example, the telephone earpiece. *Decoding* is the process of extracting a message from a code—for example, translating speech sounds into nerve impulses. *See also* **encoder.**

defensiveness. An attitude of an individual or an atmosphere in a group characterized by threats, fear, and domination; messages evidencing evaluation, control, strategy, neutrality, superiority, and certainty are thought to lead to defensiveness. *Opposed to* **supportiveness.**

delayed reaction. A reaction that a person consciously delays while analyzing the situation and evaluating possible choices for communication.

denial. One of the obstacles to the expression of emotion; the process by which you deny your emotions to yourself or to others.

denotation. The objective or descriptive aspect of a word's meaning; the meaning you'd find in a dictionary. *Opposed to* **connotation.**

depenetration. A reversal of penetration; a condition in which the **breadth** and **depth** of a relationship decrease.

depth. The degree to which the inner personality—the inner core of an individual—is penetrated in interpersonal interaction.

deterioration. In the stage model of relationships, the stage during which the connecting bonds between the partners weaken and the partners begin drifting apart.

dialogue. A form of **communication** in which each person is both speaker and listener; communication characterized by involvement, concern, and respect for the other person. *Opposed to* **monologue.**

direct speech. Speech in which the speaker's intentions are stated clearly and directly.

disclaimer. Statement that asks the listener to receive what you say without its reflecting negatively on you.

disconfirmation. The process by which someone ignores or denies the right of another individual even to define himself or herself. *Opposed to* **rejection** *and* **confirmation.**

dissolution. In the stage model of relationships, the termination or end of the relationship.

downward communication. Communication sent from the higher levels of a hierarchy to the lower levels—for example, messages sent by managers to workers or from deans to faculty members.

dyadic coalition. A two-person group formed from some larger group to achieve a particular goal.

dyadic communication. Two-person communication.

dyadic consciousness. An awareness on the part of the participants that an interpersonal relationship or pairing exists between them; distinguished from situations in which two individuals are together but do not see themselves as a unit or twosome.

dyadic effect. The tendency for the behaviors of one person to stimulate similar behaviors in the other interactant; often refers to the tendency of one person's self-disclosures to prompt the other also to self-disclose.

dyadic primacy. The significance or centrality of the two-person group, even when there are many more people interacting.

earmarker. A **marker** that identifies an item as belonging to a specific person—for example, a nameplate on a desk or initials on an attaché case.

effect. The outcome or consequence of an action or behavior; communication is assumed always to have some effect.

emblems. Nonverbal behaviors that directly translate words or phrases—for example, the signs for *OK* and *peace*.

emotion. The feelings we have—for example, our feelings of guilt, anger, or love.

emotional communication. The expression of feelings—for example, feelings of guilt, happiness, or sorrow.

emotional contagion. The transfer of emotions from one person to another, much as a contagious disease is transmitted from one person to another.

empathy. A quality of interpersonal effectiveness that involves sharing others' feelings; an ability to feel or perceive things from others' points of view.

encoder. Something that takes a message in one form (for example, nerve impulses) and translates it into another form (for example, sound waves). In human communication the encoder is the speaking mechanism; in electronic communication the encoder is, for example, the telephone mouthpiece. *Encoding* is the process of putting a message into a code—for example, translating nerve impulses into speech sounds. *See also* **decoder.**

enculturation. The process by which culture is transmitted from one generation to another.

E-prime. A form of the language that omits the verb *to be* except when used as an auxiliary or in statements of existence.

equality. An attitude that recognizes that each individual in a communication interaction is equal, that no one is superior to any other; encourages **supportiveness.** *Opposed to* **superiority.**

equilibrium theory. A theory of **proxemics** holding that intimacy and physical closeness are positively related; as a relationship becomes more intimate, the individuals will maintain shorter distances between themselves.

equity theory. A theory claiming that people experience relational satisfaction when there is an equal distribution of rewards and costs between the two persons in the relationship.

et cetera (etc.). An **extensional device** used to emphasize the notion of infinite complexity; because you can never know all about anything, any statement about the world or an event must end with an explicit or implicit "etc."

ethics. The branch of philosophy that deals with the rightness or wrongness of actions; the study of moral values; in communication, the morality of message behavior.

ethnocentrism. The tendency to see others and their behaviors through your own cultural filters, often as distortions of your own behaviors; the tendency to evaluate the values and beliefs of your own culture more positively than those of another culture.

euphemism. A polite word or phrase used to substitute for some taboo or less polite term or phrase.

evaluation. A process whereby we place a value on some person, object, or event.

excuse. An explanation designed to lessen the negative consequences of something done or said.

expectancy violations theory. A theory of **proxemics** holding that people have a certain expectancy for space relationships. When that is violated (say, a person stands too close to you or a romantic partner maintains abnormally large distances from you), the relationship comes into clearer focus and you wonder why this "normal distance" is being violated.

expressiveness. A quality of **interpersonal effectiveness** that consists of genuine involvement in speaking and listening, conveyed verbally and nonverbally.

extensional devices. Linguistic devices proposed by Alfred Korzybski to make language a more accurate means for talking about the world. The extensional devices include **et cetera, date,** and **index.**

extensional orientation. A point of view in which primary consideration is given to the world of experience and only secondary consideration is given to labels. *Opposed to* **intensional orientation.**

facial feedback hypothesis. The hypothesis or theory that your facial expressions can produce physiological and emotional effects via a feedback mechanism.

facial management techniques. Techniques used to mask certain emotions and to emphasize others; for example, intensifying your expression of happiness to make a friend feel good about a promotion.

fact–inference confusion. A misevaluation in which a person makes an inference, regards it as a fact, and acts upon it as if it were a fact.

factual statement. A statement made by the observer after observation and limited to what is observed. *Opposed to* **inferential statement.**

family. A group of people who consider themselves related and connected to one another and for whom the actions of one have consequences for others.

fear appeal. The appeal to fear to persuade an individual or group of individuals to believe or to act in a certain way.

feedback. Information that is given back to the source. Feedback may come from the source's own messages (as when you hear what you're saying) or from the receiver(s)—in forms such as applause, yawning, puzzled looks, questions, letters to the editor of a newspaper, or increased or decreased subscriptions to a magazine. *See also* **negative feedback, positive feedback.**

feedforward. Information that is sent before a regular message, telling the listener something about what is to follow; messages that are prefatory to more central messages.

feminine culture. A culture that encourages both men and women to be modest, oriented to maintaining the quality of life, and tender. Feminine cultures emphasize the quality of life and so socialize their people to be modest and to emphasize close interpersonal relationships. *Opposed to* **masculine culture.**

flexibility. The ability to adjust communication strategies and skills on the basis of the unique situation.

focus group. An in-depth interview of a small group that aims to discover what people think about an issue or product.

force. An **unproductive conflict strategy** in which you try to win an argument by emotionally or physically overpowering the other person—either by threat or by actual behavior.

friendship. An interpersonal relationship between two persons that is mutually productive, established and maintained through perceived mutual free choice, and characterized by mutual positive regard.

fundamental attribution error. The tendency to overvalue and overweight the contribution of internal factors (i.e., a person's personality) to behavior, and to undervalue and underweight the contribution of external factors (i.e., the situation the person is in or the surrounding events).

gender display rules. The cultural rules that identify what are appropriate and what are not appropriate forms of expression for men and for women.

General Semantics. The study of the relationships among language, thought, and behavior.

gossip. Oral or written **communication** about someone not present, some third party, usually about matters that are private to this third party.

gunnysacking. An **unproductive conflict strategy** of storing up grievances—as if in a gunnysack—and holding them in readiness to dump on the other person in the conflict.

halo effect. The tendency to generalize a person's virtue or expertise from one area to other areas.

haptics. The study of touch or **tactile communication.**

heterosexist language. Language that denigrates lesbians and gay men.

high-context culture. A culture in which much of the information in communication messages is left implied; it's "understood." Much information is considered to be in the context or in the person rather than explicitly coded in the verbal messages. **Collectivist cultures** are generally high context. *Opposed to* **low-context culture.**

home field advantage. The increased power that comes from being in your own territory.

home territory. Territory in which an individual has a sense of intimacy and over which he or she exercises control—for example, a teacher's office.

illustrators. Nonverbal behaviors that accompany and literally illustrate verbal messages—for example, upward movements of the head and hand that accompany the verbal "It's up there."

I-messages. Messages in which the speaker accepts responsibility for personal thoughts and behaviors and states his or her point of view explicitly. *Opposed to* **you-messages.**

immediacy. A quality of **interpersonal effectiveness** that conveys a sense of contact and togetherness, a feeling of interest in and liking for the other person.

implicit personality theory. A theory of personality, complete with rules about what characteristics go with what other characteristics, that you maintain and through which you perceive others.

inclusion (principle of). The principle of verbal interaction holding that all members should be a part of (included in) the interaction.

index. An **extensional device** symbolized by a subscript and used to emphasize the assumption that no two things are the same; for example, even though two people may both be politicians, politician$_{1[Smith]}$ is not politician$_{2[Jones]}$.

indirect speech. Speech that hides the speaker's true intentions; speech in which requests and observations are made indirectly.

indiscrimination. A misevaluation that results when you categorize people, events, or objects into a particular class and respond to them only as members of the class; a failure to recognize that each individual is unique.

individualist culture. A culture in which the individual's rather than the group's goals and preferences are given greater importance. *Opposed to* **collectivist culture.**

inevitability. A principle of communication holding that communication cannot be avoided; all behavior in an interactional setting is communication.

inferential statement. A statement that can be made by anyone, is not limited to what is observed, and can be made at any time. *Opposed to* **factual statement.**

informal time terms. Terms used to denote time periods that are approximate rather than exact, such as "soon," "early," and "in a while."

information overload. A condition in which the amount or complexity of information is too great to be dealt with effectively by an individual, group, or organization.

in-group talk. Talk about a subject or in a vocabulary that some people present understand and others do not; has the effect of excluding those who don't understand.

insulation. A reaction to **territorial encroachment** in which you erect some sort of barrier between yourself and the invaders, such as a stone wall around your property, an unlisted phone number, or caller ID.

intensional orientation. A point of view in which primary consideration is given to the way things are labeled and only secondary consideration (if any) to the world of experience. *Opposed to* **extensional orientation.**

interaction management. A quality of **interpersonal effectiveness** in which the interaction is controlled and managed to the satisfaction of both parties; effectively managing conversational turns, fluency, and message consistency.

intercultural communication. Communication that takes place between persons of different cultures or between persons who have different cultural beliefs, values, or ways of behaving.

interpersonal communication. Communication between two persons or among a small group of persons and distinguished from public or mass communication; communication of a personal nature and distinguished from impersonal communication; communication between or among connected persons or those involved in a close relationship.

interpersonal competence. The knowledge of and the ability to communicate effectively in interpersonal interactions.

interpersonal conflict. Disagreement between two connected persons.

interpersonal effectiveness. The ability to accomplish interpersonal goals; interpersonal communication that is satisfying to both individuals.

interpersonal perception. The **perception** of people; the processes through which you interpret and evaluate people and their behavior.

intimacy. The closest interpersonal relationship; usually characterizes close **primary relationships.**

intimacy claims. Obligations incurred by virtue of being in a close and intimate relationship.

intimate distance. The closest distance in **proxemics,** ranging from touching to 18 inches.

intrapersonal communication. Communication with self.

involvement. The second stage in **relationship development,** in which you further advance the relationship, first testing each other and then intensifying your interaction.

irreversibility. A principle of communication holding that communication cannot be reversed; once something has been communicated, it cannot be uncommunicated.

jargon. The technical language of any specialized group, often a professional class, which is unintelligible to individuals not belonging to the group; shop talk. This glossary is an example of the jargon of part of the **communication** field.

Johari window. A diagram of the four selves (open, blind, hidden, and unknown).

kinesics. The study of the communicative dimensions of facial and bodily movements.

language. The rules of syntax, semantics, and phonology by which sentences are created and understood; *a language* refers to the sentences that can be created in any language, such as English, Bantu, or Italian.

leave-taking cues. Verbal and nonverbal signals that indicate a desire to terminate a conversation.

linguistic relativity hypothesis. The theory that the language you speak influences your perceptions of the world and your behaviors and that therefore people speaking widely differing languages will perceive and behave differently.

listening. An active process of receiving aural stimuli consisting of five stages: receiving, understanding, remembering, evaluating, and responding.

loving. A relationship with another person in which you feel closeness, caring, warmth, and excitement.

low-context culture. A culture in which most of the information in communication is explicitly stated in the verbal message rather than being left implied or assumed to be "understood." Low-context cultures are usually **individualist cultures.** *Opposed to* **high-context culture.**

Machiavellianism. The belief that people can be manipulated easily; also, manipulative techniques or tactics one person uses to control another.

manipulation. An **unproductive conflict strategy;** a manipulative individual avoids engaging in open conflict but instead attempts to divert the conflict by being especially charming and getting the other person into a noncombative frame of mind.

manner maxim. A **conversational maxim** that holds that speakers cooperate with listeners by being clear and by organizing their thoughts into meaningful and coherent patterns.

markers. Devices that signify that a certain territory belongs to a particular person. *See also* **boundary marker, central marker,** *and* **earmarker.**

masculine culture. A culture that views men as assertive, oriented to material success, and strong; such a culture views women, on the other hand, as modest, focused on the quality of life, and tender. Masculine cultures emphasize success and so socialize their people to be assertive, ambitious, and competitive. *Opposed to* **feminine culture.**

matching hypothesis. An assumption that you date and mate people who are comparable to yourself—who match you—in physical attractiveness.

meaningfulness. A principle of **perception** that assumes that the behavior of people is sensible, stems from some logical antecedent, and therefore is meaningful rather than meaningless.

mentoring relationship. A relationship in which an experienced individual helps train someone who is less experienced; for example, an accomplished teacher might mentor a younger teacher who is newly arrived or who has never taught before.

mere exposure hypothesis. The theory that repeated or prolonged exposure to a stimulus may result in a change in attitude toward the stimulus object, generally in the direction of increased positiveness.

message. Any signal or combination of signals that serves as a stimulus for a receiver. *See also* **stimulus.**

metacommunication. Communication about communication.

metalanguage. Language that refers to language.

metamessage. A message that makes reference to another message, such as "Did I make myself clear?" or "That's a lie."

micromomentary expressions. Extremely brief movements that are not consciously controlled or recognized and that are thought to be indicative of your true emotional state.

mindfulness. A state of awareness in which you are conscious of the logic and rationality of your behaviors and of the logical connections existing among elements.

mindlessness. A lack of conscious awareness of the logic or reasons behind your thoughts or behaviors.

mixed message. A message that communicates two different and often contradictory meanings; for example, a message that asks for two different (often incompatible) responses such as "leave me alone" and "show me more attention." Often, one meaning (usually the socially acceptable meaning) is communicated verbally and the other (usually the less socially acceptable meaning) nonverbally.

model. A representation of an object or process.

monochronic time orientation. A view of time in which things are done sequentially; one thing is scheduled at a time. *Opposed to* **polychronic time orientation.**

monologue. A form of **communication** in which one person speaks and the other listens; there's no real interaction among participants. *Opposed to* **dialogue.**

negative feedback. Feedback that serves a corrective function by informing the source that his or her message is not being received in the way intended. Looks of boredom, shouts of disagreement, letters critical of newspaper policy, and teachers' instructions on how better to approach a problem are examples of negative feedback and will (ideally) serve to redirect behavior. *See also* **positive feedback.**

networking. Connecting with people who can help you accomplish a goal or help you find information related to your goal; for example, to your search for a job.

neutrality. A response pattern lacking in personal involvement; encourages defensiveness. *Opposed to* **empathy.**

noise. Anything that interferes with your receiving a message as the source intended the message to be received. Noise is present in communication to the extent that the message received is not the message sent.

nonallness. A point of view holding that you can never know all about anything and that what you know, say, or hear is only a part of what there is to know, say, or hear.

nonnegotiation. An **unproductive conflict strategy** in which an individual refuses to discuss the conflict or to listen to the other person.

nonverbal communication. Communication without words; communication by means of space, gestures, facial expressions, touching, vocal variation, or silence, for example.

nonverbal dominance. Nonverbal behavior through which one person achieves psychological dominance over another.

object-adaptors. Movements that involve manipulation of some object; for example, punching holes in a Styrofoam coffee cup, clicking a ball point pen, or chewing on a pencil.

object language. Language used to communicate about objects, events, and relations in the world (rather than about words as in **metalanguage**).

olfactory communication. Communication by smell.

openness. A quality of **interpersonal effectiveness** involving a person's willingness (1) to interact openly with others, self-disclosing as appropriate; (2) to react honestly to incoming stimuli; and (3) to own his or her own feelings and thoughts.

other talk. Talk about the listener or some third party. *Opposed to* **self talk.**

other-orientation. A quality of interpersonal effectiveness involving attentiveness, interest, and concern for the other person.

outing. The process whereby a person's affectional orientation is made public by another person without the gay man or lesbian's consent.

overattribution. The tendency to attribute to one or two characteristics most or even all of what a person does.

owning feelings. Taking responsibility for your own feelings instead of attributing them to others.

paralanguage. The vocal but nonverbal aspects of speech. Paralanguage consists of **voice qualities** (for example, pitch range, resonance, tempo); vocal characterizers (laughing or crying, yelling or whispering); vocal qualifiers (intensity, pitch height); and vocal segregates ("uh-uh" meaning "no," or "sh" meaning "silence").

pauses. Interruptions in the normally fluent stream of speech. Pauses are of two types: filled pauses (interruptions filled with such vocalizations as "er" or "um") and unfilled pauses (silences of unusually long duration).

perception. The process by which you become aware of objects and events through your senses.

perception checking. The process of verifying your understanding of some message, situation, or feeling.

perceptual accentuation. A process that leads you to see what you expect or want to see—for example, seeing people you like as better looking and smarter than people you don't like.

personal distance. The second closest distance in **proxemics,** ranging from 18 inches to 4 feet.

personal rejection. An **unproductive conflict strategy** in which you withhold love and affection and seek to win the argument by getting the other person to break down under this withdrawal.

persuasion. The process of influencing attitudes and behavior.

phatic communication. Communication that is primarily social; communication designed to open the channels of communication rather than to communicate something about the external world. "Hello" and "How are you?" in everyday interaction are examples.

pitch. In relation to **voice qualities,** the highness or lowness of the vocal tone.

polarization. A form of fallacious reasoning in which only two extremes are considered; also referred to as black-and-white or either/or thinking or as a two-valued orientation.

polychronic time orientation. A view of time in which several things may be scheduled or engaged in at the same time. *Opposed to* **monochronic time orientation.**

positive feedback. Feedback that supports or reinforces the continuation of behavior along the same lines in which it is already proceeding—for example, applause during a speech, which encourages the speaker to continue speaking the same way. *See also* **negative feedback.**

positiveness. A characteristic of **interpersonal effectiveness** involving positive attitudes and the use of positive messages expressing these attitudes (as in complimenting others) along with acceptance and approval.

power. The ability to influence or control the behavior of another person; A has power over B when A can influence or control B's behavior; an inevitable part of interpersonal relationships.

power play. A consistent pattern of behavior in which one person tries to control the behavior of another.

pragmatic implication. An assumption that is logical (and therefore appears true) but is actually not necessarily true.

pragmatics. In interpersonal communication, an approach that focuses on communication behaviors and effects and on communication effectiveness.

primacy and recency. Giving more importance to that which occurs first (primacy) or to that which occurs last or more recently (recency).

primary affect displays. The communication of the six primary emotions: happiness, surprise, fear, anger, sadness, and disgust/contempt.

primary relationship. The relationship between two people that they consider their most (or one of their most) important; for example, the relationship between husband and wife or between domestic partners.

primary territory. Areas that you consider your exclusive preserve—for example, your room or office.

process. Ongoing activity; communication is referred to as a process to emphasize that it's always changing, always in motion.

protection theory. A theory of **proxemics** holding that people establish a body-buffer zone to protect themselves from unwanted closeness, touching, or attack.

provisionalism. An attitude of open-mindedness that leads to the development of a supportive relationship and atmosphere. *Opposed to* **certainty.**

proxemics. The study of the communicative function of space; the study of how people unconsciously structure their space—the distance between people in their interactions, the organization of space in homes and offices, and even the design of cities.

proximity. As a principle of **perception,** the tendency to perceive people or events that are physically close as belonging together or representing some unit; physical closeness—one of the qualities influencing interpersonal **attraction.**

psychological time. An emphasis on or orientation toward past, present, or future time; varies from person to person.

public distance. The farthest distance in **proxemics,** ranging from 12 feet to 25 feet or more.

public territory. Areas that are open to all people—for example, restaurants or parks.

punctuation of communication. The breaking up of continuous communication sequences into short sequences with identifiable beginnings and endings or stimuli and responses.

pupil dilation. The extent to which the pupil of the eye widens; generally, large pupils indicate positive reactions.

pupillometrics. The study of communication messages reflected by changes in the size of the pupils of the eyes.

Pygmalion effect. The condition in which you make a prediction of success, act as if it is true, and thereby make it come true (as when, for example, acting toward students as if they'll be successful influences them to become successful); a type of **self-fulfilling prophecy.**

quality maxim. A **conversational maxim** that holds that speakers cooperate with listeners by saying what they think is true and by not saying what they think is false.

quantity maxim. A **conversational maxim** that holds that speakers cooperate with listeners by being only as informative as necessary to communicate their intended meanings.

racist language. Language that denigrates, demeans, or is derogatory toward members of a particular race.

rate. In relation to **voice qualities,** the speed at which you speak, generally measured in words per minute.

receiver. Any person or thing that takes in messages. Receivers may be individuals listening to or reading a message, a group of persons hearing a speech, a scattered television audience, or machines that store information.

regulators. Nonverbal behaviors that regulate, monitor, or control the communications of another person.

rejection. A response to an individual that acknowledges the person but expresses disagreement. *Opposed to* **confirmation** *and* **disconfirmation.**

relational dialectics theory. A theory that describes relationships as defined by a series of competing opposite desires or motivations, such as the desires for autonomy and belonging, for novelty and predictability, and for closedness and openness.

relation maxim. A **conversational maxim** that holds that speakers cooperate with listeners by talking about what is relevant and by not talking about what isn't.

relationship communication. Communication between or among intimates or those in close relationships; the term is used by some theorists as synonymous with **interpersonal communication.**

relationship development. The initial or beginning stage of a relationship; the stage at which two people begin to form an interpersonal relationship.

relationship maintenance. A condition of relationship stability in which the relationship does not progress or deteriorate significantly; a continuation as opposed to a dissolution (or an intensification) of a relationship.

relationship messages. Messages that comment on the relationship between the speakers rather than on matters external to them.

repair. In the stage model of relationships, a stage in which one or both parties seek to improve the relationship.

resemblance. As a principle of **perception,** the tendency to perceive people or events that are similar in appearance as belonging together.

response. Any bit of overt or covert behavior.

role. The part an individual plays in a group; an individual's function or expected behavior.

rules theory. A theory that describes relationships as interactions governed by a series of rules that a couple agrees to follow. When the rules are followed, the relationship is maintained; when they are broken, the relationship experiences difficulty.

schemata. Ways of organizing perceptions; mental templates or structures that help you organize the millions of items of information you come into contact with every day as well as those you already have in memory; general ideas about groups of people or individuals, about yourself, or about types of social roles. The word *schemata* is the plural of *schema.*

script. A type of schema; an organized body of information about some action, event, or procedure. A script provides a general idea of how some event should play out or unfold, the rules governing the events and their sequence.

secondary territory. An area that does not belong to you but that you've occupied and that is therefore associated with you—for example, the seat you normally take in class.

selective attention. The tendency to attend to those things that you want to see or that you expect to see.

selective exposure. The tendency to expose your senses to certain things and not others, to actively seek out information that supports your beliefs and to actively avoid information that contradicts these beliefs.

selective perception. The tendency to perceive certain things and not others; includes **selective attention** and **selective exposure.**

self-talk. Talk about yourself. *Opposed to* **other talk.**

semantics. The area of language study concerned with meaning.

self-acceptance. Being satisfied with yourself, your virtues and vices, your abilities and limitations.

self-adaptors. Movements that usually satisfy a physical need, especially to make you more comfortable; for example, scratching your head to relieve an itch, moistening your lips because they feel dry, or pushing your hair out of your eyes.

self-attribution. A process through which you seek to account for and understand the reasons and motivations for your own behaviors.

self-awareness. The degree to which you know yourself.

self-concept. Your self-image, the view you have of who you are.

self-disclosure. The process of revealing something about yourself to another; usually refers to information that you'd normally keep hidden.

self-esteem. The value (usually, the positive value) you place on yourself; your self-evaluation.

self-fulfilling prophecy. The situation in which you make a prediction or prophecy and fulfill it yourself—for example, expecting a person to be hostile, you act in a hostile manner toward this person, and in doing so elicit hostile behavior in the person, thus confirming your prophecy that the person will be hostile.

self-monitoring. Manipulating the image you present to others in interpersonal interactions so as to create the most favorable impression of yourself.

self-serving bias. A bias that operates in the self-attribution process, leading you to take credit for the positive consequences of your behaviors and to deny responsibility for the negative consequences.

sexist language. Language derogatory to members of one gender, generally women.

sexual harassment. Unsolicited and unwanted verbal or nonverbal sexual messages.

sharpening. A process of message distortion in which the details of messages, when repeated, are crystallized and heightened.

shyness. A condition of discomfort and uneasiness in interpersonal situations.

signal and noise, relativity of. The principle of verbal interaction that holds that what is signal (meaningful) and what is noise (interference) is relative to the communication analyst, the participants, and the context.

signal reaction. A conditioned response to a signal; a response to some signal that is immediate rather than delayed. *Opposed to* **delayed reaction.**

signal-to-noise ratio. A measure of the relationship between meaningful information (signal) and interference (noise).

silence. The absence of vocal communication; often misunderstood to refer to the absence of communication.

silencers. **Unproductive conflict strategies** (such as crying) that literally silence your opponent.

similarity. A principle of **attraction** holding that you're attracted to qualities similar to your own and to people who are similar to you. *Opposed to* **complementarity.**

slang. Language used by special groups, often not considered standard in general society.

social comparison. The processes by which you compare yourself (for example, your abilities, opinions, and values) with others and then assess and evaluate yourself on the basis of the comparison; one of the sources of **self-concept.**

social distance. The next-to-farthest distance in **proxemics,** ranging from 4 feet to 12 feet; the distance at which business is usually conducted.

social exchange theory. A theory hypothesizing that you cultivate profitable relationships (those in which your rewards are greater than your costs) and that you avoid or terminate unprofitable relationships (those in which your costs exceed your rewards).

social penetration theory. A theory concerned with relationship development from the superficial to the intimate levels (**depth**) and from few to many areas of interpersonal interaction (**breadth**). *See also* **depenetration.**

source. Any person or thing that creates messages; for example, an individual speaking, writing, or gesturing, or a computer solving a problem.

speech. Messages conveyed via a vocal–auditory channel.

spontaneity. The communication pattern in which you say what you're thinking without attempting to develop strategies for control; encourages **supportiveness.** *Opposed to* **strategy.**

stability. Principle of **perception** that states that your perceptions of things and of people are relatively consistent with your previous conceptions.

static evaluation. An orientation that fails to recognize that the world is constantly changing; an attitude that sees people and events as fixed rather than as ever changing.

status. The level a person occupies in a hierarchy relative to the levels occupied by others. In the United States occupation, financial position, age, and educational level are significant determinants of social status.

stereotype. In communication, a fixed impression of a group of people through which we then perceive specific individuals. Stereotypes are most often negative but may also be positive.

stimulus. Any external or internal change that impinges on or arouses an organism.

stimulus–response models of communication. Models of communication that assume that the process of communication is linear, beginning with a stimulus that then leads to a response.

strategy. The use of some plan for control of other members of a communication interaction, often through **manipulation;** often encourages **defensiveness.** *Opposed to* **spontaneity.**

subjectivity. The principle of **perception** that refers to the fact that your perceptions are not objective but are influenced by your wants and needs, expectations and predictions.

superiority. A point of view or attitude that assumes that others are not equal to yourself; encourages **defensiveness.** *Opposed to* **equality.**

supportiveness. An attitude of an individual or an atmosphere in a group that is characterized by **openness,** absence of fear, and a genuine feeling of **equality.** *Opposed to* **defensiveness.**

symmetrical relationship. A relation between two or more persons in which one person's behavior serves as a stimulus for the same type of behavior in the other person(s); for example, a relationship in which anger in one person encourages anger in the other, or in which a critical comment by one person leads the other to respond in kind.

taboo. Forbidden; culturally censored; frowned upon by "polite society." Taboos may include entire topics as well as specific words—for example, death, sex, certain forms of illness, and various words denoting sexual activities and excretory functions.

tactile communication. Communication by touch; communication received by the skin.

temporal communication. The messages that your time orientation and treatment of time communicate.

territorial encroachment. The trespassing on, use of, or appropriation of one person's territory by another.

territoriality. A possessive or ownership reaction to an area of space or to particular objects.

theory. A general statement or principle applicable to related phenomena.

touch avoidance. The tendency to avoid touching and being touched by others.

transactional view. A view of communication as an ongoing process in which all elements are interdependent and influence one another.

uncertainty reduction theory. Theory that as interpersonal relationships develop, uncertainty is reduced; **relationship development** is seen as a process of reducing uncertainty about each other.

universal of interpersonal communication. A feature of communication common to all interpersonal communication acts.

unproductive conflict strategies. Ways of engaging in conflict that generally prove counterproductive; for example, avoidance, force, blame, silencers, gunnysacking, manipulation, personal rejection, and fighting below the belt.

upward communication. Communication sent from the lower levels of a hierarchy to the upper levels—for example, from line worker to manager or from faculty member to dean.

value. Relative worth of an object; a quality that makes something desirable or undesirable; ideal or custom about which we have emotional responses, whether positive or negative.

verbal aggressiveness. A method of arguing in which one person attacks the other person's **self-concept.**

visual dominance. The use of your eyes to maintain a superior or dominant position; for example, when making an especially important point, you might look intently at the other person.

voice qualities. Aspects of **paralanguage**—specifically, pitch range, lip control, glottis control, pitch control, articulation control, rhythm control, resonance, and tempo.

volume. In relation to **voice qualities,** the relative loudness of the voice.

you-messages. Messages in which you deny responsibility for your own thoughts and behaviors; messages that attribute your **perception** to another person; messages of blame. *Opposed to* **I-messages.**

Glossary of Interpersonal Communication Skills

abstractions. Use both abstract and specific terms when describing or explaining.

accommodation. Accommodate to the speaking style of your listeners in moderation. Too much mirroring of the other's style may appear manipulative.

active and inactive listening. Be an active listener: paraphrase the speaker's meaning, express understanding of the speaker's feelings, and ask questions when necessary.

active interpersonal conflict. Engage in interpersonal conflict actively; be appropriately revealing, and listen to your partner.

advantages and disadvantages of relationships. In evaluating, entering, or dissolving relationships, consider both the advantages and the disadvantages.

allness. Avoid allness statements; they invariably misstate the reality and will often offend the other person.

analyzing your perceptions. Increase accuracy in interpersonal perception by identifying the influence of your physical and emotional states and making sure that you're not drawing conclusions from too little information.

anger management. Calm down as best you can; then consider your communication options and the relevant communication skills for expressing your feelings.

appreciating cultural differences. Look at cultural differences not as deviations or deficiencies but as the differences they are. Recognizing different ways of doing things, however, does not necessarily mean accepting them.

appropriateness of self-disclosure. When thinking of disclosing, consider the legitimacy of your motives, the appropriateness of the disclosure, the listener's responses (is the dyadic effect operating?), and the potential burdens such disclosures might impose.

argumentativeness. Avoid aggressiveness (attacking the other person's self-concept); instead, focus logically on the issues, emphasize finding solutions, and work to ensure that what is said will result in positive self-feelings for both individuals.

artifactual communication. Use artifacts (for example, color, clothing, body adornment, space decoration) to communicate desired messages.

body movements. Use body and hand gestures to reinforce your communication purposes.

channel. Assess your channel options (for example, face-to-face, e-mail, leaving a voicemail message) before communicating important messages.

checking perceptions. Increase accuracy in perception by: (1) describing what you see or hear and the meaning you assign to it and (2) asking the other person if your perceptions are accurate.

communicating assertively. Describe the problem, say how the problem affects you, propose solutions, confirm your understanding, and reflect on your own assertiveness.

communicating power. Avoid powerless message forms such as hesitations, excessive intensifiers, disqualifiers, tag questions, one-word answers, self-critical statements, overly polite statements, and vulgar and slang expressions.

communication apprehension management. To reduce anxiety acquire necessary communication skills and experiences, focus on prior successes, reduce unpredictability, and put apprehension in perspective.

communication options. In light of the inevitability, irreversibility, and unrepeatability of messages, assess your communication options before communicating.

confirmation. When you wish to be confirming, acknowledge (verbally and/or nonverbally) others in your group and their contributions.

conflict styles. Chose your conflict style carefully; each style has consequences. In relationship conflict, look for win–win solutions rather than solutions in which one person wins and the other loses.

conflict, culture, and gender. Approach conflict with an understanding of the cultural and gender differences in attitudes toward what constitutes conflict and toward how it should be pursued.

connotative meanings. Clarify your connotative meanings if you have any doubts that your listeners might misunderstand you; as a listener, ask questions if you have doubts about the speaker's connotations.

content and relationship. Listen to both the content and the relationship aspects of messages, distinguish between them, and respond to both.

content and relationship conflicts. Analyze conflict messages in terms of content and relationship dimensions, and respond to each accordingly.

context adjustment. Adjust your messages to the physical, cultural, social–psychological, and temporal context.

conversational maxims. Follow (generally) the basic maxims of conversation, such as the maxims of quantity, quality, relations, manner, and politeness.

conversational rules. Observe the general rules for conversation (for example, keeping speaking turns relatively short and avoiding interrupting), but break them when there seems logical reason to do so.

conversational turns. Maintain relatively short conversational turns; after taking your turn, pass the speaker's turn to another person nonverbally or verbally.

cultural differences in listening. Be especially flexible when listening in a multicultural setting, realizing that people from other cultures give different listening cues and may operate with different rules for listening.

cultural identifiers. Use cultural identifiers that are sensitive to the desires of others; when appropriate, make clear the cultural identifiers you prefer.

cultural influences. Communicate with an understanding that culture influences communication in all its forms.

cultural influences on interpersonal relationships. Culture exerts influences on all types of relationships, encouraging some and discouraging others.

cultural sensitivity. Increase your cultural sensitivity by learning about different cultures, recognizing and facing your fears, recognizing relevant differences, and becoming conscious of the cultural rules of other cultures.

culture and perception. Increase accuracy in perception by learning as much as you can about the cultures of those with whom you interact.

dating statements. Date your statements to avoid thinking of the world as static and unchanging. Reflect the inevitability of change in your messages.

deciding to self-disclose. Consider the potential benefits (for example, self-knowledge, increased communication effectiveness, and physiological health) as well as the potential personal, relationship, and professional risks.

disclaimers. Use disclaimers if you feel you might be misunderstood. But avoid them when they're not necessary; too many disclaimers can make you appear unprepared or unwilling to state an opinion.

disconfirming language. Avoid sexist, heterosexist, racist, and ageist language, which is disconfirming and insulting and invariably creates communication barriers.

emotional communication. Communicate emotions effectively: (1) Describe feelings, (2) identify the reasons for the feelings, (3) anchor feelings to the present, and (4) own your feelings and messages.

emotional display. Express emotions and interpret the emotions of others in light of the cultural rules dictating what is and what isn't "appropriate."

emotionality in interpersonal communication. Recognize the inevitable emotionality in your thoughts and feelings, and include emotion as appropriate in your verbal and nonverbal messages.

emotional understanding. Identify and describe emotions (both positive and negative) clearly and specifically. Learn the vocabulary of emotional expression.

empathic and objective listening. Punctuate the interaction from the speaker's point of view, engage in dialogue, and seek to understand the speaker's thoughts and feelings.

empathic conflict. Engage in conflict with empathy rather than blame. Also, express this empathy ("I can understand how you must have felt").

empathy. Communicate empathy when appropriate: Resist evaluating the person, focus on the person, express active involvement through facial expressions and gestures, reflect back the feelings you think are being expressed, self-disclose, and address mixed messages.

ethnocentric thinking. Recognize your own ethnocentric thinking and be aware of how it influences your verbal and nonverbal messages.

evaluating. Try first to understand fully what the speaker means and then look to identify any biases or self-interests that might lead the speaker to give an unfair presentation.

expressiveness. Communicate active involvement by using active listening, addressing mixed messages, using I-messages, and using appropriate variations in paralanguage and gestures.

eye movements. Use eye movements to seek feedback, exchange conversational turns, signal the nature of your relationship, or compensate for increased physical distance.

face-saving strategies. Use strategies that allow your opponents to save face; avoid beltlining, or hitting opponents with attacks that they will have difficulty absorbing and will resent.

facial messages. Use facial expressions to communicate involvement. In listening, look to the facial expressions of others as cues to their emotions and meaning.

facts and inferences. Distinguish facts (verifiably true past events) from inferences (guesses or hypotheses), and act on inferences with tentativeness.

feedback. Listen to both verbal and nonverbal feedback—from yourself and from others—and use these cues to help you adjust your messages.

feedforward. Use feedforward when you feel your listener needs background or when you want to ease into a particular topic, such as bad news.

flexibility. Because no two communication situations are identical, because everything is in a state of flux, and because everyone is different, cultivate flexibility and adjust your communication to the unique situation.

friendships. Establish friendships to help serve such needs as utility, ego support, stimulation, and security. At the same time, seek to serve your friends' similar needs.

fundamental attribution error. Avoid the fundamental attribution error, whereby you attribute someone's behavior solely to internal factors while minimizing or ignoring situational forces.

gender differences in listening. Understand that in general, women give more cues that they're listening and appear more supportive in their listening than men.

giving space. Give others the space they need. Look to the other person for any signs of spatial discomfort.

high- and low-context cultures. Adjust your messages and your listening in light of the differences between high- and low-context cultures.

I-messages. Use I-messages when communicating your feelings; take responsibility for your own feelings rather than attributing them to others.

immediacy. Maintain immediacy through close physical distances and eye contact and by smiling, using the other person's name, and focusing on the other's remarks.

implicit personality theory. Bring your implicit personality theory to your mindful state to subject your perceptions and conclusions to logical analysis.

increasing assertiveness. Increase assertiveness by analyzing the assertive messages of others, rehearsing assertive messages, and communicating assertively.

indirect messages. Use indirect messages when a more direct style might prove insulting or offensive, but be aware that they may create misunderstanding.

indiscrimination. Treat each situation and each person as unique (when possible) even when they're covered by the same label. Index key concepts.

individualist and collectivist cultures. Adjust your messages and your listening with an awareness of differences between individualist and collectivist cultures.

initial impressions. Guard against drawing impressions too quickly or from too little information and using initial impressions as filters; such filters can prevent you from forming more accurate perceptions on the basis of more information.

intensional orientation. Avoid intensional orientation. Look to people and things first and to labels second.

interaction management. Speak in relatively short conversational turns, avoid long and/or frequent pauses, and use verbal and nonverbal messages that are consistent.

intercultural communication. Become mindful of (1) differences between yourself and people who are culturally different, (2) differences within other cultural groups, and (3) cultural differences in meanings.

listening to the feelings of others. Empathize, focus on the other person, and encourage the person to explore his or her feelings.

making excuses. Repair conversational problems by offering excuses that demonstrate understanding, acknowledge your responsibility, acknowledge your regret, request forgiveness, and make clear that this will never happen again.

managing relationship dissolution. Break the loneliness–depression cycle, take time out, bolster self-esteem, seek support from nourishing others, and avoid repeating negative patterns.

masculine and feminine cultures. Adjust your messages and your listening to allow for differences in cultural masculinity and femininity.

meanings depend on context. Look at the context for cues as to how you should interpret the meanings of messages.

meanings in people. When deciphering meaning, the best source is the person; meanings are in people. When in doubt, find out—from the source.

message overload. Combat message overload by using and disposing of messages as they come to you, organizing, getting rid of extra copies, and distinguishing between messages to save and messages to throw away.

metacommunication. Metacommunicate when you want to clarify the way you're talking or what you're talking about by, for example, giving clear feedforward and paraphrasing your complex messages.

mindfulness. Increase your mindfulness by creating and recreating categories and being open to new information and points of view; also, beware of relying too heavily on first impressions.

negatives and positives of conflict. Approach conflict to minimize its negative aspects and to maximize the positive benefits of conflict and its resolution.

networking. Establish a network of relationships to provide insights into issues relevant to your personal and professional life, and be willing to lend your expertise to others.

noise management. Reduce physical, physiological, psychological, and semantic noise as best you can; use repetition and restatement and, when in doubt, ask if you're clear.

nonjudgmental and critical listening. Keep an open mind, avoid filtering out difficult messages, and recognize your own biases. When listening to make judgments, listen extra carefully, ask questions when in doubt, and check your perceptions before criticizing.

nonverbal communication and culture. Interpret the nonverbal cues of others with an awareness of the other person's cultural meanings (insofar as you can).

open expression in conflict. Try to express your feelings openly rather than resorting to silence or avoidance.

openness. Increase openness when appropriate by self-disclosing, responding spontaneously and honestly to those with whom you're interacting, and owning your own feelings and thoughts.

other orientation. Acknowledge the importance of the other person: use focused eye contact and appropriate facial expressions; smile, nod, and lean toward the other person.

overattribution. Avoid overattribution; rarely is any one factor an accurate explanation of complex human behavior.

packaging. Make your verbal and nonverbal messages consistent; inconsistencies often create uncertainty and misunderstanding.

paralanguage. Vary paralinguistic features to communicate nuances of meaning and to add interest and color to your messages.

perceptual shortcuts. Be mindful of your perceptual shortcuts so that they don't mislead you and result in inaccurate perceptions.

polarization. Avoid thinking and talking in extremes by using middle terms and qualifiers. But remember that too many qualifiers may make you appear unsure of yourself.

positiveness. Communicate positiveness by expressing your own satisfaction with the interaction and by complimenting others.

power distance. Adjust your messages and listening on the basis of the power-distance orientation of the culture in which you find yourself.

power plays. Respond to power plays with cooperative strategies: Express your feelings, describe the behavior to which you object, and state a cooperative response.

present-focus conflict. Focus your conflict resolution messages on the present; avoid gunnysacking, or dredging up and unloading old grievances.

problem-solving conflicts. Deal with interpersonal conflicts systematically as problems to be solved: Define the problem, examine possible solutions, test a solution, evaluate the solution, and accept or reject the solution.

receiving. Focus attention on both the verbal and the nonverbal messages; both communicate essential parts of the total meaning.

reducing uncertainty. Use passive, active, and interactive strategies to reduce uncertainty.

relationship messages. Formulate messages that are appropriate to the stage of the relationship. Also, listen to messages from relationship partners that may reveal differences in perceptions about your relationship stage.

relationship repair. Recognize the problem, engage in productive conflict resolution, pose possible solutions, affirm each other, integrate solutions into normal behavior, and take risks as appropriate.

remembering. Identify the central ideas, summarize the message in an easier-to-retain form, and repeat ideas (aloud or to yourself) to help you remember.

responding. Express support for the speaker using I-messages instead of you-messages.

responding to others' disclosures. Listen actively, support the discloser, and keep the disclosures confidential.

romantic workplace relationships. Establish romantic relationships at work with a clear understanding of the potential problems.

self-awareness. Increase self-awareness by listening to others, increasing your open self, and seeking out information to reduce blind spots.

self-concept. See yourself, as objectively as you can, through the eyes of others; compare yourself to similar (and admired) others; examine the influences of culture; and observe and evaluate your own message behaviors.

self-esteem. Raise your self-esteem: Challenge self-destructive beliefs, seek out nourishing people, work on projects that will result in success, and secure affirmation.

self-fulfilling prophecy. Take a second look at your perceptions when they correspond very closely to your initial expectations; the self-fulfilling prophecy may be at work.

self-serving bias. Become mindful of giving too much weight to internal factors (when explaining your positives) and too little weight to external factors (when explaining your negatives).

sexual harassment management. Talk to the harasser; if this doesn't stop the behavior, then consider collecting evidence, using appropriate channels within the organization, and filing a complaint.

sexual harassment messages. Avoid behaviors that are sexual in nature, that might be considered unreasonable, that are severe or pervasive, and that are unwelcome and offensive.

silence. Examine silence for meanings just as you would eye movements or body gestures.

spatial and proxemic conversational distances. Maintain distances that are comfortable and that are appropriate to the situation and to your relationship with the other person.

stereotypes. Focus on the individual rather than on the individual's membership in one group or another.

supportive conflict. Engage in conflict using a supportive approach, so as not to create defensiveness; avoid messages that evaluate or control, that are strategic or inappropriately neutral, or that express superiority or certainty.

surface and depth listening. Focus on both verbal and nonverbal messages, on both content and relationship messages, and on statements that refer back to the speaker. At the same time, do not avoid the surface or literal meaning.

talk, not force. Talk about problems rather than using physical or emotional force.

time cues. Be alert for time cues on the part of the person with whom you're interacting. Be especially sensitive to the person's leave-taking cues—remarks such as "It's getting late" or glances at his or her watch.

touch and touch avoidance. Respect the touch-avoidance tendencies of others; pay special attention to cultural and gender differences in touch preferences.

turn-taking cues. Respond to both the verbal and the nonverbal conversational turn-taking cues given you by others, and make your own cues clear to others.

understanding. Relate new information to what you already know, ask questions, and paraphrase what you think the speaker said to make sure you understand.

Bibliography

Acor, A. A. (2001). Employers' perceptions of persons with body art and an experimental test regarding eyebrow piercing (Doctoral dissertation, Marquette University, 2001). *Dissertation Abstracts International: Section B. The Sciences and Engineering, 61,* 3885.

Adrianson, L. (2001). Gender and computer-mediated communication: Group processes in problem solving. *Computers in Human Behavior, 17,* 71–94.

Albas, Daniel C., McCluskey, Ken W., & Albas, Cheryl A. (1976, December). Perception of the emotional content of speech: A comparison of two Canadian groups. *Journal of Cross-Cultural Psychology, 7,* 481–490.

Albert, Rosita, & Nelson, Gayle L. (1993, Winter). Hispanic/Anglo American differences in attributions to paralinguistic behavior. *International Journal of Intercultural Relations, 17,* 19–40.

Alberti, Robert (Ed.). (1977). *Assertiveness: Innovations, applications, issues.* San Luis Obispo, CA: Impact.

Alessandra, Tony. (1986). How to listen effectively. *Speaking of Success* (videotape series). San Diego, CA: Levitz Sommer Productions.

Altman, I. (1975). *The environment and social behavior.* Monterey, CA: Brooks/Cole.

Altman, Irwin, & Taylor, Dalmas. (1973). *Social penetration: The development of interpersonal relationships.* New York: Holt, Rinehart & Winston.

Andersen, Peter. (1991). Explaining intercultural differences in nonverbal communication. In Larry A. Samovar & Richard E. Porter (Eds.), *Intercultural communication: A reader* (6th ed., pp. 286–296). Belmont, CA: Wadsworth.

Andersen, Peter A., & Leibowitz, Ken. (1978). The development and nature of the construct touch avoidance. *Environmental Psychology and Nonverbal Behavior, 3,* 89–106.

Anderson, Claire J., & Fisher, Caroline. (1991, August). Male-female relationships in the workplace: Perceived motivations in office romance. *Sex Roles, 25,* 163–180.

Angier, N. (1995, May 9). Scientists mull role of empathy in man and beast. *New York Times,* C1, C6.

Argyle, M., & Ingham, R. (1972). Gaze, mutual gaze and distance. *Semiotica, 1,* 32–49.

Argyle, Michael. (1988). *Bodily communication* (2nd ed.). New York: Methuen.

Argyle, Michael, & Henderson, Monika. (1985). *The anatomy of relationships: And the rules and skills needed to manage them successfully.* London: Heinemann.

Aronson, E., Wilson, T. D., & Akert, R. M. (1999). *Social psychology* (3rd ed.). Boston: Allyn & Bacon.

Aronson, J., Cohen, J., & Nail, P. (1998). Self-affirmation theory: An update and appraisal. In E. Harmon-Jones & J. S. Mills (Eds.), *Cognitive dissonance theory: Revival with revisions and controversies.* Washington, DC: American Psychological Association.

Asch, Solomon. (1946). Forming impressions of personality. *Journal of Abnormal and Social Psychology, 41,* 258–290.

Ashcraft, Mark H. (1998). *Fundamentals of cognition.* New York: Longman.

Aspinwall, L. G., & Taylor, S. E. (1993). Effects of social comparison direction, threat, and self-esteem on affect, evaluation, and expected success. *Journal of Personality and Social Psychology 64,* 708–722.

Aune, Krystyna-Strzyzewski, Buller, David B., & Aune, R. Kelly. (1996, September). Display rule development in romantic relationships: Emotion management and perceived appropriateness of emotions across relationship stages. *Human Communication Research, 23,* 115–145.

Aune, R. Kelly, & Kikuchi, Toshiyuki. (1993, September). Effects of language intensity similarity on perceptions of credibility, relational attributions, and persuasion. *Journal of Language and Social Psychology, 12,* 224–238.

Authier, J., & Gustafson, K. (1982). *Microtraining: Focusing on specific skills.* In E. K. Marshall, P. D. Kurtz, and Associates (Eds.), *Interpersonal helping skills: A guide to training methods, programs, and resources* (pp. 93–130). San Francisco: Jossey-Bass.

Axtell, Roger. (1993). *Do's and taboos around the world* (3rd ed.). New York: Wiley.

Axtell, Roger E. (1990). *Do's and taboos of hosting international visitors.* New York: Wiley.

Ayres, Joe, & Hopf, Tim. (1993). *Coping with speech anxiety.* Norwood, NJ: Ablex.

Ayres, Joe, & Hopf, Tim. (1995, Fall). An assessment of the role of communication apprehension in communicating with the terminally ill. *Communication Research Reports, 12,* 227–234.

Babcock, J. C., Waltz, J., Jacobson, N. S., & Gottman, J. M. (1993, February). Power and violence: The relation between communication patterns, power discrepancies, and domestic violence. *Journal of Marriage and the Family, 60,* 70–78.

Bach, George R., & Wyden, Peter. (1968). *The intimacy enemy.* New York: Avon.

Balswick, J. O., & Peck, C. (1971). The inexpressive male: A tragedy of American society? *The Family Coordinator, 20,* 363–368.

Barbato, Carole A., & Perse, Elizabeth M. (1992, August). Interpersonal communication motives and the life position of elders. *Communication Research, 19,* 516–531.

Baringer, D. K., & McCroskey, J. C. (2000). Immediacy in the classroom: Student immediacy. *Communication Education, 49,* 178–186.

Barker, Larry, Edwards, Renee, Gaines, C., Gladney, K., & Holley, F. (1980). An investigation of proportional time spent in various communication activities by college students. *Journal of Applied Communication Research, 8,* 101–109.

Barker, L. L., & Gaut, D. (2002). *Communication* (8th ed.). Boston: Allyn & Bacon.

Barna, L. M. (1997). Stumbling blocks in intercultural communication. In L. A. Samovar & R. E. Porter (Eds.), *Intercultural communication: A reader* (7th ed., pp. 337–346). Belmont, CA: Wadsworth.

Barrett, L., & Godfrey, T. (1988, November). Listening. *Person Centered Review, 3,* 410–425.

Barta, Patrick. (1999, December 16). Sex differences in the inferior parietal lobe. *Cerebral Cortex.* Http://www.wired.com/news/technology/0,1282,33033,00.html.

Basso, K. H. (1972). To give up on words: Silence in Apache culture. In Pier Paolo Giglioli (Ed.), *Language and social context.* New York: Penguin.

Baumeister, R. F., Bushman, B. J., & Campbell, W. K. (2000, February). Self-esteem, narcissism, and aggression: Does violence result from low self-esteem or from threatened egotism? *Current Directions in Psychological Science, 9,* 26–29.

Baxter, Leslie A. (1988). A dialectical perspective on communication strategies in relationship development. In Steve W. Duck (Ed.), *Handbook of Personal Relationships.* New York: Wiley.

Baxter, Leslie A. (1990, February). Dialectical contradictions in relationship development. *Journal of Social and Personal Relationships, 7,* 69–88.

Baxter, Leslie A., & Simon, Eric P. (1993, May). Relationship maintenance strategies and dialectical contradictions in personal relationships. *Journal of Social and Personal Relationships*, 10, 225–242.

Baxter, Leslie A., & Wilmot, W. W. (1984). "Secret tests": Social strategies for acquiring information about the state of the relationship. *Human Communication Research, 11,* 171–201.

Beach, Wayne A. (1990–1991). Avoiding ownership for alleged wrongdoings. *Research on Language and Social Interaction, 24,* 1–36.

Beatty, Michael J. (1988). Situational and predispositional correlates of public speaking anxiety. *Communication Education,* 37: 28–39.

Bedford, Victoria Hilkevitch. (1996). Relationships between adult siblings. In Ann Elisabeth Auhagen & Maria von Salisch (Eds.), *The diversity of human relationships* (pp. 120–140). New York: Cambridge University Press.

Beebe, Steven A., & Masterson, John T. (2000). *Communicating in small groups: Principles and practices* (6th ed.). New York: Longman.

Behzadi, Kavous G. (1994, September). Interpersonal conflict and emotions in an Iranian cultural practice: *Qahr* and *Ashti. Culture, Medicine, and Psychiatry, 18,* 321–359.

Beier, Ernst. (1974). How we send emotional messages. *Psychology Today, 8,* 53–56.

Bell, Robert A., & Buerkel-Rothfuss, N. L. (1990). S(he) loves me, s(he) loves me not: Predictors of relational information-seeking in courtship and beyond. *Communication Quarterly, 38,* 64–82.

Bell, R. A., & Daly, J. A. (1984). The affinity-seeking function of communication. *Communication Monographs, 51,* 91–115.

Berg, John H., & Archer, Richard L. (1983). The disclosure-liking relationship. *Human Communication Research, 10,* 269–281.

Berger, Charles R., & Bradac, James J. (1982). *Language and social knowledge: Uncertainty in interpersonal relations.* London: Edward Arnold.

Berger, Charles R., & Calabrese, Richard J. (1975, Winter). Some explorations in initial interaction and beyond: Toward a theory of interpersonal communication. *Human Communication Research, 1,* 99–112.

Bernstein, W. M., Stephan, W. G., & Davis, M. H. (1979). Explaining attributions for achievement: A path analytic approach. *Journal of Personality and Social Psychology, 37,* 1810–1821.

Berry, J. W., Poortinga, Y. H., Segall, M. H., & Dasen, P. R. (1992). *Cross-cultural psychology: Research and applications.* Cambridge: Cambridge University Press.

Berscheid, E., & Reis, H. T. (1998). Attraction and close relationships. In D. Gilbert, S. Fiske, & G. Lindzey (Eds.), *The handbook of social psychology* (4th ed., Vol. 2, pp. 193–281). New York: W. H. Freeman.

Bierhoff, Hans W., & Klein, Renate. (1991, March). Dimensionen der Liebe: Entwicklung einer Deutschsprachigen Skala zur Erfassung von Liebesstilen. *Zeitschrift for Differentielle und Diagnostische Psychologie, 12,* 53–71.

Bishop, Jerry E. (1993, April 7). New research suggests that romance begins by falling nose over heels in love. *Wall Street Journal,* B1.

Blake, R. R., & Mouton, J. S. (1985). *The managerial grid III* (3rd ed.). Houston, TX: Gulf Publishing.

Blieszner, Rosemary, & Adams, Rebecca G. (1992). *Adult friendship.* Thousand Oaks, CA: Sage.

Blumstein, Philip, & Schwartz, Pepper. (1983). *American couples: Money, work, sex.* New York: Morrow.

Bochner, Arthur. (1984). The functions of human communication in interpersonal bonding. In Carroll C. Arnold & John Waite Bowers (Eds.), *Handbook of rhetorical and communication theory.* Boston: Allyn & Bacon.

Bochner, Arthur, & Kelly, Clifford. (1974). Interpersonal competence: Rationale, philosophy, and implementation of a conceptual framework. *Communication Education, 23,* 279–301.

Bochner, Arthur P., & Yerby, Janet. (1977). Factors affecting instruction in interpersonal competence. *Communication Education, 26,* 91–103.

Bochner, Stephen, & Hesketh, Beryl. (1994, June). Power distance, individualism/collectivism, and job-related attitudes in a culturally diverse work group. *Journal of Cross-Cultural Psychology, 25,* 233–257.

Bok, Sissela. (1978). *Lying: Moral choice in public and private life.* New York: Pantheon.

Bok, Sissela. (1983). *Secrets.* New York: Vintage Books.

Boneva, B., Kraut, R., & Frohlich, D. (2001). Using e-mail for personal relationships: The difference gender makes. *American Behavioral Scientist, 45,* 530–549.

Borden, George A. (1991). *Cultural orientation: An approach to understanding intercultural communication.* Englewood Cliffs, NJ: Prentice-Hall.

Bosmajian, Haig. (1974). *The language of oppression.* Washington, DC: Public Affairs Press.

Bourland, D. D., Jr. (1965–66). A linguistic note: Writing in e-prime. *General Semantics Bulletin 32–33,* 111–114.

Bower, B. (2001). Self-illusions come back to bite students. *Science News, 159,* 148.

Bravo, Ellen, & Cassedy, Ellen. (1992). *The 9 to 5 guide to combating sexual harassment.* New York: Wiley.

Bresnahan, Mary I., & Cai, Deborah H. (1996, March/April). Gender and aggression in the recognition of interruption. *Discourse Processes, 21,* 171–189.

Bridges, Carl R. (1996, July). The characteristics of career achievement perceived by African American college administrators. *Journal of Black Studies, 26,* 748–767.

Briton, Nancy J., & Hall, Judith A. (1995, January). Beliefs about female and male nonverbal communication. *Sex Roles, 32,* 79–90.

Brody, Jane E. (1991, April 28). How to foster self-esteem. *New York Times Magazine,* 26–27.

Brody, Jane E. (1994, March 21). Notions of beauty transcend culture, new study suggests. *The New York Times,* p. A14.

Brody, Leslie R. (1985, June). Gender differences in emotional development: A review of theories and research. *Journal of Personality, 53,* 102–149.

Brown, P. (1980). How and why are women more polite: Some evidence from a Mayan community. In S. McConnell-Ginet, R. Borker, & M. Furman (Eds.), *Women and language in literature and society* (pp. 111–136). New York: Praeger.

Brown, Penelope, & Levinson, S. C. (1987). *Politeness: Some universals of language usage.* Cambridge, UK: Cambridge University Press.

Brownell, J. (1987). Listening: The toughest management skill. *Cornell Hotel and Restaurant Administration Quarterly, 27,* 64–71.

Brownell, J. (2002). *Listening: Attitudes, principles, and skills* (2nd ed). Boston: Allyn & Bacon.

Bruneau, Tom. (1985). The time dimension in intercultural communication. In Larry A. Samovar & Richard E. Porter (Eds.), *Intercultural communication: A reader* (4th ed., pp. 280–289). Belmont, CA: Wadsworth.

Bruneau, Tom. (1990). Chronemics: The study of time in human interaction. In Joseph A. DeVito & Michael L. Hecht (Eds.), *The nonverbal communication reader* (pp. 301–311). Prospect Heights, IL: Waveland Press.

Buber, M. (1958). *I and thou* (2nd ed.). New York: Scribners.

Buller, David B., & Aune, R. Kelly. (1992, Winter). The effects of speech rate similarity on compliance: Application of communication accommodation theory. *Western Journal of Communication, 56,* 37–53.

Buller, David B., LePoire, Beth A., Aune, Kelly, & Eloy, Sylvie. (1992, December). Social perceptions as mediators of the effect of speech rate similarity on compliance. *Human communication research, 19,* 286–311.

Burgoon, J. K., & Bacue, A. E. (2003). Nonverbal communication skills. In J. O. Greene & B. R. Burleson (Eds.), *Handbook of communication and social interaction skills* (pp. 179–220). Mahwah, NJ: Erlbaum.

Burgoon, J. K., Berger, C. R., & Waldron, V. R. (2000). Mindfulness and interpersonal communication. *Journal of Social Issues, 56,* 105–127.

Burgoon, Judee K., Buller, David B., & Woodall, W. Gill. (1996). *Nonverbal communication: The unspoken dialogue* (2nd ed.). New York: McGraw-Hill.

Burgoon, J. K., & Hoobler, G. D. (2002). Nonverbal signals. In M. L. Knapp & J. A. Daly (Eds.), *Handbook of interpersonal communication* (3rd ed., pp. 240–299). Thousand Oaks, CA: Sage.

Burleson, B. R. (2003). Emotional support skills. In J. O. Greene & B. R. Burleson (Eds.), *Handbook of communication and social interaction skills* (pp. 551–594). Mahwah, NJ: Erlbaum.

Bushman, B. J., & Baumeister, R. F. (1998). Threatened egotism, narcissism, self-esteem, and direct and displaced aggression: Does self-love or self-hate lead to violence? *Journal of Personality and Social Psychology, 75,* 219–229.

Butler, P. E. (1981). *Talking to yourself: Learning the language of self-support.* New York: Harper & Row.

Byers, E. Sandra, & Demmons, Stephanie. (1999, May). Sexual satisfaction and sexual self-disclosure within dating relationships. *Journal of Sex Research, 36,* 180–189.

Cai, D. A., & Fink, E. L. (2002, March). Conflict style differences between individualists and collectivists. *Communication Monographs, 69,* 67–87.

Canary, D. J. (2003). Managing interpersonal conflict: A model of events related to strategic choices. In J. O. Greene & B. R. Burleson (Eds.), *Handbook of communication and social interaction skills* (pp. 515–550). Mahwah, NJ: Erlbaum.

Canary, D. J., & Hause, K. (1993). Is there any reason to research sex differences in communication? *Communication Quarterly, 41,* 129–144.

Canary, Daniel, Cupach, William R., & Messman, Susan J. (1995). *Relationship conflict.* Thousand Oaks, CA: Sage.

Cappella, Joseph N. (1993, March–June). The facial feedback hypothesis in human interaction: Review and speculation. *Journal of Language and Social Psychology, 12,* 13–29.

Carducci, B. J., with Zimbardo, P. G. (1996, November–December). Are you shy? *Psychology Today, 28,* 34–41, 64–70, 78–82.

Carli, Linda L. (1999, Spring). Gender, interpersonal power, and social influence. *Journal of Social Issues, 55,* 81–99.

Carroll, D. W. (1994). *Psychology of language* (2nd ed.). Pacific Grove, CA: Brooks/Cole.

Castleberry, S. B., & Shepherd, C. D. (1993). Effective interpersonal listening and personal selling. *Journal of personal selling and sales management, 13,* 35–49.

Cate, R., Henton, J., Koval, J., Christopher, R., & Lloyd, S. (1982). Premarital abuse: A social psychological perspective. *Journal of Family Issues, 3,* 79–90.

Cawthon, S. W. (2001). Teaching strategies in inclusive classrooms with deaf students. *Journal of Deaf Studies and Deaf Education, 6,* 212–225.

Chang, Hui-Ching, & Holt, G. Richard. (1996, Winter). The changing Chinese interpersonal world: Popular themes in interpersonal communication books in modern Taiwan. *Communication Quarterly, 44,* 85–106.

Chanowitz, B., & Langer, E. (1981). Premature cognitive commitment. *Journal of Personality and Social Psychology, 41,* 1051–1063.

Chen, Guo-Ming. (1992). Differences in self-disclosure patterns among Americans versus Chinese: A comparative study. Paper presented at the annual meeting of the Eastern Communication Association, Portland, ME.

Chen, Ling. (1993, Summer). Chinese and North Americans: An epistemological exploration of intercultural communication. *Howard Journal of Communications, 4,* 342–357.

Cherulnik, Paul D. (1979, August). Sex differences in the expression of emotion in a structured social encounter. *Sex Roles, 5,* 413–424.

Chesebro, J. L., & McCroskey, J. C. (1998, Fall). The relationship of teacher clarity and teacher immediacy with students' experiences of state receiver apprehension. *Communication Quarterly, 46,* 446–456.

Christie, Richard. (1970). Scale construction. In R. Christie & F. L. Geis (Eds.), *Studies in Machiavellianism* (pp. 35–52). New York: Academic Press.

Chung, L. C., & Ting-Toomey, S. (1999, Spring). Ethnic identity and relational expectations among Asian Americans. *Communication Research Reports, 16,* 157–166.

Cline, M. G. (1956). The influence of social context on the perception of faces. *Journal of Personality, 2,* 142–185.

Coates, J., & Cameron, D. (1989). *Women, men, and language: Studies in language and linguistics.* London: Longman.

Coats, Erik J., & Feldman, Robert S. (1996, October). Gender differences in nonverbal correlates of social status. *Personality and Social Psychology Bulletin, 22,* 1014–1022.

Cody, M. J. (1982). A typology of disengagement strategies and an examination of the role intimacy, reactions to inequity, and relational problems play in strategy selection. *Communication Monographs, 49,* 148–170.

Cohen, Joyce. (2001, January 18). On the Internet, love really is blind. *The New York Times,* pp. G1, G9.

Cohen, J. (2002, May 9). An e-mail affliction: The long goodbye. *The New York Times,* p. G6.

Coleman, P. (2002). *How to say it for couples: Communicating with tenderness, openness, and honesty.* Paramus, NJ: Prentice-Hall.

Collier, Mary Jane. (1991). Conflict competence within African, Mexican, and Anglo American friendships. In Stella Ting-Toomey & Felipe Korzenny (Eds.), *Cross-cultural interpersonal communication* (pp. 132–154). Newbury Park, CA: Sage.

Collins, Nancy L., & Miller, Lynn Carol. (1994, November). Self-disclosure and liking: A meta-analytic review. *Psychological Bulletin, 116,* 457–475.

Cooley, Charles Horton. (1922). *Human nature and the social order* (rev. ed.). New York: Scribners.

Coon, Christine A., & Schwanenflugel, Paula J. (1996, July/August). Evaluation of interruption behavior by naive encoders. *Discourse Processes, 22,* 1–24.

Cooper, A., & Sportolari, L. (1997). Romance in cyberspace: Understanding online attraction. *Journal of Sex Education and Therapy, 22,* 7–14.

Coover, G. E., & Murphy, S. T. (2000). The communicated self: Exploring the interaction between self and social context. *Human Communication Research, 26,* 125–147.

Cornwell, B., & Lundgren, D. C. (2001). Love on the Internet: Involvement and misrepresentation in romantic relationships in cyberspace vs. realspace. *Computers in Human Behavior, 17,* 197–211.

Darwin, C. (1872). *The expression of the emotions in man and animals.* Chicago: University of Chicago Press (reprinted 1965).

D'Augelli, Anthony R. (1992, September). Lesbian and gay male undergraduates' experiences of harassment and fear on campus. *Journal of Interpersonal Violence, 7,* 383–395.

Davis, Murray S. (1973). *Intimate relations.* New York: Free Press.

Davis, Ossie. (1973). The English language is my enemy. In Joseph A. DeVito (Ed.), *Language: Concepts and processes* (pp. 164–170). Englewood Cliffs, NJ: Prentice-Hall.

Deal, James E., & Wampler, Karen Smith. (1986). Dating violence: The primacy of previous experience. *Journal of Social and Personal Relationships, 3,* 457–471.

Deaux, K., & LaFrance, M. (1998). Gender. In D. Gilbert, S. Fiske & G. Lindzey (Eds.), *The Handbook of Social Psychology, Vol. 1.* (4th ed., pp. 788–828). New York: Freeman.

deBono, Edward. (1987). *The six thinking hats.* New York: Penguin.

DeCecco, John. (1988). Obligation versus aspiration. In John DeCecco (Ed.), *Gay relationships.* New York: Harrington Park Press.

DePaulo, Bella M. (1992). Nonverbal behavior and self-presentation. *Psychological Bulletin, 111,* 203–212.

Derlega, Valerian J., Winstead, Barbara A., Wong, Paul T. P., & Greenspan, Michael. (1987). Self-disclosure and relationship development: An attributional analysis. In Michael E. Roloff & Gerald R. Miller (Eds.), *Interpersonal processes: New directions in communication research* (pp. 172–187). Newbury Park, CA: Sage.

Derlega, V. J., Winstead, B. A., Wong, P. T. P., & Hunter, S. (1985). Gender effects in an initial encounter: A case where men exceed women in disclosure. *Journal of Social and Personal Relationships, 2,* 25–44.

DeTurck, Mark A. (1987). When communication fails: Physical aggression as a compliance-gaining strategy. *Communication Monographs, 54,* 106–112.

DeVito, Joseph A. (1996). *Brainstorms: How to think more creatively about communication (or about anything else).* New York: Longman.

DeVito, Joseph A., & Hecht, Michael L. (Eds.). (1990). *The nonverbal communication reader.* Prospect Heights, IL: Waveland Press.

Dewey, John. (1910). *How we think.* Boston: Heath.

Dillard, J. P., & Marshall, L. J. (2003). Persuasion as a social skill. In J. O. Greene & B. R. Burleson (Eds.), *Handbook of communication and social interaction skills* (pp. 479–514). Mahwah, NJ: Erlbaum.

Dindia, Kathryn, & Fitzpatrick, Mary Anne. (1985). Marital communication: Three approaches compared. In Steve Duck & Daniel Perlman (Eds.), *Understanding personal relationships: An interdisciplinary approach* (pp. 137–158). Thousand Oaks, CA: Sage.

Dindia, K., & Timmerman, L. (2003). Accomplishing romantic relationships. In J. O. Greene & B. R. Burleson (Eds.), *Handbook of communication and social interaction skills* (pp. 685–722). Mahwah, NJ: Erlbaum.

Dion, K., Berscheid, E., & Walster, E. (1972). What is beautiful is good. *Journal of Personality and Social Psychology, 24,* 285–290.

Dion, Karen K., & Dion, Kenneth L. (1993a, Fall). Individualistic and collectivist perspectives on gender and the cultural context of love and intimacy. *Journal of Social Issues, 49,* 53–69.

Dion, Kenneth L., & Dion, Karen K. (1993b, December). Gender and ethnocultural comparisons in styles of love. *Psychology of Women Quarterly, 17,* 464–473.

Dittman, David A. (1997, December). Reexamining curriculum. *The Cornell Hotel and Restaurant Administration Quarterly, 38,* 3.

Dolgin, Kim Gale, & Lindsay, Kristen Renee. (1999, September). Disclosure between college students and their siblings. *Journal of Family Psychology, 13,* 393–400.

Dolgin, Kim G., Meyer, Leslie, & Schwartz, Janet. (1991, September). Effects of gender, target's gender, topic, and self-esteem on disclosure to best and middling friends. *Sex Roles, 25,* 311–329.

Donohue, William A., & Kolt, Robert. (1992). *Managing interpersonal conflict.* Thousand Oaks, CA: Sage.

Douglas, W. (1994). The acquaintanceship process: An examination of uncertainty, information seeking, and social attraction during initial conversation. *Communication Research, 21,* 154–176.

Dovidio, J. F., Gaertner, S. E., Kawakami, K., & Hodson, G. (2002). Why can't we just get along? Interpersonal biases and interracial distrust. *Cultural Diversity and Ethnic Minority Psychology, 8,* 88–102.

Drass, Kriss A. (1986, December). The effect of gender identity on conversation. *Social Psychology Quarterly, 49,* 294–301.

Dresser, Norine. (1996). *Multicultural manners: New rules of etiquette for a changing society.* New York: Wiley.

Dresser, N. (1999). *Multicultural celebrations: Today's rules of etiquette for life's special occasions.* New York: Three Rivers Press.

Drews, D. R., Allison, C. K., & Probst, J. R. (2000). Behavioral and self-concept differences in tattooed and non-tattooed college students. *Psychological Reports, 86,* 475–481.

Dreyfuss, Henry. (1971). *Symbol sourcebook.* New York: McGraw-Hill.

Dsilva, M., & Whyte, L. O. (1998). Cultural differences in conflict styles: Vietnamese refugees and established residents. *The Howard Journal of Communication, 9,* 57–68.

Duncan, S. D., Jr. (1972). Some signals and rules for taking speaking turns in conversation. *Journal of Personality and Social Psychology, 23,* 283–292.

Eckstein, D., & Goldman, A. (2001). The couple's gender-based communication questionnaire (CGCQ). *Family Journal: Counseling and Therapy for Couples and Families, 9,* 62.

Eden, Dov. (1992, Winter). Leadership and expectations: Pygmalion effects and other self-fulfilling prophecies in organizations. *Leadership Quarterly, 3,* 271–305.

Eder, D., & Enke, J. L. (1991). The structure of gossip: Opportunities and constraints on collective expression among adolescents. *American Sociological Review, 56,* 494–508.

Edwards, K., & Smith, E. (1996). A disconfirmation bias in the evaluation of arguments. *Journal of Personality and Social Psychology, 71,* 5–24.

Ehrenhaus, Peter. (1988, March). Silence and symbolic expression. *Communication Monographs, 55,* 41–57.

Einstein, E. (1995). Success or sabotage: Which self-fulfilling prophecy will the stepfamily create? In D. K. Huntley (Ed.), *Understanding stepfamilies: Implications for assessment and treatment.* Alexandria, VA: American Counseling Association.

Ekman, Paul. (1985a). Communication through nonverbal behavior: A source of information about an interpersonal relationship. In S. S. Tomkins & C. E. Izard (Eds.), *Affect, cognition and personality.* New York: Springer.

Ekman, Paul. (1985b). *Telling lies: Clues to deceit in the marketplace, politics, and marriage.* New York: Norton.

Ekman, Paul, & Friesen, Wallace V. (1969). The repertoire of nonverbal behavior: Categories, origins, usage, and coding. *Semiotica, 1,* 49–98.

Ekman, Paul, Friesen, Wallace V., & Ellsworth, Phoebe. (1972). *Emotion in the human face: Guidelines for research and an integration of findings.* New York: Pergamon Press.

Elfenbein, H. A., & Ambady, N. (2002). Is there an in-group advantage in emotion recognition? *Psychological Bulletin, 128,* 243–249.

Ellis, Albert. (1988). *How to stubbornly refuse to make yourself miserable about anything, yes anything.* Secaucus, NJ: Lyle Stuart.

Ellis, Albert, & Harper, Robert A. (1975). *A new guide to rational living.* Hollywood, CA: Wilshire Books.

Elmes, Michael B., & Gemmill, Gary. (1990, February). The psychodynamics of mindlessness and dissent in small groups. *Small Group Research, 21,* 28–44.

Epstein, N., Pretzer, J. L., & Fleming, B. (1987). The role of cognitive appraisal in self-reports of marital communication. *Behavior Therapy, 18,* 51–69.

Epstein, R. M., & Hundert, E. M. (2002). Defining and assessing professional competence. *JAMA: Journal of the American Medical Association, 287,* 226–235.

Eriksen, John, & Lindsay, Jo. (1999). Unmarried cohabitation and family policy: Norway and Australia compared. *Comparative Social Research, 18,* 79–103.

Exline, R. V., Ellyson, S. L., & Long, B. (1975). Visual behavior as an aspect of power role relationships. In P. Pliner, L. Krames, & T. Alloway (Eds.), *Nonverbal communication of aggression.* New York: Plenum.

Fernald, C. D. (1995). When in London . . .: Differences in disability language preferences among English-speaking countries. *Mental Retardation, 33,* 99–103.

Fesko, S. L. (2001, November). Disclosure of HIV status in the workplace: Considerations and strategies. *Health and Social Work, 26,* 235–244.

Festinger, Leon. (1954). A theory of social comparison processes. *Human Relationships, 7,* 117–140.

Field, R. H. G. (1989, March). The self-fulfilling prophecy leader: Achieving the Metharme effect. *Journal of Management Studies, 26,* 151–175.

Fischer, Agneta H. (1993). Sex differences in emotionality: fact or stereotype? *Feminism and Psychology, 3,* 303–318.

Floyd, J. J. (1985). *Listening: A practical approach.* Glenview, IL: Scott, Foresman.

Folger, Joseph P., Poole, Marshall Scott, & Stutman, Randall K. (1997). *Working through conflict: A communication perspective* (3rd ed.). Boston: Allyn & Bacon.

Forbes, G. B. (2001). College students with tattoos and piercings: Motives, family experiences, personality factors, and perception by others. *Psychological Reports, 89,* 774–786.

Franklin, C. W., & Mizell, C. A. (1995). Some factors influencing success among African-American men: A preliminary study. *Journal of Men's Studies, 3,* 191–204.

Fraser, Bruce. (1990, April). Perspectives on politeness. *Journal of Pragmatics, 14,* 219–236.

French, J. R. P., Jr., & Raven, B. (1968). The bases of social power. In Dorwin Cartwright & Alvin Zander (Eds.), *Group dynamics: Research and theory* (3rd ed., pp. 259–269). New York: Harper & Row.

Friedman, Joel, Boumil, Marcia Mobilia, & Taylor, Barbara Ewert. (1992). *Sexual harassment.* Deerfield Beach, FL: Health Communications.

Frone, M. R. (2000). Interpersonal conflict at work and psychological outcomes: Testing a model among young workers. *Journal of Occupational Health Psychology, 5,* 246–255.

Furlow, F. Bryant. (1996, March/April). The smell of love. *Psychology Today, 29,* 38–45.

Furnham, Adrian, & Bochner, Stephen. (1986). *Culture shock: Psychological reactions to unfamiliar environments.* New York: Methuen.

Gable, Myron, Hollon, Charles, & Dangello, Frank. (1992, May). Managerial structuring of work as a moderator of the Machiavellianism and job performance relationship. *Journal of Psychology, 126,* 317–325.

Galvin, Kathleen, & Brommel, Bernard J. (2000). *Family communication: Cohesion and change* (5th ed.). Boston: Allyn & Bacon.

Gamble, T. K., & Gamble, M. W. (2003). *The gender communication connection.* Boston: Houghton Mifflin.

Gelfand, M. J., Nishii, L. H., Holcombe, K. M., Dyer, N., Ohbuchi, K., & Fukuno, M. (2001). Cultural influences on cognitive representations of conflict: Interpretations of conflict episodes in the United States and Japan. *Journal of Applied Psychology, 86,* 1059–1074.

Gelles, R., & Cornell, C. (1985). *Intimate violence in families.* Newbury Park, CA: Sage.

Gibb, J. (1961). Defensive communication. *Journal of Communication, 11,* 141–148.

Giles, Howard, Mulac, Anthony, Bradac, James J., & Johnson, Patricia. (1987). Speech accommodation theory: The first decade and beyond. In Margaret L. McLaughlin (Ed.), *Communication yearbook 10* (pp. 13–48). Thousand Oaks, CA: Sage.

Goffman, Erving. (1967). *Interaction ritual: Essays on face-to-face behavior.* New York: Pantheon.

Goffman, E. (1971). *Relations in public: Microstudies of the public order.* New York: HarperCollins.

Goldin-Meadow, S., Nusbaum, H., Kelly, S. D., & Wagner, S. (2001). Gesture—psychological aspects. *Psychological Science, 12,* 516–522.

Goleman, Daniel. (1995a). *Emotional intelligence.* New York: Bantam.

Goleman, Daniel. (1995b, February 14). For man and beast, language of love shares many traits. *The New York Times,* pp. C1, C9.

Gonzalez, Alexander, & Zimbardo, Philip G. (1985). Time in perspective. *Psychology Today, 19,* 20–26. Reprinted in DeVito & Hecht (1990).

Goode, Erica. (2000, August 8). How culture molds habits of thought. *The New York Times,* pp. F1, F8.

Goodwin, Robin, & Lee, Iona. (1994, September). Taboo topics among Chinese and English friends: A cross-cultural comparison. *Journal of Cross-Cultural Psychology, 25,* 325–338.

Gordon, Thomas. (1975). *P.E.T.: Parent effectiveness training.* New York: New American Library.

Gosling, S. D., Ko, S. J., Mannarelli, T., & Morris, M. E. (2002, March). A room with a cue: Personality judgments based on offices and bedrooms. *Journal of Personality and Social Psychology, 82,* 379–398.

Gottman, J. M. (1993). *What predicts divorce: The relationships between marital processes and marital outcomes.* Hillsdale, NJ: Erlbaum.

Gottman, J. M. (1994). *Why marriages succeed or fail.* New York: Simon & Schuster.

Gottman, John M., & Carrere, S. (1994). Why can't men and women get along? Developmental roots and marital inequities. In D. J. Canary & Laura Stafford (Eds.), *Communication and relational maintenance* (pp. 203–229). San Diego, CA: Academic Press.

Gould, Stephen Jay. (1995, June 7). No more "wretched refuse." *The New York Times,* p. A27.

Graham, E. E. (1994). Interpersonal communication motives scale. In R. B. Rubin, P. Palmgreen, & H. E. Sypher (Eds.), *Communication research measures: A sourcebook* (pp. 211–216). New York: Guilford.

Graham, E. E., Barbato, C. A., & Perse, E. M. (1993). The interpersonal communication motives model. *Communication Quarterly, 41,* 172–186.

Graham, Jean Ann, & Argyle, Michael. (1975, December). The effects of different patterns of gaze, combined with different facial expressions, on impression formation. *Journal of Movement Studies, 1,* 178–182.

Graham, Jean Ann, Bitti, Pio Ricci, & Argyle, Michael. (1975, June). A cross-cultural study of the communication of emotion by facial, and gestural cues. *Journal of Human Movement Studies, 1,* 68–77.

Grandey, Alicia A. (2000, January). Emotion regulation in the workplace: A new way to conceptualize emotional labor. *Journal of Occupational Health and Psychology, 5,* 95–110.

Greif, Esther Blank. (1980). Sex differences in parent-child conversations. *Women's Studies International Quarterly, 3,* 253–258.

Grice, H. P. (1975). Logic and conversation. In P. Cole & J. L. Morgan (Eds.), *Syntax and semantics*: Vol. 3. Speech acts (pp. 41–58). New York: Seminar Press.

Griffin, Em, & Sparks, Glenn G. (1990). Friends forever: A longitudinal exploration of intimacy in same-sex friends and platonic pairs. *Journal of Social and Personal Relationships, 7,* 29–46.

Gross, Ronald. (1991). *Peak learning.* Los Angeles: Jeremy P. Tarcher.

Gross, T., Turner, E., & Cederholm, L. (1987, June). Building teams for global operation. *Management Review,* 32–36.

Gu, Yueguo. (1990, April). Polite phenomena in modern Chinese. *Journal of Pragmatics, 14,* 237–257.

Gudykunst, W., & Nishida, T. (1984). Individual and cultural influence on uncertainty reduction. *Communication Monographs, 51,* 23–36.

Gudykunst, W. B., Nishida, T., & Chua, E. (1987). Perceptions of social penetration in Japanese-North American dyads. *International Journal of Intercultural Relations, 11,* 171–189.

Gudykunst, W., Yang, S., & Nishida, T. (1985). A cross-cultural test of uncertainty reduction theory: Comparisons of acquaintance, friend, and dating relationships in Japan, Korea, and the United States. *Human Communication Research, 11,* 407–454.

Gudykunst, W. B. (1989). Culture and the development of interpersonal relationships. In J. A. Anderson (Ed.), *Communication yearbook 12* (pp. 315–354). Thousand Oaks, CA: Sage.

Gudykunst, W. B. (1991). *Bridging differences: Effective intergroup communication.* Newbury Park, CA: Sage.

Gudykunst, W. B. (1993). Toward a theory of effective interpersonal and intergroup communication: An anxiety/uncertainty management (AUM) perspective. In R. L. Wiseman (Ed.), *Intercultural communication competence.* Thousand Oaks, CA: Sage.

Gudykunst, W. B. (1994). *Bridging differences: Effective intergroup communication* (2nd ed.). Thousand Oaks, CA: Sage.

Gudykunst, W. B. (Ed.). (1983). *Intercultural communication theory: Current perspectives.* Newbury Park, CA: Sage.

Gudykunst, W. B., & Kim, Y. W. (1992). *Communicating with strangers: An approach to intercultural communication* (2nd ed.). New York: Random House.

Guerrero, L. K., DeVito, J. A., & Hecht, M. L. (Eds.). (1999). *The nonverbal communication reader: Classic and contemporary readings* (2nd ed.). Prospect Heights, IL: Waveland Press.

Haar, Birgit Friederike, & Krahe, Barbara. (1999, November). Strategies for resolving interpersonal conflicts in adolescence: A German-Indonesian comparison. *Journal of Cross-Cultural Psychology, 30,* 667–683.

Haar, B. F., & Krabe, B. (1999). Strategies for resolving interpersonal conflicts in adolescence: A German–Indonesian comparison. *Journal of Cross-Cultural Psychology, 30,* 667–683.

Hajek, C., & Giles, H. (2003). New directions in intercultural communication competence: The process model. In J. O. Greene & B. R. Burleson (Eds.), *Handbook of communication and social interaction skills* (pp. 935–957). Mahwah, NJ: Erlbaum.

Hall, Edward T. (1959). *The silent language.* Garden City, NY: Doubleday.

Hall, E. T. (1963). A system for the notation of proxemic behavior. *American Anthropologist, 65,* 1003–1026.

Hall, Edward T. (1966). *The hidden dimension.* Garden City, NY: Doubleday.

Hall, Edward T. (1976). *Beyond culture.* Garden City, NY: Doubleday.

Hall, Edward T. (1983). *The dance of life: The other dimension of time.* New York: Doubleday.

Hall, Edward T., & Hall, Mildred Reed. (1971, June). The sounds of silence. *Playboy,* pp. 139–140, 204, 206.

Hall, Edward T., & Hall, Mildred Reed. (1987). *Hidden differences: Doing business with the Japanese.* New York: Doubleday.

Hall, Joan Kelly. (1993). Tengo una bomba: The paralinguistic and linguistic conventions of the oral practice chismeando. *Research on Language and Social Interaction, 26,* 55–83.

Hall, Judith A. (1984). *Nonverbal sex differences.* Baltimore: Johns Hopkins University Press.

Hall, Judith A. (1996, Spring). Touch, status, and gender at professional meetings. *Journal of Nonverbal Behavior, 20,* 23–44.

Hall, Judith A. (1998). How big are nonverbal sex differences? The case of smiling and sensitivity to nonverbal cues. In D. J. Canary & K. Dindia (Eds.), *Sex differences and similarities in communication: Critical essays and empirical investigations of sex and gender in interaction* (pp. 155–178). Mahwah, NJ: Erlbaum.

Haney, William (1973). *Communication and organizational behavior: Text and cases* (3rd ed.). Homewood, IL: Irwin.

Hart, Fiona. (1990, September/December). The construction of masculinity in men's friendships: Misogyny, heterosexism and homophobia. *Resources for Feminist Research, 19,* 60–67.

Hart, R. P., Carlson, R. E., & Eadie, W. F. (1980). Attitudes toward communication and the assessment of rhetorical sensitivity. *Communication Monographs, 47,* 1–22.

Hatfield, Elaine, & Rapson, Richard L. (1992). Similarity and attraction in close relationships. *Communication Monographs, 59,* 209–212.

Hatfield, Elaine, & Rapson, Richard L. (1996). *Love and sex: Cross-cultural perspectives.* Boston: Allyn & Bacon.

Havlena, William J., Holbrook, Morris B., & Lehmann, Donald R. (1989, Summer). Assessing the validity of emotional typologies. *Psychology and Marketing, 6,* 97–112.

Hayakawa, S. I., & Hayakawa, A. R. (1989). *Language in thought and action* (5th ed.). New York: Harcourt Brace Jovanovich.

Hays, Robert B. (1989). The day-to-day functioning of close versus casual friendships. *Journal of Social and Personal Relationships, 6,* 21–37.

Heasley, John B., Babbitt, Charles E., & Burbach, Harold J. (1995, Fall). Gender differences in college students' perceptions of "fighting words." *Sociological Viewpoints, 11,* 30–40.

Hecht, Michael. (1978a). The conceptualization and measurement of interpersonal communication satisfaction. *Human Communication Research, 4,* 253–264.

Hecht, Michael. (1978b). Toward a conceptualization of communication satisfaction. *Quarterly Journal of Speech, 64,* 47–62.

Hecht, Michael L., Collier, Mary Jane, & Ribeau, Sidney. (1993). *African American communication: Ethnic identity and cultural interpretation.* Thousand Oaks, CA: Sage.

Hendrick, Clyde, & Hendrick, Susan. (1990). A relationship-specific version of the love attitudes scale. In J. W. Heulip (Ed.), *Handbook of replication research in the behavioral and social sciences* [special issue]. *Journal of Social Behavior and Personality, 5,* 239–254.

Hendrick, Clyde, Hendrick, Susan, Foote, Franklin H., & Slapion-Foote, Michelle J. (1984). Do men and women love differently? *Journal of Social and Personal Relationships, 1,* 177–195.

Hesegawa, T., & Gudykunst, W. B. (1998). Silence in Japan and the United States. *Journal of Cross-Cultural Psychology, 29,* 668–684.

Hess, Eckhard H. (1975). *The tell-tale eye.* New York: Van Nostrand Reinhold.

Hess, Ursula, Kappas, Arvid, McHugo, Gregory J., Lanzetta, John T., et al. (1992, May). The facilitative effect of facial expression on the self-generation of emotion. *International Journal of Psychophysiology, 12,* 251–265.

Hewitt, J. P. (1998). *The myth of self-esteem: Finding happiness and solving problems in America.* New York: St. Martin's Press.

Hewitt, John, & Stokes, Randall. (1975). Disclaimers. *American Sociological Review, 40,* 1–11.

Hickson, Mark L., & Stacks, Don W. (1993). *NVC: Nonverbal communication: Studies and applications* (3rd ed.). Dubuque, IA: William C. Brown.

Hofstede, Geert. (1997). *Cultures and organizations: Software of the mind.* New York: McGraw-Hill.

Hoft, Nancy L. (1995). *International technical communication: How to export information about high technology.* New York: Wiley.

Holmes, Janet. (1986). Compliments and compliment responses in New Zealand English. *Anthropological Linguistic, 28,* 485–508.

Holmes, Janet. (1995). *Women, men and politeness.* New York: Longman.

Howard, P. E. N., Rainie, L., & Jones, S. (2001). Days and nights on the Internet: The impact of a diffusing technology. *American Behavioral Scientist, 45,* 383–404.

Hupka, R. (1981). Cultural determinants of jealousy. *Alternative Lifestyles, 4,* 310–356.

Infante, Dominic A. (1988). *Arguing constructively.* Prospect Heights, IL: Waveland Press.

Infante, Dominic A., & Rancer, Andrew S. (1982). A conceptualization and measure of argumentativeness. *Journal of Personality Assessment, 46,* 72–80.

Infante, Dominic A., Rancer, Andrew S., & Jordan, Felecia F. (1996, March). Affirming and nonaffirming style, dyad sex, and the perception of argumentation and verbal aggression in an interpersonal dispute. *Human Communication Research, 22,* 315–334.

Infante, D. A., Rancer, A. S., & Womack, D. F. (2002). *Building communication theory* (4th ed.). Prospect Heights, IL: Waveland Press.

Infante, Dominic A., & Wigley, C. J. (1986). Verbal aggressiveness: An interpersonal model and measure. *Communication Monographs, 53,* 61–69.

Ingram, M. P. B. (1998). A study of transformative aspects of career change experiences and implications for current models of career development (Doctoral dissertation, Texas A&M University, 1998). *Dissertation Abstracts International: Section A. Humanities and Social Sciences, 58,* 4156.

Insel, Paul M., & Jacobson, Lenore F. (Eds.). (1975). *What do you expect? An inquiry into self-fulfilling prophecies.* Menlo Park, CA: Cummings.

Jackson, Linda A., & Ervin, Kelly S. (1992, August). Height stereotypes of women and men: The liabilities of shortness for both sexes. *Journal of Social Psychology, 132,* 433–445.

Jacobson, D. (1999). Impression formation in cyberspace: Online expectations and offline experiences in text-based virtual communities. *Journal of Computer Mediated Communication, 5,* np.

Jaksa, James A., & Pritchard, Michael S. (1994). *Communication ethics: Methods of analysis* (2nd ed.). Belmont, CA: Wadsworth.

Jandt, Fred E. (2000). *Intercultural communication* (3rd ed.). Thousand Oaks, CA: Sage.

Jaworski, Adam. (1993). *The power of silence: Social and pragmatic perspectives.* Thousand Oaks, CA: Sage.

Johannesen, Richard L. (1974, Winter). The functions of silence: A plea for communication research. *Western Speech, 38,* 25–35.

Johansson, Warren, & Percy, William A. (1994). *Outing: Shattering the conspiracy of silence.* New York: Harrington Park Press.

Johnson, C. E. (1987). An introduction to powerful and powerless talk in the classroom. *Communication Education, 36,* 167–172.

Johnson, S. D., & Bechler, C. (1998). Examining the relationship between listening effectiveness and leadership emergence: Perceptions, behaviors, and recall. *Small Group Research, 29,* 452–471.

Joiner, Tomas E. (1994). Contagious depression: Existence, specificity to depressed symptoms, and the role of reassurance seeking. *Journal of Personality and Social Psychology, 67,* 287–296.

Joinson, A. N. (2001). Self-disclosure in computer-mediated communication: The role of self-awareness and visual anonymity. *European Journal of Social Psychology, 31,* 177–192.

Jones, Stanley, & Yarbrough, A. Elaine. (1985). A naturalistic study of the meanings of touch. *Communication Monographs, 52,* 19–56. (A version of this paper appears in DeVito & Hecht, 1990.)

Jourard, Sidney M. (1968). *Disclosing man to himself.* New York: Van Nostrand Reinhold.

Jourard, Sidney M. (1971). *Self-disclosure.* New York: Wiley.

Kanner, Bernice. (1989, April 3). Color schemes. *New York Magazine,* pp. 22–23.

Kearney, P., Plax, T. G., Richmond, V. P., & McCroskey, J. C. (1984). Power in the classroom IV: Alternatives to discipline. In R. N. Bostrom (Ed.), *Communication yearbook 8* (pp. 724–746). Thousand Oaks, CA: Sage.

Kearney, P., Plax, T. G., Richmond, V. P., & McCroskey, J. C. (1985). Power in the classroom III: Teacher communication techniques and messages. *Communication Education, 34,* 19–28.

Keenan, Elinor Ochs. (1976, April). The universality of conversational postulates. *Language in Society, 5,* 67–80.

Kennedy, C. W., & Camden, C. T. (1988). A new look at interruptions. *Western Journal of Speech Communication, 47,* 45–58.

Keyes, Ralph. (1980). *The height of your life.* New York: Warner Books.

Kim, Young Yun. (1988). Communication and acculturation. In Larry A. Samovar & Richard E. Porter (Eds.), *Intercultural communication: A reader* (5th ed., pp. 344–354). Belmont, CA: Wadsworth.

Kim, Young Yun. (1991). Intercultural communication competence. In Stella Ting-Toomey & Felipe Korzenny (Eds.), *Cross-cultural interpersonal communication* (pp. 259–275). Newbury Park, CA: Sage.

King, Robert, & DiMichael, Eleanor. (1992). *Voice and diction.* Prospect Heights, IL: Waveland Press.

Kleinfield, N. R. (1992, October 25). The smell of money. *The New York Times,* pp. C1, C8.

Kleinke, Chris L. (1986). *Meeting and understanding people.* New York: W. H. Freeman.

Klineberg, O., & Hull, W. F. (1979). *At a foreign university: An international study of adaptation and coping.* New York: Praeger.

Knapp, Mark L., & Hall, Judith. (1996). *Nonverbal behavior in human interaction* (3rd ed.). New York: Holt, Rinehart, & Winston.

Knapp, Mark, Hart, Roderick P., Friedrich, Gustav W., & Shulman, Gary M. (1973). The rhetoric of goodbye: Verbal and nonverbal correlates of human leave-taking. *Speech Monographs, 40,* 182–198.

Knapp, M. L., & Vangelisti, A. (2000). *Interpersonal communication and human relationships* (4th ed.). Boston: Allyn & Bacon.

Knobloch, L. K., & Solomon, D. H. (1999, Winter). Measuring the sources and content of relational uncertainty. *Communication Studies, 50,* 261–278.

Koberg, Don, & Bagnall, Jim. (1976a). *The universal traveler.* Los Altos, CA: William Kaufmann.

Koberg, Don, & Bagnall, Jim. (1976b). *Values tech: A portable school for discovering and developing decision-making skills for self-enhancing potentials.* Los Altos, CA: William Kaufmann.

Kochman, Thomas. (1981). *Black and white: Styles in conflict.* Chicago: University of Chicago Press.

Komarovsky, M. (1964). *Blue collar marriage.* New York: Random House.

Korda, M. (1975). *Power! How to get it, how to use it.* New York: Ballantine.

Korzybski, A. (1933). *Science and sanity.* Lakeville, CT: The International Non-Aristotelian Library.

Kposow, Augustine J. (2000, April). Marital status and suicide in the National Longitudinal Mortality Study. *Journal of Epidemiology and Community Health, 54,* 254–261.

Kramarae, Cheris. (1974a). Folklinguistics. *Psychology Today, 8,* 82–85.

Kramarae, Cheris. (1974b). Stereotypes of women's speech: The word from cartoons. *Journal of Popular Culture, 8,* 624–630.

Kramarae, Cheris. (1977). Perceptions of female and male speech. *Language and speech, 20,* 151–161.

Kramarae, Cheris. (1981). *Women and men speaking.* Rowley, MA: Newbury House.

Kramer, R. (1997). Leading by listening: An empirical test of Carl Rogers's theory of human relationship using interpersonal assessments of leaders by followers. *Dissertation Abstracts International: Section A. Humanities and Social Sciences, 58,* 514.

Krivonos, Paul D., & Knapp, Mark L. (1975). Initiating communication: What do you say when you say hello? *Central States Speech Journal, 26,* 115–125.

Kuhn, D., Weinstock, M., & Flaton, R. (1994). How well do jurors reason? Competence dimensions of individual variation in a juror reasoning task. *Psychological Science, 5,* 289–296.

Kurdek, Lawrence A. (1994, November). Areas of conflict for gay, lesbian, and heterosexual couples: What couples argue about influences relationship satisfaction. *Journal of Marriage and the Family, 56,* 923–934.

Labott, Susan M., Martin, Randall B., Eason, Patricia S., & Berkey, Elayne Y. (1991, September/November). Social reactions to the expression of emotion. *Cognition and Emotion, 5,* 397–417.

Laing, Milli. (1993, Spring). Gossip: Does it play a role in the socialization of nurses. *Journal of Nursing Scholarship, 25,* 37–43.

Laing, Ronald D., Phillipson, H., & Lee, A. Russell. (1966). *Interpersonal perception.* New York: Springer.

Lakoff, R. (1975). *Language and women's place.* New York: Harper & Row.

Langer, Ellen J. (1989). *Mindfulness.* Reading, MA: Addison-Wesley.

Lantz, A. (2001). Meetings in a distributed group of experts: Comparing face-to-face, chat and collaborative virtual environments. *Behaviour and Information Technology, 20,* 111–117.

Lanzetta, J. T., Cartwright-Smith, J., & Kleck, R. E. (1976). Effects of nonverbal dissimulations on emotional experience and autonomic arousal. *Journal of Personality and Social Psychology, 33,* 354–370.

Larsen, Randy J., Kasimatis, Margaret, & Frey, Kurt. (1992, September). Facilitating the furrowed brow: An unobtrusive test of the facial feedback hypothesis applied to unpleasant affect. *Cognition and Emotion, 6,* 321–338.

Lea, Martin, & Spears, Russell. (1995). Love at first byte? Building personal relationships over computer networks. In Julia T. Wood & Steve Duck (Eds.), *Understudied relationships: Off the beaten track* (pp. 197–233). Thousand Oaks, CA: Sage.

Leaper, Campbell, Carson, Mary, Baker, Carilyn, Holliday, Heithre, et al. (1995). Self-disclosure and listener verbal support in same-gender and cross-gender friends' conversations. *Sex Roles, 33,* 387–404.

Leaper, Campbell, & Holliday, Heithre. (1995, September). Gossip in same-gender and cross-gender friends' conversations. *Personal Relationships, 2,* 237–246.

Leathers, Dale G. (1997). *Successful nonverbal communication: Principles and applications* (2nd ed.). New York: Macmillan.

Lederer, W. J. (1984). *Creating a good relationship.* New York: Norton.

Lee, A. M., & Lee, E. B. (1972). *The fine art of propaganda.* San Francisco: International Society for General Semantics.

Lee, A. M., & Lee, E. B. (1995, Spring). The iconography of propaganda analysis. *ETC: A Review of General Semantics, 52,* 13–17.

Lee, Fiona. (1993, July). Being polite and keeping Mum: How bad news is communicated in organizational hierarchies. *Journal of Applied Social Psychology, 23,* 1124–1149.

Lee, John Alan. (1976). *The colors of love.* New York: Bantam.

Lee, Karen. (2000, November 1). Information overload threatens employee productivity. *Employee Benefit News,* Securities Data Publishing, p. 1.

Leung, Kwok. (1988, March). Some determinants of conflict avoidance. *Journal of Cross-Cultural Psychology, 19,* 125–136.

Lever, Janet. (1995, August 22). The 1995 advocate survey of sexuality and relationships: The women, lesbian sex survey. *The Advocate, 687/688,* 22–30.

Levine, D. (2000). Virtual attraction: What rocks your boat. *CyberPsychology and Behavior, 3,* 565–573.

LeVine, R., & Bartlett, K. (1984). Pace of life, punctuality, and coronary heart disease in six countries. *Journal of Cross-Cultural Psychology, 15,* 233–255.

LeVine, R., Sato, S., Hashimoto, T., & Verma, J. (1994). Love and marriage in eleven cultures. Unpublished manuscript. California State University, Fresno. Cited in Hatfield & Rapson (1996).

Lewis, David. (1989). *The secret language of success.* New York: Carroll & Graf.

Lindeman, Marjaana, Harakka, Tuija, & Keltikangas-Jarvinen, Liisa. (1997, June). Age and gender differences in adolescents' reactions to conflict situations: Aggression, prosociality, and withdrawal. *Journal of Youth and Adolescence, 26,* 339–351.

Lloyd, S. R. (2001). *Developing positive assertiveness* (3rd ed.). Menlo Park, CA: Crisp Publications.

Lukens, J. (1978). Ethnocentric speech. *Ethnic Groups, 2,* 35–53.

Lustig, Myron W., & Koester, Jolene. (1999). *Intercultural competence: Interpersonal communication across cultures* (3rd ed.). New York: HarperCollins.

Ma, Karen. (1996). *The modern Madame Butterfly: Fantasy and reality in Japanese cross-cultural relationships.* Rutland, VT: Charles E. Tuttle.

Ma, Ringo. (1992, Summer). The role of unofficial intermediaries in interpersonal conflicts in the Chinese culture. *Communication Quarterly, 40,* 269–278.

Mackey, R. A., Diemer, M. A., & O'Brien, B. A. (2000). Psychological intimacy in the lasting relationships of heterosexual and same-gender couples. *Sex Roles, 43,* 201–227.

MacLachlan, James. (1979). What people really think of fast talkers. *Psychology Today, 13,* 113–117.

Maggio, Rosalie. (1997). *Talking about people: A guide to fair and accurate language.* Phoenix, AZ: Oryx Press.

Malandro, Loretta A., Barker, Larry, & Barker, Deborah Ann. (1989). *Nonverbal communication* (2nd ed.). New York: Random House.

Manes, Joan, & Wolfson, Nessa. (1981). The compliment formula. In Florian Coulmas (Ed.), *Conversational routine* (pp. 115–132). The Hague: Mouton.

Manniche, Erik. (1991). Marriage and non-marriage cohabitation in Denmark. *Family Reports, 20,* 9–35.

Mao, LuMing Robert. (1994, May). Beyond politeness theory: "Face" revisited and renewed. *Journal of Pragmatics, 21,* 451–486.

Marsh, P. (1988). *Eye to eye: How people interact.* Topside, MA: Salem House.

Marshall, Evan. (1983). *Eye language: Understanding the eloquent eye.* New York: New Trend.

Marshall, Linda L., & Rose, Patricia. (1987). Gender, stress and violence in the adult relationships of a sample of college students. *Journal of Social and Personal Relationships, 4,* 299–316.

Martin, G. N. (1998). Human electroencephalographic (EEG) response to olfactory stimulation: Two experiments using the aroma of food. *International Journal of Psychophysiology, 30,* 287–302.

Martin, Matthew M., & Anderson, Carolyn M. (1995, Spring). Roommate similarity: Are roommates who are similar in their communication traits more satisfied? *Communication Research Reports, 12,* 46–52.

Marwell, G., & Schmitt, D. R. (1967). Dimensions of compliance-gaining behavior: An empirical analysis. *Sociometry, 39,* 350–364.

Matsumoto, David. (1991, Winter). Cultural influences on facial expressions of emotion. *Southern Communication Journal, 56,* 128–137.

Matsumoto, David. (1994). *People: Psychology from a cultural perspective.* Pacific Grove, CA: Brooks/Cole.

Matsumoto, D. (1996). *Culture and psychology.* Pacific Grove, CA: Brooks/Cole.

Matsumoto, David, & Kudoh, T. (1993). American-Japanese cultural differences in attributions of personality based on smiles. *Journal of Nonverbal Behavior, 17,* 231–243.

McBroom, William H., & Reed, Fred W. (1992, June). Toward a reconceptualization of attitude-behavior consistency. *Social Psychology Quarterly, 55* [Special issue. Theoretical Advances in Social Psychology], 205–216.

McConatha, Jasmin-Tahmaseb, Lightner, Eileen, & Deaner, Stephanie L. (1994, September). Culture, age, and gender as variables in the expression of emotions. *Journal of Social Behavior and Personality, 9,* 481–488.

McCroskey, James C. (1997). *Introduction to rhetorical communication* (7th ed.). Englewood Cliffs, NJ: Prentice-Hall.

McCroskey, James C. (1998). *Why we communicate the ways we do: A communibiological perspective.* Boston: Allyn & Bacon.

McCroskey, James C., Booth-Butterfield, S., & Payne, S. K. (1989). The impact of communication apprehension on college student retention and success. *Communication Quarterly, 37,* 100–107.

McCroskey, James C., & Wheeless, Lawrence. (1976). *Introduction to human communication.* Boston: Allyn & Bacon.

McGill, Michael E. (1985). *The McGill report on male intimacy.* New York: Harper & Row.

McLaughlin, Margaret L. (1984). *Conversation: How talk is organized.* Newbury Park, CA: Sage.

McLoyd, Vonnie, & Wilson, Leon. (1992, August). Telling them like it is: The role of economic and environmental factors in single mothers' discussions with their children. *American Journal of Community Psychology, 20,* 419–444.

McNamee, S., & Gergen, K. J. (Eds.). (1999). *Relational responsibility: Resources for sustainable dialogue.* Thousand Oaks, CA: Sage.

McNatt, D. B. (2001). Ancient Pygmalion joins contemporary management: A meta-analysis of the result. *Journal of Applied Psychology, 85,* 314–322.

Merton, Robert K. (1957). *Social theory and social structure.* New York: Free Press.

Messick, R. M., & Cook, K. S. (Eds.). (1983). *Equity theory: Psychological and sociological perspectives.* New York: Praeger.

Messmer, Max. (1999, August). Skills for a new millennium: Accounting and financial professionals. *Strategic Finance Magazine,* 10ff.

Metts, Sandra. (1989, May). An exploratory investigation of deception in close relationships. *Journal of Social and Personal Relationships, 6,* 159–179.

Metts, S., & Planalp, S. (2002). Emotional communication. In M. L. Knapp & J. A. Daly (Eds.) (pp. 339–373). *Handbook of Interpersonal Communication* (3rd ed.), Thousand Oaks, CA: Sage.

Meyer, Janet R. (1994, Spring). Effect of situational features on the likelihood of addressing face needs in requests. *Southern Communication Journal, 59,* 240–254.

Midooka, Kiyoski. (1990, October). Characteristics of Japanese style communication. *Media Culture and Society, 12,* 477–489.

Miller, G. R. (1978). The current state of theory and research in interpersonal communication. *Human Communication Research, 4,* 164–178.

Miller, G. R. (1990). Interpersonal communication. In G. L. Dahnke & G. W. Clatterbuck (Eds.), *Human communication: Theory and research* (pp. 91–122). Belmont, CA: Wadsworth.

Miller, Gerald R., & Parks, Malcolm R. (1982). Communication in dissolving relationships. In Steve Duck (Ed.), *Personal relationships: Vol. 4. Dissolving personal relationships* (pp. 127–154). New York: Academic Press.

Miller, LaRonda R. (1997, December). Better ways to think and communicate. *Association Management, 49,* 71–73.

Miner, Horace. (1956). Body ritual among the Nacirema. *American Anthropologist, 58,* 503–507.

Mir, Montserrat. (1993). *Direct requests can also be polite.* Paper presented at the annual meeting of the International Conference on Pragmatics and Language Learning, Champaign, IL.

Moghaddam, Fathali M., Taylor, Donald M., & Wright, Stephen C. (1993). *Social psychology in cross-cultural perspective.* New York: W. H. Freeman.

Molloy, John. (1977). *The woman's dress for success book.* Chicago: Follett.

Molloy, J. (1981). *Molloy's live for success.* New York: Bantam.

Monahan, J. L. (1998). I don't know it but I like you. *Human Communication Research, 24,* 480–500.

Montagu, Ashley. (1971). *Touching: The human significance of the skin.* New York: Harper & Row.

Moon, Dreama G. (1996, Winter). Concepts of "culture": Implications for intercultural communication research. *Communication Quarterly, 44,* 70–84.

Moore, A., Masterson, J. T., Christophel, D. M., & Shea, K. A. (1996). College teacher immediacy and student ratings of instruction. *Communication Education, 45,* 29–39.

Morreale, S. P., Osborn, M. M., & Pearson, J. C. (2000, January). Why communication is important: A rationale for the centrality of the study of communication. *Journal of the Association for Communication Administration, 29,* 1–25.

Morrill, C. (1992). Vengeance among executives. *Virginia Review of Sociology, 1,* 51–76.

Morris, Desmond. (1977). *Manwatching: A field guide to human behavior.* New York: Abrams.

Morrow, Gregory D., Clark, Eddie M., & Brock, Karla F. (1995, August). Individual and partner love styles: Implications for the quality of romantic involvements. *Journal of Social and Personal Relationships, 12,* 363–387.

Murstein, Bernard I., Merighi, Joseph R., & Vyse, Stuart A. (1991, Spring). Love styles in the United States and France: A cross-cultural comparison. *Journal of Social and Clinical Psychology, 10,* 37–46.

Naifeh, Steven, & Smith, Gregory White. (1984). *Why can't men open up? Overcoming men's fear of intimacy.* New York: Clarkson N. Potter.

Neugarten, Bernice. (1979). Time, age, and the life cycle. *American Journal of Psychiatry, 136,* 887–894.

Neuliep, J. W., Chaudoir, M., & McCroskey, J. C. (2001). A cross-cultural comparison of ethnocentrism among Japanese and United States college students. *Communication Research Reports, 18,* 137–146.

Nichols, Michael P. (1995). *The lost art of listening: How learning to listen can improve relationships.* New York: Guilford Press.

Nichols, Ralph. (1961). Do we know how to listen? Practical helps in a modern age. *Communication Education, 10,* 118–124.

Nichols, Ralph, & Stevens, Leonard. (1957). *Are you listening?* New York: McGraw-Hill.

Noble, Barbara Presley. (1994, August 14). The gender wars: Talking peace. *The New York Times,* p. 21.

Noller, Patricia, & Fitzpatrick, Mary Anne. (1993). *Communication in family relationships.* Englewood Cliffs, NJ: Prentice-Hall.

Nordhaus-Bike, Anne M. (1999, August). Learning to lead. *Hospitals & Health Networks, 73,* 28ff.

Norton, Robert, & Warnick, Barbara. (1976). Assertiveness as a communication construct. *Human Communication Research, 3,* 62–66.

Notarius, Clifford I., & Herrick, Lisa R. (1988). Listener response strategies to a distressed other. *Journal of Social and Personal Relationships, 5,* 97–108.

Oatley, Keith, & Duncan, Elaine. (1994). The experience of emotions in everyday life. *Cognition and Emotion, 8,* 369–381.

Ober, C., Weitkamp, L. R., Cox, N., Dytch, H., Kostyu, D., & Elias, S. (1997). *American Journal of Human Genetics, 61,* 494–496.

Oberg, K. (1960). Cultural shock: Adjustment to new cultural environments. *Practical Anthropology, 7,* 177–182.

Oetzel, J., Ting-Toomey, S., Masumoto, T., Yokochi, Y., Pan, X., Takai, J., & Wilcox, R. (2001). Face and facework in conflict: A cross-cultural comparison of China,

Germany, Japan, and the United States. *Communication Monographs, 68,* 235–258.

O'Hair, D., Cody, M. J., & McLaughlin, M. L. (1981). Prepared lies, spontaneous lies, Machiavellianism, and nonverbal communication. *Human Communication Research, 7,* 325–339.

Olaniran, Bolanle A. (1994, February). Group performance in computer-mediated and face-to-face communication media. *Management Communication Quarterly, 7,* 256–281.

Otaki, Midori, Durrett, Mary Ellen, Richards, Phyllis, Nyquist, Lina, & Pennebaker, James W. (1986). Maternal and infant behavior in Japan and America. *Journal of Cross-Cultural Psychology, 17,* 251–268.

Parker, Rhonda G., & Parrott, Roxanne. (1995). Patterns of self-disclosure across social support networks: Elderly, middle-aged, and young adults. *International Journal of Aging and Human Development, 41,* 281–297.

Patton, Bobby R., Giffin, Kim, & Patton, Eleanor Nyquist. (1989). *Decision-making group interaction* (3rd ed.). New York: HarperCollins.

Paul, A. M. (2001). Self-help: Shattering the myths. *Psychology Today, 34,* 60ff.

Payne, K. E. (2001). *Different but equal: Communication between the sexes.* Westport, CT: Praeger.

Pearson, J. C., Nelson, P., Titsworth, S., & Harter, L. (2003). *Human communication.* New York: McGraw-Hill.

Pearson, J. C., & Spitzberg, B. H. (1990). *Interpersonal communication: Concepts, components, and contexts* (2nd ed.). Dubuque, IA: William C. Brown.

Pearson, Judy C., West, Richard, & Turner, Lynn H. (1995). *Gender and communication* (3rd ed.). Dubuque, IA: William C. Brown.

Penfield, Joyce (Ed.). (1987). *Women and language in transition.* Albany: State University of New York Press.

Pennebacker, James W. (1991). *Opening up: The healing power of confiding in others.* New York: Avon.

Peterson, Candida C. (1996). The ticking of the social clock: Adults' beliefs about the timing of transition events. *International Journal of Aging and Human Development, 42,* 189–203.

Petrocelli, William, & Repa, Barbara Kate. (1992). *Sexual harassment on the job.* Berkeley, CA: Nolo Press.

Pilkington, C. J., & Richardson, D. R. (1988). Perceptions of risk in intimacy. *Journal of Social and Personal Relationships, 5,* 503–508.

Pilkington, C. J., & Woods, S. P. (1999). Risk in intimacy as a chronically accessible schema. *Journal of Social and Personal Relationships, 16,* 249–263.

Pilkington, Neil W., & D'Augelli, Anthony R. (1995, January). Victimization of lesbian, gay, and bisexual youth in community settings. *Journal of Community Psychology, 23,* 34–56.

Piot, Charles D. (1993, June). Secrecy, ambiguity, and the everyday in Kabre culture. *American Anthropologist, 95,* 353–370.

Pittenger, R. E., Hockett, C. F., & Danehy, J. J. (1960). *The first five minutes.* Ithaca, NY: Paul Martineau.

Plutchik, Robert. (1980). *Emotion: A psycho-evolutionary synthesis.* New York: Harper & Row.

Porter, R. H., & Moore, J. D. (1981). Human kin recognition by olfactory cues. *Physiology and Behavior, 27,* 493–495.

Porter, S., Brit, A. R., Yuille, J. C., & Lehman, D. R. (2000, November). Negotiating false memories: Interviewer and rememberer characteristics relate to memory distortion. *Psychological Science, 11,* 507–510.

Powers, W. G., & Love, D. E. (2000). Communication apprehension in the dating partner context. *Communication Research Reports, 17,* 221–228.

Pratkanis, A., & Aronson, E. (1991). *Age of propaganda: The everyday use and abuse of persuasion.* New York: W. H. Freeman.

Raney, Rebecca Fairley. (2000, May 11). Study finds Internet of social benefit to users. *The New York Times,* p. G7.

Rankin, Paul. (1929). *Listening ability.* Proceedings of the Ohio State Educational Conference's ninth annual session.

Raven, R., Centers, C., & Rodrigues, A. (1975). The bases of conjugal power. In R. E. Cromwell & D. H. Olson (Eds.), *Power in families* (pp. 217–234). New York: Halsted Press.

Rector, M., & Neiva, E. (1996). Communication and personal relationships in Brazil. In W. B. Gudykunst, S. Ting-Toomey, & T. Nishida (Eds.), *Communication in personal relationships across cultures* (pp. 156–173). Thousand Oaks, CA: Sage.

Reed, Mark D. (1993, Fall). Sudden death and bereavement outcomes: The impact of resources on grief, symptomatology and detachment. *Suicide and Life-Threatening Behavior, 23,* 204–220.

Reisman, John. (1979). *Anatomy of friendship.* Lexington, MA: Lewis.

Reisman, John M. (1981). Adult friendships. In Steve Duck, & Robin Gilmour (Eds.), *Personal relationships: Vol. 2: Developing personal relationships* (pp. 205–230). New York: Academic Press.

Rich, Andrea L. (1974). *Interracial communication.* New York: Harper & Row.

Richmond, Virginia P., Davis, L. M., Saylor, K., & McCroskey, J. C. (1984). Power strategies in organizations: Communication techniques and messages. *Human Communication Research, 11,* 85–108.

Richmond, Virginia P., & McCroskey, James C. (1998). *Communication: Apprehension, avoidance, and effectiveness* (5th ed.). Boston: Allyn & Bacon.

Riggio, Ronald E. (1987). *The charisma quotient.* New York: Dodd, Mead.

Roberts, Carlos A., & Aruguete, Mara S. (2000, February). Task and socioemotional behaviors of physicians: A test of reciprocity and social interaction theories in analogue physician-patient encounters. *Social Science and Medicine, 50,* 309–315.

Roberts, Moss. (Ed. and Trans., with the assistance of Tay, C. N.). (1979). *Chinese fairy tales and fantasies.* New York: Pantheon.

Roger, Derek, & Nesshoever, Willfried. (1987, September). Individual differences in dyadic conversational strategies: A further study. *British Journal of Social Psychology, 26,* 247–255.

Rogers, C. (1970). *Carl Rogers on encounter groups.* New York: Harrow Books.

Rogers, Carl, & Farson, Richard. (1981). Active listening. In Joseph A. DeVito (Ed.), *Communication: Concepts and processes* (3rd ed., pp. 137–147). Englewood Cliffs, NJ: Prentice-Hall.

Rokach, A. (1998). The relation of cultural background to the causes of loneliness. *Journal of Social and Clinical Psychology, 17,* 75–88.

Rokach, A., & Brock, H. (1995). The effects of gender, marital status, and the chronicity and immediacy of loneliness. *Journal of Social Behavior and Personality, 19,* 833–848.

Rose, Amanda J., & Asher, Steven R. (1999, January). Children's goals and strategies in response to conflicts within a friendship. *Developmental Psychology, 35,* 69–79.

Rosen, Emanuel. (1998, October). Think like a shrink. *Psychology Today,* 54–59.

Rosenbaum, M. E. (1986). The repulsion hypothesis. On the nondevelopment of relationships. *Journal of Personality and Social Psychology, 51,* 1156–1166.

Rosenfeld, Lawrence. (1979). Self-disclosure avoidance: Why I am afraid to tell you who I am. *Communication Monographs, 46,* 63–74.

Rosengren, A., et al. (1993, October 19). Stressful life events, social support, and mortality in men born in 1933. *British Medical Journal.* Cited in Goleman (1995a).

Rosenthal, Robert, & Jacobson, L. (1968). *Pygmalion in the classroom.* New York: Holt, Rinehart and Winston.

Rosnow, Ralph L. (1977, Winter). Gossip and marketplace psychology. *Journal of Communication, 27,* 158–163.

Ross, J. L. (1995). Conversational pitchbacks: Helping couples bat 1000 in the game of communications. *Journal of Family Psychotherapy, 6,* 83–86.

Rowland-Morin, P. A., & Carroll, J. G. (1990). Verbal communication skills and patient satisfaction: A study of doctor–patient interviews. *Evaluation and the Health Professions, 13,* 168–185.

Ruben, Brent D. (1985). Human communication and cross-cultural effectiveness. In Larry A. Samovar & Richard E. Porter (Eds.), *Intercultural communication: A reader* (4th ed., pp. 338–346). Belmont, CA: Wadsworth.

Rubenstein, Carin. (1993, June 10). Fighting sexual harassment in schools. *The New York Times,* p. C8.

Rubenstein, Carin, & Shaver, Philip. (1982). *In search of intimacy.* New York: Delacorte.

Rubin, Rebecca B., Fernandez-Collado, C., & Hernandez-Sampieri, R. (1992). A cross-cultural examination of interpersonal communication motives in Mexico and the United States. *International Journal of Intercultural Relations, 16,* 145–157.

Rubin, Rebecca B., & Martin, M. M. (1994). Development of a measure of interpersonal communication competence. *Communication Research Reports, 11,* 33–44.

Rubin, Rebecca B., Perse, Elizabeth M., & Barbato, Carole A. (1988). Conceptualization and measurement of interpersonal communication motives. *Human Communication Research, 14,* 602–628.

Rubin, Rebecca B., & Rubin, Alan M. (1992). Antecedents of interpersonal communication motivation. *Communication Quarterly, 40,* 315–317.

Rubin, Zick. (1973). *Liking and loving: An invitation to social psychology.* New York: Holt, Rinehart & Winston.

Rundquist, Suellen. (1992, November). Indirectness: A gender study of flaunting Grice's maxims. *Journal of Pragmatics, 18,* 431–449.

Rushe, R. H. (1996). Tactics of power and influence in violent marriages. Dissertation abstracts international: Section B: The Sciences and Engineering (University of Washington), 57, 1453.

Saboonchi, Fredrik, Lundh, Lars Gunnar, & Oest, Lars Goeran. (1999, September). Perfectionism and self-consciousness in social phobia and panic disorder with agoraphobia. *Behaviour Research and Therapy, 37,* 799–808.

Samovar, Larry A., & Porter, Richard E. (Eds.). (1991). *Communication between cultures.* Belmont, CA: Wadsworth.

Samter, W. (2003). Friendship interaction skills across the life-span. In J. O. Greene & B. R. Burleson (Eds.), *Handbook of communication and social interaction skills* (pp. 637–684). Mahwah, NJ: Erlbaum.

Samter, W., & Cupach, W. R. (1998). Friendly fire: Topics variations in conflict among same- and cross-sex friends. *Communication Studies, 49,* 121–138.

Sanders, Judith A., Wiseman, Richard L., & Matz, S. Irene. (1991). Uncertainty reduction in acquaintance relationships in Ghana and the United States. In Stella Ting-Toomey & Felipe Korzenny (Eds.), *Cross-cultural interpersonal* (pp. 79–98). Thousand Oaks, CA: Sage.

Sarwer, David B., Kalichman, Seth C., Johnson, Jennifer R., Early, Jamie, et al. (1993, June). Sexual aggression and love styles: An exploratory study. *Archives of Sexual Behavior, 22,* 265–275.

Saunders, Carol S., Robey, Daniel, & Vaverek, Kelly A. (1994, June). The persistence of status differentials in computer conferencing. *Human Communication Research, 20,* 443–472.

Scandura, T. (1992). Mentorship and career mobility: An empirical investigation. *Journal of Organizational Behavior, 13,* 169–174.

Schaap, C., Buunk, B., & Kerkstra, A. (1988). Marital conflict resolution. In Patricia Noller & Mary Anne Fitzpatrick (Eds.), *Perspectives on marital interaction* (pp. 203–244). Philadelphia: Multilingual Matters.

Schachter, Stanley. (1964). The interaction of cognitive and physiological determinants of emotional state. In Leonard Berkowitz (Ed.), *Advances in experimental social psychology* (Vol. 1). New York: Academic Press.

Scheetz, L. Patrick. (1995). *Recruiting trends 1995–1996: A study of 527 businesses, industries, and governmental agencies employing new college graduates.* East Lansing, MI: Collegiate Employment Research Institute, Michigan State University.

Scherer, K. R. (1986). Vocal affect expression. *Psychological Bulletin, 99,* 143–165.

Schmidt, Tracy O., & Cornelius, Randolph R. (1987). Self-disclosure in everyday life. *Journal of Social and Personal Relationships, 4,* 365–373.

Schoeneman, T. J., & Rubanowitz, E. E. (1985). Attributions in the advice columns: Actors and observers, causes and reasons. *Personality and Social Psychology Bulletin, 11,* 315–325.

Schwartz, Marilyn, & the Task Force on Bias-Free Language of the Association of American University Presses. (1995). *Guidelines for bias-free writing.* Bloomington: Indiana University Press.

Shaffer, David R., Pegalis, Linda J., & Bazzini, Doris G. (1996, May). When boy meets girl (revisited): Gender, gender role orientation, and prospect of future interaction as determinants of self-disclosure among same- and opposite-sex acquaintances. *Personality and Social Psychology Bulletin, 22,* 495–506.

Shuter, Robert. (1990, Spring). The centrality of culture. *Southern Communication Journal, 55,* 237–249.

Siegert, John R., & Stamp, Glen H. (1994, December). "Our first big fight" as a milestone in the development of close relationships. *Communication Monographs, 61,* 345–360.

Signorile, Michelangelo. (1993). *Queer in America: Sex, the media, and the closets of power.* New York: Random House.

Silverman, T. (2001). Expanding community: The Internet and relational theory. *Community, Work and Family, 4,* 231–237.

Slade, Margot. (1995, February 19). We forgot to write a headline: But it's not our fault. *The New York Times,* p. 5.

Smith, C. S. (2002, April 30). Beware of green hats in China and other cross-cultural faux pas. *The New York Times,* p. C11.

Snyder, C. R. (1984). Excuses, excuses. *Psychology Today, 18,* 50–55.

Snyder, C. R., Higgins, Raymond L., & Stucky, Rita J. (1983). *Excuses: Masquerades in search of grace.* New York: Wiley.

Snyder, M. (1992, February). A gender-informed model of couple and family therapy: Relationship enhancement therapy. *Contemporary Family Therapy: An International Journal, 14,* 15–31.

Solomon, G. B., Striegel, D. A., Eliot, J. F., Heon, S. N., et al. (1996). The self-fulfilling prophecy in college basketball: Implications for effective coaching. *Journal of Applied Sport Psychology, 8,* 44–59.

Sommers, S. (1984). Reported emotions and conventions of emotionality among college students. *Journal of Personality and Social Psychology, 46,* 207–215.

Sondel, Bess. (1968). *To win with words.* New York: Hawthorn Books.

Sorenson, Paula S., Hawkins, Katherine, & Sorenson, Ritch L. (1995, August). Gender, psychological type and conflict style preferences. *Management Communication Quarterly, 9,* 115–126.

Spangler, Diane L., & Burns, David D. (2000, Winter). Is it true that men are from Mars and women are from Venus? A test of gender differences in dependency and perfectionism. *Journal of Cognitive Psychotherapy, 13,* 339–357.

Spitzberg, B. H. (1991). Intercultural communication competence. In L. A. Samovar & R. E. Porter (Eds.), *Intercultural communication: A reader* (pp. 353–365). Belmont, CA: Wadsworth.

Spitzberg, Brian H., & Cupach, William R. (1989). *Handbook of interpersonal competence research.* New York: Springer.

Spitzberg, Brian H., & Hecht, Michael L. (1984). A component model of relational competence. *Human Communication Research, 10,* 575–599.

Sprecher, Susan. (1987). The effects of self-disclosure given and received on affection for an intimate partner and stability of the relationship. *Journal of Social and Personal Relationships, 4,* 115–127.

Stafford, L., Kline, S. L., & Dimmick, J. (1999). Home e-mail: Relational maintenance and gratification opportunities. *Journal of Broadcasting and Electronic Media, 43,* 659–669.

Steil, Lyman K., Barker, Larry L., & Watson, Kittie W. (1983). *Effective listening: Key to your success.* Reading, MA: Addison-Wesley.

Steiner, Claude. (1981). *The other side of power.* New York: Grove.

Steinfatt, Thomas M. (1987). Personality and communication: Classic approaches. In James C. McCroskey & John A. Daly (Eds.), *Personality and interpersonal communication* (pp. 42–126). Thousand Oaks, CA: Sage.

Stephan, Cookie White, & Stephan, Walter G. (1992, Winter). Reducing intercultural anxiety through intercultural contact. *International Journal of Intercultural Relations, 16,* 89–106.

Stephan, Walter G., & Stephan, Cookie White. (1985). Intergroup anxiety. *Journal of Social Issues, 41,* 157–175.

Stewart, L. P., Cooper, P. J., Stewart, A. D., with Friedley, S. A. (2003). *Communication and gender.* Boston: Allyn & Bacon.

Strecker, Ivo. (1993). Cultural variations in the concept of "face." *Multilingua, 12,* 119–141.

Szapocznik, Jose. (1995, January). Research on disclosure of HIV status: Cultural evolution finds an ally in science. *Health Psychology, 14,* 4–5.

Tannen, Deborah. (1990). *You just don't understand: Women and men in conversation.* New York: Morrow.

Tannen, Deborah. (1994a). *Gender and discourse.* New York: Oxford University Press.

Tannen, Deborah. (1994b). *Talking from 9 to 5.* New York: Morrow.

Tardiff, T. (2001). Learning to say "no" in Chinese. *Early Education and Development, 12,* 303–323.

Tavris, C. (1989). *Anger: The misunderstood emotion* (2nd ed.). New York: Simon & Schuster.

Timmerman, L. J. (2002). Comparing the production of power in language on the basis of sex. In M. Allen & R. W. Preiss (Eds.), *Interpersonal communication research: Advances through meta-analysis* (pp. 73–88). Mahwah, NJ: Erlbaum.

Ting-Toomey, S. (1981). Ethnic identity and close friendship in Chinese-American college students. *International Journal of Intercultural Relations, 5,* 383–406.

Ting-Toomey, Stella. (1985). Toward a theory of conflict and culture. *International and Intercultural Communication Annual, 9,* 71–86.

Ting-Toomey, Stella. (1986). Conflict communication styles in black and white subjective cultures. In Young Yun Kim (Ed.), *Interethnic communication: Current research.* (pp. 75–88). Thousand Oaks, CA: Sage.

Tinsley, C. H., & Brett, J. M. (2001). Managing workplace conflict in the United States and Hong Kong. *Organizational Behavior and Human Decision Processes, 85,* 360–381.

Titlow, Karen I., Rackoff, Jonathan E., & Emanuel, Ezekiel J. (1999). What will it take to restore patient trust? *Business & Health, 17,* (6A), 61–64.

Trager, George L. (1958). Paralanguage: A first approximation. *Studies in Linguistics, 13,* 1–12.

Trager, George L. (1961). The typology of paralanguage. *Anthropological Linguistics, 3,* 17–21.

Traxler, A. J. (1980). *Let's get gerontologized: Developing a sensitivity to aging.* Springfield, IL: Illinois Department of Aging.

Tyler, Patrick E. (1996, July 11). Crime (and punishment) rages anew in China. *The New York Times,* pp. A1, A8.

Unger, F. L. (2001). Speech directed at able-bodied adults, disabled adults, and disabled adults with speech impairments. Dissertation Abstracts International: Section B: The Sciences and Engineering (Hofstra University), 62, 1146.

Uris, A. (1986). *101 of the greatest ideas in management.* New York: Wiley.

VanHyning, Memory. (1993). *Crossed signals: How to say no to sexual harassment.* Los Angeles: Infotrends Press.

Veenendall, Thomas L., & Feinstein, Marjorie C. (1995). *Let's talk about relationships: Cases in study* (2nd ed.). Prospect Heights, IL: Waveland Press.

Velting, D. M. (1999). Personality and negative expectations: Trait structure of the Beck Hopelessness Scale. *Personality and Individual Differences, 26,* 913–921.

Victor, David. (1992). *International business communication.* New York: HarperCollins.

von Tetzchner, S., & Jensen, K. (1999, December). Interacting with people who have severe communication problems: Ethical considerations. *International Journal of Disability, Development and Education, 46,* 453–462.

Wade, Carole, & Tavris, Carol. (1998). *Psychology* (5th ed.). New York: Longman.

Wade, Carole, & Tavris, Carol. (1990). *Learning to think critically: The case of close relationships.* New York: HarperCollins.

Wade, N. (2002, January 22). Scent of a man is linked to a woman's selection. *New York Times,* p. F2.

Walker, L. (1998). *Telephone techniques: The essential guide to thinking and working smarter.* New York: American Management Association.

Walster, E., Walster, G. W., & Berscheid, E. (1978). *Equity: Theory and research.* Boston: Allyn & Bacon.

Watzlawick, Paul. (1977). *How real is real? Confusion, disinformation, communication: An anecdotal introduction to communications theory.* New York: Vintage.

Watzlawick, Paul. (1978). *The language of change: Elements of therapeutic communication.* New York: Basic Books.

Watzlawick, Paul, Beavin, Janet Helmick, & Jackson, Don D. (1967). *Pragmatics of human communication: A study of interactional patterns, pathologies, and paradoxes.* New York: Norton.

Weathers, M. D., Frank, E. M., & Spell, L. A. (2002). Differences in the communication of affect: Members of the same race versus members of a different race. *Journal of Black Psychology, 28,* 66–77.

Weinberg, Harry L. (1959). *Levels of knowing and existence.* New York: Harper & Row.

Weinstein, Eugene A., & Deutschberger, Paul. (1963). Some dimensions of altercasting. *Sociometry, 26,* 454–466.

Werner, E. K. (1975). *A study of communication time.* M.A. Thesis, University of Maryland, College Park. Cited in Wolvin and Coakley (1996).

Werrbach, Gail B., Grotevant, Harold D., & Cooper, Catherine R. (1990, October). Gender differences in adolescents' identity development in the domain of sex role concepts. *Sex Roles, 23,* 349–362.

West, Candace, & Zimmerman, Don H. (1977, June). Women's place in everyday talk: reflections on parent-child interaction. *Social Problems, 24,* 521–529.

Westwood, R. I., Tang, F. F., & Kirkbride, P. S. (1992, Summer). Chinese conflict behavior: Cultural antecedents and behavioral consequences. *Organizational Development Journal, 10,* 13–19.

Wetzel, Patricia J. (1988). Are "powerless" communication strategies the Japanese norm? *Language in Society, 17,* 555–564.

Wheeless, Lawrence R., & Grotz, Janis. (1977). The measurement of trust and its relationship to self-disclosure. *Human Communication Research, 3,* 250–257.

Whitty, M., & Gavin, J. (2001). Age/sex/location: Uncovering the social cues in the development of online relationships. *CyberPsychology and Behavior, 4,* 623–630.

Wiederman, Michael W., & Hurd, Catherine. (1999, April). Extradyadic involvement during dating. *Journal of Social and Personal Relationships, 16,* 265–274.

Wilkins, B. M., & Andersen, P. A. (1991). Gender differences and similarities in management communication: A meta-analysis. *Management Communication Quarterly, 5,* 6–35.

Wilmot, William W. (1987). *Dyadic communication* (3rd ed.). New York: Random House.

Wilson, J. H., & Taylor, K. W. (2001). Professor immediacy as behaviors associated with liking students. *Teaching of Psychology, 28,* 136–138.

Wilson, R. A. (1989). Toward understanding e-prime. *ETC: A Review of General Semantics, 46,* 316–319.

Wilson, S. R., & Sabee, C. M. (2003). Explicating communicative competence as a theoretical term. In J. O. Greene & B. R. Burleson (Eds.), *Handbook of communication and social interaction skills* (pp. 3–50). Mahwah, NJ: Erlbaum.

Winquist, Lynn A., Mohr, Cynthia D., & Kenny, David A. (1998, September). The female positivity effect in the perception of others. *Journal of Research in Personality, 32,* 370–388.

Witcher, S. K. (1999, August 9–15). Chief executives in Asia find listening difficult. *Asian Wall Street Journal Weekly, 21,* p. 11.

Witt, P. L., & Wheeless, L. R. (2001). An experimental study of teachers' verbal and nonverbal immediacy and students' affective and cognitive learning. *Communication Education, 50,* 327–342.

Wolfson, Nessa. (1988). The bulge: A theory of speech behaviour and social distance. In J. Fine (Ed.), *Second language discourse: A textbook of current research.* Norwood, NJ: Ablex.

Wolvin, A. D., & Coakley, C. G. (1996). *Listening.* Dubuque, IA: William C. Brown.

Won-Doornink, Myong-Jin. (1991). Self-disclosure and reciprocity in South Korean and U.S. male dyads. In Stella Ting-Toomey & Felipe Korzenny (Eds.), *Cross-cultural interpersonal communication* (pp. 116–131). Thousand Oaks, CA: Sage.

Wood, Julia T. (1994). *Gendered lives: Communication, gender, and culture.* Belmont, CA: Wadsworth.

Wright, Paul H. (1978). Toward a theory of friendship based on a conception of self. *Human Communication Research, 4,* 196–207.

Wright, Paul H. (1984). Self-referent motivation and the intrinsic quality of friendship. *Journal of Social and Personal Relationships, 1,* 115–130.

Wright, Paul H. (1988). Interpreting research on gender differences in friendship: A case for moderation and a plea for caution. *Journal of Social and Personal Relationships, 5,* 367–373.

Yau-fair Ho, D., Chan, S. F., Peng, S., & Ng, A. K. (2001). The dialogical self: Converging East–West constructions. *Culture and Psychology, 7,* 393–408.

Yovetich, Nancy A., & Drigotas, Stephen M. (1999, September). Secret transmission: A relative intimacy hypothesis. *Personality and Social Psychology Bulletin, 25,* 1135–1146.

Yun, Hum. (1976). The Korean personality and treatment considerations. *Social Casework, 57,* 173–178.

Zimmerman, Don H., & West, Candace. (1975). Sex roles, interruptions and silences in conversations. In B. Thorne & N. Henley (Eds.), *Language and sex: Differences and dominance.* Rowley, MA: Newbury House.

Zuckerman, M., Klorman, R., Larrance, D. T., & Spiegel, N. H. (1981). Facial, autonomic, and subjective components of emotion: The facial feedback hypothesis versus the externalizer-internalizer distinction. *Journal of Personality and Social Psychology, 41,* 929–944.

Zunin, Leonard M., & Zunin, Hilary Stanton. (1991). *The art of condolence: What to write, what to say, what to do at a time of loss.* New York: Harper Perennial.

Zunin, Leonard M., & Zunin, Natalie B. (1972). *Contact: The first four minutes.* Los Angeles: Nash.

Credits

··

Index

Note: Italicized letters *f* and *t* following page numbers indicate figures and tables, respectively; italicized page numbers indicate glossary terms.

Culture(s) *(continued)*
  perception and, *288*
  power and, 263–264
  relationships and, 213
  self-concept and, 33–34
  self-disclosure and, 37–38
  U.S. demographics, 25–26, 25*f*
  weak-uncertainty-avoidance, 66–67
Culture shock, 204–206

Date, *279*
Dating statements, *288*
Deaf and hearing persons, 74, 75*t*
Deception, nonverbal, 118
Deciding to self-disclosure, *288*
Decoders, 8, 8*f*, *279*
Decoration of body and space, 128–129
Defensiveness, 248, *279*
Defining a conflict, 242–243, 242*f*
Delayed reaction, *279*
Denial, 151, *279*
Denotative meanings, 92–93, *279*
Depenetration, *279*
Depth listening, 82, *290*
Depth of relationship, *279*
Describing feelings, 153
Deterioration of relationships, 214*f*, 216, *279*
Dialogue, 174–175, 175*f*, *279*
Differences. *See also* Cultural differences; Gender
    differences
  in meaning, 203
  perceiving, 63
Direct messages, 93–95
Direct speech, 86, *279*
Disabled and able persons, 205*t*
Disclaimers, 164–165, *279, 288*
Disclosure. *See* Self-disclosure
Disconfirmation. *See* Confirmation and disconfirmation
Disengagement strategies, 229
Displays. *See also* Cultural display rules
  of affect, 120, 121*t*
  culture-based, 128
  gender-based, 149
Disqualifiers, power and, 260
Dissolution of relationships, 214*f*, 217–218, *279, 289*
Distance in relationships
  change strategies for, 229
  cultural, power and, 263
  proxemic, 125–126, 125*t*
Distinctions in verbal messages, obscuring, 110–111
Domestic partners, 228
Downward communication, *279*
Dyadic coalition, *279*
Dyadic communication, *279*
Dyadic consciousness, *279*

Dyadic effect, 39, *279*
Dyadic primacy, *279*

E′ (E-prime), 107, *279*
Earmarkers, 127, *279*
Effect(s)
  dyadic, 39, *279*
  halo effect, 58, *281*
  of messages, 8, *279*
  primacy–recency, 59–60, *284*
  Pygmalion, 59, *284*
Effectiveness, *281*
E-mail. *See* Online communication
Emblems, 119–120, 121*t, 279*
Emotion(s), *279*
  anchoring, 154
  arousal sequence of, 146, 146*f*
  communicating. *See* Emotional communication
  describing, 153
  versus emotional expression, 147
  expressing understanding of, 84
  identifying, 153
  influences on, 144–145
  owning, 154–155
  primary *versus* blended, 145–146, 145*f*
Emotional communication, 144, *279, 288*
  affect displays, 120, 121*t*
  of anger, 155–157
  in conflict situations. *See* Conflict management
  display rules for, 148–149
  facial, 121–125
  guidelines for, 152–157
  influence of, 149–150
  listening to, 153
  nonverbal, 118–119, 148
  obstacles to, 150–152
  self-test of, 147
  silence as, 131–132
  skill exercises, 149, 152
  tactile, 129
  verbal, 146–148
Emotional contagion, 149–150, *279*
Emotional display, *288*
Emotional understanding, *288*
Emotionality in interpersonal communication, *288*
Empathic conflict, *288*
Empathic listening, *288*
Empathy, *279, 288*
  communicating, 183
  conflict and, 243, 250
  listening with, 79–80
Empowerment
  apprehension and, 48
  of others, 262, 266
Encoders, 8, 8*f*, *279*

Self-destructive beliefs, self-esteem and, 268
Self-disclosure, 36–43, *285*
 dangers of, 40–41
 deciding on, *288*
 factors influencing, 37–39
 guidelines for, 41–43
 outing as, 37
 in relationships, 44
 resisting, 43
 rewards of, 39–40
 skills of, 42, 44
Self-esteem, *285, 290*
 power and, 267–269
 relationship dissolution and, 218
Self-fulfilling prophecy, 58–59, *285, 290*
Self-knowledge, self-disclosure and, 39–40
Self-monitoring, *285*
Self-references, 168
Self-serving bias, 62, *285, 290*
Self-talk, 36, *285*
Self-tests, xi
Semantics, *285*
Sensitivity. *See* Cultural sensitivity
Sex role stereotyping, 100
Sexism, 100
Sexist language, 100, *285*
Sexual harassment, *285*
 managing, 265, *290*
 messages of, 264–265, *290*
Sexual orientation identifiers, 104
Sharpening, *285*
Shyness, *285*
Sighted and blind persons, 11, 12*t*
Signal and noise, relativity of, *285*
Signal reaction, *285*
Signals, communication as, 18
Signal-to-noise ratio, 11, *285*
Silence, *285, 290*
 communication through, 131–132
 cross-cultural variance in, 137–138
 ethical aspects of, 132
Silencers, 250, *285*
Similarity rule, *285*
Skill building exercises, xii–xiii
Skills, xi
 apprehension-related, 47
 competence-related, 14–15, 14*f*
 complaint management, 246
 conversational, general, 180–182
 conversational, specific, 179, 182–186
 coping with difficult listeners, 87
 creating lasting relationships, 223
 emotional communication, 152, 154
 exerting power, 260
 intercultural communication, 197

 nonverbal communication with power, 135
 online communication, 7, 105
 relationship communication, 220
 self-disclosure, 43
 telephone etiquette, 65
Slang, 260, *285*
Smell messages, 134–135
Social clock, 139
Social comparisons, 32–33, *285*
Social distance, 125*t*, 126, *285*
Social exchange theory, *285*
Social penetration theory, *285*
Social rules/customs. *See* Beliefs; Rules
Solution messages, 83
Source, 8, *285*
Source–receiver relationship, 8, 8*f*
Space
 decorating, 128–129
 giving, *288*
Spamming, 237
Spatial distance messages, 125–127, 125*t*, *290*
Speaker cues, 175–176, 175*f*
Speech, *285*
 conversational cues, 175–177, 175*f*
 direct *versus* indirect, 86
 face-to-face, 10
Speech and language disorders, 162, 163*t*
Spontaneity, conflict and, 248, *285*
Stability, *285*
Stage talk, 219
Static evaluation, 111, *285*
Status, *286*
STEP system, 14–15
Stereotypes, *286, 290*
Stereotyping
 perception and, 60–62
 sex role bias and, 100
Sticky relationships, 223
Stimulation, perception and, 52–53
Stimulus, 52, *286*
Stimulus–response models of communication, *286*
Storge love, 225–226
Strategy, 248, *286*
Styles of conflict, 240–241, 240*f*
Subjectivity, *286*
Success
 apprehension and, 47
 self-esteem and, 269
Superiority, 248–249, *286*
Supportiveness, *286*
 in conflict management, *290*
 in relationships, 218, 223
Surface listening, 82, *290*
Symbolism, language as, 107–108
Symmetrical relationship, *286*

Contents